ACCA

S
T
U
D
Y

T
E
X
T

PAPER F3

FINANCIAL ACCOUNTING (INTERNATIONAL)

In this edition, approved by ACCA

- We **discuss** the **best strategies** for studying for ACCA exams
- We **highlight** the **most important elements** in the syllabus and the **key skills** you will need
- We **signpost** how each chapter links to the syllabus and the study guide
- We **provide** lots of **exam focus points** demonstrating what the examiner will want you to do
- We **emphasise key points** in regular **fast forward summaries**
- We **test your knowledge** of what you've studied in **quick quizzes**
- We **examine your understanding** in our **exam question bank**
- We **reference all the important topics** in our **full index**

BPP's **i-Learn** and **i-Pass** products also support this paper.

FOR EXAMS UNTIL 30 NOVEMBER 2011

BPP
LEARNING MEDIA

First edition 2007
Third edition June 2009

ISBN 9780 7517 6364 5
(Previous ISBN 9870 7517 4723 2)

British Library Cataloguing-in-Publication Data
A catalogue record for this book
is available from the British Library

Published by

BPP Learning Media Ltd
BPP House, Aldine Place
London W12 8AA

www.bpp.com/learningmedia

Printed in Great Britain

We are grateful to the Association of Chartered Certified
Accountants for permission to reproduce past
examination questions. The suggested solutions in the
exam answer bank have been prepared by BPP Learning
Media Ltd, unless where otherwise stated.

Contents

Review form and free prize draw

A note about copyright

Dear Customer

What does the little © mean and why does it matter?

Your market-leading BPP books, course materials and e-learning materials do not write and update themselves. People write them: on their own behalf or as employees of an organisation that invests in this activity. Copyright law protects their livelihoods. It does so by creating rights over the use of the content.

Breach of copyright is a form of theft – as well as being a criminal offence in some jurisdictions, it is potentially a serious breach of professional ethics.

With current technology, things might seem a bit hazy but, basically, without the express permission of BPP Learning Media:
- Photocopying our materials is a breach of copyright
- Scanning, ripcasting or conversion of our digital materials into different file formats, uploading them to facebook or emailing them to your friends is a breach of copyright

You can, of course, sell your books, in the form in which you have bought them – once you have finished with them. (Is this fair to your fellow students? We update for a reason.) But the e-products are sold on a single user licence basis: we do not supply 'unlock' codes to people who have bought them second-hand.

And what about outside the UK? BPP Learning Media strives to make our materials available at prices students can afford by local printing arrangements, pricing policies and partnerships which are clearly listed on our website. A tiny minority ignore this and indulge in criminal activity by illegally photocopying our material or supporting organisations that do. If they act illegally and unethically in one area, can you really trust them?

How the BPP ACCA-approved Study Text can help you pass – AND help you with your Practical Experience Requirement!

Before you can qualify as an ACCA member, you do not only have to pass all your exams but also fulfil a three year **practical experience requirement** (PER). To help you to recognise areas of the syllabus that you might be able to apply in the workplace to achieve different performance objectives, we have introduced the '**PER alert**' feature. You will find this feature throughout the Study Text to remind you that what you are **learning to pass** your ACCA exams is **equally useful to the fulfilment of the PER requirement**.

Tackling studying

Studying can be a daunting prospect, particularly when you have lots of other commitments. The **different features** of the text, the **purposes** of which are explained fully on the **Chapter features** page, will help you whilst studying and improve your chances of **exam success**.

Developing exam awareness

Our Texts are completely **focused** on helping you pass your exam.

Our advice on **Studying F3** outlines the **content** of the paper, the **necessary skills** the examiner expects you to demonstrate and any **brought forward knowledge** you are expected to have.

Exam focus points are included within the chapters to provide information about skills that you will need in the exam and reminders of important points within the specific subject areas.

Using the Syllabus and Study Guide

You can find the syllabus, Study Guide and other useful resources for F3 on the ACCA web site:

www.accaglobal.com/students/study_exams/qualifications/acca_choose/acca/fundamentals.

The Study Text covers **all aspects** of the syllabus to ensure you are as fully prepared for the exam as possible.

Testing what you can do

Testing yourself helps you develop the skills you need to pass the exam and also confirms that you can recall what you have learnt.

We include **Exam-style Questions** – lots of them - both within chapters and in the **Exam Question Bank**, as well as **Quick Quizzes** at the end of each chapter to test your knowledge of the chapter content.

Chapter features

Each chapter contains a number of helpful features to guide you through each topic.

Topic list

Topic list	Syllabus reference

Tells you what you will be studying in this chapter and the relevant section numbers, together with the ACCA syllabus references.

Introduction

Puts the chapter content in the context of the syllabus as a whole.

Study Guide

Links the chapter content with ACCA guidance.

Exam Guide

Highlights how examinable the chapter content is likely to be and the ways in which it could be examined.

FAST FORWARD ▶▶

Summarises the content of main chapter headings, allowing you to preview and review each section easily.

Examples

Demonstrate how to apply key knowledge and techniques.

Key terms

Definitions of important concepts that can often earn you easy marks in exams.

Exam focus points

Provide information about skills you will need in the exam and reminders of important points within the specific subject area.

Formula to learn

Formulae that are not given in the exam but which have to be learnt.

 PER alert

This is a new feature that gives you a useful indication of syllabus areas that closely relate to performance objectives in your PER.

 Question

Give you essential practice of techniques covered in the chapter.

 Case Study

Provide real world examples of theories and techniques.

Chapter Roundup

A full list of the Fast Forwards included in the chapter, providing an easy source of review.

Quick Quiz

A quick test of your knowledge of the main topics in the chapter.

Exam Question Bank

Found at the back of the Study Text with more comprehensive chapter questions.

Studying F3

As the name suggests, this paper examines basic financial accounting topics and is fundamental for all financial accountants.

The examiner for this paper is **Nicola Ventress**. She is a member of the ICAEW and an experienced accounting and financial reporting author and tutor.

1 What F3 is about

Paper F3 aims to develop your knowledge and understanding of the underlying principles, concepts and regulations relating to financial accounting. You will need to demonstrate technical proficiency in the use of double entry techniques, including the preparation of basic financial statements for sole traders, partnerships and limited liability companies. The skills you learn at F3 will be built upon in papers F7 and P2.

2 What skills are required?

You are expected to demonstrate Level 1 skills throughout the syllabus. This means that you need to show 'knowledge and comprehension'. It is not sufficient to merely know the subject, you need to understand it and show that you understand. Therefore you will need to not only know an accounting standard but also show how to use it in practice.

Double entry bookkeeping is a basic skill that you will need throughout all the financial accounting papers. Therefore it is essential that you master it at this stage or you will find the higher papers very difficult to understand.

For paper F3, you also need to be able to prepare basic financial statements. Once again, your basic knowledge from paper F3 will be built upon in papers F7 and P2. Therefore you must understand the basics of preparing financial statements now.

3 How to improve your chances of passing

Examiners have repeatedly emphasised that students must know the **whole syllabus**. This is particularly important for paper F3, as all fifty questions are compulsory and the examiner aims to cover most of the syllabus. If you miss out a syllabus area, you will severely limit your chances of passing the exam.

Above all you must practise questions. The text gives you some exam style questions but you really need a large question bank to practise on as given in BPP's Practice and Revision Kit. Do keep to the timing specified. The exam is 2 hours for 90 marks, which means 1.3 minutes per mark or just over 2.5 minutes for a 2 mark question. In the exam question bank we suggest that you allow 1 minute for a 1 mark question and 2 minutes for a 2 mark question.

The exam paper

The exam is a two-hour paper.

There will be fifty questions and they are all compulsory. The format of the paper based Pilot Paper is 50 MCQs, 40 being 2 mark questions and 10 being 1 mark questions. The examiner has confirmed that this will be the format for future exams.

All exams are marked by computer and so no marks will be given for workings.

Analysis of pilot paper

		Number of marks
40	2 mark compulsory MCQs	80
10	1 mark compulsory MCQs	10
		90

Computer based exam

You can also sit the exam as a computer based assessment. Feedback from students implies that the 40 2 mark questions are divided approximately 50:50 between MCQs and data entry style questions. Data entry style questions may require you to enter the answer to a calculation or words to complete a sentence and are very similar to the non-MCQ style questions found in the Quick Quizzes.

Technical articles

There have been a number of technical articles on exams in recent editions of *Student Accountant*.

Fundamental Knowledge, 7 February 2008 (why all the questions in Fundamentals level exams are compulsory)

Be Prepared – multiple choice questions, 7 July 2008 (practical guidance on how to maximise marks in MCQs)

Computer-based exams put to the test, 19 August 2008.

The context and purpose of
financial reporting

Introduction to accounting

Topic list	Syllabus reference
1 The purpose of financial reporting	A1(a)
2 Types of business entity	A1(b) – (d)
3 Nature, principles and scope of financial reporting	A1(e)
4 Users' and stakeholders' needs	A2(a)
5 The main elements of financial reports	A3(a) – (b)

Introduction

We will begin by looking at the aim of Paper F3, as laid out in ACCA's syllabus and Study Guide and discussed already in the introductory pages to this text (if you haven't read through the introductory pages, do so now – the information in there is extremely important).

> 'Aim of Paper F3
>
> To develop knowledge and understanding of the underlying principles and concepts relating to financial accounting and technical proficiency in the use of double-entry accounting techniques including the preparation of basic financial statements.'

Before you learn **how** to prepare financial reports, it is important to understand **why** they are prepared. Sections 1 – 3 of this chapter introduce some basic ideas about financial reports and give an indication of their purpose. You will also be introduced to the **functions** which accountants carry out: financial accounting and management accounting. These functions will be developed in detail in your later studies for the ACCA qualification.

Section 4 identifies the main **users** of financial statements and their **needs**.

Finally, in Section 5, we will look at the **main financial statements:** the **statement of financial position** and the **income statement**; as well as the main elements of assets, liabilities, equity, revenue and expense.

Study guide

		Intellectual level
A1	**The reasons for and objectives of financial reporting**	
(a)	Define financial reporting – recording, analysing and summarising financial data.	1
(b)	Identify and define types of business entity – sole trader, partnership, limited liability company.	1
(c)	Recognise the legal differences between a sole trader, partnership and a limited liability company.	1
(d)	Identify the advantages and disadvantages of operating as a limited liability company, sole trader or partnership.	1
(e)	Understand the nature, principles and scope of financial reporting.	1
A2	**Users' and stakeholders' needs**	
(a)	Identify the users of financial statements and state and differentiate between their information needs.	1
A3	**The main elements of financial reports**	
(a)	Understand and identify the purpose of each of the main financial statements.	1
(b)	Define and identify assets, liabilities, equity, revenue and expense.	1

Exam guide

The exam consists of 10 1 mark and 40 2 mark MCQs. Any of the topics in this chapter could form the basis of a 1 or 2 mark question.

Remember that all fifty questions are compulsory and will cover most of the syllabus. Therefore, do not neglect these introductory topics. Just because the exam is composed of MCQs, do not assume that it is easy (it's not). Also the format means that no method marks are available

Exam focus point

> At the 2009 ACCA Teachers' Conference, the examiner reminded students that they need to study the full breadth of the syllabus.

1 The purpose of financial reporting

1.1 What is financial reporting?

FAST FORWARD

> **Financial reporting** is a way of recording, analysing and summarising financial data.

Financial data is the name given to the actual transactions carried out by a business eg sales of goods, purchases of goods, payment of expenses.

These transactions are **recorded** in **books of prime entry** (which we will study in detail in Chapter 4).

The transactions are **analysed** in the books of prime entry and the totals are posted to the ledger accounts (see Chapter 5).

Finally, the transactions are **summarised** in the financial statements, which we will meet in section 5 of this chapter (and will study in detail in Chapter 6).

Financial reporting means the financial statements produced only by a large quoted company.

Is this statement correct?

A   Yes

B   No

Answer

The correct answer is B. Financial reporting is carried out by all businesses, no matter what their size or structure.

2 Types of business entity

2.1 What is a business?

FAST FORWARD

Businesses of whatever size or nature exist to make a **profit**.

There are a number of different ways of looking at a business. Some ideas are listed below.

- A business is a **commercial or industrial concern** which exists to deal in the manufacture, re-sale or supply of goods and services.
- A business is an **organisation which uses economic resources** to create goods or services which customers will buy.
- A business is an **organisation providing jobs** for people.
- A business invests **money in resources** (for example: buildings, machinery, employees) in order to make even more money for its owners.

This last definition introduces the important idea of profit. Businesses vary from very small businesses (the local shopkeeper or plumber) to very large ones (ICI, IKEA, Corus). However all of them want to earn profits.

Key term

> **Profit** is the excess of revenue (income) over expenditure. When expenditure exceeds revenue, the business is running at a loss.

One of the jobs of an accountant is to measure revenue and expenditure, and so profit. It is not such a straightforward problem as it may seem and in later chapters we will look at some of the theoretical and practical difficulties involved.

2.2 Types of business entity

There are three main types of business entity.

- Sole traders
- Partnerships
- Limited liability companies

Sole traders are people who work for themselves. Examples include the local shopkeeper, a plumber and a hairdresser. The term sole trader refers to the **ownership** of the business, sole traders can have employees.

Partnerships occur when **two or more** people decide to run a business together. Examples include an accountancy practice, a medical practice and a legal practice.

Limited liability companies are incorporated to take advantage of 'limited liability' for their owners (shareholders). This means that, while sole traders and partners are **personally responsible** for the amounts owed by their businesses, the shareholders of a limited liability company are only responsible for the **amount to be paid for their shares**. Limited liability companies are dealt with in more detail in Chapter 20.

In law sole traders and partnerships are not separate entities from their owners. However, a limited liability company is legally a separate entity from its owners and it can issue contracts in the company's name.

For **accounting purposes**, all three entities are treated as separate from their owners. This is called the **business entity concept**. We will see the practical consequence in Chapter 5.

2.3 Advantages of trading as a limited liability company

(a)   **Limited liability** makes investment less risky than investing in a sole trader or partnership. However, lenders to a small company may ask for a shareholder's personal guarantee to secure any loans.

(b)   It is **easier to raise finance** because of limited liability and there is no limit on the number of shareholders.

(c)   A limited liability company has a **separate legal identity** from its shareholders. So a company continues to exist regardless of the identity of its owners. In contrast, a partnership ceases, and a new one starts, whenever a partner joins or leaves the partnership.

(d)   There are **tax advantages** to being a limited liability company. The company is taxed as a separate entity from its owners and the tax rate on companies may be lower than the tax rate for individuals.

(e)   It is relatively easy to **transfer shares** from one owner to another. In contrast, it may be difficult to find someone to buy a sole trader's business or to buy a share in a partnership.

2.4 Disadvantages of trading as a limited liability company

(a)   Limited liability companies have to **publish annual financial statements**. This means that anyone (including competitors) can see how well (or badly) they are doing. In contrast, sole traders and partnerships do not have to publish their financial statements.

(b)   Limited liability company financial statements have to comply with **legal and accounting requirements**. In particular the financial statements have to comply with accounting standards. Sole traders and partnerships may comply with accounting standards, but are not compelled to do so.

(c)   The financial statements of larger limited liability companies have to be **audited**. This means that the statements are subject to an independent review to ensure that they comply with legal requirements and accounting standards. This can be inconvenient, time consuming and expensive.

(d)   **Share issues** are regulated by law. For example, it is difficult to reduce share capital. Sole traders and partnership can increase or decrease capital as and when the owners wish.

3 Nature, principles and scope of financial reporting

You should be able to distinguish the following:

*   Financial accounting
*   Management accounting

You may have a wide understanding of what accounting and financial reporting is about. Your job may be in one area or type of accounting, but you must understand the breadth of work which an accountant undertakes.

3.1 Financial accounting

So far in this chapter we have dealt with **financial** accounts. Financial accounting is mainly a method of reporting the results and financial position of a business. It is not primarily concerned with providing information towards the more efficient running of the business. Although financial accounts are of interest to management, their principal function is to satisfy the information needs of persons not involved in running the business. They provide **historical** information.

3.2 Management accounting

The information needs of management go far beyond those of other account users. Managers have the responsibility of planning and controlling the resources of the business. Therefore they need much more detailed information. They also need to **plan for the future** (eg budgets, which predict future revenue and expenditure).

Key term

> **Management (or cost) accounting** is a management information system which analyses data to provide information as a basis for managerial action. The concern of a management accountant is to present accounting information in the form most helpful to management.

You need to understand this distinction between management accounting and financial accounting.

Question	Accountants

They say that America is run by lawyers and Britain is run by accountants, but what do accountants do in your organisation or country? Before moving on to the next section, think of any accountants you know and the kind of jobs they do.

4 Users' and stakeholders' needs

4.1 The need for financial statements

FAST FORWARD

> There are various groups of people who need information about the activities of a business.

Why do businesses need to produce financial statements? If a business is being run efficiently, why should it have to go through all the bother of accounting procedures in order to produce financial information?

The International Accounting Standards Board states in its document *Framework for the preparation and presentation of financial statements* (which we will examine in detail later in this Study Text):

> 'The objective of financial statements is to provide information about the **financial position, performance** and **changes in financial position** of an entity that is useful to a wide range of users in making economic decisions.'

In other words, a business should produce information about its activities because there are various groups of people who want or need to know that information. This sounds rather vague: to make it clearer, we will study the classes of people who need information about a business. We need also to think about what information in particular is of interest to the members of each class.

Large businesses are of interest to a greater variety of people and so we will consider the case of a large public company, whose shares can be purchased and sold on a stock exchange.

4.2 Users of financial statements and accounting information

The following people are likely to be interested in financial information about a large company with listed shares.

(a)   **Managers of the company** appointed by the company's owners to supervise the day-to-day activities of the company. They need information about the company's financial situation as it is currently and as it is expected to be in the future. This is to enable them to manage the business efficiently and to make effective decisions.

(b) **Shareholders of the company**, ie the company's owners, want to assess how well the management is performing. They want to know how profitable the company's operations are and how much profit they can afford to withdraw from the business for their own use.

(c) **Trade contacts** include suppliers who provide goods to the company on credit and customers who purchase the goods or services provided by the company. **Suppliers** want to know about the company's ability to pay its debts; **customers** need to know that the company is a secure source of supply and is in no danger of having to close down.

(d) **Providers of finance to the company** might include a bank which allows the company to operate an overdraft, or provides longer-term finance by granting a loan. The bank wants to ensure that the company is able to keep up interest payments, and eventually to repay the amounts advanced.

(e) **The taxation authorities** want to know about business profits in order to assess the tax payable by the company, including sales taxes.

(f) **Employees of the company** should have a right to information about the company's financial situation, because their future careers and the size of their wages and salaries depend on it.

(g) **Financial analysts and advisers** need information for their clients or audience. For example, stockbrokers need information to advise investors; credit agencies want information to advise potential suppliers of goods to the company; and journalists need information for their reading public.

(h) **Government and their agencies** are interested in the allocation of resources and therefore in the activities of business entities. They also require information in order to provide a basis for national statistics.

(i) **The public**. Entities affect members of the public in a variety of ways. For example, they may make a substantial contribution to a local economy by providing employment and using local suppliers. Another important factor is the effect of an entity on the environment, for example as regards pollution.

Accounting information is summarised in financial statements to satisfy the **information needs** of these different groups. Not all will be equally satisfied.

4.3 Needs of different users

Managers of a business need the most information, to help them make their planning and control decisions. They obviously have 'special' access to information about the business, because they are able to demand whatever internally produced statements they require. When managers want a large amount of information about the costs and profitability of individual products, or different parts of their business, they can obtain it through a system of cost and management accounting.

Question	Information for managers

Which of the following statements is particularly useful for managers?

A   Financial statements for the last financial year
B   Tax records for the past five years
C   Budgets for the coming financial year
D   Bank statements for the past year

Answer

The correct answer is C. Managers need to look forward and make plans to keep the business profitable. Therefore the most useful information for them would be the budgets for the coming financial year.

In addition to management information, financial statements are prepared (and perhaps published) for the benefit of other user groups, which may demand certain information.

(a) The **national laws** of a country may provide for the provision of some accounting information for shareholders and the public.

(b) **National taxation** authorities will receive the information they need to make tax assessments.

(c) A **bank** might demand a forecast of a company's expected future cash flows as a pre-condition of granting an overdraft.

(d) The **International Accounting Standards Board (IASB)** has been responsible for issuing **International Financial Reporting Standards (IFRSs and IASs)** and these require companies to publish certain additional information. Accountants, as members of professional bodies, are placed under a strong obligation to ensure that company financial statements conform to the requirements of IFRS/IAS.

(e) Some companies provide, voluntarily, specially prepared financial information for issue to their employees. These statements are known as 'employee reports'.

Exam focus point

The needs of users can easily be examined by means of a MCQ. For example, you could be given a list of types of information and asked which user group would be most interested in this information.

5 The main elements of financial reports

FAST FORWARD

The principle financial statements of a business are the **statement of financial position** and the **income statement**.

5.1 Statement of financial position

Key term

The **statement of financial position** is simply a *list* of all the *assets owned* and all the *liabilities owed* by a business as at a particular date. It is a snapshot of the financial position of the business at a particular moment. Monetary amounts are attributed to each of the assets and liabilities.

5.1.1 Assets

Key term

An **asset** is something valuable which a business owns or has the use of.

Examples of assets are factories, office buildings, warehouses, delivery vans, lorries, plant and machinery, computer equipment, office furniture, cash and goods held in store awaiting sale to customers.

Some assets are held and used in operations for a long time. An office building is occupied by administrative staff for years; similarly, a machine has a productive life of many years before it wears out.

Other assets are held for only a short time. The owner of a newsagent shop, for example, has to sell his newspapers on the same day that he gets them. The more quickly a business can sell the goods it has in store, the more profit it is likely to make; provided, of course, that the goods are sold at a higher price than what it cost the business to acquire them.

5.1.2 Liabilities

Key term

A **liability** is something which is owed to somebody else. 'Liabilities' is the accounting term for the debts of a business.

Examples of liabilities are amounts owed to a supplier for goods bought on credit, amounts owed to a bank (or other lender), a bank overdraft and amounts owed to tax authorities (eg in respect of sales tax).

Some liabilities are due to be repaid fairly quickly eg suppliers. Other liabilities may take some years to repay (eg a bank loan).

5.1.3 Capital or equity

The amounts invested in a business by the owner are amounts that the business owes to the owner. This is a special kind of liability, called **capital**. In a limited liability company, capital usually takes form of shares. Share capital is also known as **equity**.

5.1.4 Form of statement of financial position

A statement of financial position used to be called a balance sheet. The former name is apt because assets will always be equal to liabilities plus capital (or equity). A very simple statement of financial position for a sole trader is shown below.

A TRADER
STATEMENT OF FINANCIAL POSITION AS AT 30 APRIL 20X7

	$	$
Assets		
Plant and machinery		55,000
Inventory	5,000	
Receivables (from customers)	1,500	
Bank	500	
		7,000
Total assets		62,000
Capital		
Balance brought forward		25,000
Profit for the year		10,400
Balance carried forward		35,400
Liabilities		
Bank loan		25,000
Payables (to suppliers)		1,600
Total capital plus liabilities		62,000

We will be looking at a statement of financial position in a lot more detail later in this Study Text. This example is given simply to illustrate what a statement of financial position looks like.

5.2 Income statement

Key term

> An **income statement** is a *record* of *revenue generated* and *expenditure incurred* over a given period. The statement shows whether the business has had more revenue than expenditure (a profit) or vice versa (loss).

5.2.1 Revenue and expenses

Revenue is the income for a period. The **expenses** are the costs of running the business for the same period.

5.2.2 Form of income statement

The period chosen will depend on the purpose for which the statement is produced. The income statement which forms part of the published annual financial statements of a **limited liability company** will usually be for the period of a **year**, commencing from the date of the previous year's statements. On the other hand, **management** might want to keep a closer eye on a company's profitability by making up **quarterly or monthly** statements.

A simple income statement for a sole trader is shown on the next page.

A TRADER
INCOME STATEMENT FOR THE YEAR ENDED 30 APRIL 20X7

	$
Revenue	150,000
Cost of sales	75,000
Gross profit	75,000
Other expenses	64,600
Net profit	10,400

Once again, this example is given purely for illustrative purposes. We will be dealing with an income statement in detail later in this Study Text.

5.3 Purpose of financial statements

Both the statement of financial position and the income statement are **summaries of accumulated data**. For example, the income statement shows a figure for revenue earned from selling goods to customers. This is the total amount of revenue earned from all the individual sales made during the period. One of the jobs of an accountant is to devise methods of recording such individual transactions, so as to produce summarised financial statements from them.

The statement of financial position and the income statement form the basis of the financial statements of most businesses. For limited liability companies, other information by way of statements and notes may be required by national legislation and/or accounting standards, for example a **statement of comprehensive income** and a **statement of cash flows**. These are considered in detail later in this Study Text.

Question

Accounting information

The financial statements of a limited liability company will consist solely of the statement of financial position and income statement.

Is this statement correct?

A   True
B   False

Answer

The correct answer is B. As shown above other statements, such as a statement of cash flows, are usually needed.

One of the competences you require to fulfil performance objective 4 of the PER is the ability to prioritise and plan your work to meet objectives, managing conflicting pressures and making best use of time and resources. In the course of your F3 studies, you will be demonstrating this competence.

Chapter Roundup

- **Financial reporting** is a way of recording, analysing and summarizing financial data.

- Businesses of whatever size or nature exist to make a **profit**.

- You should be able to distinguish the following.
    - Financial accounting
    - Management accounting

- There are **various groups of people** who need information about the activities of a business.

- The principal financial statements of a business are the **statement of financial position** and the **income statement**.

Quick Quiz

1   What is financial reporting?
2   A business entity is owned and run by Alpha, Beta and Gamma.

    What type of business is this an example of?

    A   Sole trader
    B   Partnership
    C   Limited liability company
    D   Don't know
3   Identify seven user groups who need accounting information.
4   What are the two main financial statements drawn up by accountants?
5   Which of the following is an example of a liability?

    A   Inventory
    B   Receivables
    C   Plant and machinery
    D   Loan

Answers to Quick Quiz

1   A way of recording, analysing and summarising financial data.
2   B.   A partnership, as it is owned and run by 3 people.
3   See paragraph 4.2.
4   The income statement and the statement of financial position.
5   D.   A loan. The rest are all assets.

Now try the question below from the Exam Question Bank			
Number	**Level**	**Marks**	**Time**
Q1	Examination	2	2 mins

The regulatory framework

Topic list	Syllabus reference
1 The regulatory system	A4(a)
2 The International Accounting Standards Board (IASB)	A4(a)
3 International Financial Reporting Standards (IFRSs) and International Accounting Standards (IASs)	A4(b)

Introduction

In this chapter, we introduce the regulatory system run by the International Accounting Standards Board (IASB). We are concerned with the **IASB's relationship with other bodies**, and with the way the IASB operates.

You must try to understand and appreciate the contents of this chapter. The examiner is not only interested in whether you can add up; she wants to know whether you can think about a subject which, after all, is your future career. This chapter can and **will be examined**.

	Intellectual level
including the roles of the e Foundation (IASCF), the SB), the Standards Advisory Reporting Interpretations	1
cial Reporting Standards.	1

ble background information. Expect at least one
system. The examiner is also likely to test you on
area that is consistently answered badly in the

FAST FORWARD

> A number of factors have shaped the **development** of financial accounting.

1.1 Introduction

Although new to the subject, you will be aware from your reading of the press that there have been some considerable upheavals in financial reporting, mainly in response to criticism. The **details** of the regulatory framework of accounting, and the technical aspects of the changes made, will be covered later in this chapter and in your more advanced studies. The purpose of this section is to give a **general picture** of some of the factors which have shaped financial accounting. We will concentrate on the accounts of limited liability companies, as these are the accounts most closely regulated by statute or otherwise.

The following factors can be identified.

- National/local legislation
- Accounting concepts and individual judgement
- Accounting standards
- Other international influences
- Generally accepted accounting principles (GAAP)
- Fair presentation

1.2 National/local legislation

Limited liability companies may be required by law to prepare and publish accounts annually. The form and content of the accounts may be regulated primarily by national legislation, but must also comply with International Accounting Standards (IASs) and International Financial Reporting Standards (IFRSs).

1.3 Accounting concepts and individual judgement

FAST FORWARD

> Many figures in financial statements are derived from the **application of judgement** in applying fundamental accounting assumptions and conventions. This can lead to subjectivity.

Financial statements are prepared on the basis of a number of **fundamental accounting assumptions and conventions**. Many figures in financial statements are derived from the application of judgement in putting these assumptions into practice.

It is clear that different people exercising their judgement on the same facts can arrive at very different conclusions.

 Case Study

An accountancy training firm has an excellent **reputation** amongst students and employers. How would you value this? The firm may have relatively little in the form of assets that you can touch, perhaps a building, desks and chairs. If you simply drew up a statement of financial position showing the cost of the assets owned, then the business would not seem to be worth much, yet its income earning potential might be high. This is true of many service organisations where the people are among the most valuable assets.

Other examples of areas where the judgement of different people may vary are as follows.

(a)   Valuation of buildings in times of rising property prices.

(b)   Research and development: is it right to treat this only as an expense? In a sense it is an investment to generate future revenue.

(c)   Accounting for inflation.

(d)   Brands such as 'Snickers' or 'Walkman'. Are they assets in the same way that a fork lift truck is an asset?

Working from the same data, different groups of people produce very different financial statements. If the exercise of judgement is completely unfettered, there will be no comparability between the accounts of different organisations. This will be all the more significant in cases where deliberate manipulation occurs, in order to present accounts in the most favourable light.

1.4 Accounting standards

In an attempt to deal with some of the subjectivity, and to achieve comparability between different organisations, **accounting standards** were developed. These are developed at both a national level (in most countries) and an international level. In this text we are concerned with **International Accounting Standards** (IASs) and **International Financial Reporting** Standards (IFRSs).

1.4.1 International Financial Reporting Standards and the IASB

International Financial Reporting Standards (IFRSs) are produced by the **International Accounting Standards Board (IASB)**. The IASB develops IFRSs through an international process that involves the world-wide accountancy profession, the preparers and users of financial statements, and national standard setting bodies. Prior to 2003 standards were issued as International Accounting Standards (IASs). In 2003 IFRS 1 was issued and all new standards are now designated as IFRSs. Throughout this Study Text, we will use the abbreviation IFRSs to include **both** IFRSs **and** IASs.

The objectives of the IASB are:

(a)   To **develop**, in the public interest, a single set of high quality, understandable and enforceable **global accounting standards** that require high quality, transparent and comparable information in financial statements and other financial reporting to help participants in the world's capital markets and other users make economic decisions.

(b)   To promote the use and **rigorous application** of those standards.

(c)   To bring about **convergence of national accounting standards** and International Financial Reporting Standards to high quality solutions.

In the UK the consolidated accounts of listed companies have had to be produced in accordance with IFRS from January 2005.

1.4.2 Standards Advisory Council (SAC)

The Standards Advisory Council assists the IASB in standard setting. It has about 50 members drawn from organisations all over the world, such as national standard–setting bodies, accountancy firms, the IMF and the World Bank.

The SAC meets the IASB at least three times a year and puts forward the views of its members on current standard–setting projects.

1.4.3 International Financial Reporting Interpretations Committee (IFRIC)

IFRIC was set up in December 2001 and issues guidance in cases where unsatisfactory or conflicting interpretations of accounting standards have developed. In these situations, IFRIC works closely with similar national committees with a view to reaching consensus on the appropriate accounting treatment.

1.4.4 The International Accounting Standards Committee Foundation (IASCF)

The IASCF is an independent body that oversees the IASB. It was formed as a not-for-profit corporation in the USA.

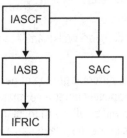

Exam focus point

In the December 2007 exam, there was a 1 mark MCQ on the roles of the IASB and its associated bodies. The examiner commented that there was roughly an even split between the two options, suggesting that this area 'is not given adequate attention'. The examiner also commented that she regards this area to be an important part of the F3 syllabus.

1.4.5 The use and application of IASs and IFRSs

IASs and IFRSs have helped to both improve and harmonise financial reporting around the world. The standards are used in the following ways.

(a)   As **national requirements**, often after a national process
(b)   As the **basis** for all or some **national requirements**
(c)   As an **international benchmark** for those countries which develop their own requirements
(d)   By **regulatory authorities** for domestic and foreign companies
(e)   **By companies** themselves

1.4.6 Benchmark and allowed alternatives

IASs often allowed more than one accounting treatment (a benchmark (or preferred) treatment and an allowed alternative). Recent IFRSs and amendments to IASs have sought to disallow alternative treatments.

1.5 Generally Accepted Accounting Practice (GAAP)

We also need to consider some important terms which you will meet in your financial accounting studies. GAAP, as a term, has sprung up in recent years and signifies all the rules, from whatever source, which govern accounting.

Key term

> **GAAP** is a set of rules governing accounting. The rules may derive from:
>
> - Local (national) company legislation
> - National and international accounting standards
> - Statutory requirements in other countries (particularly the US)
> - Stock exchange requirements

1.6 Fair presentation

FAST FORWARD

> Financial statements are required to give a **fair presentation** or **present fairly in all material respects** the financial results of the entity. These terms are not defined and tend to be decided in courts of law on the facts.

It is a requirement of both national legislation (in some countries) and International Standards on Auditing that the financial statements should give a **fair presentation** of the financial position of the entity as at the end of the financial year.

1.6.1 Fair presentation 'override'

The term fair presentation is not defined in accounting or auditing standards. Despite this, a company's managers may depart from any of the provisions of accounting standards if these are inconsistent with the requirement to give a fair presentation. This is commonly referred to as the ' fair presentation override'. It has been treated as an important loophole in the law in different countries and has been the cause of much argument and dissatisfaction within the accounting profession.

2 The International Accounting Standards Board (IASB)

FAST FORWARD

> The main objectives of the IASB are to raise the standard of financial reporting and to eventually bring about global harmonisation of accounting standards.

2.1 International harmonisation

The IASB is an **independent private sector body**. Its objective is to achieve **uniformity** in the accounting principles which are used by businesses and other organisations for financial reporting around the world. This is known as **international harmonisation**.

2.2 Current position of the IASB

There were 41 IASs, as well as the *Framework for the preparation and presentation of financial statements*, (which is discussed in Chapter 3). A substantial number of multinational companies prepare financial statements in accordance with IASs. IASs are also endorsed by many countries as their own standards, either unchanged or with minor amendments. The IASB has adopted the extant IASs and issued 8 IFRSs. **From 1 January 2005 listed companies in the EU have been required to prepare consolidated accounts in accordance with IFRS.**

3 International Financial Reporting Standards (IFRSs) and International Accounting Standards (IASs)

FAST FORWARD

> In this section, we examine the process by which IFRSs are created and we will list the full range of IFRSs currently in force, so you can place the standards you will study into context.

3.1 Standard setting process

The IASB prepares IFRSs in accordance with **due process**. You do not need to know this for your exam, but the following diagram may be of interest.

The procedure can be summarised as follows.

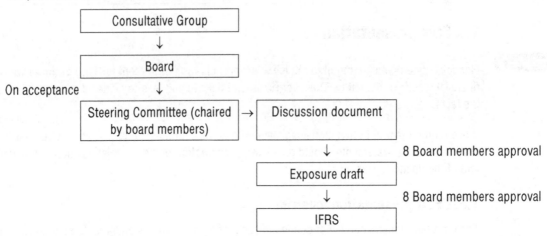

3.1.1 Current IASs/IFRSs

The current list is as follows. Those examinable in Paper F3 are highlighted*.

IAS 1*   Presentation of financial statements
IAS 2*   Inventories
IAS 7*   Statement of cash flows
IAS 8*   Accounting policies, changes in accounting estimates and errors
IAS 10*   Events after the reporting period
IAS 11   Construction contracts
IAS 12   Income taxes
IAS 16*   Property, plant and equipment
IAS 17   Leases
IAS 18*   Revenue
IAS 19   Employee benefits
IAS 20   Accounting for government grants and disclosure of government assistance
IAS 21   The effects of changes in foreign exchange rates
IAS 23   Borrowing costs
IAS 24   Related party disclosures
IAS 27   Consolidated and separate financial statements
IAS 28   Investments in associates
IAS 29   Financial reporting in hyperinflationary economies
IAS 31   Interests in joint ventures
IAS 32   Financial instruments: presentation
IAS 33   Earnings per share
IAS 34   Interim financial reporting
IAS 36   Impairment of assets
IAS 37*   Provisions, contingent liabilities and contingent assets
IAS 38*   Intangible assets
IAS 39   Financial instruments: recognition and measurement
IAS 40   Investment property
IAS 41   Agriculture

Notes

IAS 37   Only paragraphs 10, 27-35, 85-92, Appendices A and B are examinable in so far as they
            relate to contingent liabilities and contingent assets

IAS 38   Only paragraphs 7, 39-47, 55, 79, 88, 107 and 115 relating to R & D are examinable

Framework for the Preparation and Presentation of Financial Statements*

IFRS 1   First time adoption of International Financial Reporting Standards
IFRS 2   Share based payment
IFRS 3   Business combinations
IFRS 5   Non-current assets held for sale and discontinued operations
IFRS 6   Exploration for the evaluation of mineral resources
IFRS 7   Financial Instruments: disclosures
IFRS 8   Operating segments

Various exposure drafts and discussion papers are currently at different stages within the IFRS process, but these are not of concern to you at this stage. By the end of your financial accounting studies, however, you will know *all* the standards, exposure drafts and discussion papers!

Question	Standards 1

Why do you think that those standards highlighted above have been included in your syllabus?

Answer

These standards affect the content and format of almost all financial statements. You therefore need to know about them in order to prepare a basic set of accounts. Most of the other standards will only affect larger and more complex organisations.

3.2 Interpretation of IASs/IFRSs – IFRIC

The IASB has now also developed a procedure for issuing interpretations of its standards. In March 2002 the International Financial Reporting Interpretations Committee (IFRIC) was set up.

The IFRIC will consider accounting issues that are likely to receive divergent or unacceptable treatment in the absence of authoritative guidance. Its review will be within the context of existing IASs/IFRSs and the IASB *Framework*.

The IFRIC will deal with issues of reasonably widespread importance, and not issues of concern to only a small set of enterprises. The interpretations will cover both:

(a)   **Mature issues** (unsatisfactory practice within the scope of existing standards).

(b)   **Emerging issues** (new topics relating to an existing standard but not actually considered when the standard was developed).

In developing interpretations, the 11-person IFRIC will work closely with similar national committees. If it reached consensus on an interpretation the IFRIC will ask the Board to approve the interpretation for issue. Interpretations will be formally published after approval by the Board.

3.3 Scope and application of IASs and IFRS

3.3.1 Scope

Any limitation of the applicability of a specific IAS or IFRS is made clear within that standard. IASs/IFRSs are **not intended to be applied to immaterial items, nor are they retrospective**. Each individual standard lays out its scope at the beginning of the standard.

3.3.2 Application

Within each individual country **local regulations** govern, to a greater or lesser degree, the issue of financial statements. These local regulations include accounting standards issued by the national regulatory bodies and/or professional accountancy bodies in the country concerned.

The IASB **concentrates on essentials** when producing standards. This means that the IASB tries not to make standards too complex, because otherwise they would be impossible to apply on a worldwide basis.

Question	Standards 2

How far do the accounting standards in force in your country diverge from the IFRSs you will cover in this text?

If you have the time and energy, perhaps you could find out.

3.4 Worldwide effect of international standards and the IASB

As far as **Europe** is concerned, the consolidated financial statements of many of Europe's top multinationals are prepared in conformity with national requirements, EC directives and IASs/IFRSs. Furthermore, IFRSs are having a growing influence on national accounting requirements and practices. Many of these developments have been given added impetus by the internationalisation of capital markets. There was a 2005 deadline for implementation of IASs/IFRSs.

In **Japan**, the influence of the IASB had, until recently, been negligible. This was mainly because of links in Japan between tax rules and financial reporting. The Japanese Ministry of Finance set up a working committee to consider whether to bring national requirements into line with IFRSs. The Tokyo Stock Exchange has now announced that it will accept financial statements from foreign issue that conform with home country standards. This was widely seen as an attempt to attract foreign issuers, in particular companies from Hong Kong and Singapore. As these countries base their accounting on international standards, this action is therefore implicit acknowledgement by the Japanese Ministry of Finance of IFRS requirements.

America and Japan have been two of the developed countries which have been most reluctant to accept accounts prepared under IFRSs, but recent developments suggest that such financial statements may soon be acceptable on these important stock exchanges.

In **America**, the Securities and Exchange Commission (SEC) agreed in 1993 to allow foreign issuers (of shares, etc) to follow IFRS treatments on certain issues, including statement of cash flows under IAS 7. The overall effect is that, where IASB treatments differ from US GAAP, these treatments will now be acceptable. The SEC is now supporting the IASB because it wants to attract foreign listings.

Now that you are aware of the workings and impact of the IASB, we will spend the rest of this chapter looking at some of the problems and criticisms which the IASB is faced with, and how it has tackled some of them. We begin at the end of this section by looking at the problem of choice in IASs/ IFRSs.

3.5 Accounting standards and choice

It is sometimes argued that companies should be given a **choice** in matters of financial reporting on the grounds that accounting standards are detrimental to the quality of such reporting. There are arguments on both sides.

In favour of accounting standards (both national and international), the following points can be made.

(a)   They **reduce or eliminate** confusing **variations** in the methods used to prepare accounts.

(b)   They provide a **focal point** for debate and discussions about accounting practice.

(c)   They oblige companies to **disclose** the accounting policies used in the preparation of accounts.

(d)   They are a **less rigid alternative** to enforcing conformity by means of **legislation**.

(e)   They have obliged companies to **disclose more accounting information** than they would otherwise have done if accounting standards did not exist, for example IAS 33 *Earnings per share*.

Many companies are reluctant to disclose information which is not required by national legislation. However, the following arguments may be put forward against standardisation and in **favour of choice**.

(a)   A **set of rules** which give backing to one method of preparing accounts **might be inappropriate** in some circumstances.

(b)   Standards may be **subject to lobbying** or government pressure (in the case of national standards). For example, in the USA, the accounting standard FAS 19 on the accounts of oil and gas companies led to a powerful lobby of oil companies, which persuaded the SEC (Securities and Exchange Commission) to step in. FAS 19 was then suspended.

(c)   Many national standards are **not based on a conceptual framework** of accounting, although IASs and IFRSs are (see Chapter 3).

(d)   There may a **trend towards rigidity**, and away from flexibility in applying the rules.

Exam focus point

The examiner has indicated that, while Sections 3.4 and 3.5 give useful background information, you are unlikely to be directly examined on these points.

Chapter Roundup

- A number of factors have shaped the **development** of financial accounting.

- Many figures in financial statements are derived from the **application of judgement** in applying fundamental accounting assumptions and conventions. This can lead to subjectivity.

- Financial statements are required to give a **true and fair view** or **present fairly in all material respects** the financial results of the entity. These terms are not defined and tend to be decided in courts of law on the facts.

- The main objectives of the IASB are to raise the standard of financial reporting and to eventually bring about global harmonisation of accounting standards.

- In this section, we examine the process by which IFRSs are created and we will list the full range of IFRSs currently in force, so you can place the standards you will study into context.

Quick Quiz

1   What are the objectives of the IASB?
     A   To enforce IFRSs
     B   To issue IFRSs

2   What development at the IASB aids users' interpretation of IFRSs?

3   Which of the following arguments is not in favour of accounting standards, but is in favour of accounting choice?
     A   They reduce variations in methods used to produce accounts
     B   They oblige companies to disclose their accounting policies
     C   They are a less rigid alternative to legislation
     D   They may tend towards rigidity in applying the rules

4   What happened in 2005 for listed companies in the EU?
     A   IFRSs to be used for all financial statements
     B   IFRSs to be used for consolidated financial statements

5   The IASB guides the standard setting process. True or false?

Answers to Quick Quiz

1   B   The IASB has no powers of enforcement.
2   The International Financial Reporting Interpretations Committee (IFRIC).
3   D   The other arguments are all in favour of accounting standards.
4   B   IFRSs to be used in consolidated financial statements.
5   True. The IASB is responsible for the standard setting process.

Now try the question below from the Exam Question Bank

Number	Level	Marks	Time
Q2	Examination	1	1 min

P
A
R
T

B

The qualitative characteristics of financial information and the fundamental bases of accounting

Accounting conventions

Topic list	Syllabus reference
1 Background	B1(a)
2 IAS 1 *Presentation of financial statements*	B1(a)
3 The IASB's Framework	B1(a) – (b)
4 Criticisms of accounting conventions	B1(b)
5 Bases of valuation	B2(a) – (b)
6 IAS 8 *Accounting policies, changes in accounting estimates and errors*	B2(c) – (d)

Introduction

The purpose of this chapter is to encourage you to think more deeply about the **assumptions** on which financial statements are prepared.

This chapter deals with the accounting conventions which lie behind accounts preparation and which you will meet in Part C in the chapters on bookkeeping.

In Part D, you will see how conventions and assumptions are **put into practice.** You will also deal with certain items which are the subject of accounting standards.

The first part of this chapter deals with two important standards: IAS 1 and the *Framework*. Do not neglect these sections as they contain **very important** basic ideas which underlie the whole of accounting.

In the second half of this chapter, you will consider the bases of valuation of items in the financial statements and IAS 8 on changes in accounting policies.

Study guide

		Intellectual level
B1	**The qualitative characteristics of financial reporting**	
(a)	Define, understand and apply accounting concepts and qualitative characteristics:	1
(i)	Fair presentation	
(ii)	Going concern	
(iii)	Accruals	
(iv)	Consistency	
(v)	Materiality	
(vi)	Relevance	
(vii)	Reliability	
(viii)	Faithful representation	
(ix)	Substance over form	
(x)	Neutrality	
(xi)	Prudence	
(xii)	Completeness	
(xiii)	Comparability	
(xiv)	Understandability	
(xv)	Business entity concept	
(b)	Understand the balance between qualitative characteristics.	1
B2	**Alternative bases used in the preparation of financial information**	
(a)	Identify and explain the main characteristics of alternative valuation bases eg historical cost, replacement cost, net realisable value, economic value.	1
(b)	Understand the advantages and disadvantages of historical cost accounting.	1
(c)	Understand the provision of International Financial Reporting Standards governing financial statements regarding changes in accounting policies.	1
(d)	Identify the appropriate accounting treatment if a company changes a material accounting policy.	1

Exam guide

This is a very important chapter, which set the basis of accounting ideas and conventions. Expect questions on all aspects, including the *Framework*. Accounting conventions have been called into question and you may be asked to **question them** yourself in an exam. Pay particular attention to Section 4 of this chapter.

Exam focus point

Always **read the question carefully** before answering. Make sure that you understand the requirement and have picked out the main points of the question. Remember that the distracters (wrong options) will include common errors made by students, so always **check your answer** before moving on.

1 Background

FAST FORWARD

In preparing financial statements, accountants follow certain **fundamental assumptions**.

Accounting practice has developed gradually over a matter of centuries. Many of its procedures are operated automatically by people who have never questioned whether alternative methods exist which have equal validity. However, the procedures in common use imply the acceptance of certain concepts which are by no means self-evident; nor are they the only possible concepts which could be used to build up an accounting framework.

Our next step is to look at some of the more important concepts which are taken for granted in preparing accounts. In this chapter we shall single out the following assumptions and concepts for discussion.

(a)   Fair presentation
(b)   Going concern
(c)   Accruals or matching
(d)   Consistency concept
(e)   Prudence
(f)   Materiality
(g)   Substance over form
(h)   Relevance
(i)   Reliability
(j)   Faithful representation
(k)   Neutrality
(l)   Completeness
(m)   Comparability
(n)   Understandability
(o)   Business entity concept.

We begin by considering **accounting policies** and those **fundamental assumptions** which are the subject of IAS 1 *Presentation of financial statements* (items (a) – (g) of the above list).

2 IAS 1 Presentation of financial statements

FAST FORWARD

IAS 1 identifies **four fundamental assumptions** that must be taken into account when preparing statements:

• Fair presentation
• Going concern
• Accruals
• Consistency

IAS 1 also considers three other concepts extremely important. **Prudence, substance over form and materiality** should govern the selection and application of accounting policies.

IAS 1 *Presentation of financial statements* was published in 1997 and revised in 2004 and again in 2007. Here we will look at the general requirements of IAS 1 and what it says about **accounting policies** and **fundamental assumptions**. The rest of the standard, on the format and content of financial statements will be covered in Chapter 21.

2.1 Objectives and scope

The main objective of IAS 1 is:

> 'To prescribe the basis for presentation of general purpose financial statements, to ensure comparability both with the entity's financial statements of previous periods and with the financial statements of other entities.'

Part B The qualitative characteristics of financial information and the fundamental bases of accounting | **3: Accounting conventions**   27

IAS 1 applies to all **general purpose financial statements** prepared and presented in accordance with International Financial Reporting Standards (IFRSs).

2.2 Purpose of financial statements

The **objective of financial statements** is to provide information about the financial position, performance and cash flows of an entity that is useful to a wide range of users in making economic decisions. They also show the result of **management's stewardship** of the resources entrusted to it.

In order to fulfil this objective, financial statements must provide information about the following aspects of an entity's results.

- Assets
- Liabilities
- Equity
- Income and expenses (including gains and losses)
- Other changes in equity
- Cash flows

Along with other information in the notes and related documents, this information will assist users in predicting the entity **future cash flows**.

According to IAS 1, a complete set of financial statements includes the following components.

(a) Statement of financial position

(b) Income statement and/or statement of comprehensive income

(c) Statement of changes in equity

(d) Statement of cash flows

(e) Accounting policies and explanatory notes

The preparation of these statements is the responsibility of the **board of directors**. IAS 1 also encourages a **financial review** by management and the production of any other reports and statements which may aid users.

2.3 Fair presentation and compliance with IASs/IFRSs

Most importantly, financial statements should **present fairly** the financial position, financial performance and cash flows of an entity. **Compliance with IASs/IFRS** will almost always achieve this.

The following points made by IAS 1 expand on this principle.

(a) **Compliance with IASs/IFRSs** should be disclosed

(b) **All relevant IASs/IFRSs** must be followed if compliance with IASs/IFRSs is disclosed

(c) Use of an **inappropriate accounting treatment** cannot be rectified either by disclosure of accounting policies or notes/explanatory material

There may be (very rare) circumstances when management decides that compliance with a requirement of an IAS/IFRS would be misleading. **Departure from the IAS/IFRS** is therefore required to achieve a fair presentation. The following should be disclosed in such an event.

(a) Management confirmation that the financial statements fairly present the entity's financial position, performance and cash flows

(b) Statement that all IASs/IFRSs have been complied with *except* departure from one IAS/IFRS to achieve a fair presentation

(c) Details of the nature of the departure, why the IAS/IFRS treatment would be misleading, and the treatment adopted

(d) Financial impact of the departure

IAS 1 states what is required for a fair presentation.

(a) Selection and application of **accounting policies**

(b) **Presentation of information** in a manner which provides relevant, reliable, comparable and understandable information

(c) **Additional disclosures** where required

2.4 Accounting policies

We will look at accounting policies in more detail in Section 6 of this Chapter. However, accounting policies should be chosen in order **to comply with International Financial Reporting Standards.** Where there is **no specific requirement** in an IAS or IFRS, policies should be developed so that information provided by the financial statements is:

(a) **Relevant** to the decision-making needs of users.

(b) **Reliable** in that they:

    (i) Represent faithfully the **results and financial position** of the entity.

    (ii) Reflect the **economic substance** of events and transactions and not merely the legal form.

    (iii) Are **neutral**, that is free from bias.

    (iv) Are **prudent**.

    (v) Are **complete in all material respects**.

(c) Comparable

(d) Understandable

We will look at these four characteristics in more detail in Section 3 of this chapter. IAS 1 then considers certain important assumptions which underpin the preparation and presentation of financial statements.

2.5 Going concern

Key term

> The entity is normally viewed as a **going concern**, that is, as continuing in operation for the foreseeable future. It is assumed that the entity has neither the intention nor the necessity of liquidation or of curtailing materially the scale of its operations.

This concept assumes that, when preparing a normal set of accounts, the business will **continue to operate** in approximately the same manner for the foreseeable future (at least the next 12 months). In particular, the entity will not go into liquidation or scale down its operations in a material way.

The main significance of a going concern is that the assets **should not be valued at their 'break-up' value;** the amount they would sell for if they were sold off piecemeal and the business were broken up.

2.6 Example: Going concern

Emma acquires a T-shirt printing machine at a cost of $60,000. The asset has an estimated life of six years, and it is normal to write off the cost of the asset to the income statement over this time. In this case a depreciation cost of $10,000 per year is charged.

Using the going concern assumption, it is presumed that the business will continue its operations and so the asset will live out its full six years in use. A depreciation charge of $10,000 is made each year, and the value of the asset in the statement of financial position is its cost less the accumulated depreciation charged to date. After one year, the **net book value** of the asset is $(60,000 - 10,000) = $50,000, after two years it is $40,000, after three years $30,000 etc, until it is written down to a value of 0 after 6 years.

This asset has no other operational use outside the business and, in a forced sale, it would only sell for scrap. After one year of operation, its scrap value is $8,000.

The net book value of the asset, applying the going concern assumption, is $50,000 after one year, but its immediate sell-off value only $8,000. It can be argued that the asset is over-valued at $50,000, that it should be written down to its break-up value ($8,000) and the balance of its cost should be treated as an expense. However, provided that the going concern assumption is valid, it is appropriate accounting practice to value the asset at its net book value.

A retailer commences business on 1 January and buys inventory of 20 washing machines, each costing $100. During the year he sells 17 machines at $150 each. How should the remaining machines be valued at 31 December in the following circumstances?

(a)   He is forced to close down his business at the end of the year and the remaining machines will realise only $60 each in a forced sale.

(b)   He intends to continue his business into the next year.

Answer

(a)   If the business is to be closed down, the remaining three machines must be valued at the amount they will realise in a forced sale, ie 3 × $60 = $180.

(b)   If the business is regarded as a going concern, the inventory unsold at 31 December will be carried forward into the following year, when the cost of the three machines will be matched against the eventual sale proceeds in computing that year's profits. The three machines will therefore be valued at cost, 3 × $100 = $300.

If the going concern assumption is not followed, that fact must be disclosed, together with the following information.

(a)   The basis on which the financial statements have been prepared.

(b)   The reasons why the entity is not considered to be a going concern.

2.7 Accruals basis of accounting

Key term

> **In the accruals basis of accounting**, items are recognised as assets, liabilities, equity, income and expenses (the elements of financial statements) when they satisfy the definitions and recognition criteria for those elements in the *Framework*.   *(IAS 1)*

Entities should prepare their financial statements on the basis that transactions are recorded in them, not as the cash is paid or received, but as the revenues or expenses are **earned or incurred** in the accounting period to which they relate.

According to the accrual assumption, in computing profit revenue earned must be **matched against** the expenditure incurred in earning it. This is also known as the **matching convention**.

2.8 Example: Accrual

Emma prints 20 T-shirts in her first month of trading (May) at a cost of $5 each. She then sells all of them for $10 each. Emma has therefore made a profit of $100, by matching the revenue ($200) earned against the cost ($100) of acquiring them.

If, however, Emma only sells 18 T-shirts, it is incorrect to charge her income statement with the cost of 20 T-shirts, as she still has two T-shirts in inventory. If she sells them in June, she is likely to make a profit on the sale. Therefore, only the purchase cost of 18 T-shirts ($90) should be matched with her sales revenue ($180), leaving her with a profit of $90.

Her statement of financial position will look like this.

	$
Assets	
Inventory (at cost, ie 2 × $5)	10
Accounts receivable (18 × $10)	180
	190
Capital and liabilities	
Proprietor's capital (profit for the period)	90
Accounts payable (20 × $5)	100
	190

However, if Emma had decided to give up selling T-shirts, then the going concern assumption no longer applies and the value of the two T-shirts in the statement of financial position is break-up valuation not cost. Similarly, if the two unsold T-shirts are unlikely to be sold at more than their cost of $5 each (say, because of damage or a fall in demand) then they should be recorded on the statement of financial position at their *net realisable value* (ie the likely eventual sales price less any expenses incurred to make them saleable) rather than cost. This shows the application of the **prudence concept**, which we will look at shortly.

In this example, the concepts of going concern and accrual are linked. Since the business is assumed to be a going concern, it is possible to carry forward the cost of the unsold T-shirts as a charge against profits of the next period.

2.9 Consistency of presentation

To maintain consistency, the presentation and classification of items in the financial statements should **stay the same from one period to the next**, except as follows.

(a)   There is a significant change in the **nature of the operations** or a review of the financial statements indicates a **more appropriate presentation.**

(b)   A change in presentation is **required by an IFRS.**

2.10 Materiality and aggregation

All material items should be **disclosed** in the financial statements.

Amounts which are **immaterial** can be aggregated with amounts of a similar nature or function and need not be presented separately.

Key term

> **Materiality.** Information is material if its omission or misstatement could influence the economic decisions of users taken on the basis of the financial statements.   *(IAS 1)*

An error which is too trivial to affect anyone's understanding of the accounts is referred to as **immaterial**. In preparing accounts it is important to assess what is material and what is not, so that time and money are not wasted in the pursuit of excessive detail.

Determining whether or not an item is material is a very **subjective exercise**. There is no absolute measure of materiality. It is common to apply a convenient rule of thumb (for example material items are those with a value greater than 5% of net profits). However some items disclosed in the accounts are regarded as particularly sensitive and even a very small misstatement of such an item is taken as a material error. An example, in the accounts of a limited liability company, is the amount of remuneration paid to directors of the company.

The assessment of an item as material or immaterial may **affect its treatment in the accounts**. For example, the income statement of a business shows the expenses incurred grouped under suitable captions (heating and lighting, rent and local taxes, etc); but in the case of very small expenses it may be appropriate to lump them together as 'sundry expenses', because a more detailed breakdown is inappropriate for such immaterial amounts.

In assessing whether or not an item is material, it is not only the value of the item which needs to be considered. The **context** is also important.

(a) If a statement of financial position shows non-current assets of $2 million and inventories of $30,000, an error of $20,000 in the depreciation calculations might not be regarded as material. Whereas an error of $20,000 in the inventory valuation is material. In other words, the total of which the error forms part must be considered.

(b) If a business has a bank loan of $50,000 and a $55,000 balance on bank deposit account, it will be a material misstatement if these two amounts are displayed on the statement of financial position as 'cash at bank $5,000'. In other words, incorrect presentation may amount to material misstatement even if there is no monetary error.

Question
Materiality

Would you treat the following items as assets in the accounts of a company?

(a) A box file
(b) A computer
(c) A small plastic display stand

Answer

(a) No. You would write it off to the income statement as an expense.

(b) Yes. You would capitalise the computer and charge depreciation on it.

(c) Your answer depends on the size of the company and whether writing off the item has a material effect on its profits. A larger organisation might well write this item off under the heading of advertising expenses, while a small one might capitalise it and depreciate it over time. This is because the item is material to the small company, but not to the large company.

2.11 Offsetting

IAS 1 does not allow **assets and liabilities to be offset** against each other unless such a treatment is required or permitted by another IFRS.

Income and expenses can be offset only when one of the following applies.

(a) An IFRS requires/permits it.
(b) Gains, losses and related expenses arising from the same/similar transactions are not material.

2.12 Comparative information

IAS 1 requires comparative information to be disclosed for the previous period for all **numerical information**, unless another IFRS permits/requires otherwise. Comparatives should also be given in narrative information where helpful.

Comparatives should be **restated** when the presentation or classification of items in the financial statements is amended.

2.13 Prudence

Key term

> **Prudence.** The inclusion of a degree of caution in the exercise of the judgements needed in making the estimates required under conditions of uncertainty, such that assets or income are not overstated and liabilities or expenses are not understated.

Prudence must be exercised when preparing financial statements because of the **uncertainty** surrounding many transactions. It is not permitted, however, to create secret or hidden reserves using prudence as a justification.

There are three important issues to bear in mind.

(a)   Where **alternative procedures or valuations** are possible, the one selected should be the one which gives the most cautious result. For example, you may have wondered why the three washing machines in Question Going Concern were stated in the statement of financial position at their cost ($100 each) rather than their selling price ($150 each). This is simply an aspect of prudence: to value the machines at $150 would be to anticipate making a profit before the profit had been realised.

(b)   Where a **loss is foreseen,** it should be anticipated and taken into account immediately. Even when the exact amount of the loss is not known, an estimate of the loss should be made, based on the best information available. If a business purchases inventory for $1,200 but, because of a sudden slump in the market, only $900 is likely to be realised when the inventory is sold; the prudence concept dictates that the inventory is valued at $900. It is not enough to wait until the inventory is sold, and then recognise the $300 loss; it must be recognised as soon as it is foreseen.

(c)   Profits should only be recognised when **realised** in the form of cash or another asset with a reasonably certain cash value.

2.14 Examples: Prudence

Some examples might help to explain the application of prudence.

(a)   A company begins trading on 1 January 20X5 and sells goods worth $100,000 during the year to 31 December. At 31 December there are accounts receivable outstanding of $15,000. Of these, the company is now doubtful whether $6,000 will ever be paid.

The company should make an *allowance for receivables* of $6,000. Sales for 20X5 are shown in the income statement at their full value of $100,000, but the allowance for receivables is a charge of $6,000. Since there is some uncertainty that the sales will be realised in the form of cash, prudence dictates that the $6,000 should not be included in the profit for the year.

(b)   Samson Feeble trades as a carpenter. He undertakes to make a range of kitchen furniture for a customer at an agreed price of $1,000. At the end of Samson's accounting year the job is unfinished (being two thirds complete) and the following data has been assembled.

	$
Costs incurred in making the furniture to date	800
Further estimated costs to completion of the job	400
Total cost	1,200

The incomplete job represents *work in progress* at the end of the year which is an asset, like inventory. Its cost to date is $800, but by the time the job is completed Samson will make a loss of $200.

The full $200 loss should be charged against profits of the current year. The value of work in progress at the year end is its *net realisable value*, which is lower than its cost. The net realisable value can be calculated in either of two ways.

	(i)		(ii)
	$		$
Eventual sales value	1,000	Work in progress at cost	800
Less further costs to completion			
In order to make the sale	400	Less loss foreseen	200
Net realisable value	600		600

2.15 Substance over form

Substance over form. The principle that transactions and other events are accounted for and presented in accordance with their substance and economic reality and not merely their legal form.

Substance over form usually applies to transactions which are fairly complicated. It is very important because it acts as a 'catch-all' to stop entities distorting their results by following the **letter of the law,** instead of showing what the entity has really been doing.

2.16 Presentation of accounting policies

There should be a specific section for accounting policies in the notes to the financial statements and the following should be disclosed there.

(a)   **Measurement bases** used in preparing the financial statements (see Section 5)

(b)   Each **specific accounting policy** necessary for a proper understanding of the financial statements (see Section 6)

To be clear and understandable it is essential that financial statements disclose the accounting policies used in their preparation. This is because **policies may vary**, not only from entity to entity, but also from country to country. As an aid to users, all the major accounting policies used should be disclosed in the same note.

There is a wide range of policies available in many accounting areas. Examples where such differing policies exist are as follows, although the list is not exhaustive and it has been selected from the standard to reflect the limited areas covered in your syllabus.

Area	Policy
General	– Overall valuation policy (eg historical cost, replacement value) – Events subsequent to the reporting period
Assets	– Receivables – Inventories and related cost of goods sold – Depreciable assets and depreciation – Research and development
Liabilities and provisions	– Commitments and contingencies
Profits and losses	– Methods of revenue recognition – Maintenance, repairs and improvements – Gains and losses on disposals of property

3 The IASB's Framework

The **IASB's Framework** provides the basis of its **conceptual framework**. IASs and IFRSs are based on this framework. The key elements are:

- Financial statements should provide **useful information** to users.
- **Financial position** is shown in the statement of financial position.
- **Financial performance** is shown in the income statement.
- **Changes in financial position** are shown in the statement of cash flows.
- The main **underlying assumptions** are **accruals** and **going concern.**
- Financial statements should be: – Understandable
  - Relevant
  - Reliable
  - Comparable

The *Framework for the preparation and presentation of financial statements* (*'Framework'*) is, in effect, the **conceptual** framework upon which all IASs and IFRSs are based and hence which determines how financial statements are prepared and the information they contain.

The *Framework* consists of several sections or chapters, following on after a preface and introduction. These chapters are as follows.

- The objective of financial statements.
- Underlying assumptions
- Qualitative characteristics of financial statements
- The elements of financial statements
- Recognition of the elements of financial statements
- Measurement of the elements of financial statements
- Concepts of capital and capital maintenance

We will look briefly at the preface and introduction to the *Framework* as these will place the document in context with the rest of what you will study for this paper. We will then look only at the first three of the chapters listed above, because a detailed knowledge of the remainder of the *Framework* is not examinable. A brief summary of the remaining chapters is given at the end of this section.

3.1 Preface

The preface to the *Framework* points out the fundamental reason why financial statements are produced worldwide, ie to **satisfy the requirements of external users**, but that practice varies due to the individual pressures in each country. These pressures may be social, political, economic or legal, but they result in variations in practice from country to country, including the form of statements, the definition of their component parts (assets, liabilities etc), the criteria for recognition of items and both the scope and disclosure of financial statements.

It is these differences which the IASB wishes to narrow by **harmonising** all aspects of financial statements, including the regulations governing their accounting standards and their preparation and presentation.

The preface emphasises the way **financial statements are used to make economic decisions** and thus financial statements should be prepared to this end. The types of economic decisions for which financial statements are likely to be used include the following.

- Decisions to buy, hold or sell equity investments
- Assessment of management stewardship and accountability
- Assessment of the enterprise's ability to pay employees
- Assessment of the security of amounts lent to the enterprise
- Determination of taxation policies
- Determination of distributable profits and dividends
- Inclusion in national income statistics
- Regulations of the activities of enterprises

Any additional requirements imposed by **national governments** for their own purposes should not affect financial statements produced for the benefit of other users.

The *Framework* recognises that financial statements can be prepared using a **variety of models**. Although the most common is based on historical cost and a nominal unit of currency (ie pound sterling, US dollar etc), the *Framework* can be applied to financial statements prepared under a range of models.

3.2 Introduction

The introduction to the *Framework* lays out the purpose, status and scope of the document. It then looks at different users of financial statements and their information needs.

3.2.1 Purpose and status

The introduction gives a list of the purposes of the *Framework*.

(a) Assist the Board of the IASB in the **development of future** IFRSs and in its review of existing IASs.

(b) Assist the Board of the IASB in **promoting harmonisation** of regulations, accounting standards and procedures relating to the presentation of financial statements by providing a basis for reducing the number of alternative accounting treatments permitted by IASs.

(c) Assist **national standard-setting bodies** in developing national standards.

(d) Assist **preparers of financial statements** in applying IFRSs and in dealing with topics that have yet to form the subject of an IFRS.

(e) Assist **auditors** in forming an opinion as to whether financial statements conform with IASs.

(f) Assist **users of financial statements** in interpreting the information contained in financial statements prepared in conformity with IFRSs.

(g) Provide those who are interested in the work of IASB with **information** about its approach to the **formulation of IFRSs.**

Exam focus point

The **purpose** of the IASB *Framework* is given as background information, it is unlikely to be tested in the exam.

The *Framework* is not an IFRS and so does not overrule any individual IFRS. In the (rare) cases of conflict between an IAS or IFRS and the *Framework*, the IAS or IFRS will prevail. These cases will diminish over time as the *Framework* will be used as a guide in the production of future IFRSs. The *Framework* itself will be revised occasionally depending on the experience of the IASB in using it.

3.2.2 Scope

The *Framework* deals with:

(a) The **objective** of financial statements

(b) The **qualitative characteristics** that determine the usefulness of information in financial statements

(c) The **definition, recognition and measurement** of the elements from which financial statements are constructed

(d) Concepts of **capital and capital maintenance**

We are only concerned with (a) and (b) here.

The *Framework* is concerned with **'general purpose' financial statements** (ie a normal set of annual statements), but it can be applied to other types of accounts. A complete set of financial statements includes:

(a) A statement of financial position

(b) An income statement

(c) A statement of changes in financial position (eg a statement of cash flows)

(d) Notes, other statements and explanatory material

Supplementary information may be included, but some items are not included, namely commentaries and reports by the directors, the chairman, management etc.

All types of financial reporting entities are included (commercial, industrial, business; public or private sector).

Key term

A **reporting entity** is an entity for which there are users who rely on the financial statements as their major source of financial information about the entity.   (*Framework*)

3.2.3 Users and their information needs

We have already looked at the users of accounting information in Chapter 1. They consist of investors, employees, lenders, suppliers and other trade payables, customers, government and their agencies and the public.

Financial statements cannot meet all these users' needs, but financial statements which meet the **needs of investors** (providers of risk capital) will meet most of the needs of other users.

The *Framework* emphasises that the preparation and presentation of financial statements is primarily the **responsibility of an entity's management**. Management also has an interest in the information appearing in financial statements.

3.3 The objective of financial statements

The *Framework* states that:

> 'The objective of financial statements is to provide information about the financial position performance and changes in financial position of an entity that is useful to a wide range of users in making economic decisions.'

Such financial statements will meet the needs of most users. The information is, however, restricted.

(a)   It is **based on past events** not expected future events.
(b)   It does not necessarily contain **non-financial information**.

The statements also show the results of the **management's stewardship**.

3.3.1 Financial position, performance and changes in financial position

It is important for users to assess the **ability of an entity to produce cash and cash equivalents** to pay employees, lenders etc.

Financial position information is affected by the following and information about each one can aid the user.

(a)   **Economic resources controlled:** to predict the ability to generate cash
(b)   **Financial structure:** to predict borrowing needs, the distribution of future profits/cash and likely success in raising new finance
(c)   **Liquidity and solvency:** to predict whether financial commitments will be met as they fall due (liquidity relates to short-term commitments, solvency is longer-term)

In all these areas, the capacity to adapt to changes in the environment in which the entity operates is very important.

Financial performance (income statement) information, particularly profitability, is used to assess potential changes in the economic resources the entity is likely to control in future. Information about performance variability is therefore important.

Changes in financial position (ie statement of cash flows) information is used to assess the entity's investing, financing and operating activities. They show the entity's ability to produce cash and the needs which utilise those cash flows.

All parts of the financial statements are **interrelated**, reflecting different aspects of the same transactions or events. Each statement provides different information; none can provide all the information required by users.

3.4 Underlying assumptions

We have met two of the assumptions discussed here in Section 2 and the other in Chapter 1. Here is a quick revision.

(a) **Accruals basis**
Financial statements prepared under the accruals basis show users past transactions involving cash and also obligations to pay cash in the future and resources which represent cash to be received in the future.

(b) **Going concern**
It is assumed that the entity has no intention to liquidate or curtail major operations. If it did, then the financial statements would be prepared on a different (disclosed) basis.

(c) **Business entity concept**
Financial statements are prepared on the basis that the business is a separate entity from the owner(s) regardless of the legal position.

3.5 Qualitative characteristics of financial statements

The *Framework* states that qualitative characteristics are the attributes that make the information provided in financial statements useful to users. The four principal qualitative characteristics are **understandability, relevance, reliability and comparability**. These and the other qualitative characteristics are discussed in detail in Sections 3.6 to 3.15 that follow.

Exam focus point

While the previous sections have been mainly background information, make sure that you learn Sections 3.6 to 3.15 as these are specifically listed in the syllabus. At the 2009 ACCA Teachers' Conference, the examiner emphasised that students need to be aware of the theoretical aspects of the syllabus eg the *Framework*.

3.6 Understandability

Users must be able to understand financial statements. They are assumed to have some business, economic and accounting knowledge and to be able to apply themselves to study the information property. **Complex matters should not be left out** of financial statements simply due to its difficulty if it is relevant information.

3.7 Relevance

Only relevant information can be useful. Information is relevant when it helps users evaluate past, present or future events, or it confirms or corrects previous evaluations. The predictive and confirmatory roles of information are interrelated.

Information on financial position and performance is often used to predict future position and performance and other things of interest to the user, eg likely dividend, wage rises. The **manner of showing information** will enhance the ability to make predictions, eg by highlighting unusual items.

The relevance of information is affected by its nature and **materiality**. Information may be judged relevant simply because of its nature (eg remuneration of management). In other cases, both the nature and materiality of the information are important. Materiality is not a primary qualitative characteristic itself (like reliability or relevance), because it is merely a threshold or cut-off point.

3.8 Reliability

Information must also be **reliable** to be useful, ie **free from material error and bias**. The user must be able to depend on it being a faithful representation.

Point to note

Even if information is relevant, if it is very unreliable it may be misleading to recognise it, eg a disputed claim for damages in a legal action.

3.9 Faithful representation

Information must **represent faithfully** the transactions it purports to represent in order to be reliable. There is a risk that this may not be the case, not due to bias, but due to **inherent difficulties in identifying the transactions** or finding an **appropriate method** of measurement or presentation.

Where measurement of the financial effects of an item is so uncertain, enterprises should not recognise such an item, eg internally generated goodwill.

3.10 Substance over form

Faithful representation of a transaction is only possible if it is accounted for according to its **substance and economic reality**, not with its legal form.

3.11 Neutrality

Information **must be free from bias to be reliable**. Neutrality is lost if the financial statements are prepared so as to influence the user to make a judgement or decision in order to achieve a predetermined outcome.

3.12 Prudence

Uncertainties exist in the preparation of financial information, eg the collectability of doubtful receivables. These uncertainties are recognised through disclosure and through the application of prudence.

Point to note

Prudence does not, however, allow the creation of hidden reserves or excessive provisions, understatement of assets or income or overstatement of liabilities or expenses.

3.13 Completeness

Financial information must be complete, within the restrictions of materiality and cost, to be reliable. Omission may cause information to be misleading.

3.14 Comparability

Users must be able to compare an entity's financial statements:

(a)   **through time** to identify trends; and

(b)   **with other entity's statements**, to evaluate their relative financial position, performance and changes in financial position.

The consistency of treatment is therefore important across like items over time, within the entity and across all entities.

The **disclosure of accounting policies** is particularly important here. Users must distinguish between different accounting policies to be able to make a valid comparison of similar items in the accounts of different entities.

Comparability is **not the same as uniformity**. Entities should change accounting policies if they become inappropriate.

Corresponding information for **preceding** periods should be shown to enable comparison over time.

3.15 Constraints on relevant and reliable information

3.15.1 Timeliness

Information may become irrelevant if there is a delay in reporting it. **There is a balance between timeliness and the provision of reliable information.** Information may be reported on a timely basis when not all aspects of the transaction are known, thus compromising reliability.

> If every detail of a transaction is known, it may be too late to publish the information because it has become irrelevant. The overriding consideration is how best to satisfy the economic decision-making needs of the users.

3.15.2 Balance between benefits and cost

This is a pervasive constraint, not a qualitative characteristic. When information is provided, its benefits must exceed the costs of obtaining and presenting it. This is a **subjective** area and there are other difficulties: others than the intended users may gain a benefit; also the cost may be paid by someone other than the users. It is therefore difficult to apply a cost-benefit analysis, but preparers and users should be aware of the constraint.

3.15.3 Balance between qualitative characteristics

A **trade off between qualitative characteristics** of often necessary, the aim being to achieve an appropriate balance to meet the objective of financial statements. It is a matter for professional judgement as to the relative importance of these characteristics in each case. We will look at this in Section 4 of this chapter.

We have now covered those parts of the IASB's *Framework* which you need to understand in detail. A summary of the rest of the document is given below.

3.16 The elements of financial statements

This section defines the important items which make up the financial statements and looks at their sub-classification.

(a) **Financial position**

    (i)   Assets

Key term

> An **asset** is a resource controlled by the entity as a result of past events and from which future economic benefits are expected to flow to the entity. *Framework*

    (ii)   Liabilities

Key term

> A **liability** is a present obligation of the entity arising from past events, the settlement of which is expected to result in a outflow from the entity of resource embodying economic benefits. *Framework*

    (iii)   Equity

Key term

> **Equity** is the residual interest in the assets of the entity after deducting all its liabilities. *Framework*

(b) **Performance**

    (i)   Income

Key term

> **Income** is increases in economic benefits during the accounting period in the form of inflows or enhancement of assets or decrease of liabilities that result in increases in equity, other than those relating to contributions from equity participants. *Framework*

    (ii)   Expenses

Key term

> **Expenses** are decreases in economic benefits during the accounting period in the form of outflows or depletions of assets or incurrences of liabilities that result in decreases in equity, other than those relating to distributions to equity participants. *Framework*

(iii)   Capital maintenance adjustments

We have looked at most of these items in detail in Chapter 1. We will look at capital maintenance later in this section.

Exam focus point

You do need to know the *Framework* definitions of assets, liabilities, equity, revenue and expenses.

3.17 Recognition of the elements of financial statements

Having defined the elements, the *Framework* then lays out the criteria for when items should be recognised (ie included in the financial statements). The section looks at the recognition of assets, liabilities, income and expenditure in turn, based on the concept of outflows and inflows of future economic benefit.

3.18 Measurement of the element of financial statements

This brief section simply mentions some of the different measurement bases available, including historical cost and current cost.

3.19 Concepts of capital and capital maintenance

The different concepts are examined briefly, the main two concepts are:

(a)   **financial capital maintenance**; and
(b)   physical (or operating) capital maintenance.

Capital maintenance is an idea that capital must be preserved before any payments can be made to shareholders. In times of high inflation, a company may appear to have made a profit. However, if the inflation factor is applied to the capital, there may well have been a loss.

For example, a company may have capital of $100,000 and make profits of $10,000. However, inflation is running at 10%. Therefore capital maintenance requires that the $10,000 is needed to maintain capital (10% × $100,000) and so no dividend is paid to the shareholders.

Question	Revision of concepts

See if you can write a short sentence explaining each of the following concepts.

(a)   Relevance
(b)   Reliability
(c)   Faithful representation
(d)   Neutrality
(e)   Completeness
(f)   Comparability
(g)   Understandability

Answer

(a)   **Relevance**. The information provided satisfies the needs of users.

(b)   **Reliability**. The information is free from material error or bias.

(c)   **Faithful representation**. The information gives full details of its effects on the financial statements and is only recognised if its financial effects are certain.

(d)   **Neutrality**. The information is free from bias.

(e)   **Completeness**. The information must present a rounded picture of its economic activities.

(f)   **Comparability**. The information should be produced on a consistent basis so that valid comparisons can be made with previous periods and with other entities.

(g)   **Understandability**. Information may be difficult to understand if it is incomplete, but too much detail can also confuse the issue.

Consistency

Which of the following statements **best** describes the consistency concept?

A   Only material items are disclosed
B   The way an item is presented always remains the same
C   Presentation and classification of items should remain the same unless a change is required by an IFRS

Answer

The correct answer is C.

4 Criticisms of accounting conventions

Accounting conventions are not 'set in stone'. They can be, and have been, criticised.

It is easy to assume that these accounting conventions are the best ones we could use. However, this is not necessarily the case. This is potentially a vast topic, so we will look at only to two or three examples.

Exam focus point

The syllabus and study guide show that you must understand the balance between qualitative characteristics. Do not neglect this section.

4.1 Criticisms of the prudence concept

'Prudence' and 'accountant' would appear to go together. Surely this bedrock of accounting is unassailable?

Question   Prudence

Before we go any further, can you remember exactly what prudence is?

Answer

The prudence concept lays down that revenue and profits are not anticipated but should only be recorded when earning is reasonably certain. Expenses and liabilities should, however, be recorded when anticipated, as best estimates if no actual figures are available.

Loss in value of assets, whether realised or not, should be recorded when it arises, but a gain in value of an asset should not be recorded except via an unrealised reserve and only then if properly warranted.

An example of the application of the prudence concept is the requirement to value inventory at the lower of cost and net realisable value.

This is all very well, but it can lead to problems, of which the following can be identified as the most significant.

(a) **Prudence** most obviously conflicts with the **accrual** assumption because it requires that the matching of costs and revenues should not take place if there is any doubt about the future recoverability of deferred costs. This conflict has been summarised as 'should we report the worst possible situation (prudence) or the most likely position?'

(b) **Prudence** also conflicts with the **going concern** assumption because it may not be prudent to assume that a business is a going concern (although it is realistic).

(c) **Prudence makes it difficult to treat items consistently** because circumstances in one period may require a different treatment from previous periods in order to be prudent.

(d) **Prudence** also undermines several other assumptions. For instance, **objectivity** is regarded as important by most users of accounts but prudence (or conservatism as it is sometimes called) implies a subjectivity in coming to accounting judgements. It is also difficult to reconcile prudence with the use of anything other than the **historical cost convention** for valuing assets (see Section 5).

4.2 Criticisms of the accruals assumption

Try this question before you go any further.

Question	Accruals

Can you remember what the accruals assumption is?

Answer

Under the accruals assumption, revenue and expenditure are matched and recorded in the accounts when earned or incurred, rather than being dependent on the associated cash movement.

This applies most obviously for credit sales, but also results in the identification of inventory at the end of each accounting period rather than writing all purchases off to the trading account. Only purchases which result in a sale recorded in the period or are used for promotional or similar purposes should be matched with sales for the period. Therefore, if purchased goods still on hand at the period end are of saleable quality and the company will still be trading in the next period (ie the prudence and going concern concepts are satisfied) then any unsold goods can be treated as current assets and their value can be deducted from purchases and opening inventory.

What could possibly be wrong with that? The main criticism relates to the conflict with historical cost accounting.

It can be argued that the accrual assumption is not applied in historical cost accounting. The assumption states that revenue earned must be matched against expenditure incurred in earning it. The cost of goods sold in the income statement is normally computed on the basis of their historical cost. However, a continuing business will want to replace inventories sold and will have to do so at ever higher prices. This means that some of the 'profit' shown by the accounts is not profit at all, but must be spent in restoring the assets of the business to their previous level.

It may be argued that the accrual assumption could be better applied under a system of replacement cost. Thus the historical cost profit would be adjusted by the 'cost of sales adjustment' which aims to charge the income statement with the current cost of each item of inventory sold at the date of sale.

Other criticisms of the accrual assumption include the following.

(a) The nature of the matching process is often **arbitrary**, for example in selecting a depreciation method.

(b) The accrual assumption **conflicts with the prudence concept** as indicated above.

(c)   The accrual assumption is about getting the income statement figure right. This is an admirable aim in itself, but it may mean that the **statement of financial position contains rather arbitrary figures**. For example, when an asset is depreciated, the statement of financial position figure is simply the unexpired cost to be allocated to future accounting periods. In other words, it is what is left over after matching has taken place, not in itself a meaningful figure.

5 Bases of valuation

FAST FORWARD

Items in the financial statements can be valued under a number of bases. For your syllabus, you need to know the following bases.

- Historical cost
- Replacement cost
- Net realisable value
- Economic value

5.1 Historical cost

A basic principle of accounting (some writers include it in the list of fundamental accounting assumptions) is that items are normally stated in accounts at historical cost, ie at the amount which the business paid to acquire them. An important advantage of this procedure is that the objectivity of accounts is maximised: there is usually documentary evidence to prove the amount paid to purchase an asset or pay an expense.

Key term

> **Historical cost** means that transactions are recorded at the cost when they occurred.

In general, accountants prefer to deal with costs, rather than with 'values'. This is because valuations tend to be subjective and to vary according to what the valuation is for.

5.2 Replacement cost

Key term

> **Replacement cost** means the amount needed to replace an items with an identical item.

Example: Replacement cost

XY Co bought a machine five years ago for $15,000. It is now worn out and needs replacing. An identical machine can be purchased for $20,000.

> **Historical cost** is $15,000
> **Replacement cost** is $20,000

5.3 Net realisable value

Key term

> **Net realisable value** is the expected price less any costs still to be incurred in getting the item ready for sale and then selling it.

Example: Net realisable value

XY Co's machine from the example above can be restored to working order at a cost of $5,000. It can then be sold for $10,000. What is its net realisable value?

> **Net realisable value** = $10,000 – $5,000
> = $5,000

5.4 Economic value

> **Economic value** is the value derived from an asset's ability to generate income.

A machine's economic value is the amount of profits it is expected to generate for the remains of its useful life.

Example: Economic value

Suppose XY Co buy the new machine for $20,000. It is estimated that the new machine will generate profits of $4,000 per year for its useful life of 8 years. What is its economic value?

$$\text{Economic value} = \$4,000 \times 8$$
$$= \$32,000$$

5.5 Advantages and disadvantages of historical cost accounting

The **advantage** of historical cost accounting is that the cost is known and can be proved (eg by the invoice). There is no subjectivity or bias in the valuation.

There are a number of **disadvantages** and these usually arise in times of rising prices (inflation). When inflation is low, then historical cost accounting is usually satisfactory. However, when inflation is high the following problems can occur.

5.5.1 Non-current asset values are unrealistic

The most striking example is property. Although some entities have periodically updated the statement of financial position values, in general there has been a lack of consistency in the approach adopted and a lack of clarity in the way in which the effects of these changes in value have been expressed.

If non-current assets are retained in the books at their historical cost, **unrealised holding gains are not recognised**. This means that the total holding gain, if any, will be brought into account during the year in which the asset is realised, rather than spread over the period during which it was owned.

There are, in essence, two contradictory points to be considered.

(a)   Although it has long been accepted that a statement of financial position prepared under the historical cost concept is an historical record and not a statement of current worth, many people now argue that the statement of financial position should at least give an indication of the current value of the company's tangible net assets.

(b)   The prudence concept requires that profits should only be recognised when realised in the form either of cash or of other assets, the ultimate cash realisation of which can be assessed with reasonable certainty. It may be argued that recognising unrealised holding gains on non-current assets is contrary to this concept.

On balance, the weight of opinion is now in favour of restating asset values. It is felt that the criticism based on prudence can be met by ensuring that valuations are made as objectively as possible (eg in the case of property, by having independent expert valuations) and by not taking unrealised gains through the income statement, but instead through reserves.

5.5.2 Depreciation is inadequate to finance the replacement of non-current assets

Depreciation is not provided for in order to enforce retention of profits and thus ensure that funds are available for asset replacement. It is intended as a measure of the contribution of non-current assets to the company's activities in the period. However, an incidental effect of providing for depreciation is that not all liquid funds can be paid out to investors and so funds for asset replacement are on hand. What is important is not the replacement of one asset by an identical new one (something that rarely happens) but the replacement of the *operating capability* represented by the old asset.

5.5.3 Holding gains on inventories are included in profit

Another criticism of historical cost depreciation is that it does not fully reflect the value of the asset consumed during the accounting year.

During a period of high inflation the monetary value of inventory held may increase significantly while they are being processed. The conventions of historical cost accounting lead to the unrealised part of this holding gain (known as *inventory appreciation*) being included in profit for the year.

Example: Holding gain

This problem can be illustrated using a simple example. At the beginning of the year a company has 100 units of inventory and no other assets. Its trading account for the year is shown below.

TRADING ACCOUNT

	Units	$		Units	$
Opening inventory	100	200	Sales (made 31 December)	100	500
Purchases (made 31 December)	100	400			
	200	600			
Closing inventory (FIFO basis)	100	400			
	100	200			
Gross profit	–	300			
	100	500		100	500

Apparently the company has made a gross profit of $300. But, at the beginning of the year the company owned 100 units of inventory and at the end of the year it owned 100 units of inventory and $100 (sales $500 less purchases $400). From this it would seem that a profit of $100 is more reasonable. The remaining $200 is inventory appreciation arising as the purchase price increased from $2 to $4.

The criticism can be overcome by using a **capital maintenance concept** based on physical units rather than money values.

5.5.4 Profits (or losses) on holdings of net monetary items are not shown

In periods of inflation the purchasing power, and thus the value, of money falls. It follows that an investment in money will have a lower real value at the end of a period of time than it did at the beginning. A loss has been incurred. Similarly, the real value of a monetary liability will reduce over a period of time and a gain will be made.

5.5.5 The true effect of inflation on capital maintenance is not shown

To a large extent this follows from the points already mentioned. It is a widely held principle that distributable profits should only be recognised after full allowance has been made for any erosion in the capital value of a business. In historical cost accounts, although capital is maintained in *nominal money terms*, it may not be in *real terms*. In other words, profits may be distributed to the detriment of the long-term viability of the business. This criticism may be made by those who advocate capital maintenance in physical terms.

5.5.6 Comparisons over time are unrealistic

This will tend to an exaggeration of growth. For example, if a company's profit in 1966 was $100,000 and in 1999 $500,000, a shareholder's initial reaction might be that the company had done rather well. If, however, it was then revealed that with $100,000 in 1966 he could buy exactly the same goods as with $500,000 in 1999, the apparent growth would seem less impressive.

6 IAS 8 Accounting policies, changes in accounting estimates and errors

FAST FORWARD

IAS 8 Accounting policies, changes in accounting estimates and errors is an important standard. Here, you need to be able to understand the provisions and identify the appropriate accounting treatment in respect of **changes in accounting policies**.

IAS 8 lays down the criteria for selecting and changing accounting policies and specifies the accounting treatment and disclosure of changes in accounting policies, changes in accounting estimates, and errors.

6.1 Definitions

The following definitions are given in the standard.

Key terms

> **Accounting policies** are the specific principles, bases, conventions, rules and practices applied by an entity in preparing and presenting financial statements.
>
> A **change in accounting estimate** is an adjustment of the carrying amount of an asset or a liability, or the amount of the periodic consumption of an asset.
>
> **Material**: Omissions or misstatements of items are material if they could, individually or collectively, influence the economic decisions of users taken on the basis of the financial statements.
>
> **Prior period errors** are omissions from, and misstatements in, the entity's financial statements for one or more prior periods.
>
> **Impracticable**: Applying a requirement is impracticable when the entity cannot apply it after making every reasonable effort to do so.

6.2 Changes in accounting policies

The same accounting policies are usually adopted from period to period, to allow users to analyse trends over time in profit, cash flows and financial position. **Changes in accounting policy will therefore be rare** and should be made only if required.

(a) By an **standard or an interpretation (of a standard)**
(b) If the change will result in a **more appropriate presentation** of events or transactions in the financial statements of the entity

A change in accounting policy is a change in measurement, presentation or recognition of an item eg a business has written off all development expenditure in the past, but now decides to capitalise qualifying development expenditure in the statement of financial position.

The standard highlights two types of event which do not constitute changes in accounting policy.

(a) Adopting an accounting policy for a **new type of transaction** or event not dealt with previously by the entity.
(b) Adopting a **new accounting policy** for a transaction or event which has not occurred in the past or which was not material.

In the case of property, plant and equipment, if a policy of revaluation is adopted for the first time then this is treated, not as a change of accounting policy under IAS 8, but as a revaluation under IAS 16 *Property, plant and equipment* (see Chapter 9). The following paragraphs do not therefore apply to revaluations.

A change in accounting policy should be applied retrospectively. Where an entity cannot determine the effect of applying the new policy to all prior periods, the new policy should be applied prospectively from the start of the earliest period practicable.

(a) **Retrospective application**

The new accounting policy is applied to transactions and events as if it had always been in use. In other words, at the earliest date such transactions or events occurred, the policy is applied from that date.

(b) **Prospective application**

The new policy will be applied only to transactions or events occurring after the date of the change in policy. Existing balances are not recalculated so no change is made to the opening balance on retained reserves or to net profit or loss for the current period relating to prior periods. Only changes caused by the new accounting policy in the existing period are necessary.

Where retrospective application is impracticable, the standard allows prospective application.

6.2.1 Adoption of an IFRS

Where a new IFRS is adopted, IAS 8 requires any transitional provisions in the new IFRS itself to be followed. If none are given in the IFRS which is being adopted, then retrospective application is required.

6.2.2 Other changes in accounting policy:

IAS 8 requires **retrospective application**, *unless* the amount of any resulting adjustment that relates to prior periods is **not reasonably determinable**. Any resulting adjustment should be reported as an adjustment to the opening balance of retained earnings. Comparative information should be restated unless it is impracticable to do so.

This means that all comparative information must be restated **as if the new policy had always been in force**, with amounts relating to earlier periods reflected in an adjustment to opening reserves of the earliest period presented.

Prospective application is allowed in certain circumstances, when the amount of the adjustment to the opening balance of retained earnings required by the benchmark treatment cannot be reasonably determined.

Certain **disclosures** are required when a change in accounting policy has a material effect on the current period or any prior period presented, or when it may have a material effecting subsequent periods.

(a) Reasons for the change

(b) Amount of the adjustment for the current period and for each period presented

(c) Amount of the adjustment relating to periods prior to those included in the comparative information

(d) The fact that comparative information has been restated or that it is impracticable to do so

Disclosures are required when a change in accounting policy has a material effect on the current period or any prior period presented, or when it may have a material effect in subsequent periods.

(a) Reasons for the change

(b) Amount of the adjustment recognised in net profit/loss in the current period

(c) The amount of the adjustment included in each period for which prior information is presented and the amount of the adjustment relating to periods prior to those included in the financial statements

Question   Change of accounting policy

Wick Co was established on 1 January 20X0. In the first three years' accounts development expenditure was carried forward as an asset in the statement of financial position. During 20X3 the managers decided that for the current and future years, all development expenditure should be written off as it is incurred. This decision has not resulted from any change in the expected outcome of development projects on hand, but rather from a desire to favour the prudence concept. The following information is available.

(a) Movements on the development account.

Year	Development expenditure incurred and capitalised during year $'000	Transfer from capitalised development expenditure account to income statement $'000
20X0	525	–
20X1	780	215
20X2	995	360

(b) The 20X2 accounts showed the following.

	$'000
Retained earnings b/f	2,955
Retained earnings for the year	1,825
Retained earnings c/f	4,780

(c) The retained profit for 20X3 after charging the actual development expenditure for the year was $2,030,000.

Required

Show how the change in accounting policy should be reflected in the reserves in the company's 20X3 accounts per IAS 8.

Ignore taxation.

Answer

If the new accounting policy had been adopted since the company was incorporated, the additional income statement charges for development expenditure would have been:

	$'000
20X0	525
20X1 (780 – 215)	565
	1,090
20X2 (995 – 360)	635
	1,725

This means that the reserves brought forward at 1 January 20X3 would have been $1,725,000 less than the reported figure of $4,780,000; while the reserves brought forward at 1 January 20X2 would have been $1,090,000 less than the reported figure of $2,955,000.

The statement of reserves in Wick Co's 20X3 accounts should, therefore, appear as follows.

	20X3 $'000	Comparative (previous year) figures 20X2 $'000
Retained earnings at the beginning of year		
Previously reported	4,780	2,955
Retrospective change in accounting policy (note 1)	1,725	1,090
Restated	3,055	1,865
Retained earnings for the year	2,030	1,190 (note 2)
Retained earnings at the end of the year	5,085	3,055

Notes

1 The accounts should include a note explaining the reasons for and consequences of the changes in accounting policy. (See above workings for 20X3 and 20X2.)

2 The retained profit shown for 20X2 is after charging the additional development expenditure of $635,000.

Part B The qualitative characteristics of financial information and the fundamental bases of accounting | **3: Accounting conventions** 49

Attention!

> You will deal with limited company financial statements in Chapter 21. We suggest that you flag this example and return to it after you have studied Chapter 21.

Question

AB Co decides to change its accounting policy following the issue of a new IFRS. The IFRS includes provisions for accounting for transitional changes.

How should it account for the change in policy?

A   According to IAS 8
B   According to the new IFRS

Answer

The correct answer is B. The new IFRs includes accounting requirements on the transition. IAS 8 is only followed if the new IFRS does not include transitional arrangements.

Chapter Roundup

- In preparing financial statements, accountants follow certain *fundamental assumptions*.

- IAS 1 identifies **four fundamental assumptions** that must be taken into account when preparing statements:

  - Fair presentation
  - Going concern
  - Accruals
  - Consistency

  IAS 1 also considers three other concepts extremely important. **Prudence, substance over form and materiality** should govern the selection and application of accounting policies.

- The **IASB's Framework** provides the basis of its **conceptual framework**. IASs and IFRSs are based on this framework. The key elements are:

  - Financial statements should provide **useful information** to users.

  - **Financial position** is shown in the statement of financial position.

  - **Financial performance** is shown in the income statement.

  - Changes in financial position are shown in the statement of cash flows.

  - The main **underlying assumptions** are **accruals** and **going concern**.

  - Financial statements should be: – Understandable
    - Relevant
    - Reliable
    - Comparable

- **Accounting conventions** are not 'set in stone'. They can be, and have been, criticised.

- Items in the financial statements can be valued under a number of bases. For your syllabus, you need to know the following bases.

  - Historical cost
  - Replacement cost
  - Net realisable value
  - Economic value

- IAS 8 Accountancy policies, changes in accounting estimates and errors is an important standard. Here, you need to be able to understand the provisions and identify the appropriate accounting treatment in respect of **changes in accounting policies**.

Quick Quiz

1   Which IAS deals with accounting assumptions?

2   Which of the following assumptions are included in IAS 1?

    A   Money measurement

    B   Objectivity

    C   Going concern

    D   Business entity

3   Define 'going concern'.

4   What is meant by the prudence concept?

5   Only items which have a monetary value can be included in accounts. Which of the following is a basis of valuation?

    A   Historical cost

    B   Money measurement

    C   Realisation

    D   Business entity

6   Suggest four possible values which might be attributed to an asset in the statement of financial position of a business.

7   Making an allowance for receivables is an example of which concept?

    A   Accruals

    B   Going concern

    C   Materiality

    D   Prudence

8   Why is a conceptual framework necessary?

    A   To provide a theoretical basics for financial statements

    B   To provide concepts on which to build a framework

9   Which of the following sections are not included in the IASB's *Framework*?

    A   Users of financial statements

    B   Underlying assumptions

    C   Qualitative characteristics

    D   Concept of capital maintenance

10 What does 'reliability' mean in the context of financial statements?

Answers to Quick Quiz

1   IAS 1 *Presentation of Financial Statements.*

2   C   Only going concern is included in IAS 1, the others are assumptions and concepts generally used in accountancy, but not mentioned in IAS 1.

3   The assumption that a business will continue in operation for the foreseeable future, without going into liquidation or materially scaling down its operations.

4   Prudence means to be cautious when exercising judgement. In particular profits should not be recognised until realised, but a loss should be recognised as soon as it is foreseen.

5   A   This is the only valuation basis.

6   •   Historical cost
    •   Replacement value
    •   Net realisable value
    •   Economic value

7   D   Prudence

8   A   It forms the theoretical basis for determining what is included in financial statements, how they are measured and how they are communicated.

9   A

10 Free from material error and bias.

Now try the questions below from the Exam Question Bank

Number	Level	Marks	Time
Q3	Examination	2	2 mins
Q4	Examination	2	2 mins
Q5	Examination	2	2 mins
Q6	Examination	2	2 mins

Part B The qualitative characteristics of financial information and the fundamental bases of accounting | **3: Accounting conventions**   **53**

The use of double entry and accounting systems

Sources, records and books of prime entry

Topic list	Syllabus reference
1 The role of source documents	C1(a)–(b), (f)
2 The need for books of prime entry	C2(a)
3 Sales and purchase day books	D1(a)–(b)
4 Cash book	D2(a)
5 Petty cash	D2(b)–(e)

Introduction

From your studies of the first three chapters you should have grasped some important points about the nature and purpose of accounting.

- Most organisations provide products and services in the hope of making a profit for their owners, by receiving payment in money for those goods and services.

- The role of the accounting system is to record these monetary effects and create information about them.

You should also, by now, understand the basic principles underlying the statement of financial position and income statement and have an idea of what they look like.

We now turn our attention to the process by which a business transaction works its way through to the financial statements.

It is usual to record a business transaction on a **document**. Such documents include invoices, orders, credit notes and goods received notes, all of which will be discussed in Section 1 of this chapter. In terms of the accounting system these are known as **source documents**. The information on them is processed by the system by, for example, aggregating (adding together) or classifying.

Records of source documents are kept in 'books of prime entry', which, as the name suggests, are the first stage at which a business transaction enters into the accounting system. The various types of books of prime entry are discussed in Sections 2 to 4. We will also look at the treatment of petty cash in Section 5.

In the next chapter we consider what happens to transactions after the books of prime entry stage.

Study guide

		Intellectual level
C1	**Double-entry bookkeeping principles including the maintenance of accounting records and sources of information**	
(a)	Identify and explain the function of the main data sources in an accounting system	1
(b)	Outline the contents and purpose of different types of business documentation, including: quotation, sales order, purchase order, goods received note, goods dispatched note, invoice, statement, credit note, debit note, remittance advice, receipt.	1
(f)	Identify the main types of business transactions, eg sales, purchases, payments, receipts.	1
C2	**Ledger accounts, books of prime entry and journals**	
(a)	Identify the main types of ledger accounts and books of prime entry, and understand their nature and function.	1
D1	**Sales and purchases**	
(a)	Record sale and purchase transactions in ledger accounts and in day books.	1
(b)	Understand and record sales and purchase returns.	1
D2	**Cash**	
(a)	Record cash transactions in ledger accounts.	1
(b)	Understand the need for a record of petty cash transactions.	1
(c)	Describe the features and operations of a petty cash imprest system.	1
(d)	Account for petty cash using imprest and non-imprest methods.	1
(e)	Understand the importance of, and identify controls and security over the petty cash system.	1

Exam guide

These topics are likely to be examined by means of asking which books of prime entry you could use to record a set of transactions.

1 The role of source documents

FAST FORWARD

Business transactions are recorded on **source documents**. Examples include sales and purchase orders, invoices and credit notes.

1.1 Types of source documents

Whenever a business transaction takes place, involving sales or purchases, receiving or paying money, or owing or being owed money, it is usual for the transaction to be recorded on a document. These documents are the source of all the information recorded by a business.

Documents used to record the business transactions in the 'books of account' of the business include the following.

- **Quotation.** A business makes a written offer to a customer to produce or deliver goods or services for a certain amount of money.

- **Sales order**. A customer writes out or signs an order for goods or services he requires.
- **Purchase order**. A business orders from another business goods or services, such as material supplies.
- **Goods received note.** A list of goods that a business has received from a supplier. This is usually prepared by the business's own warehouse or goods receiving area.
- **Goods despatched note.** A list of goods that a business has sent out to a customer.
- **Invoice**. This is discussed further below.
- **Statement.** A document sent out by a supplier to a customer listing all invoices, credit notes and payments received from the customer.
- **Credit note.** A document sent by a supplier to a customer in respect of goods returned or overpayments made by the customer. It is a 'negative' invoice.
- **Debit note.** A document sent by a customer to a supplier in respect of goods returned or an overpayment made. It is a formal request for the supplier to issue a credit note.
- **Remittance advice.** A document sent with a payment, detailing which invoices are being paid and which credit notes offset.
- **Receipt.** A written confirmation that money has been paid. This is usually in respect of cash sales, eg a till receipt from a cash register.

1.2 Invoices

Key term

> An **invoice** relates to a sales order or a purchase order.
>
> - When a business sells goods or services on credit to a customer, it sends out an invoice. The details on the invoice should match the details on the sales order. The invoice is a request for the customer to pay what he owes.
>
> - When a business buys goods or services on credit it receives an invoice from the supplier. The details on the invoice should match the details on the purchase order.

The invoice is primarily a demand for payment, but it is used for other purposes as well, as we shall see. Since it has several uses, an invoice is often produced on multi-part stationery, or photocopied, or carbon-copied. The top copy will go to the customer and other copies will be used by various people within the business.

1.2.1 What does an invoice show?

Most invoices are numbered, so that the business can keep track of all the invoices it sends out. Information usually shown on an invoice includes the following.

(a)   Name and address of the seller and the purchaser
(b)   Date of the sale
(c)   Description of what is being sold
(d)   Quantity and unit price of what has been sold (eg 20 pairs of shoes at $25 a pair)
(e)   Details of trade discount, if any (eg 10% reduction in cost if buying over 100 pairs of shoes)
(f)   Total amount of the invoice including (usually) details any of sales tax
(g)   Sometimes, the date by which payment is due, and other terms of sale

1.2.2 Uses of multi-part invoices

As stated above invoices may be used for different purposes.

- Top copy to customer as a request for payment
- Second copy to accounts department to match to eventual payment
- Third copy to ware house to generate a despatch of goods, as evidenced by a goods despatched note.
- Fourth copy stapled to sales order and kept in sales department as a record of sales.

Please note that businesses will design their own invoices and there may be other copies for other departments. Not all businesses will need four part invoices. A very small business may use the customer copy of the invoice as a despatch note as well. In addition, the sales invoice may be stapled to the sales order and both documents passed to the accounts department.

1.3 The credit note

China Supplies sent out an invoice for 20 dinner plates, but the typist accidentally typed in a total of $162.10, instead of $62.10. The china shop has been **overcharged** by $100. What is China Supplies to do?

Alternatively, when the china shop received the plates it found that they had all been broken in the post and that it was going to send them back. Although the china shop has received an invoice for $62.10, it has no intention of paying it because the plates were useless. Again, what is China Supplies to do?

The answer is that China Supplies sends out a **credit note**. A credit note is sometimes printed in red to distinguish it from an invoice. Otherwise, it will be made out in much the same way as an invoice, but with less detail and 'Credit Note Number' instead of 'Invoice Number'.

Key term

> A **credit note** is a document relating to returned goods or refunds when a customer has been overcharged. It can be regarded as a **negative invoice**.

1.4 Other documents

The following documents are sometimes used in connection with sales and purchases.

(a)   Debit notes
(b)   Goods received notes

A **debit note** might be issued to **adjust an invoice** already issued. This is also commonly achieved by issuing a revised invoice after raising a credit or debit note purely for internal purposes (ie to keep the records straight).

More commonly, a debit note is issued to a supplier as a means of formally requesting a credit note.

Goods received notes (GRNs) record a receipt of goods, most commonly in a warehouse. They may be used in addition to suppliers' advice notes. Often the accounts department will require to see the relevant GRN before paying a supplier's invoice. Even where GRNs are not routinely used, the details of a consignment from a supplier which arrives without an advice note must always be recorded.

Question	Credit note

Fill in the blanks.

'China Supplies sends out a . . . . to a credit customer in order to correct an error where a customer has been overcharged on an . . . .'

Answer

Credit note; invoice.

2 The need for books of prime entry

In the course of business, source documents are created. The details on these source documents need to be summarised, as otherwise the business might forget to ask for some money, or forget to pay some, or even accidentally pay something twice. In other words, it needs to keep records of source documents – of transactions – so that it knows what is going on. Such records are made in **books of prime entry**.

Books of prime entry are books in which we first record transactions.

The main **books of prime entry** are as follows.

(a)   Sales day book
(b)   Purchase day book
(c)   Sales returns day book
(d)   Purchase returns day book
(e)   Journal (described in the next chapter)
(f)   Cash book
(g)   Petty cash book

It is worth bearing in mind that, for convenience, this chapter describes books of prime entry as if they are actual books written by hand. However, books of prime entry are often not books at all, but rather files hidden in the memory of a computer. However, the principles remain the same whether they are manual or computerised.

You may get a question on books of prime entry, also you need to know where the entries to the ledger accounts come from and how they are posted.

3 Sales and purchase day books

Invoices and credit notes are recorded in **day books**.

3.1 The sales day book

The **sales day book** is the book of prime entry for credit sales.

The sales day book is used to keep a list of all invoices sent out to customers each day. An extract from a sales day book might look like this.

SALES DAY BOOK

Date	Invoice	Customer	Total amount invoiced
20X0			$
Jan 10	247	Jones & Co	105.00
	248	Smith Co	86.40
	249	Alex & Co	31.80
	250	Enor College	1,264.60
			1,487.80

Most businesses 'analyse' their sales. For example, this business sells boots and shoes. The sale to Smith was entirely boots, the sale to Alex was entirely shoes, and the other two sales were a mixture of both.

Then the sales day book might look like this.

SALES DAY BOOK

Date	Invoice	Customer	Total amount invoiced	Boot sales	Shoe sales
20X0			$	$	$
Jan 10	247	Jones & Co	105.00	60.00	45.00
	248	Smith Co	86.40	86.40	
	249	Alex & Co	31.80		31.80
	250	Enor College	1,264.60	800.30	464.30
			1,487.80	946.70	541.10

The analysis gives the managers of the business useful information which helps them to decide how best to run the business.

3.2 The purchase day book

A business also keeps a record in the purchase day book of all the invoices it receives.

The **purchase day book** is the book of prime entry for credit purchases.

An extract from a purchase day book might look like this.

PURCHASE DAY BOOK

Date	Supplier	Total amount Invoiced	Purchases	Electricity etc
20X8		$	$	$
Mar 15	Cook & Co	315.00	315.00	
	W Butler	29.40	29.40	
	EEB	116.80		116.80
	Show Fair Co	100.00	100.00	
		561.20	444.40	116.80

- There is no 'invoice number' column, because the purchase day book records **other people's invoices**, which have all sorts of different numbers.
- Like the sales day book, the purchase day book analyses the invoices which have been sent in. In this example, three of the invoices related to goods which the business intends to re-sell (called simply 'purchases') and the other invoice was an electricity bill.

3.3 The sales returns day book

When customers return goods for some reason, a credit note is raised. All credit notes are recorded in the sales returns day book. An extract from the sales returns day book follows.

SALES RETURNS DAY BOOK

Date	Credit note	Customer and goods	Amount
20X8			$
30 April	CR008	Owen Plenty	
		3 pairs 'Texas' boots	135.00

The **sales returns day book** is the book of prime entry for credit notes raised.

Not all sales returns day books analyse what goods were returned, but it makes sense to keep as complete a record as possible. Where a business has very few sales returns, it may record a credit note as a negative entry in the sales day book.

3.4 The purchase returns day book

Not surprisingly, the purchase returns day book records credit notes received in respect of goods which the business sends back to its suppliers.

An extract from the purchase returns day book follows.

PURCHASE RETURNS DAY BOOK

Date	Supplier and goods	Amount
20X8		$
29 April	Boxes Co	
	300 cardboard boxes	46.60

> The **purchase returns day book** is the book of prime entry for credit notes received from suppliers.

Once again, a business with very few purchase returns may record a credit note received as a negative entry in the purchase day book.

4 Cash book

> The **cash book** may be a manual record or a computer file. It records all transaction that go through the bank account.

4.1 The cash book

The cash book is also a day book, used to keep a record of money received and money paid out by the business. The cash book deals with money paid into and out of the business **bank account**. This could be money received on the business premises in notes, coins and cheques, subsequently paid into the bank. There are also receipts and payments made by bank transfer, standing order, direct debit and bank interest and charges, directly by the bank.

Some cash, in notes and coins, is usually kept on the business premises in order to make occasional payments for odd items of expense. This cash is usually accounted for separately in a **petty cash book** (which we will look at shortly).

One side (the left) of the cash book is used to record receipts of cash, and the other side (the right) is used to record payments. The best way to see how the cash book works is to follow through an example. For convenience, we are showing the cash receipts and cash payments sides separately, but they are part of the same book.

> The **cash book** is the book of prime entry for cash receipts and payments.

4.2 Example: Cash book

At the beginning of 1 September, Robin Plenty had $900 in the bank.

During 1 September 20X7, Robin Plenty had the following receipts and payments.

(a)   Cash sale: receipt of $80
(b)   Payment from credit customer Hay $400 less discount allowed $20
(c)   Payment from credit customer Been $720
(d)   Payment from credit customer Seed $150 less discount allowed $10
(e)   Cheque received for cash to provide a short-term loan from Len Dinger $1,800
(f)   Second cash sale: receipt of $150
(g)   Cash received for sale of machine $200
(h)   Payment to supplier Kew $120
(i)   Payment to supplier Hare $310
(j)   Payment of telephone bill $400
(k)   Payment of gas bill $280
(l) $100 in cash withdrawn from bank for petty cash
(m)   Payment of $1,500 to Hess for new plant and machinery

If you look through these transactions, you will see that seven of them are receipts and six of them are payments.

The receipts part of the cash book for 1 September would look like this.

CASH BOOK (RECEIPTS)

Date 20X7	Narrative	Total $
1 Sept	Balance b/d*	900
	Cash sale	80
	Accounts receivable: Hay	380
	Accounts receivable: Been	720
	Accounts receivable: Seed	140
	Loan: Len Dinger	1,800
	Cash sale	150
	Sale of non-current asset	200
		4,370

* 'b/d' = brought down (ie brought forward)

Points to note

- There is space on the right hand side of the cash book so that the receipts can be analysed under various headings – for example, 'cash from receivables', 'cash sales' and 'other receipts'.
- The cash received in the day amounted to $3,470. Added to the $900 at the start of the day, this comes to $4,370. This is not the amount to be carried forward to the next day, because first we have to subtract all the payments made during 1 September.

The payments part of the cash book for 1 September would look like this.

CASH BOOK (PAYMENTS)

Date 20X7	Narrative	Total $
1 Sept	Accounts payable: Kew	120
	Accounts payable: Hare	310
	Telephone	400
	Gas bill	280
	Petty cash	100
	Machinery purchase	1,500
	Balance c/d (balancing figure)	1,660
		4,370

As you can see, this is very similar to the receipts part of the cash book. The only points to note are as follows.

(a) The analysis on the right would be under headings like 'payments to payables, 'payments into petty cash', 'wages' and 'other payments'.

(b) Payments during 1 September totalled $2,710. We know that the total of receipts was $4,370. That means that there is a balance of $4,370 – $2,710 = $1,660 to be 'carried down' to the start of the next day. As you can see this 'balance carried down' is noted at the end of the payments column, so that the receipts and payments totals show the same figure of $4,370 at the end of 1 September.

With analysis columns completed, the cash book given in the examples above might look as follows.

CASH BOOK (RECEIPTS)

Date 20X7	Narrative	Total $	Accounts receivable $	Cash sales $	Other $
1 Sept	Balance b/d	900			
	Cash sale	80		80	
	Accounts receivable: Hay	380	380		
	Accounts receivable: Been	720	720		
	Accounts receivable: Seed	140	140		
	Loan: Len Dinger	1,800			1,800
	Cash sale	150		150	
	Sale of non-current asset	200			200
		4,370	1,240	230	2,000

CASH BOOK (PAYMENTS)

Date	Narrative	Total $	Accounts payable $	Petty cash $	Wages $	Other $
20X7						
1 Sept	Account payable: Kew	120	120			
	Account payable: Hare	310	310			
	Telephone	400				400
	Gas bill	280				280
	Petty cash	100		100		
	Machinery purchase	1,500				1,500
	Balance c/d	1,660				
		4,370	430	100	–	2,180

4.3 Bank statements

Weekly or monthly, a business will receive a **bank statement**. Bank statements should be used to check that the amount shown as a balance in the cash book agrees with the amount on the bank statement, and that no cash has 'gone missing'. This agreement or 'reconciliation' of the cash book with a bank statement is the subject of a later chapter.

5 Petty cash

FAST FORWARD

Most businesses keep **petty cash** on the premises, which is topped up from the main bank account. Under the **imprest system**, the petty cash is kept at an agreed sum, so that each topping up is equal to the amount paid out in the period.

5.1 What is petty cash?

Most businesses keep a small amount of cash on the premises to make occasional small payments in cash, eg staff refreshments, postage stamps, to pay the office cleaner, taxi fares, etc. This is often called the cash float or **petty cash** account. The cash float can also be the resting place for occasional small receipts, eg cash paid by a visitor to make a phone call, etc.

5.2 Security

As you will appreciate, keeping cash (even in small amounts) on the premises is a security risk. Therefore a petty cash system is usually subject to strict controls.

- Payment is only made in respect of **authorised** claims.
- All claims are supported by **evidence**.

In addition, the business may use the **imprest system** (see Section 5.4 below).

5.2.1 Authorisation

An employee must complete a **petty cash voucher** detailing the expenses claimed. Usually receipts must be attached to the voucher (see below: evidence). The completed voucher then needs to be signed by (say) the employee's manager to **authorise** payment. Some times the petty cashier may be authorised to sign vouchers for small amounts (eg $5 or less) if these are supported by receipts.

5.2.2 Evidence

All petty cash vouchers must have receipts for the expenditure attached, as **evidence** that the employee has really incurred that cost. Sometimes receipts may not be available (eg taxi fares) and the employer may then have systems in place to authorise claims without evidence.

5.3 The petty cash book

A **petty cash book** is a cash book for small payments.

Although the amounts involved are small, petty cash transactions still need to be recorded; otherwise the cash float could be abused for personal expenses or even stolen.

There are usually more payments than receipts, and petty cash must be 'topped up' from time to time with cash from the business bank account. A typical layout follows.

PETTY CASH BOOK

Receipts $	Date 20X7	Narrative	Total $	Milk $	Postage $	Travel $	Other $
250	1 Sept	Bal b/d					
		Milk bill	25	25			
		Postage stamps	5		5		
		Taxi fare	10			10	
		Flowers for sick staff	15				15
		Bal c/d	195				
250			250	25	5	10	15

5.4 Imprest system

Under what is called the **imprest system**, the amount of money in petty cash is kept at an agreed sum or 'float' (say $250). This is called the **imprest amount**. Expense items are recorded on vouchers as they occur, so that at any time:

	$
Cash still held in petty cash	195
Plus voucher payments (25+5+10+15)	55
Must equal the imprest amount	250

The total float is made up regularly (to $250, or whatever the imprest amount is) by means of a cash payment from the bank account into petty cash. The amount of the 'top-up' into petty cash will be the total of the voucher payments since the previous top-up.

The **imprest system** makes a refund of the total paid out in a period.

The June 2008 exam included a question asking students to calculate the imprest amount. Many students didn't read the question carefully enough and so arrived at a wrong answer. Make sure that you follow the example below, which demonstrates the correct technique.

5.5 Example: petty cash and the imprest system

DEF operates an imprest system for petty cash. During February 20X9, the following petty cash transactions took place.

		$
2.2.X9	Stamps	12.00
3.2.X9	Milk	25.00
8.2.X9	Taxi fare	15.00
17.2.X9	Stamps	5.00
18.2.X9	Received from staff for photocopying	8.00
28.2.X9	Stationery	7.50

The amount remaining in petty cash at the end of the month was $93.50. What is the imprest amount?

A $166.00
B $150.00
C $72.50
D $56.50

The solution is B.

	$	
Opening balance (imprest amount)	150.00	(balancing figure)
Add: amount received from staff	8.00	
	158.00	
Less: expenditure	(64.50)	(12 + 25 + 15 + 5 + 7.50)
Cash in hand at end of month	93.50	

Question   Books of prime entry

State which books of prime entry the following transactions would be entered into.

(a)   Your business pays A Brown (a supplier) $450.00.
(b)   You send D Smith (a customer) an invoice for $650.
(c)   Your accounts manager asks you for $12 urgently in order to buy some envelopes.
(d)   You receive an invoice from A Brown for $300.
(e)   You pay D Smith $500.
(f)   F Jones (a customer) returns goods to the value of $250.
(g)   You return goods to J Green to the value of $504.
(h)   F Jones pays you $500.

Answer

(a)   Cash book
(b)   Sales day book
(c)   Petty cash book
(d)   Purchases day book
(e)   Cash book
(f)   Sales returns day book
(g)   Purchase returns day book
(h)   Cash book

Chapter Roundup

- Business transactions are recorded on **source documents**. Examples include sales and purchase orders, invoices and credit notes.

- The main **books of prime entry** are as follows.

  - Sales day book
  - Purchase day book
  - Sales returns day book
  - Purchase returns day book
  - Journal (described in the next chapter)
  - Cash book
  - Petty cash book

- Invoices and credit notes are recorded in **day books**.

- The **cash book** may be a manual record or a computer file. It records all transactions that go through the bank account.

- Most businesses keep **petty cash** on the premises which is topped up from the main bank account. Under the **imprest system** the petty cash is kept at an agreed sum so that each topping up is equal to the amount paid out in the period.

Quick Quiz

1 Name four pieces of information normally shown on an invoice.

2 Which of the following is not a book of prime entry.

   A   Sales invoice

   B   Purchase day book

   C   Sales day book

   D   Journal

3 Which of the following is a source document for petty cash.

   A   Purchase invoice

   B   Quotation

   C   Sales invoice

   D   Receipt and claim form

4 What is the purchase returns day book used to record?

   A   Supplier's invoices

   B   Customer's invoices

   C   Details of goods returned to suppliers

   D   Details of goods returned by customers

5 What is the difference between the cash book and the petty cash book?

6 Petty cash is controlled under an imprest system. The imprest amount is $100. During a period, payments totalling $53 have been made. How much needs to be reimbursed at the end of the period to restore petty cash to the imprest account?

   A $100

   B $53

   C $47

   D $50

7 All petty cash claims are automatically paid from petty cash.

   Is this statement:

   A   True

   B   False

1   **Four** from the following
- Invoice number
- Seller's name and address
- Purchaser's name and address
- Date of sale
- Description of goods or services
- Quantity and unit price
- Trade discount (if any)
- Total amount, including sales tax (if any)
- Any special terms

2   A   Sales invoice is a source document

3   D   The claim form and receipt form the source document for the petty cash system.

4   C   Supplier's invoices (A) are recorded in the purchase day book, customer's invoices (B) are recorded in the sales day book and goods returned by customers (D) are recorded in the sales returns day book.

5   The cash book records amounts paid into or out of the bank account. The petty cash book records payments of small amounts of cash.

6   B   Under the imprest system, a reimbursement is made of the amount of the vouchers (or payments made) for the period.

7   B   Only **authorised** and **evidenced** petty cash claims are paid out of petty cash.

Now try the questions below from the Exam Question Bank

Number	Level	Marks	Time
Q7	Examination	2	2 mins
Q8	Examination	1	1 min

4: Sources, records and books of prime entry | Part C The use of double entry and accounting systems

Ledger accounts and double entry

Topic list	Syllabus reference
1 Why do we need ledger accounts?	C1(e)
2 The nominal ledger	C1(e), C2(a), C3(a)
3 The accounting equation	C1(d), D8(a)
4 Double entry bookkeeping	C1(c), D2(a)
5 The journal	C2(b)–(c)
6 Day book analysis	D1(a)–(b)
7 The imprest system	D2(d)
8 The receivables and payables ledgers	D1(a)–(b), D8(a)

Introduction

In the previous chapter we saw how to organise transactions into lists (ie entered into books of prime entry). It is not easy, however, to see how a business is doing from the information scattered throughout these books of prime entry. The lists need to be summarised. This is **ledger accounting**, which we look at in Sections 1 and 2.

The summary is produced in the nominal ledger by a process you may have heard of known as **double entry bookkeeping**. This is the cornerstone of accounts preparation and is surprisingly simple, once you have grasped the rules. We will look at the essentials in Sections 3 and 4.

In Section 5, we will deal with the final book of prime entry: **the journal**.

We will then look in detail at posting transactions from the day books to the ledgers in Sections 6 and 7.

Finally, we will consider how to deal with credit transactions in Section 8.

Study guide

		Intellectual level
C1	**Double entry bookkeeping principles including the maintenance of accounting records and sources of information**	
(c)	Understand and apply the concept of double entry accounts and the duality concept.	1
(d)	Understand and apply the accounting equation.	1
(e)	Understand how the accounting system contributes to providing useful accounting information and complies with organisational deadlines.	1
C2	**Ledger accounts, books of prime entry and journals**	
(a)	Identify the main types of ledger accounts and books of prime entry, and understand their nature and function.	1
(b)	Understand and illustrate the uses of journals and the posting of journal entries into ledger accounts.	1
(c)	Identify correct journals from given narrative.	1
C3	**Accounting systems and the impact of information technology on financial reporting**	
(a)	Understand the basic function and form of accounting records in a typical manual system	1
D1	**Sales purchases**	
(a)	Record sale and purchase transactions in ledger accounts and in day books.	1
(b)	Understand and record sales and purchase returns.	1
D2	**Cash**	
(a)	Record cash transactions in ledger accounts.	1
(d)	Account for petty cash using imprest and non imprest methods	1
D8	**Receivable and payables**	
(a)	Explain and identify examples of receivables and payables.	1

Exam guide

This chapter is the fundamental background for all accounting. It is, therefore, **extremely important** and is highly likely to be examined.

1 Why do we need ledger accounts?

FAST FORWARD

> Ledger accounts **summarise** all the individual transactions listed in the books of prime entry.

A business is continually making transactions, eg buying and selling, and we do not want to prepare an income statement and a statement of financial position on completion of every individual transaction. To do so would be a time-consuming and cumbersome administrative task.

It is common sense that a business should keep a record of the transactions that it makes, the assets it acquires and liabilities it incurs. When the time comes to prepare an income statement and a statement of financial position, the relevant information can be taken from those records.

The **records of transactions, assets and liabilities** should be kept in the following ways.

(a)   In **chronological order**, and **dated** so that transactions can be related to a particular period of time.

(b)   Built up in **cumulative totals**.

      (i)   Day by day (eg total sales on Monday, total sales on Tuesday)
      (ii)   Week by week
      (iii)   Month by month
      (iv)   Year by year

We have already seen the first step in this process, which is to list all the transactions in various books of prime entry. Now we will look at the method used to summarise these records: **ledger accounting** and **double entry**.

This system of summarising information speeds up the provision of useful information to managers and so helps managers to keep to organisational deadlines (eg provision of monthly profit figures for management purposes).

2 The nominal ledger

> The principal accounts are contained in a ledger called the **general** or **nominal ledger**.

Key term

> The **nominal ledger** is an accounting record which summarises the financial affairs of a business.

The nominal ledger is sometimes called the **'general ledger'**. The information contained in the books of prime entry (see Chapter 4) is **summarised** and **posted** to accounts in the nominal ledger.

It contains details of assets, liabilities, capital, income and expenditure, and so profit and loss. It consists of a large number of different accounts, each account having its own purpose or 'name' and an identity or code.

There may be various subdivisions, whether for convenience, ease of handling, confidentiality, security, or to meet the needs of computer software design. For example, the ledger may be split alphabetically, with different clerks responsible for sections A-F, G-M, N-R and S-Z. This can help to stop fraud, as there would have to be collusion between the different section clerks.

Examples of accounts in the nominal ledger include the following.

(a)   Plant and machinery at cost (non-current asset)
(b)   Motor vehicles at cost (non-current asset)
(c)   Plant and machinery, provision for depreciation (liability)
(d)   Motor vehicles, provision for depreciation (liability)
(e)   Proprietor's capital (liability)
(f)   Inventories – raw materials (current asset)
(g)   Inventories – finished goods (current asset)
(h)   Total trade accounts receivable (current asset)
(i)   Total trade accounts payable (current liability)
(j)   Wages and salaries (expense item)
(k)   Rent and local taxes (expense item)
(l)   Advertising expenses (expense item)
(m)   Bank charges (expense item)
(n)   Motor expenses (expense item)
(o)   Telephone expenses (expense item)
(p)   Sales (revenue item)
(q)   Total cash or bank overdraft (current asset or liability)

When it comes to drawing up the financial statements, the revenue and expense accounts will help to form the income statement; while the asset and liability accounts go into the statement of financial position.

2.1 The format of a ledger account

If a ledger account were to be kept in an actual book, rather than as a computer record, it might look like this:

ADVERTISING EXPENSES

Date 20X6	Narrative	Ref.	$	Date	Narrative	Ref.	$
15 April	JFK Agency for quarter to 31 March	PL 348	2,500				

For the rest of this chapter, we will assume that a manual system is being used, in order to illustrate fully the working of the ledger accounts. However, a computerised system performs the same functions although the actual ledger accounts may be 'hidden' inside the computer!

There are two sides to the account, and an account heading on top, and so it is convenient to think in terms of 'T' accounts.

(a) On top of the account is its name.
(b) There is a left hand side, or debit side.
(c) There is a right hand side, or credit side.

NAME OF ACCOUNT

DEBIT SIDE	$	CREDIT SIDE	$

We will look at 'debits' and 'credits' in detail in Section 4, but first we shall consider the accounting equation.

3 The accounting equation

FAST FORWARD

The **accounting equation** emphasises the equality between assets and liabilities (including capital as a liability).

We will start by showing how to account for a business's transactions from the time that trading first begins. We will use an example to illustrate the 'accounting equation', ie the rule that the assets of a business will at all times equal its liabilities. This is also known as the **statement of financial position equation**.

3.1 Example: The accounting equation

Key term

> **Business entity concept**. Regardless of how a business is legally set up, in accounting a business is always treated separately from its owners(s).

Liza Doolittle starts a business. The business begins by owning the cash that Liza has put into it, $2,500. The business is a separate entity in accounting terms and so it owes the money to Liza as **capital**.

Key term

> In accounting, **capital** is an investment of money (funds) with the intention of earning a return. A business proprietor invests capital with the intention of earning profit. As long as that money is invested, accountants will treat the capital as money owed to the proprietor by the business.

When Liza Doolittle sets up her business:

Capital invested	=	$2,500
Cash	=	$2,500

Capital invested is a form of liability, because it is an amount owed by the business to its owner(s). Adapting this to the idea that assets and liabilities are always equal amounts, we can state the accounting equation as follows.

The accounting equation is:

$$ASSETS = CAPITAL + LIABILITIES$$

For Liza Doolittle, as at 1 July 20X6:

Assets	=	*Capital*	+	*Liabilities*
$2,500 (cash)	=	$2,500	+	$0

3.2 Example continued

Liza Doolittle purchases a market stall from Len Turnip, who is retiring from his fruit and vegetables business. The cost of the stall is $1,800.

She also purchases some flowers and potted plants from a trader in the wholesale market, at a cost of $650. This leaves $50 in cash, after paying for the stall and goods for resale, out of the original $2,500.

The assets and liabilities of the business have now altered, and at 3 July before trading begins, the state of her business is as follows.

Assets		=	*Capital*	+	*Liabilities*
	$				
Stall	1,800	=	$2,500	+	$0
Flower and plants	650				
Cash	50				
	2,500				

The stall and the flowers and plants are physical items, but they must be given a money value. This money value is usually what they cost the business (called **historical cost** in accounting terms).

3.3 Profit introduced into the accounting equation

On 3 July Liza has a very successful day. She sells all of her flowers and plants for $900 cash.

Since Liza has sold goods costing $650 to earn revenue of $900, we can say that she has **earned a profit of $250 on the day's trading.**

Profits belong to the owners of a business. In this case, the $250 belongs to Liza Doolittle. However, so long as the business retains the profits and does not pay anything out to its owners, the **retained profits** are accounted for as an addition to the proprietor's capital.

Assets		=	*Capital*		+	*Liabilities*
	$			$		
Stall	1,800		Original investment	2,500		
Flower and plants	0		Retained profit			
Cash (50 + 900)	950		(900 – 650)	250		
	2,750			2,750	+	$0

We can re-arrange the accounting equation to help us to calculate the capital balance.

Assets – liabilities	=	Capital, which is the same as
Net assets	=	Capital

At the beginning and end of 3 July 20X6, Liza Doolittle's financial position was as follows.

		Net assets	*Capital*
(a)	At the beginning of the day:	$(2,500 – 0) = $2,500 =	$2,500
(b)	At the end of the day:	$(2,750 – 0) = $2,750 =	$2,750

There has been an increase of $250 in net assets, which is the amount of profits earned during the day.

3.4 Drawings

> **Drawings** are amounts of money taken out of a business by its owner.

Since Liza Doolittle has made a profit of $250 from her first day's work, she might want to withdraw some money from the business. After all, business owners, like everyone else, need income for living expenses. Liza decides to pay herself $180 in 'wages'. However, the $180 is not an expense to be deducted in arriving at the figure of net profit. In other words, it is incorrect to calculate the net profit earned by the business as follows.

	$
Profit on sale of flowers etc	250
Less 'wages' paid to Liza	180
Net profit earned by business (incorrect)	70

This is because any amounts paid by a business to its proprietor are treated by accountants as withdrawals of profit (the usual term is **drawings**) and not as expenses incurred by the business. In the case of Liza's business, the true position is that the net profit earned is the $250 surplus on sale of flowers.

	$
Net profit earned by business	250
Less profit withdrawn by Liza	180
Net profit retained in the business	70

Profits are capital as long as they are retained in the business. Once they are **withdrawn**, the business suffers a reduction in capital.

The withdrawals of profit are taken in cash, and so the business loses $180 of its cash assets. After the withdrawals have been made, the accounting equation would be restated.

(a)

Assets		=	*Capital*		+	*Liabilities*
	$			$		
Stall	1,800		Original investment	2,500		
Flowers and plants	0		Retained profit			
Cash (950 – 180)	770		(250 – 180)	70		
	2,570			2,570	+	$0

(b) Alternatively

Net assets		*Capital*
$(2,570 – 0)	=	$2,570

The increase in net assets since trading operations began is now only $(2,570 – 2,500) = $70, which is the amount of the retained profits.

Question

Capital

Which of the following is correct?

A   Capital = assets + liabilities
B   Capital = liabilities – assets
C   Capital = assets – liabilities
D   Capital + assets = liabilities

Answer

The correct answer is C. As assets = liabilities + capital, then capital = assets – liabilities

3.5 Example continued

FAST FORWARD

You should now be aware that, when business transactions are accounted for it should be possible to **restate the assets and liabilities** of the business after the transactions have taken place.

The next market day is on 10 July and Liza purchases more flowers and plants for cash, at a cost of $740. She is not feeling well, because of a heavy cold, and so she decides to accept help for the day from her cousin Ethel. Ethel is to be paid a wage of $40 at the end of the day.

Trading on 10 July was again very brisk, and Liza and Ethel sold all their goods for $1,100 cash. Liza paid Ethel her wage of $40 and drew out $200 for herself.

Required

(a)   State the accounting equation before trading began on 10 July.
(b)   State the accounting equation at the end of 10 July, after paying Ethel:
    (i)   but before drawings are made.
    (ii)   after drawings have been made.

You are reminded that the accounting equation for the business at the end of transactions for 3 July is given in Paragraph 3.4.

Solution

(a)   After the purchase of the goods for $740.

Assets		=	Capital	+	Liabilities
	$				
Stall	1,800				
Goods	740				
Cash (770 – 740)	30				
	2,570 =		$ 2,570	+	$0

(b)   (i)   On 10 July, all the goods are sold for $1,100 cash, and Ethel is paid $40. The profit for the day is $320.

	$	$
Sales		1,100
Less cost of goods sold	740	
Ethel's wage	40	
		780
Profit		320

Assets		=	Capital		+	Liabilities
	$			$		
Stall	1,800		At beginning of 10 July	2,570		
Goods	0		Profits earned on 10 July	320		
Cash						
(30+ 1,100 – 40)	1,090					
	2,890			2,890	+	$0

(ii)   After Liza has withdrawn $200 in cash, retained profits will be only $(320 – 200) = $120.

Assets		=	Capital		+	Liabilities
	$			$		
Stall	1,800		At beginning of 10 July	2,570		
Goods	0		Retained profits	120		
Cash			for 10 July			
(1,090 – 200)	890					
	2,690			2,690	+	$0

It is very important you should understand the principles described so far. Do not read on until you are confident that you understand the solution to this example.

3.6 Payables and receivables

Trade accounts payable are liabilities. Trade accounts receivable are assets.

3.6.1 Trade accounts payable and trade accounts receivable

Key term

A **payable** is a person to whom a business owes money.

A **trade payable** is a person to whom a business owes money for debts incurred in the course of trading operations. In the accounts of a business, debts still outstanding which arise from the purchase of materials, components or goods for resale are called **trade accounts payable**, sometimes abbreviated to 'accounts payable' or 'payables'.

A business does not always pay immediately for goods or services it buys. It is a common business practice to make purchases on credit, with a promise to pay within 30 days, or two months or three months, of the date of the invoice for the goods. For example, A buys goods costing $2,000 on credit from B, B sends A an invoice for $2,000, dated 1 March, with credit terms that payment must be made within 30 days. If A then delays payment until 31 March, B will be a payable of A between 1 and 31 March for $2,000. From A's point of view, the amount owed to B is a **trade account payable.**

A trade account payable is a **liability** of a business.

Key term

Just as a business might buy goods on credit, so too might it sell goods to customers on credit. A customer who buys goods without paying cash for them straight away is a **receivable**.

For example, suppose that C sells goods on credit to D for $6,000 on terms that the debt must be settled within two months of the invoice date 1 October. If D does not pay the $6,000 until 30 November, D will be a receivable of C for $6,000 from 1 October until 30 November. In the accounts of the business, amounts owed by receivables are called **trade accounts receivable,** sometimes abbreviated to 'accounts receivable' or 'receivables'.

A trade account receivable is an **asset** of a business. When the debt is finally paid, the trade account receivable 'disappears' as an asset, to be replaced by 'cash at bank and in hand'.

3.6.2 Example continued

The example of Liza Doolittle's market stall is continued, by looking at the consequences of the following transactions in the week to 17 July 20X6. (See Paragraph 3.5 for the situation as at the end of 10 July.)

(a) Liza Doolittle realises that she is going to need more money in the business and so she makes the following arrangements.

(i) She invests immediately a further $250 of her own capital.

(ii) She persuades her Uncle Henry to lend her $500 immediately. Uncle Henry tells her that she can repay the loan whenever she likes, but in the meantime, she must pay him interest of $5 each week at the end of the market day. They agree that it will probably be quite a long time before the loan is eventually repaid.

(b) She decides to buy a second hand van to pick up flowers and plants from her supplier and bring them to her stall in the market. She finds a car dealer, Laurie Loader, who agrees to sell her a van on credit for $700. Liza agrees to pay for the van after 30 days' trial use.

(c) During the week, Liza's Uncle George telephones her to ask whether she would sell him some garden gnomes and furniture for his garden. Liza tells him that she will look for a supplier. After some investigations, she buys what Uncle George has asked for, paying $300 in cash to the supplier. Uncle George accepts delivery of the goods and agrees to pay $350, but he asks if she can wait until the end of the month for payment. Liza agrees.

(d)   Liza buys flowers and plants costing $800. Of these purchases $750 are paid in cash, with the remaining $50 on seven days' credit. Liza decides to use Ethel's services again as an assistant on market day, at an agreed wage of $40.

(e)   On 17 July, Liza succeeds in selling all her goods earning revenue of $1,250 (all in cash). She decides to withdraw $240 for her week's work. She also pays Ethel $40 in cash. She decides to make the interest payment to her Uncle Henry the next time she sees him.

(f)   We shall ignore any van expenses for the week, for the sake of relative simplicity.

Required

State the accounting equation:

(i)   After Liza and Uncle Henry have put more money into the business and after the purchase of the van.

(ii)   After the sale of goods to Uncle George.

(iii) After the purchase of goods for the weekly market

(iv)   At the end of the day's trading on 17 July, and after withdrawals have been appropriated out of profit.

Solution

There are a number of different transactions to account for here. This solution deals with them one at a time in chronological order. (In practice, it is possible to do one set of calculations which combines the results of all the transactions.)

(i)   *The addition of Liza's extra capital and Uncle Henry's loan*

An investment analyst might call Uncle Henry's loan a capital investment, on the grounds that it will probably be for the long term. Uncle Henry is not the owner of the business, however, even though he has made an investment of a loan in it. He would only become an owner if Liza offered him a partnership in the business, and she has not done so. To the business, Uncle Henry is a long-term payable, and it is more appropriate to define his investment as a liability of the business and not as business capital.

The accounting equation after $(250 + 500) = $750 cash is put into the business will be:

Assets		=	Capital		+	Liabilities	
	$			$			$
Stall	1,800		As at end of 10 July	2,690		Loan	500
Goods	0		Additional capital put in	250			
Cash (890+750)	1,640						
	3,440	=		2,940	+		500

The purchase of the van (cost $700) on credit

Assets		=	Capital		+	Liabilities	
	$			$			$
Stall	1,800		As at end of 10 July	2,690		Loan	500
Van	700		Additional capital	250		Payables	700
Cash	1,640						
	4,140	=		2,940	+		1,200

(ii) *The sale of goods to Uncle George on credit ($350) which cost the business $300 (cash paid)*

Assets	$	=	Capital	$	+	Liabilities	$
Stall	1,800		As at end of 10 July	2,690		Loan	500
Van	700		Additional capital	250		Payables	700
Receivable	350		Profit on sale to				
Cash			Uncle George (350 – 300)	50			
(1,640 – 300)	1,340						
	4,190	=		2,990	+		1,200

(iii) *After the purchase of goods for the weekly market ($750 paid in cash and $50 of purchases on credit)*

Assets	$	=	Capital	$	+	Liabilities	$
Stall	1,800		As at end of 10 July	2,690		Loan	500
Van	700		Additional capital	250		Payables	
Goods	800		Profit on sale to			(van)	700
Receivables	350		Uncle George	50		Payables	
Cash						(goods)	50
(1,340 – 750)	590						
	4,240	=		2,990	+		1,250

(iv) *After market trading on 17 July*

Sales of goods costing $800 earned revenues of $1,250. Ethel's wages were $40 (paid), Uncle Henry's interest charge is $5 (not paid yet) and withdrawals on account of profits were $240 (paid). The profit for 17 July may be calculated as follows, taking the full $5 of interest as a cost on that day.

	$	$
Sales		1,250
Cost of goods sold	800	
Wages	40	
Interest	5	
		845
Profit earned on 17 July		405
Profit on sale of goods to Uncle George		50
Profit for the week		455
Drawings		240
Retained profit		215

Assets	$	=	Capital	$	+	Liabilities	$
Stall	1,800		As at end of 10 July	2,690		Loan	500
Van	700		Additional capital	250		Payable for	
Goods (800 – 800)	0		Profits retained	215		van	700
Receivables	350					Payable for	
Cash (590+						goods	50
1,250 – 40 – 240)	1,560					Payable for	
						interest	
						payment	5
	4,410			3,155			1,255

3.7 Matching

BPP
LEARNING MEDIA

In the example above, we have 'matched' the revenue earned with the expenses incurred in earning it. So in part (iv), we included all the costs of the goods sold of $800, even though $50 had not yet been paid in cash. Also the interest of $5 was deducted from revenue, even though it had not yet been paid. This is known as the **matching convention**, or accruals convention.

Question

How would each of these transactions affect the accounting equation?

(a) Purchasing $800 worth of inventory on credit
(b) Paying the telephone bill $25
(c) Selling $450 worth of inventory for $650
(d) Paying $800 to the supplier

Answer

(a)	Increase in liabilities (payables)	$800
	Increase in assets (inventory)	$800
(b)	Decrease in assets (cash)	$25
	Decrease in capital (profit)	$25
(c)	Decrease in assets (inventory)	$450
	Increase in assets (cash)	$650
	Increase in capital (profit)	$200
(d)	Decrease in liabilities (payables)	$800
	Decrease in assets (cash)	$800

4 Double entry bookkeeping

Double entry bookkeeping is based on the idea that each transaction has an equal but opposite effect. Every accounting event must be entered in ledger accounts both as a debit and as an equal but opposite credit.

4.1 Dual effect (duality concept)

Double entry bookkeeping is the method used to transfer our weekly/monthly totals from our books of prime entry into the nominal ledger.

Central to this process is the idea that every transaction has two effects, the **dual effect**. This feature is not something peculiar to businesses. If you were to purchase a car for $1,000 cash for instance, you would be affected in two ways.

(a) You own a car worth $1,000.
(b) You have $1,000 less cash.

If instead you got a bank loan to make the purchase:

(a) You own a car worth $1,000.
(b) You owe the bank $1,000.

A month later if you pay a garage $50 to have the exhaust replaced:

(a) You have $50 less cash.
(b) You have incurred a repairs expense of $50.

Ledger accounts, with their debit and credit sides, are kept in a way which allows the two-sided nature of every transaction to be recorded. This is known as the **'double entry'** system of bookkeeping, because **every transaction is recorded twice** in the accounts.

4.2 The rules of double entry bookkeeping

FAST FORWARD

A debit entry will:

- increase an asset
- decrease a liability
- increase an expense

A credit entry will:

- decrease an asset
- increase a liability
- increase income

The basic rule, which must always be observed, is that **every financial transaction gives rise to two accounting entries, one a debit and the other a credit**. The total value of debit entries in the nominal ledger is therefore always equal at any time to the total value of credit entries. Which account receives the credit entry and which receives the debit depends on the nature of the transaction.

Key terms

- An **increase** in an **expense** (eg a purchase of stationery) or an **increase in an asset** (eg a purchase of office furniture) is a **debit**.
- An **increase** in **revenue** (eg a sale) or an **increase in a liability** (eg buying goods on credit) is a **credit**.
- A **decrease** in an **asset** (eg making a cash payment) is a **credit**.
- A **decrease** in a **liability** (eg paying a creditor) is a **debit**.

In terms of 'T' accounts:

ASSET			LIABILITY			CAPITAL		
DEBIT	$	CREDIT $	DEBIT	$	CREDIT $	DEBIT	$	CREDIT $
Increase		Decrease	Decrease		Increase	Decrease		Increase

For income and expenses, think about profit. Profit retained in the business increases capital. Income increases profit and expenses decrease profit.

INCOME			EXPENSE		
DEBIT	$	CREDIT $	DEBIT	$	CREDIT $
Decrease		Increase	Increase		Decrease

Have a go at the question below before you learn about this topic in detail.

Question   **Debits and credits**

Complete the following table relating to the transactions of a bookshop. (The first two are done for you.)

(a)   Purchase of books on credit

(i)	accounts payable increase	CREDIT	accounts payable	(increase in liability)
(ii)	purchases expense increases	DEBIT	purchases	(item of expense)

(b)   Purchase of cash register

(i)	own a cash register	DEBIT	cash register	(increase in asset)
(ii)	cash at bank decreases	CREDIT	cash at bank	(decrease in asset)

(c) Payment received from a credit customer

    (i)   accounts receivable decrease

    (ii)   cash at bank increases

(d) Purchase of van

    (i)   own a van

    (ii)   cash at bank decreases

Answer

(c) Payment received from a credit customer

(i)	accounts receivable decrease	CREDIT	accounts receivable	decrease in asset
(ii)	cash at bank increases	DEBIT	cash at bank	increase in asset

(d) Purchase of van

(i)	own a van	DEBIT	van	increase in asset
(ii)	cash at bank decreases	CREDIT	cash at bank	decrease in asset

How did you get on? Students coming to the subject for the first time often have difficulty in knowing where to begin. A good starting point is the cash account, ie the nominal ledger account in which receipts and payments of cash are recorded. The rule to remember about the cash account is as follows.

(a) A cash **payment** is a **credit** entry in the cash account. Here the **asset is decreasing**. Cash may be paid out, for example, to pay an expense (such as tax) or to purchase an asset (such as a machine). The matching debit entry is therefore made in the appropriate expense or asset account.

(b) A cash **receipt** is a **debit** entry in the cash account. Here the **asset is increasing**. Cash might be received, for example, by a retailer who makes a cash sale. The credit entry would then be made in the sales account.

Key term

> **Double entry bookkeeping** is the method by which a business records financial transactions. An account is maintained for every asset, liability, income and expense. Every transaction is recorded twice so that every *debit* is balanced by a *credit*.

4.3 Example: Double entry for cash transactions

In the cash book of a business, the following transactions have been recorded.

(a) A cash sale (ie a receipt) of $250

(b) Payment of a rent bill totalling $150

(c) Buying some goods for cash at $100

(d) Buying some shelves for cash at $200

How would these four transactions be posted to the ledger accounts and to which ledger accounts should they be posted? Don't forget that each transaction will be posted twice, in accordance with the rule of double entry.

Solution

(a) The two sides of the transaction are:

    (i)   Cash is received (debit entry in the cash at bank account).

    (ii)   Sales increase by $250 (credit entry in the sales account).

CASH AT BANK ACCOUNT

	$		$
Sales a/c	250		

SALES ACCOUNT

	$		$
		Cash a/c	250

(Note how the entry in the cash at bank account is cross-referenced to the sales account and vice-versa. This enables a person looking at one of the accounts to trace where the other half of the double entry can be found.)

(b)　The two sides of the transaction are:

　　(i)　Cash is paid (credit entry in the cash at bank account).
　　(ii)　Rent expense increases by $150 (debit entry in the rent account).

CASH AT BANK ACCOUNT

	$		$
		Rent a/c	150

RENT ACCOUNT

	$		$
Cash at bank a/c	150		

(c)　The two sides of the transaction are:

　　(i)　Cash is paid (credit entry in the cash at bank account).
　　(ii)　Purchases increase by $100 (debit entry in the purchases account).

CASH AT BANK ACCOUNT

	$		$
		Purchases a/c	100

PURCHASES ACCOUNT

	$		$
Cash at bank a/c	100		

(d)　The two sides of the transaction are:

　　(i)　Cash is paid (credit entry in the cash at bank account).
　　(ii)　Assets – in this case, shelves – increase by $200 (debit entry in shelves account).

CASH AT BANK ACCOUNT

	$		$
		Shelves a/c	200

SHELVES (ASSET) ACCOUNT

	$		$
Cash at bank a/c	200		

4.4 Credit transactions

FAST FORWARD

Some accounts in the nominal ledger represent the total of very many smaller balances. For example, the **trade accounts receivable** account represents all the balances owed by individual customers of the business while the **trade accounts payable account** represents all money owed by the business to its suppliers.

Not all transactions are settled immediately in cash or by cheque. A business can purchase goods or non-current assets on credit terms, so that the suppliers would be trade accounts payable until settlement was made in cash. Equally, the business might grant credit terms to its customers who would then be trade accounts receivable of the business. Clearly no entries can be made in the cash book when a credit transaction occurs, because no cash has been received or paid, so where can the details of the transactions be entered?

The solution to this problem is to use **trade accounts receivable and trade accounts payable accounts**. When a business acquires goods or services on credit, the credit entry is made in an account designated 'trade accounts payable' instead of in the cash at bank account. The debit entry is made in the appropriate expense or asset account, exactly as in the case of cash transactions. Similarly, when a sale is made to a credit customer the entries made are a debit to the total trade accounts receivable account (instead of cash at bank account) and a credit to sales account.

4.5 Example: Credit transactions

Recorded in the sales day book and the purchase day book are the following transactions.

(a)   The business sells goods on credit to a customer Mr A for $2,000.
(b)   The business buys goods on credit from a supplier B Inc for $100.

How and where are these transactions posted in the ledger accounts?

Solution

(a)

TRADE ACCOUNTS RECEIVABLE			
	$		$
Sales a/c	2,000		

SALES ACCOUNT			
	$		$
		Trade accounts receivable account	2,000

(b)

TRADE ACCOUNTS PAYABLE			
	$		$
		Purchases a/c	100

PURCHASES ACCOUNT			
	$		$
Trade accounts payable a/c	100		

4.5.1 When cash is paid to suppliers or by customers

What happens when a credit transaction is eventually settled? Suppose that, in the example above, the business paid $100 to B Inc one month after the goods were acquired. The two sides of this new transaction are:

(a)   Cash is paid (credit entry in the cash at bank account).
(b)   The amount owing to trade accounts payable is reduced (debit entry in the trade accounts payable account).

CASH AT BANK ACCOUNT

	$		$
		Trade accounts payable a/c	100

TRADE ACCOUNTS PAYABLE

	$		$
Cash a/c	100		

If we now bring together the two parts of this example, the original purchase of goods on credit and the eventual settlement in cash, we find that the accounts appear as follows.

CASH AT BANK ACCOUNT

	$		$
		Trade accounts payable a/c	100

PURCHASES ACCOUNT

	$		$
Trade accounts payable a/c	100		

TRADE ACCOUNTS PAYABLE

	$		$
Cash at bank a/c	100	Purchases a/c	100

The two entries in trade accounts payable cancel each other out, indicating that no money is owing to suppliers any more. We are left with a credit entry of $100 in the cash at bank account and a debit entry of $100 in the purchases account. These are exactly the same as the entries used to record a **cash** purchase of $100 (compare example above). This is what we would expect: after the business has paid off its trade accounts payable, it is in exactly the same position as if it had made a cash purchase, and the accounting records reflect this similarity.

Similar reasoning applies when a customer settles his debt. In the example above when Mr A pays his debt of $2,000 the two sides of the transaction are:

(a)   Cash is received (debit entry in the cash at bank account).

(b)   The amount owed by trade accounts receivable is reduced (credit entry in the trade accounts receivable account).

CASH AT BANK ACCOUNT

	$		$
Trade accounts receivable a/c	2,000		

TRADE ACCOUNTS RECEIVABLE

	$		$
		Cash at bank a/c	2,000

The accounts recording this sale to, and payment by, Mr A now appear as follows.

CASH AT BANK ACCOUNT

	$		$
Trade accounts receivable a/c	2,000		

SALES ACCOUNT

	$		$
		Trade accounts receivable a/c	2,000

TRADE ACCOUNTS RECEIVABLE

	$		$
Sales a/c	2,000	Cash at bank a/c	2,000

The two entries in trade accounts receivable cancel each other out; while the entries in the cash at bank account and sales account reflect the same position as if the sale had been made for cash (see above).

Now try the following questions.

Question

Debit and credit

See if you can identify the debit and credit entries in the following transactions.

(a) Bought a machine on credit from A, cost $8,000.
(b) Bought goods on credit from B, cost $500.
(c) Sold goods on credit to C, value $1,200.
(d) Paid D (a credit supplier) $300.
(e) Collected $180 from E, a credit customer.
(f) Paid wages $4,000.
(g) Received rent bill of $700 from landlord G.
(h) Paid rent of $700 to landlord G.
(i) Paid insurance premium $90.
(j) Received a credit note for $450 from supplier, H
(k) Sent out a credit note for $200 to customer, I

Answer

			$	$
(a)	DEBIT	Machine account (non-current asset)	8,000	
	CREDIT	Trade accounts payable		8,000
(b)	DEBIT	Purchases account	500	
	CREDIT	Trade accounts payable		500
(c)	DEBIT	Trade accounts receivable	1,200	
	CREDIT	Sales		1,200
(d)	DEBIT	Trade accounts payable	300	
	CREDIT	Cash at bank		300
(e)	DEBIT	Cash at bank	180	
	CREDIT	Trade accounts receivable		180
(f)	DEBIT	Wages account	4,000	
	CREDIT	Cash at bank		4,000
(g)	DEBIT	Rent account	700	
	CREDIT	Trade accounts payable		700

			$	$
(h)	DEBIT	Trade accounts payable	700	
	CREDIT	Cash at bank		700
(i)	DEBIT	Insurance costs	90	
	CREDIT	Cash at bank		90
(j)	DEBIT	Trade accounts payable	450	
	CREDIT	Purchase returns		450
(k)	DEBIT	Sales returns	200	
	CREDIT	Trade accounts receivable		200

Question

See now whether you can record the ledger entries for the following transactions. Ron Knuckle set up a business selling keep fit equipment, trading under the name of Buy Your Biceps Shop. He put $7,000 of his own money into a business bank account (transaction A) and in his first period of trading, the following transactions occurred.

Transaction		$
B	Paid rent of shop for the period	3,500
C	Purchased equipment (inventories) on credit	5,000
D	Raised loan from bank	1,000
E	Purchase of shop fittings (for cash)	2,000
F	Sales of equipment: cash	10,000
G	Sales of equipment: on credit	2,500
H	Payments for trade accounts payable	5,000
I	Payments from trade accounts receivable	2,500
J	Interest on loan (paid)	100
K	Other expenses (all paid in cash)	1,900
L	Drawings	1,500

Try to do as much of this question as you can by yourself before reading the solution.

Answer

Clearly, there should be an account for cash at bank, trade accounts receivable, trade accounts payable, purchases, a shop fittings account, sales, a loan account and a proprietor's capital account. It is also useful to keep a separate account for **drawings** until the end of each accounting period. Other accounts should be set up as they seem appropriate and in this exercise, accounts for rent, bank interest and other expenses would seem appropriate.

It has been suggested to you that the cash at bank account is a good place to start, if possible. You should notice that cash transactions include the initial input of capital by Ron Knuckle, subsequent drawings, the payment of rent, the loan from the bank, the interest, some cash sales and cash purchases, and payments for trade accounts payable and from trade accounts receivable. (The transactions are identified below by their reference, to help you to find them.)

CASH AT BANK

	$		$
Capital – Ron Knuckle (A)	7,000	Rent (B)	3,500
Bank loan (D)	1,000	Shop fittings (E)	2,000
Sales (F)	10,000	Trade accounts payable (H)	5,000
Trade accounts receivable (I)	2,500	Bank loan interest (J)	100
		Other expenses (K)	1,900
		Drawings (L)	1,500

CAPITAL (RON KNUCKLE)

	$		$
		Cash at bank (A)	7,000

BANK LOAN

	$		$
		Cash at bank (D)	1,000

PURCHASES

	$		$
Trade accounts payable (C)	5,000		

TRADE ACCOUNTS PAYABLE

	$		$
Cash at bank (H)	5,000	Purchases (C)	5,000

RENT

	$		$
Cash at bank (B)	3,500		

NON-CURRENT ASSETS (SHOP FITTINGS)

	$		$
Cash at bank (E)	2,000		

SALES

	$		$
		Cash at bank (F)	10,000
		Trade accounts receivable (G)	2,500

TRADE ACCOUNTS RECEIVABLE

	$		$
Sales (G)	2,500	Cash at bank (I)	2,500

BANK LOAN INTEREST

	$		$
Cash at bank (J)	100		

OTHER EXPENSES

	$		$
Cash at bank (K)	1,900		

DRAWINGS ACCOUNT

	$		$
Cash at bank (L)	1,500		

(a) If you want to make sure that this solution is complete, you should go through the transactions A to L and tick off each of them twice in the ledger accounts, once as a debit and once as a credit. When you have finished, all transactions in the 'T' account should be ticked.

(b) In fact, there is an easier way to check that the solution to this sort of problem does 'balance' properly, which we will meet in the next chapter.

(c) On asset and liability accounts, the debit or credit balance represents the amount of the asset or liability outstanding at the period end. For example, on the cash at bank account, debits exceed credits by $6,500 and so there is a debit balance of cash in hand of $6,500. On the capital account, there is a credit balance of $7,000 and so the business owes Ron $7,000.

(d) The balances on the revenue and expense accounts represent the total of each revenue or expense for the period. For example, sales for the period total $12,500.

5 The journal

FAST FORWARD

The **journal** is the record of prime entry for transactions which are not recorded in any of the other books of prime entry.

You should remember that one of the books of prime entry was the **journal**.

Key term

The **journal** keeps a record of unusual movement between accounts. It is used to record any double entries made which do not arise from the other books of prime entry. For example, journal entries are made when errors are discovered and need to be corrected.

Whatever type of transaction is being recorded, the **format of a journal entry** is:

Date	Debit	Credit
	$	$
Account to be debited	X	
Account to be credited		X
(Narrative to explain the transaction)		

(Remember: in due course, the ledger accounts will be written up to include the transactions listed in the journal.)

A **narrative explanation** must accompany each journal entry. It is required for audit and control, to indicate the purpose and authority of every transaction which is not first recorded in a book of original entry.

Exam focus point

An examination question might ask you to 'journalise' transactions which would not in practice be recorded in the journal at all. If you are faced with such a problem, you should simply record the debit and credit entries for every transaction.

5.1 Examples: Journal entries

The following is a summary of the transactions of Hair by Fiona Middleton hairdressing business of which Fiona is the sole proprietor.

1 January	Put in cash of $2,000 as capital
	Purchased brushes and combs for cash $50
	Purchased hair driers from Gilroy Ltd on credit $150
30 January	Paid three months rent to 31 March $300
	Collected and paid in takings $600
31 January	Gave Mrs Sullivan a perm, highlights etc on credit $80

Show the transactions by means of journal entries.

Solution

JOURNAL

			$	$
1 January	DEBIT	Cash at bank	2,000	
	CREDIT	Fiona Middleton – capital account		2,000
		Initial capital introduced		
1 January	DEBIT	Brushes and combs account	50	
	CREDIT	Cash at bank		50
		The purchase for cash of brushes and combs as non-current		
		assets		
1 January	DEBIT	Hair dryer account	150	
	CREDIT	Sundry accounts payable *		150
		The purchase on credit of hair driers as non-current assets		
30 January	DEBIT	Rent account	300	
	CREDIT	Cash at bank		300
		The payment of rent to 31 March		
30 January	DEBIT	Cash at bank	600	
	CREDIT	Sales account		600
		Cash takings		
31 January	DEBIT	Trade accounts receivable	80	
	CREDIT	Sales account		80
		The provision of a hair-do on credit		

* *Note*. Suppliers who have supplied non-current assets are included amongst sundry accounts payable, as distinct from trade suppliers (who have supplied raw materials or goods for resale) who are trade accounts payable. It is quite common to have separate 'total accounts payable' accounts, one for trade accounts payable and another for sundry other accounts payable.

5.2 The correction of errors

The journal is most commonly used to record corrections to errors that have been made in writing up the nominal ledger accounts. Errors corrected by the journal must be **capable of correction by means of a double entry** in the ledger accounts. In other words the error must not have caused total debits and total credits to be unequal.

Special rules apply when errors are made which break the rule of double entry.

We will deal with errors in Chapter 16.

6 Day book analysis

Entries in the daybooks are totalled and analysed before posting to the nominal ledger.

6.1 Sales day book

In the previous chapter, we used the following example of four transactions entered into the sales day book.

SALES DAY BOOK

Date 20X0	Invoice	Customer	Total amount invoiced $	Boot sales $	Shoe sales
Jan 10	247	Jones & Co	105.00	60.00	45.00
	248	Smith Ltd	86.40	86.40	
	249	Alex & Co	31.80		31.80
	250	Enor College	1,264.60	800.30	464.30
			1,487.80	946.70	541.10

We have already seen that in theory these transactions are posted to the ledger accounts as follows.

DEBIT	Trade accounts receivable	$1,487.80
CREDIT	Sales account	$1,487.80

However a total sales account is not very informative, particularly if the business sells lots of different products. So, using our example, the business might open up a 'sale of shoes' account and a 'sale of boots' account. Then the ledger account postings are:

		$	$
DEBIT	Trade accounts receivable	1,487.80	
CREDIT	Sale of shoes account		541.10
	Sale of boots account		946.70

That is why the analysis of sales is kept. Exactly the same reasoning lies behind the analyses kept in the other books of prime entry.

6.2 Sales returns day book

We will now look at the sales returns day book from Chapter 4.

SALES RETURNS DAY BOOK

Date 20X8	Credit note	Customer and goods	Amount $
30 April	CR008	Owen Plenty	
		3 pairs 'Texas' boots	135.00

This will be posted as follows:

		$	$
DEBIT	Sales returns book	135.00	
CREDIT	Trade accounts receivable		135.00

6.3 Purchase day book and purchases returns day book

The purchase day book and purchases returns day book in Chapter 4 can be posted in a similar way.

6.3.1 Purchases

		$	$
DEBIT	Purchases	444.40	
	Electricity	116.80	
CREDIT	Trade accounts payable		561.20

6.3.2 Purchase returns

		$	$
DEBIT	Trade accounts payable	46.60	
CREDIT	Purchases returns		46.60

7 The imprest system

FAST FORWARD

In the last chapter, we saw how the petty cash book was used to operate the imprest system. It is now time to see how the **double entry** works.

A business starts with a cash float on 1.3.20X7 of $250. This will be a payment from cash at bank to petty cash, ie:

DEBIT	Petty cash	$250	
CREDIT	Cash at bank		$250

Five payments were made out of petty cash during March 20X7. The petty cash book might look as follows.

Receipts $	Date	Narrative	Total $	Payments Postage $	Travel $
250.00	1.3.X7	Cash			
	2.3.X7	Stamps	12.00	12.00	
	8.3.X7	Stamps	10.00	10.00	
	19.3.X7	Travel	16.00		16.00
	23.3.X7	Travel	5.00		5.00
	28.3.X7	Stamps	11.50	11.50	
250.00			54.50	33.50	21.00

At the end of each month (or at any other suitable interval) the total payments in the petty cash book are **posted** to ledger accounts. For March 20X7, $33.50 would be debited to postage account and $21.00 to travel account. The total payments of $54.50 are credited to the petty cash account. This completes the double entry.

The cash float needs to be topped up by a payment of $54.50 from the main cash book, ie:

		$	$
DEBIT	Petty cash	54.50	
CREDIT	Cash		54.50

So the rules of double entry have been satisfied, and the petty cash book for the month of March 20X7 will look like this.

Receipts $	Date	Narrative	Total $	Payments Postage $	Travel $
250.00	1.3.X7	Cash			
	2.3.X7	Stamps	12.00	12.00	
	8.3.X7	Stamps	10.00	10.00	
	19.3.X7	Travel	16.00		16.00
	23.3.X7	Travel	5.00		5.00
	28.3.X7	Stamps	11.50	11.50	
	31.3.X7	Balance c/d	195.50		
250.00			250.00	33.50	21.00
195.50	1.4.X7	Balance b/d			
54.50	1.4.X7	Cash			

As you can see, the cash float is back up to $250 on 1.4.X7, ready for more payments to be made.

The petty cash account in the ledger will appear as follows.

PETTY CASH

		$			$
1.3.20X7	Cash	250.00	31.3.20X7	Payments	54.50
1.4.20X7	Cash	54.50	1.4.20X7	Balance c/d	250.00
		304.50			304.50
1.4.20X7	Balance b/d	250.00			

Summit Glazing operates an imprest petty cash system. The imprest amount is $150.00. At the end of the period the totals of the four analysis columns in the petty cash book were as follows.

	$
Column 1	23.12
Column 2	6.74
Column 3	12.90
Column 4	28.50

How much cash is required to restore the imprest amount?

Answer

$71.26. This is the total amount of cash that has been used.

8 The receivables and payables ledgers

FAST FORWARD

> The receivables and payables ledgers contain the **personal accounts** of individual customers and suppliers. They do not normally form part of the double-entry system.

8.1 Impersonal accounts and personal accounts

The accounts in the nominal ledger (ledger accounts) relate to types of income, expense, asset, liability – rent, sales, trade receivables, payables etc – rather than to the person to whom the money is paid or from whom it is received. They are therefore called **impersonal** accounts. However, there is also a need for **personal** accounts, most commonly for receivables and payables, and these are contained in the receivables ledger and payables ledger.

8.2 The receivables ledger

The sales day book provides a chronological record of invoices sent out by a business to credit customers. For many businesses, this might involve very large numbers of invoices per day or per week. The same customer might appear in several different places in the sales day book, for sales made on credit at different times. So a customer may owe money on several unpaid invoices.

In addition to keeping a chronological record of invoices, a business should also keep a record of how much money each individual credit customer owes, and what this total debt consists of. The need for a **personal account for each customer** is a practical one.

(a) A customer might telephone, and ask how much he currently owes. Staff must be able to tell him.

(b) It is a common practice to send out statements to credit customers at the end of each month, showing how much they still owe, and itemising new invoices sent out and payments received during the month.

(c) The managers of the business will want to keep a check on the credit position of an individual customer, and to ensure that no customer is exceeding his credit limit by purchasing more goods.

(d) Most important is the need to match payments received against debts owed. If a customer makes a payment, the business must be able to set off the payment against the customer's debt and establish how much he still owes on balance.

Key term

> The **receivables ledger** is a ledger for customers' personal accounts.

Receivables ledger accounts are written up as follows.

(a) When entries are made in the sales day book (invoices sent out), they are subsequently also made in the **debit side** of the relevant customer account in the receivables ledger.

(b) Similarly, when entries are made in the cash book (payments received), or in the sales returns day book, they are also made in the **credit side** of the relevant customer account.

Each customer account is given a reference or code number, and it is that reference which appears in the **sales day book**. We say that amounts are **posted** from the sales day book to the receivables ledger.

Here is an example of how a receivables ledger account is laid out.

ENOR COLLEGE

A/c no: RL 9

	$		$
Balance b/f	250.00		
10.1.X0 Sales – SDB 48			
(invoice no 250)	1,264.60	Balance c/d	1,514.60
	1,514.60		1,514.60
11.1.X0 Balance b/d	1,514.60		

The debit side of this personal account, then, shows amounts owed by Enor College. When Enor pays some of the money it owes it will be entered into the cash book (receipts) and subsequently 'posted' to the credit side of the personal account. For example, if the college paid $250 on 10.1.20X0, it would appear as follows.

ENOR COLLEGE

A/c no: RL 9

	$			$
Balance b/f	250.00	10.1.X0	Cash	250.00
10.1.X0 Sales – SDB 48				
(invoice no 250)	1,264.60	Balance c/d		1,264.60
	1,514.60			1,514.60
11.1.X0 Balance b/d	1,264.60			

The opening balance owed by Enor College on 11.1.X0 is now $1,264.60 instead of $1,514.60, because of the $250 receipt which came in on 10.1.X0.

8.3 The payables ledger

The payables ledger, like the receivables ledger, consists of a number of personal accounts. These are separate accounts for **each individual supplier**, and they enable a business to keep a continuous record of how much it owes each supplier at any time.

Key term

> The **payables ledger** is a ledger for suppliers' personal accounts.

After entries are made in the purchase day book, cash book, or purchase returns day book – ie after entries are made in the books of prime entry – they are also made in the relevant supplier account in the payables ledger. Again we say that the entries in the purchase day book are **posted** to the suppliers' personal accounts in the payables ledger.

Here is an example of how a payables ledger account is laid out.

COOK & CO

A/c no: PL 31

	$		$
Balance c/d	515.00	Balance b/f	200.00
		15 Mar 20X8	
		Invoice received	
		PDB 37	315.00
	515.00		515.00
		16 March 20X8	
		Balance b/d	515.00

The credit side of this personal account, then, shows amounts owing to Cook & Co. If the business paid Cook & Co some money, it would be entered into the cash book (payments) and subsequently be posted to the debit side of the personal account. For example, if the business paid Cook & Co $100 on 15 March 20X8, it would appear as follows:

COOK & CO

A/c no: PL 31

		$			$
15.3.X8	Cash	100.00		Balance b/f	200.00
			15.3.X8	Invoice received	
	Balance c/d	415.00	PDB 37		315.00
		515.00			515.00
			16.3.X8	Balance b/d	415.00

The opening balance owed to Cook & Co on 16 March 20X8 is now $415.00 instead of $515.00 because of the $100 payment made during 15 March 20X8.

The remainder of the balance brought forward of $100.00 ($200.00 brought forward less payment of $100.00) is in dispute and Cook & Co send the business a credit note for $100.00 on 17 March 20X8.

COOK & CO

A/c no: PL 31

		$			$
17.3.X8	Credit note received	100.00	16.3.X8	Balance b/f	415.00
	Balance c/d	315.00			
		415.00			415.00
			12.3.X8	Balance b/d	315.00

The business now owes Cook & Co the amount of the invoice received on 15 March 20X8.

Important

Please note that, in a manual system, the account is not 'balanced off' after each transaction. It is more likely to be done once a month. However, we have done this to show the effect of the transactions.

Chapter Roundup

- Ledger accounts **summarise** all the individual transactions listed in the books of prime entry.

- The principal accounts are contained in a ledger called the **general** or **nominal ledger**.

- The **accounting equation** emphasises the equality between assets and liabilities (including capital as a liability).

- You should now be aware that, when business transactions are accounted for it should be possible to **restate the assets and liabilities** of the business after the transactions have taken place.

- **Trade accounts payable** are **liabilities. Trade accounts receivable** are **assets**.

- The **matching convention** requires that revenue earned is matched with the expenses incurred in earning it.

- **Double entry bookkeeping** is based on the idea that each transaction has an equal but opposite effect. Every accounting event must be entered in ledger accounts both as a debit and as an equal but opposite credit.

- A debit entry will:

    - increase an asset
    - decrease a liability
    - increase an expense

    A credit entry will:

    - decrease an asset
    - increase a liability
    - increase income

- Some accounts in the nominal ledger represent the total of very many smaller balances. For example, the **trade accounts receivable** account represents all the balances owed by individual customers of the business while the **trade accounts payable account** represents all money owed by the business to its suppliers.

- The **journal** is the record of prime entry for transactions which are not recorded in any of the other books of prime entry.

- Entries in the daybooks are totalled and analysed before posting to the nominal ledger.

- In the last chapter, we saw how the petty cash book was used to operate the imprest system. It is now time to see how the **double entry** works.

- The receivables and payables ledgers contain the **personal accounts** of individual customers and suppliers. They do not normally form part of the double-entry system.

Quick Quiz

1   What is the double entry to record a cash sale of $50?
2   What is the double entry to record a credit sale of $50?

    A   Debit cash $50, credit sales $50
    B   Debit receivables $50, credit sales $50
    C   Debit sales $50, credit receivables $50
    D   Debit sales $50, credit cash $50

3   What is the double entry to record a purchase of office chairs for $1,000?

    A   Debit non-current assets $1,000, credit cash $1,000
    B   Debit cash $1,000, credit purchases $1,000

4   What is the double entry to record a credit sale of $500 to A?

    A   Debit receivables $500, credit sales $500
    B   Debit receivables ledger (A's account) $500, credit sales $500

5   Name one reason for making a journal entry.
6   Individual customer accounts are kept in which ledger?

    A   General ledger
    B   Trade accounts receivable
    C   Receivables ledger
    D   Nominal ledger

Answers to Quick Quiz

1			$	$
	DEBIT	Cash a/c	50	
	CREDIT	Sales a/c		50

2   B

3   A

4   A   The receivables ledger is a memorandum account and not part of the double entry system.

5   Most commonly to correct an error, although it can be used to make any entry that is not recorded in a book of prime entry (eg prepayments, accrued expenses, depreciation).

6   C   The receivables ledger contains the individual customer accounts. The general ledger (A) and nominal ledger (D) are different names for the same ledger. This contains the trade accounts receivable account (B) which is the **total** of all the individual customer accounts.

Now try the question below from the Exam Question Bank

Number	Level	Marks	Time
Q9	Examination	1	1 min

From trial balance to financial statements

Topic list	Syllabus reference
1 The trial balance	C2(d), E1(a)–(d)
2 The income statement	A3(a)
3 The statement of financial position	A3(a)
4 Balancing accounts and preparing financial statements	C2(d), A3(a)

Introduction

In the previous chapter you learned the principles of double entry and how to post to the ledger accounts. The next step in our progress towards the financial statements is the **trial balance**.

Before transferring the relevant balances at the year end to the income statement and putting closing balances carried forward into the statement of financial position, it is usual to test the accuracy of double entry bookkeeping records by preparing **a list of account balances**. This is done by taking all the balances on every account; because of the self-balancing nature of the system of double entry, **the total of the debit balances will be exactly equal to the total of the credit balances.**

In very straightforward circumstances, where no complications arise and where the records are complete, it is possible to prepare accounts directly from a trial balance. This is covered in Section 4.

Study guide

		Intellectual level
A3	**The main elements of financial reports**	
(a)	Understand and identify the purpose of each of the main financial statements.	1
C2	**Ledger accounts, books of prime entry and journals**	
(d)	Illustrate how to balance and close a ledger account	1
E1	**Trial balance**	
(a)	Identify the purpose of a trial balance.	1
(b)	Extract ledger balances into a trial balance.	1
(c)	Prepare extracts of an opening trial balance.	1
(d)	Identify and understand the limitations of a trial balance.	1

Exam guide

Exam questions at all levels in financial accounting can involve preparation of final accounts from a trial balance. Last but not least, you may end up having to do it in 'real life'.

1 The trial balance

FAST FORWARD

> At suitable intervals, the entries in each ledger account are totalled and a **balance** is struck. Balances are usually collected in a **trial balance** which is then used as a basis for preparing an income statement and a statement of financial position.

You have a list of transactions, and have been asked to post them to the relevant ledger accounts. You do it as quickly as possible and find that you have a little time left over at the end of the day. How do you check that you have posted all the debit and credit entries properly?

There is no foolproof method, but a technique which shows up the more obvious mistakes is to prepare a **trial balance**.

Key term

> A **trial balance** is a list of ledger balances shown in debit and credit columns.

1.1 The first step

Before you draw up a list of account balances, you must have a collection of ledger accounts. For the sake of convenience, we will use the accounts of Ron Knuckle, which we drew up in the previous chapter.

CASH AT BANK

	$		$
Capital: Ron Knuckle	7,000	Rent	3,500
Bank loan	1,000	Shop fittings	2,000
Sales	10,000	Trade accounts payable	5,000
Trade accounts receivable	2,500	Bank loan interest	100
		Other expenses	1,900
		Drawings	1,500

CAPITAL (RON KNUCKLE)

	$		$
		Cash at bank	7,000

BANK LOAN

	$		$
		Cash at bank	1,000

PURCHASES

	$		$
Trade accounts payable	5,000		

TRADE ACCOUNTS PAYABLE

	$		$
Cash at bank	5,000	Purchases	5,000

RENT

	$		$
Cash at bank	3,500		

SHOP FITTINGS

	$		$
Cash at bank	2,000		

SALES

	$		$
		Cash at bank	10,000
		Trade accounts receivable	2,500

TRADE ACCOUNTS RECEIVABLE

	$		$
Sales	2,500	Cash at bank	2,500

BANK LOAN INTEREST

	$		$
Cash at bank	100		

OTHER EXPENSES

	$		$
Cash at bank	1,900		

DRAWINGS

	$		$
Cash at bank	1,500		

The next step is to 'balance' each account.

1.2 Balancing ledger accounts

At the end of an accounting period, a balance is struck on each account in turn. This means that all the debits on the account are totalled and so are all the credits. **If the total debits exceed the total credits there is said to be a debit balance on the account; if the credits exceed the debits then the account has a credit balance.**

In our simple example, there is very little balancing to do.

(a) Both the trade accounts payable and the trade accounts receivable balance off to zero.
(b) The cash at bank account has a debit balance of $6,500.
(c) The total on the sales account is $12,500, which is a credit balance.

CASH AT BANK

	$		$
Capital: Ron Knuckle	7,000	Rent	3,500
Bank loan	1,000	Shop fittings	2,000
Sales	10,000	Trade accounts payable	5,000
Trade accounts receivable	2,500	Bank loan interest	100
		Other expenses	1,900
		Drawings	1,500
			14,000
		Balancing figure – the amount of cash left over after payments have been made	6,500
	20,500		20,500

TRADE ACCOUNTS PAYABLE

	$		$
Cash at bank	5,000	Purchases	5,000

SALES

	$		$
		Cash at bank	10,000
		Trade accounts receivable	2,500
			12,500

TRADE ACCOUNTS RECEIVABLE

	$		$
Sales	2,500	Cash at bank	2,500

Otherwise, the accounts have only one entry each, so there is no totalling to do to arrive at the balance on each account.

1.3 Collecting the balances

If the basic principle of double entry has been correctly applied throughout the period it will be found that the credit balances equal the debit balances in total. This can be illustrated by collecting together the balances on Ron Knuckle's accounts.

	Debit $	Credit $
Cash at bank	6,500	
Capital		7,000
Bank loan		1,000
Purchases	5,000	
Trade accounts payable	–	–
Rent	3,500	
Shop fittings	2,000	
Sales		12,500
Trade accounts receivable	–	–
Bank loan interest	100	
Other expenses	1,900	
Drawings	1,500	
	20,500	20,500

This is called a **trial balance**. It does not matter in what order the various accounts are listed. It is just a method used to test the accuracy of the double entry bookkeeping.

1.4 What if the trial balance shows unequal debit and credit balances?

A trial balance can be used to test the accuracy of the accounting records. It lists the balances on ledger accounts and totals them. Total debits should equal total credits.

If the two columns of the list are not equal, there must be an error in recording the transactions in the accounts. A list of account balances, however, will **not** disclose the following types of errors.

(a) The **complete omission** of a transaction, because neither a debit nor a credit is made.

(b) The posting of a debit or credit to the correct side of the ledger, but to a **wrong account**.

(c) **Compensating errors** (eg an error of $100 is exactly cancelled by another $100 error elsewhere).

(d) **Errors of principle**, eg cash from receivables being debited to trade accounts receivable and credited to cash at bank instead of the other way round.

1.5 Example: Trial balance

As at 30.3.20X7, your business has the following balances on its ledger accounts.

Accounts	Balance $
Bank loan	12,000
Cash at bank	11,700
Capital	13,000
Local business taxes	1,880
Trade accounts payable	11,200
Purchases	12,400
Sales	14,600
Sundry payables	1,620
Trade accounts receivable	12,000
Bank loan interest	1,400
Other expenses	11,020
Vehicles	2,020

During the year the business made the following transactions.

(a) Bought materials for $1,000, half for cash and half on credit

(b) Made $1,040 sales, $800 of which was for credit

(c) Paid wages to shop assistants of $260 in cash

You are required to draw up a trial balance showing the balances as at the end of 31.3.X7.

Solution

First it is necessary to decide which of the original balances are debits and which are credits.

Account	Dr $	Cr $
Bank loan (liability)		12,000
Cash at bank (asset; overdraft = liability)	11,700	
Capital (liability)		13,000
Local taxes (expense)	1,880	
Trade accounts payable (liability)		11,200
Purchases (expense)	12,400	
Sales (revenue)		14,600
Sundry payables (liability)		1,620
Trade accounts receivable (asset)	12,000	
Bank loan interest (expenses)	1,400	
Other expenses	11,020	
Vehicles (non-current asset)	2,020	
	52,420	52,420

Now we must take account of the effects of the three transactions which took place on 31.3.X7.

			$	$
(a)	DEBIT	Purchases	1,000	
	CREDIT	Cash at bank		500
		Trade accounts payable		500
(b)	DEBIT	Cash at bank	240	
		Trade accounts receivable	800	
	CREDIT	Sales		1,040
(c)	DEBIT	Other expenses	260	
	CREDIT	Cash at bank		260

When these figures are included in the trial balance, it becomes:

Account	Dr $	Cr $
Bank loan		12,000
Cash at bank (11,700 + 240 – 500 – 260)	11,180	
Capital		13,000
Local taxes	1,880	
Trade accounts payable (11,200 + 500)		11,700
Purchases (12,400 + 1,000)	13,400	
Sales (14,600 + 1,040)		15,640
Sundry payables		1,620
Trade accounts receivable (12,000 + 800)	12,800	
Bank loan interest	1,400	
Other expenses (11,020 + 260)	11,280	
Vehicles	2,020	
	53,960	53,960

2 The income statement

> **FAST FORWARD**
>
> An **income and expense** ledger account is opened up to gather all items relating to income and expenses. When rearranged, these items make up the **income statement**.

The first step in the process of preparing the financial statements is to open up another ledger account, called the **income and expense account**. In it a business summarises its results for the period by gathering together all the ledger account balances relating to the income statement. This account is still part of the double entry system, so the basic rule of double entry still applies: every debit must have an equal and opposite credit entry.

This income and expense account contains the same information as the financial statement we are aiming for, ie the income statement, and in fact there are very few differences between the two. However, the income statement lays the information out differently and it may be much less detailed.

So what do we do with this new ledger account? The first step is to look through the ledger accounts and identify which ones relate to income and expenses. In the case of Ron Knuckle, these accounts consist of purchases, rent, sales, bank loan interest, and other expenses.

The balances on these accounts are transferred to the new income and expense account. For example, the balance on the purchases account is $5,000 DR. To balance this to zero, we write in $5,000 CR. But to comply with the rule of double entry, there has to be a debit entry somewhere, so we write $5,000 DR in the income and expense (I & E) account. Now the balance on the purchases account has been moved to the income and expense account.

If we do the same thing with all the separate accounts of Ron Knuckle dealing with income and expenses, the result is as follows.

PURCHASES

	$		$
Trade account payables	5,000	I & E a/c	5,000

RENT

	$		$
Cash at bank	3,500	I & E a/c	3,500

SALES

	$		$
I & E a/c	12,500	Cash at bank	10,000
		Trade accounts receivable	2,500
	12,500		12,500

BANK LOAN INTEREST

	$		$
Cash at bank	100	I & E a/c	100

OTHER EXPENSES

	$		$
Cash at bank	1,900	I & E a/c	1,900

INCOME AND EXPENSE ACCOUNT

	$		$
Purchases	5,000	Sales	12,500
Rent	3,500		
Bank loan interest	100		
Other expenses	1,900		

(Note that the income and expense account has not yet been balanced off but we will return to that later.)

If you look at the items we have gathered together in the income and expense account, they should strike a chord in your memory. They are the same items that we need to draw up the income statement.

Question	Income statement

Draw up Ron Knuckle's income statement.

RON KNUCKLE: INCOME STATEMENT

	$	$	
Sales		12,500	Trading
Cost of sales (= purchases in this case)		(5,000)	account
Gross profit		7,500	
Expenses			
Rent	3,500		Income and
Bank loan interest	100		expenditure
Other expenses	1,900		account
		(5,500)	
Net profit		2,000	

3 The statement of financial position

FAST FORWARD

The balances on all remaining ledger accounts (including the income and expense account) can be listed and rearranged to form the **statement of financial position**.

Look back at the ledger accounts of Ron Knuckle. Now that we have dealt with those relating to income and expenses, which ones are left? The answer is that we still have to find out what to do with the cash, capital, bank loan, trade accounts payable, shop fittings, trade accounts receivable and the drawings accounts.

Are these the only ledger accounts left? No: don't forget there is still the last one we opened up, called the **income and expense account**. The balance on this account represents the profit earned by the business, and if you go through the arithmetic, you will find that it has a credit balance – a profit – of $2,000. (Not surprisingly, this is the figure that is shown in the income statement.)

These remaining accounts must also be balanced and ruled off, but since they represent assets and liabilities of the business (not income and expenses) their balances are not transferred to the income and expense account. Instead they are *carried down* in the books of the business. This means that they become opening balances for the next accounting period and indicate the value of the assets and liabilities at the end of one period and the beginning of the next.

The conventional method of ruling off a ledger account at the end of an accounting period is illustrated by the bank loan account in Ron Knuckle's books.

BANK LOAN ACCOUNT

	$		$
Balance carried down (c/d)	1,000	Cash (D)	1,000
		Balance brought down (b/d)	1,000

Ron Knuckle therefore begins the new accounting period with a credit balance of $1,000 on this account. A **credit balance brought down** denotes a liability. An asset would be represented by a **debit balance brought down**.

One further point is worth noting before we move on to complete this example. You will remember that a proprietor's capital comprises any cash introduced by him, plus any profits made by the business, less any drawings made by him. At the stage we have now reached, these three elements are contained in different ledger accounts: cash introduced of $7,000 appears in the capital account; drawings of $1,500 appear in drawings; and the profit made by the business is represented by the $2,000 credit balance on the income and expense account. It is convenient to gather together all these amounts into one **capital account**, in the same way as we earlier gathered together income and expense accounts into one income and expense account.

If we go ahead and gather the three amounts together, the results are as follows.

DRAWINGS

	$		$
Cash at bank	1,500	Capital a/c	1,500

INCOME AND EXPENSE ACCOUNT

	$		$
Purchases	5,000	Sales	12,500
Rent	3,500		
Bank loan interest	100		
Other expenses	1,900		
Capital a/c	2,000		
	12,500		12,500

CAPITAL

	$		$
Drawings	1,500	Cash at bank	7,000
Balance c/d	7,500	I & E a/c	2,000
	9,000		9,000
		Balance b/d	7,500

| Question | Statement of financial position |

You can now complete Ron Knuckle's simple statement of financial position.

Answer

RON KNUCKLE
STATEMENT OF FINANCIAL POSITION AT END OF FIRST TRADING PERIOD

	$
Assets	
Non-current assets	
Shop fittings	2,000
Current assets	
Cash at bank	6,500
Total assets	8,500
Capital and liabilities	
Proprietor's capital	7,500
Non-current liabilities	
Bank loan	1,000
Total capital and liabilities	8,500

When a statement of financial position is drawn up for an accounting period which is not the first one, then it ought to show the capital at the start of the accounting period and the capital at the end of the accounting period. This will be illustrated in the next example.

In an examination question, you might not be given the ledger accounts – you might have to draw them up in the first place. That is the case with the following exercise – see if you can do it by yourself before looking at the solution.

4 Balancing accounts and preparing financial statements

The exercise which follows is by far the most important in this text so far. It uses all the accounting steps from entering up ledger accounts to preparing the financial statements. It is **very important that you try the question by yourself:** if you do not, you will be missing out a vital part of this text.

Question
Financial statements

A business is established with capital of $2,000, and this amount is paid into a business bank account by the proprietor. During the first year's trading, the following transactions occurred:

	$
Purchases of goods for resale, on credit	4,300
Payments to trade accounts payable	3,600
Sales, all on credit	5,800
Payments from trade accounts receivable	3,200
Non-current assets purchased for cash	1,500
Other expenses, all paid in cash	900

The bank has provided an overdraft facility of up to $3,000.

Required

Prepare the ledger accounts, an income statement for the year and a statement of financial position as at the end of the year.

Answer

The first thing to do is to open ledger accounts so that the transactions can be entered up. The relevant accounts which we need for this example are: cash at bank; capital; trade accounts payable; purchases; non-current assets; sales; trade accounts receivable and other expenses.

The next step is to work out the double entry bookkeeping for each transaction. Normally you would write them straight into the accounts, but to make this example easier to follow, they are first listed below.

		Debit	Credit
(a)	Establishing business ($2,000)	Cash at bank	Capital
(b)	Purchases ($4,300)	Purchases	Trade accounts payable
(c)	Payments to trade accounts payable ($3,600)	Trade accounts payable	Cash at bank
(d)	Sales ($5,800)	Trade accounts receivable	Sales
(e)	Payments from trade accounts receivable ($3,200)	Cash at bank	Trade accounts receivable
(f)	Non-current assets ($1,500)	Non-current assets	Cash at bank
(g)	Other (cash) expenses ($900)	Other expenses	Cash at bank

So far, the ledger accounts will look like this.

CASH AT BANK

	$		$
Capital	2,000	Trade accounts payable	3,600
Trade account receivables	3,200	Non-current assets	1,500
		Other expenses	900

CAPITAL

	$		$
		Cash at bank	2,000

TRADE ACCOUNTS PAYABLE

	$		$
Cash at bank	3,600	Purchases	4,300

PURCHASES

	$		$
Trade accounts payable	4,300		

NON-CURRENT ASSETS

	$		$
Cash at bank	1,500		

SALES

	$		$
		Trade accounts receivable	5,800

TRADE ACCOUNTS RECEIVABLE

	$		$
Sales	5,800	Cash at bank	3,200

OTHER EXPENSES

	$		$
Cash at bank	900		

The next thing to do is to balance all these accounts. It is at this stage that you could, if you wanted to, draw up a trial balance to make sure the double entry is accurate. There is not very much point in this simple example, but if you did, it would look like this.

	Dr	Cr
	$	$
Cash at bank		800
Capital		2,000
Trade accounts payable		700
Purchases	4,300	
Non-current assets	1,500	
Sales		5,800
Trade accounts receivable	2,600	
Other expenses	900	
	9,300	9,300

After balancing the accounts, the income and expense account should be opened. Into it should be transferred all the balances relating to income and expense (ie purchases, other expenses, and sales). At this point, the ledger accounts will be as follows.

CASH AT BANK

	$		$
Capital	2,000	Trade accounts payable	3,600
Trade accounts receivable	3,200	Non-current assets	1,500
Balance c/d	800	Other expenses	900
	6,000		6,000
		Balance b/d	800*

* A credit balance b/d means that this cash item is a liability, not an asset. This indicates a bank overdraft of $800, with cash income of $5,200 falling short of payments of $6,000 by this amount.

CAPITAL

	$		$
Balance c/d	2,600	Cash at bank	2,000
		I & E a/c	600
	2,600		2,600

TRADE ACCOUNTS PAYABLE

	$		$
Cash at bank	3,600	Purchases	4,300
Balance c/d	700		
	4,300		4,300
		Balance b/d	700

PURCHASES ACCOUNT

	$		$
Trade accounts payable	4,300	I & E a/c	4,300

NON-CURRENT ASSETS

	$		$
Cash at bank	1,500	Balance c/d	1,500
Balance b/d	1,500		

SALES

	$		$
I & E a/c	5,800		5,800

TRADE ACCOUNTS RECEIVABLE

	$		$
Sales	5,800	Cash at bank	3,200
		Balance c/d	2,600
	5,800		5,800
Balance b/d	2,600		

OTHER EXPENSES

	$		$
Cash at bank	900	I & E a/c	900

INCOME AND EXPENSE ACCOUNT

	$		$
Purchases account	4,300	Sales	5,800
Gross profit c/d	1,500		
	5,800		5,800
Other expenses	900	Gross profit b/d	1,500
Net profit (transferred to capital account)	600		
	1,500		1,500

So the income statement will be:

INCOME STATEMENT
FOR THE ACCOUNTING PERIOD

	$
Sales	5,800
Cost of sales (purchases)	4,300
Gross profit	1,500
Expenses	900
Net profit	600

Listing and then rearranging the balances on the ledger accounts gives the statement of financial position as:

STATEMENT OF FINANCIAL POSITION AS AT THE END OF THE PERIOD

	$	$
Assets		
Non-current assets		1,500
Current assets		
Trade accounts receivable		2,600
Total assets		4,100
Capital and liabilities		
Capital		
At start of period	2,000	
Net profit for period	600	
At end of period		2,600
Current liabilities		
Bank overdraft	800	
Trade accounts payable	700	
		1,500
Total capital and liabilities		4,100

Exam focus point

> The above example is highly detailed. This detail is given to help you to work through the example properly. You may wish to do things this way yourself until you get more practised in accounting techniques and are confident enough to take short cuts.
>
> The techniques are worth practising as you may well get a MCQ requiring you to calculate a figure for the income statement or statement of financial position from a trial balance.

Question

Alpha has the following opening balances on its ledger accounts.

	$
Fixtures	5,000
Trade accounts receivable	2,000
Bank account	1,000
Loan	3,000

(a)   What is the total assets figure?

    A $6,000
    B $5,000
    C $8,000
    D $3,000

(b)   What is the opening figure for capital?

    A $6,000
    B $5,000
    C $8,000
    D $3,000

Answer

(a)   C   Assets = 5,000 + 2,000 + 1,000
                   = 8,000

(b)   B   Capital = assets – liabilities
                  = (5,000 + 2,000 + 1,000) – 3,000
                  = 5,000

Chapter Roundup

- At suitable intervals, the entries in each **ledger account** are totalled and a **balance** is struck. Balances are usually collected in a **trial balance** which is then used as a basis for preparing an income statement and a statement of financial position.

- A trial balance can be used to **test the accuracy of the double entry accounting** records. It works by listing the balances on ledger accounts, some of which will be debits and some credits. The total debits should equal total credits.

- An **income and expense ledger account** is opened up to gather all items relating to income and expenses. When **rearranged**, the items make up the **income statement**.

- The balances on all **remaining ledger accounts** (including the income and expense account) can be listed and **rearranged** to form the **statement of financial position**.

Quick Quiz

1   What is the purpose of a trial balance?

2   A trial balance may still balance if some of the balances are wrong.

    Is this statement correct?

    A   Yes
    B   No

3   In a period, sales are $140,000, purchases $75,000 and other expenses $25,000. What is the figure for net profit to be transferred to the capital account?

    A $40,000
    B $65,000
    C $75,000
    D $140,000

4   The balance on an expense account will go to the I & E account. However, the balance on a liability account is written off to capital.

    Is this statement correct?

    A   Yes
    B   No

5   The balance brought forward on the bank account is a debit figure. This means that the balance is overdrawn. True or false?

Answers to Quick Quiz

1 To test the accuracy of the double entry bookkeeping.

2 A See Section 1.4.

3 A

INCOME & EXPENSE ACCOUNT

	$		$
Purchases	75,000	Sales	140,000
Gross profit c/d	65,000		
	140,000		140,000
Other expenses	25,000	Gross profit b/d	65,000
Net profit – to capital a/c	40,000		
	65,000		65,000

B is the **gross** profit figure, while C is the figure for purchases and D sales.

4 B When an expense account is balanced off, the balance is transferred to the income and expense account. When a liability account is balanced off, the balance is carried forward to the next accounting period.

5 False. A debit balance b/f is an asset and means that the bank account is **not** overdrawn.

Now try the question below from the Exam Question Bank

Number	Level	Marks	Time
Q10	Examination	2	2 mins

Recording transactions and events

Sales tax

Topic list	Syllabus reference
1 The nature of sales tax and how it is collected	D1(c)–(d)
2 Accounting for sales tax	D1(d)

Introduction

Many business transactions involve sales tax (eg VAT in the UK). Invoices and bills show any sales tax charged separately.

Sales tax is charged on the supply of goods and services. It is an **indirect tax**.

Section 1 explains how sales tax works.

Section 2 deals with the accounting treatment of sales tax. If you understand the principle behind the tax and how it is collected, you will understand the accounting treatment.

Study guide

		Intellectual level
D1	**Sales and purchases**	
(c)	Understand the general principles of the operation of a sales tax.	1
(d)	Calculate sales tax on transactions and record the consequent accounting entries.	1

Exam guide

This topic could well be examined as part of another topic eg whether sales tax needs to be included when accounting for non-current assets. Be prepared for a range of rates to be used in the exam.

1 The nature of sales tax and how it is collected

FAST FORWARD

Sales tax is an indirect tax levied on the sale of goods and services. It is usually administered by the local tax authorities.

1.1 How is sales tax levied?

Sales tax is a cumulative tax, collected at various stages of a product's life. In the illustrative example below, a manufacturer of a television buys materials and components and then sells the television to a wholesaler, who in turn sells it to a retailer, who then sells it to a customer. It is assumed that the rate for sales tax is 15% on all items. All the other figures are for illustration only.

1.2 Example

			Price net of sales tax $	Sales tax 15% $	Total price $
(a)	(i)	Manufacturer purchases raw materials and components	40	6	46
	(ii)	Manufacturer sells the completed television to a wholesaler	200	30	230
		The manufacturer hands over to tax authorities		24	
(b)	(i)	Wholesaler purchases television for	200	30	230
	(ii)	Wholesaler sells television to a retailer	320	48	368
		Wholesaler hands over to tax authorities		18	
(c)	(i)	Retailer purchases television for	320	48	368
	(ii)	Retailer sells television	480	72	552
		Retailer hands over to tax authorities		24	
(d)		Customer purchases television for	480	72	552

The total tax of $72 is borne by the ultimate consumer. However, the tax is handed over to the authorities in stages. If we assume that the sales tax of $6 on the initial supplies to the manufacturer is paid by the supplier, the tax authorities would collect the sales tax as follows.

	$
Supplier of materials and components	6
Manufacturer	24
Wholesaler	18
Retailer	24
Total sales tax paid	72

1.3 Input and output sales tax

Sales tax charged on goods and services sold by a business is referred to as **output** sales tax. Sales tax paid on goods and services 'bought in' by a business is referred to as **input** sales tax.

If output sales tax exceeds input sales tax, the business pays the difference in tax to the authorities. If output sales tax is less than input sales tax in a period, the tax authorities will refund the difference to the business.

The example above assumes that the supplier, manufacturer, wholesaler and retailer are all sales tax registered traders.

A sales tax registered trader must carry out the following tasks.

(a)   Charge sales tax on the goods and services sold at the rate prescribed by the government. This is output sales tax.

(b)   Pay sales tax on goods and services purchased from other businesses. This is input sales tax.

(c)   Pay to the tax authorities the difference between the sales tax collected on sales and the sales tax paid to suppliers for purchases. Payments are made at quarterly intervals.

1.4 Irrecoverable sales tax

There are some circumstances in which traders are not allowed to reclaim sales tax paid on their inputs. In these cases the trader must bear the cost of sales tax and account for it accordingly. So the cost of expenses and any non-current assets purchased will include any irrecoverable sales tax.

Where sales tax is not recoverable it must be regarded as part of the cost of the items purchased and included in the I/S charge or in the statement of financial position as appropriate.

2 Accounting for sales tax

Registered businesses charge output sales tax on sales and suffer input sales tax on purchases. Sales tax does not affect the income statement, but is simply being collected on behalf of the tax authorities to whom a quarterly payment is made.

2.1 Income statement

A business does not make any profit out of the sales tax it charges. It therefore follows that its income statement figures should not include sales tax. For example, if a business sells goods for $600 + sales tax $90, ie for $690 total price, the sales account should only record the $600 excluding sales tax. The accounting entries to record the sale would be as follows.

DEBIT	Cash or trade receivables	$690	
CREDIT	Sales		$600
CREDIT	Sales tax payable (output sales tax)		$90

If input sales tax is recoverable, the cost of purchases should exclude the sales tax and be recorded net of tax. For example, if a business purchases goods on credit for $400 + sales tax $60, the transaction would be recorded as follows.

DEBIT	Purchases	$400	
DEBIT	Sales tax payables (input sales tax recoverable)	$60	
CREDIT	Trade payables		$460

If the input sales tax is not recoverable, the cost of purchases must include the tax, because it is the business itself which must bear the cost of the tax.

	Purchases	Sales
Income statement	Irrecoverable input sales tax: include Recoverable input sales tax: exclude	Exclude sales tax

2.2 Sales tax in the cash book, sales day book and purchase day book

When a business makes a credit sale the total amount invoiced, including sales tax, will be recorded in the sales day book. The analysis columns will then separate the sales tax from the sales income of the business as follows.

Date	Total $	Sales income $	Sales tax $
A Detter and Sons	230	200	30

When a business is invoiced by a supplier the total amount payable, including sales tax, will be recorded in the purchase day book. The analysis columns will then separate the recoverable input sales tax from the net purchase cost to the business as follows.

Date	Total $	Purchase $	Sales tax $
A Splier (Merchants)	184	160	24

When receivables pay what they owe, or payables are paid, there is **no need to show** the sales tax in an analysis column of the cash book, because input and output sales tax arise when the sale is made, not when the debt is settled.

However, sales tax charged on **cash sales** or sales tax paid on **cash purchases** will be analysed in a separate column of the cash book. This is because output sales tax has just arisen from the cash sale and must be credited to the sales tax payables in the ledger accounts. Similarly input sales tax paid on cash purchases, having just arisen, must be debited to the sales tax payable.

For example, the receipts side of a cash book might be written up as follows.

				Analysis columns	
Date	Narrative	Total $	Sales ledger $	Cash sales $	Output sales tax on cash sales $
	A Detter & Sons	230	230		
	Owen	660	660		
	Cash sales	322		280	42
	Newgate Merchants	184	184		
	Cash sales	92		80	12
		1,488	1,074	360	54

The payments side of a cash book might be written up as follows.

				Analysis columns	
Date	Narrative	Total $	Purchase ledger $	Cash purchases and sun- dry items $	Input sales tax on cash purchases $
	A Splier (Merchants)	184	184		
	Telephone bill paid	138		120	18
	Cash purchase of stationery	46		40	6
	Sales tax paid to tax authorities	1,400		1,400	
		1,768	184	1,560	24

Question

Are trade receivables and trade payables shown in the accounts inclusive of sales tax or exclusive of sales tax?

Answer

They are shown **inclusive** of sales tax, as the statement of financial position must reflect the total amount due from receivables and due to payables.

Exam focus point

A small element of sales tax is quite likely in questions. It is worth spending a bit of time ensuring that you understand the logic behind the way sales tax is accounted for, rather than trying to learn the rules by rote. This will ensure that even if you forget the rules, you will be able to work out what should be done.

2.3 Payable for sales tax

FAST FORWARD

An outstanding payable for sales tax will appear as a current liability in the statement of financial position.

The sales tax paid to the authorities each quarter is the difference between recoverable input sales tax on purchases and output sales tax on sales. For example, if a business is invoiced for input sales tax of $8,000 and charges sales tax of $15,000 on its credit sales and sales tax of $2,000 on its cash sales, the sales tax payable account would be as follows.

SALES TAX PAYABLE

	$		$
Payables (input sales tax)	8,000	Receivables (output sales	
Cash (payment to authorities)	9,000	tax invoiced)	15,000
		Cash (output sales tax on cash sales)	2,000
	17,000		17,000

Payments to the authorities do not coincide with the end of the accounting period of a business, and so at the reporting date there will be a balance on the sales tax payable account. If this balance is for an amount payable to the authorities, the outstanding payable for sales tax will appear as a current liability in the statement of financial position.

Occasionally, a business will be owed money back by the authorities, and in such a situation, the sales tax refund owed by the authorities would be a current asset in the statement of financial position.

Question

A business in its first period of trading charges $4,000 of sales tax on its sales and suffers $3,500 of sales tax on its purchases which include $250 sales tax on business entertaining. Prepare the sales tax payable account.

Answer

SALES TAX PAYABLE ACCOUNT

	$		$
Payables	3,250	Receivables	4,000
Balance c/d (owed to tax authorities)	750		
	4,000		4,000
		Balance b/d	750

The main points

(a) **Credit sales**

   (i) Include sales tax in sales day book; separately

   (ii) Include gross receipts from receivables in cashbook; no need to show sales tax separately

   (iii) Exclude sales tax element from income statement

   (iv) Credit sales tax payable with output sales tax element of receivables invoiced

(b) **Credit purchases**

   (i) Include Sales tax in purchases day book; show it separately

   (ii) Include gross payments in cashbook; no need to show sales tax separately

   (iii) Exclude recoverable sales tax from income statement

   (iv) Include irrecoverable sales tax in income statement

   (v) Debit sales tax payable with recoverable input sales tax element of credit purchases

(c) **Cash sales**

   (i) Include gross receipts in cashbook; show sales tax separately

   (ii) Exclude sales tax element from income statement

   (iii) Credit sales tax payable with output sales tax element of cash sales

(d) **Cash purchases**

   (i) Include gross payments in cashbook: show sales tax separately

   (ii) Exclude recoverable sales tax from income statement

   (iii) Include irrecoverable sales tax in income statement

   (iv) Debit sales tax payable with recoverable input sales tax element of cash purchases

---

Exam focus point

In sales tax questions, remember to check the tax rate used. If you are required to calculate sales tax, the rate will always to be given.

Chapter Roundup

- **Sales tax** is an indirect tax levied on the sale of goods and services. It is usually administered by the local tax authorities.

- If output sales tax exceeds input sales tax, the business pays the difference in tax to the authorities. If output sales tax is less than input sales tax in a period, the tax authorities will refund the difference to the business.

- Where sales tax is not recoverable, for any of the reasons described above, it must be regarded as part of the cost of the items purchased and included in the I/S charge or in the statement of financial position as appropriate.

- Registered businesses charge output sales tax on sales and suffer input sales tax on purchases. Sales tax does not affect the income statement, but is simply being collected on behalf of the tax authorities to whom a quarterly payment is made.

- An outstanding payable for sales tax will appear as a current liability in the statement of financial position.

Quick Quiz

1   Sales tax is:

    A   A direct tax levied on sales of goods and services

    B   An indirect tax levied on the sales of goods and services

    C   Administered by the Treasury

    D   Charged by businesses on taxable supplies

2   Sales tax is due on all sales. Is this statement correct?

    A   Yes

    B   No

3   When sales tax is not recoverable on the cost of a motor car, it should be treated in which of the following ways?

    A   Deducted from the cost of the asset capitalised

    B   Included in the cost of the asset capitalised

    C   Deducted from output tax for the period

    D   Written off to I/S as an expense

4   Purchases of goods costing $500 subject to sales tax at 15% occur. Which of the following correctly records the **credit purchase**?

A	Debit	Purchases	$500.00	
	Debit	Sales tax	$75.00	
	Credit	Payables		$575.00
B	Debit	Purchases	$575.00	
	Credit	Payables		$575.00
C	Debit	Purchases	$436.78	
	Debit	Sales tax	$65.22	
	Credit	Payables		$500.00
D	Debit	Purchases	$500.00	
	Credit	Sales tax		$65.22
	Credit	Payables		$434.78

5   A business purchases goods valued at $400. Sales tax is charged at 15%. The double entry to record the purchase is:

    Debit   .... $...............

    Debit   .... $...............

    Credit   .... $...............

6   Fill in the blanks.

    Input sales tax is .... , output sales tax is ....

7   When a cash sale is made for $115.00 (including sales tax at 15%) the entries made are:

Debit   .... account $..............

Credit   .... account $...............

Credit   .... account $...............

8   When a cash purchase of $115.00 is made (including sales tax at 15%) the entries are:

A	Debit	Purchases	115.00	
	Credit	Cash		115.00
B	Debit	Purchases	100.00	
	Debit	Sales tax	15.00	
	Credit	Cash		115.00
C	Debit	Cash	100.00	
	Debit	Sales tax	15.00	
	Credit	Purchases		115.00
D	Debit	Cash	115.00	
	Credit	Purchases		115.00

9   The sales tax paid to the tax authorities each quarter is the difference between ....
.... and ....

Answers to Quick Quiz

1	B	Correct
	A	Incorrect, the consumer has a choice as to whether or not to consume so sales tax is only chargeable when this choice is exercised.
	C	Incorrect, sales tax is administrated by the tax authorities.
	D	Only sales tax registered traders can charge sales tax.
2	B	Sales tax is only due on taxable outputs.
3	B	Correct the statement of financial position value will therefore include sales tax and the depreciation charge will rise accordingly
	A	Incorrect, it must be added.
	C	Incorrect.
	D	Incorrect, the motor car is a non-current asset not an expense, sales tax will form part of the depreciable amount of the asset.
4	A	Correct, recoverable input tax is debited to the sales tax a/c and the purchases account is debited net of sales tax.
	B	Incorrect, the sales tax has not been reclaimed.
	C	Incorrect, the $500 is subject to sales tax.
	D	Incorrect, reversal of the sales tax transaction has occurred.

5   DEBIT: PURCHASES $400
                                SALES TAX $60
          CREDIT: CASH or PAYABLES $460

6   Input sales tax is sales tax suffered on goods and services brought by a business, output sales tax is the sales tax collected on sales.

7   DEBIT   Cash account $115.00
          CREDIT   Sales account $100.00
          CREDIT   Sales tax account $15.00

8   B

9   The sales tax paid to the tax authorities each quarter is the difference between output sales tax collected on sales and input sales tax suffered on purchases and expenses.

Now try the question below from the Exam Question Bank

Number	Level	Marks	Time
Q11	Examination	2	2 mins

Inventory

Topic list	Syllabus reference
1 Cost of goods sold	D3(a)
2 Accounting for opening and closing inventories	D3(a), (b)
3 Counting inventories	D3(f)
4 Valuing inventories	D3(c), (g), (i)
5 IAS 2 *Inventories*	D3(d), (e), (h)

Introduction

Inventory is one of the most important assets in a company's statement of financial position. As we will see, it also affects the income statement, having a direct impact on gross profit.

So far you have come across inventories in the preparation of a simple statement of financial position. Here we will look at in the calculation of the cost of goods sold. This chapter also explores the **difficulties of valuing inventories**.

This is the first time that you will be required to consider the impact of the relevant International Accounting Standard on the valuation and presentation of an item in the accounts: IAS 2 *Inventories*.

Study guide

		Intellectual level
D3	Inventory	
(a)	Recognise the need for adjustments for inventory in preparing financial statements.	1
(b)	Record opening and closing inventory	1
(c)	Identify the alternative methods of valuing inventory	1
(d)	Understand and apply the IASB requirements for valuing inventories	1
(e)	Recognise which costs should be included in valuing inventories	1
(f)	Understand the use of continuous and period end inventory records	1
(g)	Calculate the value of closing inventory using FIFO (first in, first out) and AVCO (average cost)	1
(h)	Understand the impact of accounting concepts on the valuation of inventory	1
(i)	Identify the impact of inventory valuation methods on profit and on assets	1

Exam guide

You will definitely be examined on inventories. You might have to calculate closing inventory or cost of sales.

1 Cost of goods sold

FAST FORWARD

The **cost of goods sold** is calculated as:

Opening inventory + purchases – closing inventory.

1.1 Unsold goods in inventory at the end of an accounting period

Goods might be unsold at the end of an accounting period and so still be **held in inventory**. The purchase cost of these goods should not be included therefore in the cost of sales of the period.

1.2 Example: Closing inventory

Perry P Louis, trading as the Umbrella Shop, ends his financial year on 30 September each year. On 1 October 20X4 he had no goods in inventory. During the year to 30 September 20X5, he purchased 30,000 umbrellas costing $60,000 from umbrella wholesalers and suppliers. He resold the umbrellas for $5 each, and sales for the year amounted to $100,000 (20,000 umbrellas). At 30 September there were 10,000 unsold umbrellas left in inventory, valued at $2 each.

What was Perry P Louis's gross profit for the year?

Solution

Perry P Louis purchased 30,000 umbrellas, but only sold 20,000. Purchase costs of $60,000 and sales of $100,000 do not represent the same quantity of goods.

The gross profit for the year should be calculated by 'matching' the sales value of the 20,000 umbrellas sold with the cost of those 20,000 umbrellas. The cost of sales in this example is therefore the cost of purchases minus the cost of goods in inventory at the year end.

	$	$
Sales (20,000 units)		100,000
Purchases (30,000 units)	60,000	
Less closing inventory (10,000 units @ $2)	20,000	
Cost of sales (20,000 units)		40,000
Gross profit		60,000

1.3 Example continued

We shall continue the example of the Umbrella Shop into its next accounting year, 1 October 20X5 to 30 September 20X6. During the course of this year, Perry P Louis purchased 40,000 umbrellas at a total cost of $95,000. During the year he sold 45,000 umbrellas for $230,000. At 30 September 20X6 he had 5,000 umbrellas left in inventory, which had cost $12,000.

What was his gross profit for the year?

Solution

In this accounting year, he purchased 40,000 umbrellas to add to the 10,000 he already had in inventory at the start of the year. He sold 45,000, leaving 5,000 umbrellas in inventory at the year end. Once again, gross profit should be calculated by matching the value of 45,000 units of sales with the cost of those 45,000 units.

The cost of sales is the value of the 10,000 umbrellas in inventory at the beginning of the year, plus the cost of the 40,000 umbrellas purchased, less the value of the 5,000 umbrellas in inventory at the year end.

	$	$
Sales (45,000 units)		230,000
Opening inventory (10,000 units) *	20,000	
Add purchases (40,000 units)	95,000	
	115,000	
Less closing inventory (5,000 units)	12,000	
Cost of sales (45,000 units)		103,000
Gross profit		127,000

* Taken from the closing inventory value of the previous accounting year, see paragraph 1.3.

1.4 The cost of goods sold

The cost of goods sold is found by applying the following formula.

Formula to learn

	$
Opening inventory value	X
Add cost of purchases (or, in the case of a manufacturing company, the cost of production)	X
	X
Less closing inventory value	(X)
Equals cost of goods sold	X

In other words, to match 'sales' and the 'cost of goods sold', it is necessary to adjust the cost of goods manufactured or purchased to allow for increases or reduction in inventory levels during the period.

The 'formula' above is based on a logical idea. You should learn it, because it is fundamental among the principles of accounting.

Test your knowledge of the formula with the following example.

1.5 Example: Cost of goods sold and variations in inventory levels

On 1 January 20X6, the Grand Union Food Stores had goods in inventory valued at $6,000. During 20X6 its proprietor purchased supplies costing $50,000. Sales for the year to 31 December 20X6 amounted to $80,000. The cost of goods in inventory at 31 December 20X6 was $12,500.

Calculate the gross profit for the year.

Solution

GRAND UNION FOOD STORES
TRADING ACCOUNT FOR THE YEAR ENDED 31 DECEMBER 20X6

	$	$
Sales		80,000
Opening inventories	6,000	
Add purchases	50,000	
	56,000	
Less closing inventories	12,500	
Cost of goods sold		43,500
Gross profit		36,500

1.6 The cost of carriage inwards and outwards

FAST FORWARD

Carriage inwards is included in the cost of purchases.
Carriage outwards is a selling expense.

'Carriage' refers to the **cost of transporting purchased goods** from the supplier to the premises of the business which has bought them. Someone has to pay for these delivery costs: sometimes the supplier pays, and sometimes the purchaser pays. When the purchaser pays, the cost to the purchaser is carriage inwards (**into** the business). When the supplier pays, the cost to the supplier is known as carriage outwards (**out** of the business).

The **cost of carriage inwards** is usually added to the **cost of purchases**.

The **cost of carriage outwards** is a **selling and distribution expense** in the **income statement**.

1.7 Example: Carriage inwards and carriage outwards

Gwyn Tring, trading as Clickety Clocks, imports and resells clocks. He pays for the costs of delivering the clocks from his supplier in Switzerland to his shop in Wales.

He resells the clocks to other traders throughout the country, paying the costs of carriage for the consignments from his business premises to his customers.

On 1 July 20X5, he had clocks in inventory valued at $17,000. During the year to 30 June 20X6 he purchased more clocks at a cost of $75,000. Carriage inwards amounted to $2,000. Sales for the year were $162,100. Other expenses of the business amounted to $56,000 excluding carriage outwards which cost $2,500. Gwyn Tring took drawings of $20,000 from the business during the course of the year. The value of the goods in inventory at the year end was $15,400.

Required

Prepare the income statement of Clickety Clocks for the year ended 30 June 20X6.

Solution

CLICKETY CLOCKS
INCOME STATEMENT FOR THE YEAR ENDED 30 JUNE 20X6

	$	$
Sales		162,100
Opening inventory	17,000	
Purchases	75,000	
Carriage inwards	2,000	
	94,000	
Less closing inventory	15,400	
Cost of goods sold		78,600
Gross profit		83,500
Carriage outwards	2,500	
Other expenses	56,000	
		58,500
Net profit (transferred to statement of financial position)		25,000

1.8 Goods written off or written down

A trader might be unable to sell all the goods that he purchases, because a number of things might happen to the goods before they can be sold. For example:

(a) Goods might be lost or stolen.

(b) Goods might be damaged, become worthless and so be thrown away.

(c) Goods might become obsolete or out of fashion. These might be thrown away, or sold off at a very low price in a clearance sale.

When goods are **lost, stolen or thrown away** as worthless, the business will make a loss on those goods because their **'sales value' will be nil**.

Similarly, when goods lose value because they have become **obsolete** or out of fashion, the business will **make a loss** if their clearance sales value is less than their cost. For example, if goods which originally cost $500 are now obsolete and could only be sold for $150, the business would suffer a loss of $350.

If, at the end of an accounting period, a business still has goods in inventory which are either worthless or worth less than their original cost, the value of the inventories should be **written down** to:

(a) Nothing, if they are worthless

(b) Their net realisable value, if this is less than their original cost

This means that the loss will be reported as soon as the loss is foreseen, even if the goods have not yet been thrown away or sold off at a cheap price. This is an application of the prudence concept, which we looked at in Chapter 3.

The costs of inventory written off or written down should not usually cause any problems in calculating the gross profit of a business, because the cost of goods sold will include the cost of inventories written off or written down, as the following example shows.

1.9 Example: Inventories written off and written down

Lucas Wagg, trading as Fairlock Fashions, ends his financial year on 31 March. At 1 April 20X5 he had goods in inventory valued at $8,800. During the year to 31 March 20X6, he purchased goods costing $48,000. Fashion goods which cost $2,100 were still held in inventory at 31 March 20X6, and Lucas Wagg believes that these could only now be sold at a sale price of $400. The goods still held in inventory at 31 March 20X6 (including the fashion goods) had an original purchase cost of $7,600. Sales for the year were $81,400.

Required

Calculate the gross profit of Fairlock Fashions for the year ended 31 March 20X6.

Solution

Initial calculation of closing inventory values:

INVENTORY COUNT

	At cost $	Realisable value $	Amount written down $
Fashion goods	2,100	400	1,700
Other goods (balancing figure)	5,500	5,500	
	7,600	5,900	1,700

FAIRLOCK FASHIONS
TRADING ACCOUNT FOR THE YEAR ENDED 31 MARCH 20X6

	$	$
Sales		81,400
Value of opening inventory	8,800	
Purchases	48,000	
	56,800	
Less closing inventory	5,900	
Cost of goods sold		50,900
Gross profit		30,500

By using the figure of $5,900 for closing inventories, the cost of goods sold automatically includes the inventory written down of $1,700.

Question

Gross profit

Gross profit for 20X7 can be calculated from:

A   purchases for 20X7, plus inventory at 31 December 20X7, less inventory at 1 January 20X7
B   purchases for 20X7, less inventory at 31 December 20X7, plus inventory at 1 January 20X7
C   cost of goods sold during 20X7, plus sales during 20X7
D   net profit for 20X7, plus expenses for 20X7

Answer

The correct answer is D. Gross profit less expenses = net profit. Therefore net profit plus expenses = gross profit.

2 Accounting for opening and closing inventories

FAST FORWARD

Opening inventories brought forward in the inventory account are transferred to the trading account, and so at the end of the accounting year the balance on the inventory account ceases to be the opening inventory value b/f and becomes instead the closing inventory value c/f.

2.1 Recap

In Section 1, we saw that in order to calculate **gross profit** it is necessary to work out the **cost of goods sold**, and in order to calculate the cost of goods sold it is necessary to have values for the **opening inventory** (ie inventory in hand at the beginning of the accounting period) and **closing inventory** (ie inventory in hand at the end of the accounting period).

You should remember, in fact, that the trading part of an income statement includes:

	$
Opening inventory	X
Plus purchases	X
Less closing inventory	(X)
Equals cost of goods sold	X

However, just writing down this formula hides three basic problems.

(a) How do you manage to get a **precise count** of inventory in hand at any one time?

(b) Even once it has been counted, how do you **value** the inventory?

(c) Assuming the inventory is given a value, how does the **double entry bookkeeping** for inventory work?

The purpose of this chapter is to answer all three of these questions. In order to make the presentation a little easier to follow, it is convenient to take the last one first.

2.2 Ledger accounting for inventories

FAST FORWARD

The value of **closing inventories** is accounted for in the nominal ledger by debiting an inventory account and crediting the trading account at the end of an accounting period. Inventory will therefore have a debit balance at the end of a period, and this balance will be shown in the statement of financial position as a current asset.

It has already been shown that purchases are introduced to the trading section of the income statement by means of the double entry:

DEBIT	Trading account	$X	
CREDIT	Purchases account		$X

But what about opening and closing inventories? How are their values accounted for in the double entry bookkeeping system? The answer is that a inventory account must be kept. This inventory account is only ever used *at the end of an accounting period*, when the business counts up and values the inventory in hand, in a inventory count.

(a) When a inventory count is made, the business will have a value for its closing inventory, and the double entry is:

DEBIT	Inventory account (closing inventory value)	$X	
CREDIT	Trading account		$X

However, rather than show the closing inventory as a 'plus' value in the trading account (by adding it to sales) it is usual to show it as a 'minus' figure in arriving at cost of sales. This is illustrated in Paragraph 2.1 above. The debit balance on inventory account represents an asset, which will be shown as part of current assets in the statement of financial position.

(b) Closing inventory at the end of one period becomes opening inventory at the start of the next period. The inventory account remains unchanged until the end of the next period, when the value of opening inventory is taken to the trading account:

DEBIT	Trading account	$X	
CREDIT	Inventory account (value of opening inventory)		$X

Partly as an example of how this ledger accounting for inventories works, and partly as revision on ledger accounting in general, try the following exercise. It is an example from an earlier part of this text which has had a closing inventory figure included.

Question

Inventories

A business is established with capital of $2,000 and this amount is paid into a business bank account by the proprietor. During the first year's trading, the following transactions occurred.

	$
Purchases of goods for resale, on credit	4,300
Payments for trade accounts payable	3,600
Sales, all on credit	4,000
Payments from trade accounts receivable	3,200
Non-current assets purchased for cash	1,500
Other expenses, all paid in cash	900

The bank has provided an overdraft facility of up to $3,000.

All 'other expenses' relate to the current year.

Closing inventory is valued at $1,800. (Because this is the first year of the business, there are no opening inventories.)

Ignore depreciation and withdrawals on account of profit.

Required

Prepare the ledger accounts, a trading, income and expense account for the year and a statement of financial position as at the end of the year.

Answer

CASH

	$		$
Capital	2,000	Trade accounts payable	3,600
Trade accounts receivable	3,200	Non-current assets	1,500
Balance c/d	800	Other expenses	900
	6,000		6,000
		Balance b/d	800

CAPITAL

	$		$
Balance c/d	2,600	Cash	2,000
		I & E a/c	600
	2,600		2,600
		Balance b/d	2,600

TRADE ACCOUNTS PAYABLE

	$		$
Cash	3,600	Purchases	4,300
Balance c/d	700		
	4,300		4,300
		Balance b/d	700

PURCHASES ACCOUNT

	$		$
Trade accounts payable	4,300	Trading a/c	4,300

NON-CURRENT ASSETS

	$		$
Cash	1,500	Balance c/d	1,500
Balance b/d	1,500		

SALES

	$		$
Trading a/c	4,000	Trade accounts receivable	4,000

TRADE ACCOUNTS RECEIVABLE

	$		$
Sales	4,000	Cash	3,200
		Balance c/d	800
	4,000		4,000
Balance b/d	800		

OTHER EXPENSES

	$		$
Cash	900	I & E a/c	900

TRADING, INCOME AND EXPENSE ACCOUNT

	$		$
Purchases account	4,300	Sales	4,000
Gross profit c/d	1,500	Closing inventory (inventory a/c)	1,800
	5,800		5,800
Other expenses	900	Gross profit b/d	1,500
Net profit (transferred to			
capital account)	600		
	1,500		1,500

Alternatively, closing inventory could be shown as a minus value on the debit side of the trading account, instead of a credit entry, giving purchases $4,300 less closing inventory $1,800 equals cost of goods sold $2,500.

INVENTORY ACCOUNT

	$		$
Trading a/c (closing inventory)	1,800	Balance c/d	1,800
Balance b/d (opening inventory)	1,800		

STATEMENT OF FINANCIAL POSITION AS AT THE END OF THE PERIOD

	$	$
Assets		
Non-current assets		1,500
Current assets		
Goods in inventory	1,800	
Trade accounts receivable	800	
		2,600
Total assets		4,100
Capital and liabilities		
Capital		
At start of period	2,000	
Profit for period	600	
At end of period		2,600
Current liabilities		
Bank overdraft	800	
Trade accounts payable	700	
		1,500
Total capital and liabilities		4,100

Make sure you can see what has happened here. The balance on the inventory account was $1,800, which appears in the statement of financial position as a current asset. As it happens, the $1,800 closing inventory was the only entry in the inventory account – there was no figure for opening inventory.

If there had been, it would have been eliminated by transferring it as a debit balance to the trading account, ie:

DEBIT   Trading account (with value of opening inventory)
CREDIT   Inventory account (with value of opening inventory)

The debit in the trading account would then have increased the cost of sales, ie opening inventory is added to purchases in calculating cost of sales. Again, this is illustrated in Paragraph 2.1 above.

So if we can establish the value of inventories on hand, the above paragraphs and exercise show us how to account for that value. That takes care of one of the problems noted at the beginning of this chapter. But now another of those problems becomes apparent – how do we establish the **value** of inventories on hand? The first step must be to establish **how much inventory is held**.

3 Counting inventories

FAST FORWARD

The **quantity** of inventories held at the year end is established by means of a **physical court** of inventory in an annual counting exercise, or by a 'continuous' inventory court.

Business trading is a continuous activity, but accounting statements must be drawn up at a particular date. In preparing a statement of financial position it is necessary to '**freeze**' the activity of a business so as to determine its assets and liabilities at a given moment. This includes establishing the quantities of inventories on hand, which can create problems.

In simple cases, when a business holds easily counted and relatively small amounts of inventory, quantities of inventories on hand at the reporting date can be determined by physically counting them in an **inventory count**.

In more complicated cases, where a business holds considerable quantities of varied inventory, an alternative approach to establishing quantities is to maintain **continuous inventory records**. This means that a card is kept for every item of inventory, showing receipts and issues from the stores, and a running total. A few inventory items are counted each day to make sure their record cards are correct – this is called a 'continuous' count because it is spread out over the year rather than completed in one count at a designated time.

One obstacle is overcome once a business has established how much inventory is on hand. But another of the problems noted in the introduction immediately raises its head. What value should the business place on those inventories?

4 Valuing inventories

FAST FORWARD

The value of inventories is calculated at the lower **cost** and **net realisable value** for each separate item or group of items. **Cost** can be arrived at by using **FIFO** (first in-first out) or **AVCO** (weighted average costing).

4.1 The basic rule

There are **several methods** which, in theory, might be used for the valuation of inventory.

(a)   Inventories might be valued at their *expected selling price*.

(b)   Inventories might be valued at their expected selling price, less any costs still to be incurred in getting them ready for sale and then selling them. This amount is referred to as the *net realisable value* (NRV) of the inventories.

(c)   Inventories might be valued at their *historical cost* (ie the cost at which they were originally bought).

(d)   Inventories might be valued at the amount it would cost to replace them. This amount is referred to as the *current replacement cost* of inventories.

Current replacement costs are not used in the type of accounts dealt with in this syllabus.

The use of selling prices in inventory valuation is ruled out because this would create a profit for the business before the inventory has been sold.

A simple example might help to explain this. A trader buys two items of inventory, each costing $100. He can sell them for $140 each, but in the accounting period we shall consider, he has only sold one of them. The other is closing inventory in hand.

Since only one item has been sold, you might think it is common sense that profit ought to be $40. But if closing inventory is valued at selling price, profit would be $80, ie profit would be taken on the closing inventory as well.

This would contradict the accounting concept of **prudence**, ie to claim a profit before the item has actually been sold.

The same objection **usually** applies to the use of NRV in inventory valuation. The item purchased for $100 requires $5 of further expenditure in getting it ready for sale and then selling it (eg $5 of processing costs and distribution costs). If its expected selling price is $140, its NRV is $(140 – 5) = $135. To value it at $135 in the statement of financial position would still be to anticipate a $35 profit.

	$	$
Sales		140
Opening inventory	–	
Purchases (2 × $100)	200	
	200	
Less closing inventory (at selling price)	140	
Cost of sale		60
Profit		80

We are left with **historical cost** as the normal basis of inventory valuation. **The only time when historical cost is not used is in the exceptional cases where the prudence concept requires a lower value to be used.**

Staying with the example above, suppose that the market in this kind of product suddenly slumps and the item's expected selling price is only $90. The item's NRV is then $(90 – 5) = $85 and the business has in effect made a loss of $15 ($100 – $85). The prudence concept requires that losses should be recognised as soon as they are foreseen. This can be achieved by valuing the inventory item in the statement of financial position at its NRV of $85.

The argument developed above suggests that the rule to follow is that inventories should be valued at cost, or if lower, net realisable value. The accounting treatment of inventory is governed by an accounting standard, IAS 2 *Inventories*. IAS 2 states that **inventory should be valued at the lower of cost and net realisable value** as we will see below. This is an important rule and one which you should learn by heart.

Rule to learn

Inventory should be valued at the lower of cost and net realisable value.

4.2 Applying the basic valuation rule

If a business has many inventory items on hand the comparison of cost and NRV should theoretically be carried out for each item separately. It is not sufficient to compare the total cost of all inventory items with their total NRV. An example will show why.

Suppose a company has four items of inventory on hand at the end of its accounting period. Their cost and NRVs are as follows.

Inventory item	Cost $	NRV $	Lower of cost/NRV $
1	27	32	27
2	14	8	8
3	43	55	43
4	29	40	29
	113	135	107

It would be incorrect to compare total costs ($113) with total NRV ($135) and to state inventories at $113 in the statement of financial position. The company can foresee a loss of $6 on item 2 and this should be recognised. If the four items are taken together in total the loss on item 2 is masked by the anticipated profits on the other items. By performing the cost/NRV comparison for each item separately the prudent valuation of $107 can be derived. This is the value which should appear in the statement of financial position.

However, for a company with large amounts of inventory this procedure may be impracticable. In this case it is acceptable to group similar items into categories and perform the comparison of cost and NRV category by category, rather than item by item.

Question

Valuation

The following figures relate to inventory held at the year end.

	A $	B $	C $
Cost	20	9	12
Selling price	30	12	22
Modification cost to enable sale	–	2	8
Marketing costs	7	2	2
Units held	200	150	300

Required

Calculate the value of inventory held.

Answer

Item	Cost $	NRV $	Valuation $	Quantity Units	Total value $
A	20	23	20	200	4,000
B	9	8	8	150	1,200
C	12	12	12	300	3,600
					8,800

So have we now solved the problem of how a business should value its inventories? It seems that all the business has to do is to choose the lower of cost and net realisable value. This is true as far as it goes, but there is one further problem, perhaps not so easy to foresee: for a given item of inventory, **what was the cost**?

4.3 Determining the purchase cost

Inventories may be **raw materials** or components bought from suppliers, **finished goods** which have been made by the business but not yet sold, or work in the process of production, but only part-completed (this type of inventory is called **work in progress** or WIP). It will simplify matters, however, if we think about the historical cost of purchased raw materials and components, which ought to be their purchase price.

A business may be continually purchasing consignments of a particular component. As each consignment is received from suppliers they are stored in the appropriate bin or on the appropriate shelf or pallet, where they will be mingled with previous consignments. When the storekeeper issues components to production he will simply pull out from the bin the nearest components to hand, which may have arrived in the latest consignment or in an earlier consignment or in several different consignments. Our concern is to devise a pricing technique, a rule of thumb which we can use to attribute a cost to each of the components issued from stores.

There are several techniques which are used in practice.

- **FIFO (first in, first out)**. Using this technique, we assume that components are used in the order in which they are received from suppliers. The components issued are deemed to have formed part of the oldest consignment still unused and are costed accordingly.
- **AVCO (average cost)**. As purchase prices change with each new consignment, the average price of components in the bin is constantly changed. Each component in the bin at any moment is assumed to have been purchased at the average price of all components in the bin at that moment.

If you are preparing **financial accounts** you would normally expect to use FIFO or average costs for the valuation of inventory. **IAS 2 (revised) does not permit the use of LIFO**. You should note furthermore that terms such as AVCO and FIFO refer to **pricing techniques** only. The *actual* components can be used in any order.

To illustrate the various pricing methods, the following transactions will be used in each case.

TRANSACTIONS DURING MAY 20X7

	Quantity	Unit cost	Total cost	Market value per unit on date of transactions
	Units	$	$	$
Opening balance 1 May	100	2.00	200	
Receipts 3 May	400	2.10	840	2.11
Issues 4 May	200			2.11
Receipts 9 May	300	2.12	636	2.15
Issues 11 May	400			2.20
Receipts 18 May	100	2.40	240	2.35
Issues 20 May	100			2.35
Closing balance 31 May	200			2.38
			1,916	

Receipts mean goods are received into store and issues represent the issue of goods from store. The problem is to put a valuation on the following.

(a)   The issues of materials
(b)   The closing inventory

How would issues and closing inventory be valued using each of the following in turn?

(a)   FIFO
(b)   AVCO

4.4 FIFO (first in, first out)

FIFO assumes that materials are **issued out of inventory in the order in which they were delivered into inventory**, ie issues are priced at the cost of the earliest delivery remaining in inventory.

The cost of issues and closing inventory value in the example, using FIFO, would be as follows (note that OI stands for opening inventory).

Date of issue	Quantity Units	Value issued	Cost of issues $	$
4 May	200	100 OI at $2	200	
		100 at $2.10	210	
				410
11 May	400	300 at $2.10	630	
		100 at $2.12	212	
				842
20 May	100	100 at $2.12		212
				1,464
Closing inventory value	200	100 at $2.12	212	
		100 at $2.40	240	
				452
				1,916

Note that the cost of materials issued plus the value of closing inventory equals the cost of purchases plus the value of opening inventory ($1,916).

4.5 AVCO (average cost)

There are various ways in which average costs may be used in pricing inventory issues. The most common (cumulative weighted average pricing) is illustrated below.

The **cumulative weighted average pricing method** calculates a weighted average price for all units in inventory. Issues are priced at this average cost, and the balance of inventory remaining would have the same unit valuation.

A new weighted average price is calculated whenever a new delivery of materials into store is received. This is the key feature of cumulative weighted average pricing.

In our example, issue costs and closing inventory values would be as follows.

Date	Received Units	Issued Units	Balance Units	Total inventory value $	Unit cost $	Price of issue $
Opening inventory			100	200	2.00	
3 May	400			840	2.10	
			500	1,040	2.08 *	
4 May		200		(416)	2.08 **	416
			300	624	2.08	
9 May	300			636	2.12	
			600	1,260	2.10 *	
11 May		400		(840)	2.10 **	840
			200	420	2.10	
18 May	100			240	2.40	
			300	660	2.20 *	
20 May		100		(220)	2.20 **	220
						1,476
Closing inventory value			200	440	2.20	440
						1,916

* A new unit cost of inventory is calculated whenever a new receipt of materials occurs.

** Whenever inventories are issued, the unit value of the items issued is the current weighted average cost per unit at the time of the issue.

For this method too, the cost of materials issued plus the value of closing inventory equals the cost of purchases plus the value of opening inventory ($1,916).

4.6 Inventory valuations and profit

In the previous descriptions of FIFO and AVCO the example used raw materials as an illustration. Each method of valuation produced different costs both of closing inventories and also of material issues. Since raw material costs affect the cost of production, and the cost of production works through eventually into the cost of sales, it follows that different methods of inventory valuation will provide different profit figures. An example may help to illustrate this point.

4.7 Example: Inventory valuations and profit

On 1 November 20X2 a company held 300 units of finished goods item No 9639 in inventory. These were valued at $12 each. During November 20X2 three batches of finished goods were received into store from the production department, as follows.

Date	Units received	Production cost per unit
10 November	400	$12.50
20 November	400	$14
25 November	400	$15

Goods sold out of inventory during November were as follows.

Date	Units sold	Sale price per unit
14 November	500	$20
21 November	500	$20
28 November	100	$20

What was the profit from selling inventory item 9639 in November 20X2, applying the following principles of inventory valuation?

(a) FIFO
(b) AVCO (using cumulative weighted average costing)

Ignore administration, sales and distribution costs.

Solution

(a) FIFO

Date	Issue costs	Issue cost Total $	Closing inventory $
14 November	300 units × $12 plus		
	200 units × $12.50	6,100	
21 November	200 units × $12.50 plus		
	300 units × $14	6,700	
28 November	100 units × $14	1,400	
Closing inventory	400 units × $15		6,000
		14,200	6,000

(b)   AVCO *(cumulative weighted average cost)*

			Unit cost	Balance in inventory	Total cost of issues	Closing inventory
			$	$	$	$
1 November	Opening inventory	300	12.000	3,600		
10 November	400		12.500	5,000		
	700		12.286	8,600		
14 November	500		12.286	6,143	6,143	
	200		12.286	2,457		
20 November	400		14.000	5,600		
	600		13.428	8,057		
21 November	500		13.428	6,714	6,714	
	100		13.428	1,343		
25 November	400		15.000	6,000		
	500		14.686	7,343		
28 November	100		14.686	1,469	1,469	
30 November	400		14.686	5,874	14,326	5,874

Summary: profit

	FIFO	AVCO
	$	$
Opening inventory	3,600	3,600
Cost of production	16,600	16,600
	20,200	20,200
Closing inventory	6,000	5,874
Cost of sales	14,200	14,326
Sales (1,100 × $20)	22,000	22,000
Profit	7,800	7,674

Different inventory valuations have produced different cost of sales figures, and therefore different profits. In our example opening inventory values are the same, therefore the difference in the amount of profit under each method is the same as the difference in the valuations of closing inventory.

The profit differences are only temporary. In our example, the opening inventory in December 20X2 will be $6,000 or $5,874, depending on the inventory valuation used. Different opening inventory values will affect the cost of sales and profits in December, so that in the long run inequalities in cost of sales each month will even themselves out.

Question   FIFO

A firm has the following transactions with its product R.

Year 1
Opening inventory: nil
Buys 10 units at $300 per unit
Buys 12 units at $250 per unit
Sells 8 units at $400 per unit
Buys 6 units at $200 per unit
Sells 12 units at $400 per unit

Year 2
Buys 10 units at $200 per unit
Sells 5 units at $400 per unit
Buys 12 units at $150 per unit
Sells 25 units at $400 per unit

Required

Using FIFO, calculate the following on an item by item basis for both year 1 and year 2.

(i)   The closing inventory
(ii) The sales
(iii) The cost of sales
(iv) The gross profit

Answer

Year 1

Purchases (units)	Sales (units)	Balance (units)	Inventory value $	Unit cost $	Cost of sales $	Sales $
10		10	3,000	300		
12			3,000	250		
		22	6,000			
	8		(2,400)		2,400	3,200
		14	3,600			
6			1,200	200		
		20	4,800			
	12		(3,100)*		3,100	4,800
		8	1,700		5,500	8,000

* 2 @ $300 + 10 @ $250 = $3,100

Year 2

Purchases (units)	Sales (units)	Balance (units)	Inventory value $	Unit cost $	Cost of sales $	Sales $
B/f		8	1,700			
10			2,000	200		
		18	3,700			
	5		(1,100)*		1,100	2,000
		13	2,600			
12		25	1,800	150		
			4,400			
	25		(4,400)**		4,400	10,000
		0	0		5,500	12,000

* 2 @ $250 + 3 @ $200 = $1,100
** 13 @ $200 + 12 @ $150 = $4,400

Trading account

	FIFO $	$
Year 1		
Sales	FIFO	8,000
Opening inventory	$	
Purchases	7,200	
	7,200	
Closing inventory	1,700	
Cost of sales		5,500
Gross profit		2,500

	FIFO	
	$	$
Year 2		
Sales		12,000
Opening inventory	1,700	
Purchases	3,800	
	5,500	
Closing inventory	0	
Cost of sales		5,500
Gross profit		6,500

5 IAS 2 Inventories

Inventory should be valued at the lower of cost and net realisable value.

IAS 2 lays out the required accounting treatment for inventories (sometimes called stocks) under the historical cost system. The major area of contention is the cost **value of inventory** to be recorded. This is recognised as an asset of the enterprise until the related revenues are recognised (ie the item is sold) at which point the inventory is recognised as an expense (ie cost of sales). Part or all of the cost of inventories may also be expensed if a write-down to **net realisable value** is necessary.

In other words, the fundamental accounting assumption of **accrual** requires costs to be matched with associated revenues. In order to achieve this, costs incurred for goods which remain unsold at the year end must be carried forward in the statement of financial position and matched against future revenues.

5.1 Scope

The following items are **excluded** from the scope of the standard.

- Work in progress under **construction contracts** (covered by IAS 11 *Construction contracts,* which you will study in later financial accounting papers).
- **Financial instruments** (ie shares, bonds)
- **Livestock**, agricultural and forest products, and mineral ores

5.2 Definitions

The standard gives the following important definitions.

Key terms

- **Inventories** are assets:
    - held for sale in the ordinary course of business;
    - in the process of production for such sale; or
    - in the form of materials or supplies to be consumed in the production process or in the rendering of services.

- **Net realisable value** is the estimated selling price in the ordinary course of business less the estimated costs of completion and the estimated costs necessary to make the sale. *(IAS 2)*

Inventories can **include** any of the following.

- **Goods purchased and held for resale**, eg goods held for sale by a retailer, or land and buildings held for resale
- **Finished goods** produced
- **Work in progress** being produced
- Materials and supplies awaiting use in the production process (**raw materials**)

5.3 Measurement of inventories

The standard states that **'Inventories should be measured at the lower of cost and net realisable value.'**

5.4 Cost of inventories

The cost of inventories will consist of all the following costs.

(a) **Purchase**
(b) **Costs of conversion**
(c) Other costs incurred in bringing the inventories to their **present location and condition**

5.4.1 Costs of purchase

The standard lists the following as comprising the costs of purchase of inventories.

(a) **Purchase price**; *plus*
(b) **Import duties** and other taxes; *plus*
(c) Transport, handling and any other cost **directly attributable** to the acquisition of finished goods, services and materials; *less*
(d) **Trade discounts**, rebates and other similar amounts.

5.4.2 Costs of conversion

Costs of conversion of inventories consist of two main parts.

(a) Costs **directly related** to the units of production, eg direct materials, direct labour
(b) Fixed and variable **production overheads** that are incurred in converting materials into finished goods, allocated on a systematic basis.

You may have come across the terms 'fixed production overheads' or 'variable production overheads' elsewhere in your studies. The standard defines them as follows.

Key terms

> • **Fixed production overheads** are those indirect costs of production that remain relatively constant regardless of the volume of production, eg the cost of factory management and administration.
> • **Variable production overheads** are those indirect costs of production that vary directly, or nearly directly, with the volume of production, eg indirect materials and labour.   *(IAS 2)*

The standard emphasises that fixed production overheads must be allocated to items of inventory on the basis of the **normal capacity of the production facilities**. This is an important point.

(a) **Normal capacity** is the expected achievable production based on the average over several periods/seasons, under normal circumstances.
(b) The above figure should take account of the capacity lost through **planned maintenance**.
(c) If it approximates to the normal level of activity then the **actual level of production** can be used.
(d) **Low production** or **idle plant** will *not* result in a higher fixed overhead allocation to each unit.
(e) **Unallocated overheads** must be recognised as an expense in the period in which they were incurred.
(f) When production is **abnormally high**, the fixed production overhead allocated to each unit will be reduced, so avoiding inventories being stated at more than cost.
(g) The allocation of variable production overheads to each unit is based on the **actual use** of production facilities.

5.4.3 Other costs

Any other costs should only be recognised if they are incurred in bringing the inventories to their **present location and condition**.

The standard lists types of cost which **would not be included** in cost of inventories. Instead, they should be recognised as an **expense** in the period they are incurred.

- **Abnormal amounts** of wasted materials, labour or other production costs
- **Storage costs** (except costs which are necessary in the production process before a further production stage)
- **Administrative overheads** not incurred to bring inventories to their present location and conditions
- **Selling costs**

5.4.4 Techniques for the measurement of cost

Two techniques are mentioned by the standard, both of which produce results which **approximate to cost**, and so both of which may be used for convenience.

(a) **Standard costs** are set up to take account of normal production values: amount of raw materials used, labour time etc. They are reviewed and revised on a regular basis.

(b) **Retail method**: this is often used in the retail industry where there is a large turnover of inventory items, which nevertheless have similar profit margins. The only practical method of inventory valuation may be to take the total selling price of inventories and deduct an overall average profit margin, thus reducing the value to an approximation of cost. The percentage will take account of reduced price lines. Sometimes different percentages are applied on a department basis.

5.5 Cost formulas

Cost of inventories should be assigned by **specific identification** of their individual costs.

(a) Items that are **not ordinarily interchangeable**
(b) Goods or services produced and segregated for **specific projects**.

Specific costs should be attributed to individual items of inventory when they are segregated for a specific project, but not where inventories consist of a large number of interchangeable (ie identical or very similar) items. In the latter circumstances, one of **two approaches** may be taken.

The cost formula is that the cost of inventories should be assigned by using the **first-in, first-out (FIFO)** or **weighted average** cost formulas.

Under the weighted average cost method, a recalculation can be made after each purchase (as we calculated), **or alternatively only at the period end**.

LIFO is no longer permitted under IAS 2.

Question	Inventory valuation

You are the accountant at Water Pumps Co, and you have been asked to calculate the valuation of the company's inventory at cost at its year end of 30 April 20X5.

Water Pumps manufactures a range of pumps. The pumps are assembled from components bought by Water Pumps (the company does not manufacture any parts).

The company does not use a standard costing system, and work in progress and finished goods are valued as follows.

(a) Material costs are determined from the product specification, which lists the components required to make a pump.

(b) The company produces a range of pumps. Employees record the hours spent on assembling each type of pump, this information is input into the payroll system which prints the total hours spent each week assembling each type of pump. All employees assembling pumps are paid at the same rate and there is no overtime.

(c) Overheads are added to the inventory value in accordance with IAS 2 *Inventories*. The financial accounting records are used to determine the overhead cost, and this is applied as a percentage based on the direct labour cost.

For direct labour costs, you have agreed that the labour expended for a unit in work in progress is half that of a completed unit.

The draft accounts show the following materials and direct labour costs in inventory.

	Raw materials	Work in progress	Finished goods
Materials ($)	74,786	85,692	152,693
Direct labour ($)		13,072	46,584

The costs incurred in April, as recorded in the financial accounting records, were as follows.

	$
Direct labour	61,320
Selling costs	43,550
Depreciation and finance costs of production machines	4,490
Distribution costs	6,570
Factory manager's wage	2,560
Other production overheads	24,820
Purchasing and accounting costs relating to production	5,450
Other accounting costs	7,130
Other administration overheads	24,770

For your calculations assume that all work in progress and finished goods were produced in April 20X5 and that the company was operating at a normal level of activity.

Required

Calculate the value of overheads which should be added to work in progress and finished goods in accordance with IAS 2 *Inventories*.

Note. You should include details and a description of your workings and all figures should be calculated to the nearest $.

Answer

Calculation of overheads for inventory

Production overheads are as follows.

	$
Depreciation/finance costs	4,490
Factory manager's wage	2,560
Other production overheads	24,820
Accounting/purchase costs	5,450
	37,320

Direct labour = $61,320

$\therefore$ Production overhead rate = $\dfrac{37,320}{61,320}$ = 60.86%

Inventory valuation

	Raw materials $	WIP $	Finished goods $	Total $
Materials	74,786	85,692	152,693	313,171
Direct labour	–	13,072	46,584	59,656
Production overhead (at 60.86% of labour)	–	7,956	28,351	36,307
	74,786	106,720	227,628	409,134

Variable overheads will be included in the cost of inventory.

5.6 Net realisable value (NRV)

As a general rule assets should not be carried at amounts greater than those expected to be realised from their sale or use. In the case of inventories this amount could fall below cost when items are **damaged or become obsolete**, or where the **costs to completion have increased** in order to make the sale.

In fact we can identify the principal situations in which **NRV is likely to be less than cost.**

(a) An **increase in costs** or a **fall in selling price**
(b) A **physical deterioration** in the condition of inventory
(c) **Obsolescence** of products
(d) A decision as part of the company's marketing strategy to manufacture and sell products at a **loss**
(e) **Errors in production or purchasing**

A write down of inventories would normally take place on an item by item basis, but similar or related items may be **grouped together**. This grouping together is acceptable for, say, items in the same product line, but it is not acceptable to write down inventories based on a whole classification (eg finished goods) or a whole business.

The assessment of NRV should take place **at the same time** as estimates are made of selling price, using the most reliable information available. Fluctuations of price or cost should be taken into account if they relate directly to **events after the reporting period,** which confirm conditions existing at the end of the period.

The reasons why inventory is held must also be taken into account. Some inventory, for example, may be held to satisfy a firm contract and its NRV will therefore be the **contract price**. Any additional inventory of the same type held at the period end will, in contrast, be assessed according to general sales prices when NRV is estimated.

Net realisable value must be reassessed at the end of each period and compared again with cost. If the NRV has risen for inventories held over the end of more than one period, then the previous write down must be **reversed** to the extent that the inventory is then valued at the lower of cost and the new NRV. This may be possible when selling prices have fallen in the past and then risen again.

On occasion a write down to NRV may be of such size, incidence or nature that it must be **disclosed separately**.

5.7 Recognition as an expense

The following treatment is required **when inventories are sold**.

(a) The **carrying amount** is recognised as an expense in the period in which the related revenue is recognised
(b) The amount of any **write-down of inventories** to NRV and all losses of inventories are recognised as an expense in the period the write-down or loss occurs
(c) The amount of any **reversal of any write-down of inventories**, arising from an increase in NRV, is recognised as a reduction in the amount of inventories recognised as an expense in the period in which the reversal occurs

Chapter Roundup

- The **cost of goods sold** is calculated as:

  Opening inventory + purchases − closing inventory.

- **Opening inventories** brought forward in the inventory account are **transferred to the trading account**, and so at the end of the accounting year, the balance on the inventory account ceases to be the opening inventory value b/f, and becomes instead the closing inventory value c/f.

- The value of **closing inventories** is accounted for in the **nominal ledger** by debiting an inventory account and crediting the trading account at the end of an accounting period. The inventory will therefore always have a debit balance at the end of a period, and this balance will be shown in the statement of financial position as a current asset for inventories.

- The **quantity** of inventories held at the year end is established by means of a **physical count** of inventory in an annual counting exercise, or by a 'continuous' inventory count.

- The **value** of these inventories is then **calculated, taking the lower of cost and net realisable value for each separate item or group of inventory items.**

- Inventory should be valued at the lower of cost and net realisable value.

Quick Quiz

1   When is an inventory account used?

2   How is closing inventory incorporated in the financial statements?

    A   Debit: income statement   Credit: statement of financial position

    B   Debit: statement of financial position   Credit: income statement

3   What is 'continuous' inventory counting?

4   An item of inventory was purchased for $10. However, due to a fall in demand, its selling price will be only $8. In addition further costs will be incurred prior to sale of $1. What is the net realisable value?

    A $7

    B $8

    C $10

    D $11

5   Why is inventory not valued at expected selling price?

6   When valuing inventory at historical cost, the following methods are available.

    (1)   FIFO

    (2)   AVCO

    (3)   LIFO

    (4)   Standard cost

    Which methods are allowable under IAS 2 *Inventories*?

    A   (1), (2), (3)

    B   (1), (2), (3), (4)

    C   (1) only

    D   (1), (2)

7   What is included in the cost of purchase of inventories according to IAS 2?

    A   Purchase price less trade discount

    B   Purchase price plus transport costs less trade discount

    C   Purchase price less import duties less trade discount

    D   Purchase price plus import duties plus transport costs less trade discount

8   What type of costs should be recognised as an expense, not as part of the cost of inventory?

9   What are the most likely situations when the NRV of inventories falls below cost?

Answers to Quick Quiz

1   Only at the end of an accounting period.

2   B   DEBIT: Inventory in hand (statement of financial position)

               CREDIT: Closing inventory (trading account)

3   A card is kept for every item of inventory. It shows receipts and issues, with a running total. A few inventory items are counted each day to test that the cards are correct.

4   A   Net realisable value is selling price ($8) less further costs to sale ($1), ie $7.

5   Mainly because this would result in the business taking a profit before the goods have been sold.

6   D   Only FIFO and AVCO are allowed.

7   D   Purchase price **plus** import duties (and other taxes) **plus** transport costs **less** trade discount.

8   See Paragraph 5.4.3.

9
- Increase in costs or a fall in selling price
- Physical deterioration of inventory
- Obsolescence
- Marketing strategy
- Errors in production or purchasing

Now try the questions below from the Exam Question Bank

Number	Level	Marks	Time
Q12	Examination	2	2 mins
Q13	Examination	2	2 mins

Tangible non-current assets

Topic list	Syllabus reference
1 Capital and revenue expenditure	D4(a)-(d)
2 Depreciation accounting	D5(a)
3 Depreciation: the mechanics	D5(b)–(g)
4 Revaluation of non-current assets	D4(g), D5(e)
5 Non-current asset disposals	D4(e), (f), (h)
6 IAS 16 *Property, plant and equipment*	D4(i)
7 The asset register	D4(j)
8 Worked example	D4(a)–(i), D5(a)–(g)

Introduction

We start by looking at capital and revenue expenditure and the distinction between **non-current and current assets**, a non-current asset being one bought for ongoing use in the business.

Non-current assets might be held and used by a business for a number of years, but they **wear out** or lose their usefulness in the course of time. Every tangible non-current asset has a limited life; the only exception is land.

The accounts of a business try to recognise that the cost of a non-current asset is gradually consumed as the asset wears out. This is done by gradually **writing off the asset's cost in the income statement over several accounting periods**. For example, in the case of a machine costing $1,000 and expected to wear out after ten years, it might be appropriate to reduce the value by $100 each year. This process is known as **depreciation.** We will look at the definitions, before going on to the mechanics in Sections 2 and 3.

Occasionally, particularly in the case of land or buildings, the market value of a non-current asset will rise with time. The asset may then be **revalued**. The accounting treatment of revaluations and the effect on depreciation are considered in Section 4. Section 5 deals with disposals of non-current assets. A profit may arise on the sale of a non-current asset if too much depreciation has been charged.

The main categories of non-current tangible assets are governed by IAS 16 **Property, plant and equipment**, which codifies much of the information in Sections 2, 4 and 5.

Non-current assets need to be controlled, as they are usually valuable. One way of doing this is by an **assets register**. This is looked at in Section 7. We bring everything together in a worked example on the **final accounts for a sole trader** in Section 8.

Study guide

		Intellectual level
D4	**Tangible non-current assets**	
(a)	Define non-current assets	1
(b)	Recognise the difference between current and non-current assets	1
(c)	Explain the difference between capital and revenue items	1
(d)	Classify expenditure as capital or revenue expenditure	1
(e)	Prepare ledger entries to record the acquisition and disposal of non-current assets	1
(f)	Calculate and record profits or losses on disposal of non-current assets in the income statement including part exchange transactions	1
(g)	Record the revaluation of a non-current asset in ledger accounts, the statement of comprehensive income and in the statement of financial position	1
(h)	Calculate the profit or loss on disposal of a revalued asset	1
(i)	Illustrate how non-current asset balances and movements are disclosed in financial statements	1
(j)	Explain the purpose and function of an asset register.	1
D5	**Depreciation**	
(a)	Understand and explain the purpose of depreciation	1
(b)	Calculate the charge for depreciation using straight line and reducing balance methods	1
(c)	Identify the circumstances where different methods of depreciation would be appropriate	1
(d)	Illustrate how depreciation expense and accumulated depreciation are recorded in ledger accounts	1
(e)	Calculate depreciation on a revalued non-current asset including the transfer of excess depreciation between the revaluation reserve and retained earnings	1
(f)	Calculate the adjustments to depreciation necessary if changes are made in the estimated useful life and/or residual value of a non-current asset	2
(g)	Record depreciation in the income statement and statement of financial position	1

Exam guide

This topic is vitally important and will be examined!

1 Capital and revenue expenditure

Capital expenditure is expenditure which results in the **acquisition of non-current assets**.

Revenue expenditure is expenditure incurred for the **purpose of the trade** or to **maintain non current assets**.

You need to be familiar with an important distinction, the distinction between **capital and revenue expenditure**.

Key terms

> **Capital expenditure** is expenditure which results in the acquisition of non-current assets, or an improvement in their earning capacity.
>
> (a) Capital expenditure is not charged as an expense in the income statement, although a depreciation charge will usually be made to write off the capital expenditure gradually over time. Depreciation charges are expenses in the income statement.
>
> (b) Capital expenditure on non-current assets results in the appearance of a non-current asset in the statement of financial position of the business.
>
> **Revenue expenditure** is expenditure which is incurred for either of the following reasons.
>
> (a) For the purpose of the trade of the business. This includes expenditure classified as selling and distribution expenses, administration expenses and finance charges.
>
> (b) To maintain the existing earning capacity of non-current assets.

Revenue expenditure is charged to the income statement of a period, provided that it relates to the trading activity and sales of that particular period. For example, if a business buys ten steel bars for $200 ($20 each) and sells eight of them during an accounting period, it will have two steel bars left in inventory at the end of the period. The full $200 is revenue expenditure but only $160 is a cost of goods sold during the period. The remaining $40 (cost of two units) will be included in the statement of financial position in inventory, ie as a current asset valued at $40.

A business purchases a building for $30,000. It then adds an extension to the building at a cost of $10,000. The building needs to have a few broken windows mended, its floors polished and some missing roof tiles replaced. These cleaning and maintenance jobs cost $900.

In this example, the original purchase ($30,000) and the cost of the extension ($10,000) are capital expenditures, because they are incurred to acquire and then improve a non-current asset. The other costs of $900 are revenue expenditure, because these merely maintain the building and thus the 'earning capacity' of the building.

1.1 Capital income and revenue income

Capital income is the proceeds from the sale of non-trading assets (ie proceeds from the sale of non-current assets, including long-term investments). The profits (or losses) from the sale of non-current assets are included in the income statement of a business, for the accounting period in which the sale takes place. For instance, the business may sell vehicles or machinery which it no longer needs – the proceeds will be capital income.

Revenue income is income derived from the following sources.

(a) The sale of trading assets, such as goods held in inventory
(b) The provision of services
(c) Interest and dividends received from investments held by the business

1.2 Capital transactions

The categorisation of capital and revenue items given above does not mention raising additional capital from the owner(s) of the business, or raising and repaying loans.

(a) These transactions add to the cash assets of the business, thereby creating a corresponding liability (capital or loan).

(b)   When a loan is repaid, it reduces the liabilities (loan) and the assets (cash).

None of these transactions would be reported through the income statement.

1.3 Why is the distinction between capital and revenue items important?

Revenue expenditure results from the purchase of goods and services for one of the following reasons.

(a)   To be used fully in the accounting period in which they are purchased, and so be a cost or expense in the income statement.
OR

(b)   To result in a current asset as at the end of the accounting period because the goods or services have not yet been consumed or made use of. The current asset would be shown in the statement of financial position and is not yet a cost or expense in the income statement.

For instance, inventory which is purchased for resale will either be sold during the period as per (a) or still be in inventory as per (b).

Capital expenditure results in the **purchase or improvement of non-current assets**, which are assets that will provide benefits to the business in more than one accounting period, and which are not acquired with a view to being resold in the normal course of trade. The cost of purchased non-current assets is not charged in full to the income statement of the period in which the purchase occurs. Instead, the non-current asset is gradually depreciated over a number of accounting periods.

Examples of non-current assets are computers for the office, delivery vans, factory machines.

Since revenue items and capital items are accounted for in different ways, the correct and consistent calculation of profit for any accounting period depends on the correct and consistent classification of items as revenue or capital.

This may seem rather confusing at the moment, but things will become clearer in the next few chapters. You must get used to the terminology used as these words appear in the accounting standards themselves, as we will see.

Question	Capital or revenue

State whether each of the following items should be classified as 'capital' or 'revenue' expenditure or income for the purpose of preparing the income statement and the statement of financial position of the business.

(a)   The purchase of a property (eg an office building)

(b)   The annual depreciation of such a property

(c)   Solicitors' fees in connection with the purchase of such a property

(d)   The costs of adding extra storage capacity to a mainframe computer used by the business

(e)   Computer repairs and maintenance costs

(f)   Profit on the sale of an office building

(g)   Revenue from sales by credit card

(h)   The cost of new plant

(i)   Customs duty charged on the plant when imported into the country

(j)   The 'carriage' costs of transporting the new plant from the supplier's factory to the premises of the business purchasing the plant

(k)   The cost of installing the new plant in the premises of the business

(l)   The wages of the machine operators

(a)   Capital expenditure

(b)   Depreciation of a non-current asset is a revenue expenditure.

(c)   The legal fees associated with the purchase of a property may be added to the purchase price and classified as capital expenditure. The cost of the property in the statement of financial position of the business will then include the legal fees.

(d)   Capital expenditure (enhancing an existing non-current asset)

(e)   Revenue expenditure

(f)   Capital income (net of the costs of sale)

(g)   Revenue income

(h)   Capital expenditure

(i)   If customs duties are borne by the purchaser of the non-current asset, they may be added to the cost of the machinery and classified as capital expenditure.

(j)   Similarly, if carriage costs are paid for by the purchaser of the non-current asset, they may be included in the cost of the non-current asset and classified as capital expenditure.

(k)   Installation costs of a non-current asset are also added to the non-current asset's cost and classified as capital expenditure

(l)   Revenue expenditure

Exam focus point

> Exam questions are highly likely on the distinction between capital and revenue expenditure.

2 Depreciation accounting

FAST FORWARD

> The **cost** of a non-current asset, less its **estimated residual value**, is allocated fairly between accounting periods by means of **depreciation**. Depreciation is both:
>
> - charged against profit; and
> - deducted from the value of the non-current asset in the statement of financial position.

Where assets held by an enterprise have a **limited useful life**, it is necessary to apportion the value of an asset used in a period against the revenue it has helped to create. If an asset's life extends over more than one accounting period, it earns profits over more than one period. It is a **non-current asset**. **Current assets**, such as stock and cash, are continually being used and replaced. **Non-current assets** such as plant and vehicles are intended for long-term use in the business.

With the exception of land held on freehold or very long leasehold, **every non-current asset eventually wears out over time**. Machines, cars and other vehicles, fixtures and fittings, and even buildings do not last for ever. When a business acquires a non-current asset, it will have some idea about how long its useful life will be.

(a)   To keep on using the non-current asset until it becomes **completely worn out**, useless, and worthless.

(b)   To **sell off** the non-current asset at the end of its useful life, as a second-hand item or as scrap.

Since a non-current asset has a cost, a limited useful life, and its value eventually declines, it follows that a charge should be made in the income statement to reflect the use that is made of the asset by the business. This charge is called **depreciation**.

Depreciation accounting is governed by IAS 16 *Property, plant and equipment*, which will be looked at in detail in Section 5 of this Chapter. However, this section will deal with some of the IAS 16 definitions of depreciation.

- **Depreciation** is the allocation of the depreciable amount of an asset over its estimated useful life. Depreciation for the accounting period is charged to net profit or loss for the period either directly or indirectly.
- **Depreciable assets** are assets which:
    - are expected to be used during more than one accounting period;
    - have a limited useful life; and
    - are held by an enterprise for use in the production or supply of goods and service, for rental to others, or for administrative purposes.
- **Useful life** is either:
    - the period over which a depreciable asset is expected to be used by the enterprise; or
    - the number of production or similar units expected to be obtained from the asset by the enterprise.
- **Depreciable amount** of a depreciable asset is the historical cost or other amount substituted for historical cost in the financial statements, less the estimated residual value. *(IAS 16)*

An 'amount substituted for historical cost' will normally be a **current market value** after a revaluation has taken place.

2.1 Depreciation

IAS 16 requires the depreciable amount to be allocated on a **systematic basis** to each accounting period during the useful life of the asset.

One way of defining depreciation is to describe it as a means of **spreading the cost** of a non-current asset over its useful life, and so matching the cost against the full period during which it earns profits for the business. Depreciation charges are an example of the application of the accrual assumption to calculate profits.

There are situations where, over a period, an asset has **increased in value**, ie its current value is greater than the carrying value in the financial statements. You might think that in such situations it would not be necessary to depreciate the asset. The standard states, however, that this is irrelevant, and that depreciation should still be charged to each accounting period, based on the depreciable amount, irrespective of a rise in value.

2.2 Useful life

The following factors should be considered when **estimating the useful life** of a depreciable asset.

- Expected **physical wear and tear**
- **Obsolescence**
- Legal or other **limits** on the use of the assets

Once decided, the useful life should be **reviewed periodically** and depreciation rates adjusted for the current and future periods if expectations vary significantly from the original estimates. The effect of the change should be disclosed in the accounting period in which the change takes place.

The assessment of useful life requires **judgement** based on previous experience with similar assets or classes of asset. When a completely new type of asset is acquired (ie through technological advancement or through use in producing a brand new product or service) it is still necessary to estimate useful life, even though the exercise will be much more difficult.

The standard also points out that the physical life of the asset might be longer than its useful life to the enterprise in question. One of the main factors to be taken into consideration is the **physical wear and tear** the asset is likely to endure. This will depend on various circumstances, including the number of shifts for which the asset will be used, the enterprise's repair and maintenance programme and so in. Other factors to be considered include obsolescence (due to technological advances/improvements in production/reduction in demand for the product/service produced by the asset) and legal restrictions, eg length of a related lease.

2.3 Residual value

In most cases the residual value of an asset is **likely to be immaterial**. If it is likely to be of any significant value, that value must be estimated at the date of purchase or any subsequent revaluation. The amount of residual value should be estimated based on the current situation with other similar assets, used in the same way, which are now at the end of their useful lives. Any expected costs of disposal should be offset against the gross residual value.

(a)   A non-current asset costing $20,000 which has an expected life of five years and an expected residual value of nil should be depreciated by $20,000, in total over the five year period.

(b)   A non-current asset costing $20,000 which has an expected life of five years and an expected residual value of $3,000 should be depreciated by $17,000 in total over the five year period.

2.4 Depreciation methods

Consistency is important. The depreciation method selected should be applied consistently from period to period unless altered circumstances justify a change. When the method *is* changed, the effect should be quantified and disclosed and the reason for the change should be stated.

Various methods of allocating depreciation to accounting periods are available, but whichever is chosen must be applied **consistently** (as required by IAS 1: see Chapter 3), to ensure comparability from period to period. Change of policy is not allowed simply because of the profitability situation of the enterprise.

The various accepted methods of allocating depreciation and the relevant calculations and accounting treatments are discussed in the next section.

2.5 Disclosure

An accounting policy note should disclose the **valuation bases** used for determining the amounts at which depreciable assets are stated, along with the other accounting policies: see IAS 1.

IAS 16 also requires the following to be disclosed for each major class of depreciable asset.

- **Depreciation methods** used
- **Useful lives** or the depreciation rates used
- **Total depreciation** allocated for the period
- **Gross amount** of depreciable assets and the related accumulated depreciation

2.6 What is depreciation?

The need to depreciate non-current assets arises from the **accrual assumption**. If money is expended in purchasing an asset then the amount must at some time be charged against profits. If the asset is one which contributes to an enterprise's revenue over a number of accounting periods it would be inappropriate to charge any single period (eg the period in which the asset was acquired) with the whole of the expenditure. Instead, some method must be found of spreading the cost of the asset over its useful economic life.

This view of depreciation as a process of allocation of the cost of an asset over several accounting periods is the view adopted by IAS 16. It is worth mentioning here two **common misconceptions** about the purpose and effects of depreciation.

(a)   It is sometimes thought that the net book value (NBV) of an asset is equal to its net realisable value and that the object of charging depreciation is to **reflect the fall in value of an asset over its life**. This misconception is the basis of a common, but incorrect, argument which says that freehold properties (say) need not be depreciated in times when property values are rising. It is true that historical cost statements of financial position often give a misleading impression when a property's NBV is much below its market value, but in such a case it is open to a business to incorporate a revaluation into its books, or even to prepare its accounts based on current costs. This is a separate problem from that of allocating the property's cost over successive accounting periods.

(b)   Another misconception is that depreciation is provided **so that an asset can be replaced at the end of its useful life**. This is not the case.

(i)   If there is no intention of replacing the asset, it could then be argued that there is no need to provide for any depreciation at all.

(ii)   If prices are rising, the replacement cost of the asset will exceed the amount of depreciation provided.

3 Depreciation: the mechanics

FAST FORWARD

Two methods of depreciation are specified in your syllabus:

*   the straight line method
*   the reducing balance method

3.1 Methods of depreciation

When a non-current asset is depreciated, two things must be accounted for.

(a)   The **charge for depreciation** is a cost or expense of the accounting period. For the time being, we shall charge depreciation as an expense in the income statement.

(b)   At the same time, the non-current asset is wearing out and diminishing in value, and so the value of the non-current asset in the statement of financial position must be reduced by the amount of depreciation charged. The value of the non-current asset will be its '**net book value**' or '**carrying value**', which is its cost less accumulated depreciation.

The amount of depreciation deducted from the cost of a non-current asset to arrive at its carrying value will build up (or 'accumulate') over time, as more depreciation is charged in each successive accounting period. This accumulated depreciation is a 'provision' because it provides for the fall in value of the non-current asset. The term 'provision for depreciation' refers to the 'accumulated depreciation' or 'aggregate depreciation' of a non-current asset.

For example, if a non-current asset costing $40,000 has an expected life of four years and an estimated residual value of nil, it might be depreciated by $10,000 per annum.

	Depreciation charge for the year (I & E a/c) (A) $	Aggregate depreciation at end of year (B) $	Cost of the asset (C) $	Carrying value at end of year (C – B) $
At beginning of its life	–	–	40,000	40,000
Year 1	10,000	10,000	40,000	30,000
Year 2	10,000	20,000	40,000	20,000
Year 3	10,000	30,000	40,000	10,000
Year 4	10,000	40,000	40,000	0
	40,000			

At the end of year 4, the full $40,000 of depreciation charges have been made in the income statements of the four years. The carrying value of the non-current asset is now nil. In theory (although perhaps not in practice) the business will no longer use the non-current asset, which now needs replacing.

There are several different methods of depreciation. Of these, the ones which are specified in the Paper F3 Study Guide are:

- Straight-line method
- Reducing balance method

3.2 The straight line method

This is the most commonly used method of all. The total depreciable amount is charged in equal instalments to each accounting period over the expected useful life of the asset. (In this way, the carrying value of the non-current asset declines at a steady rate, or in a 'straight line' over time.)

The annual depreciation charge is calculated as: $\dfrac{\text{Cost of asset minus residual value}}{\text{Expected useful life of the asset}}$

3.3 Example: Straight line depreciation

(a) A non-current asset costing $20,000 with an estimated life of 10 years and no residual value would be depreciated at the rate of:

$$\frac{\$20,000}{10 \text{ years}} = \$2,000 \text{ per annum}$$

(b) A non-current asset costing $60,000 has an estimated life of 5 years and a residual value of $7,000. The annual depreciation charge using the straight line method would be:

$$\frac{\$(60,000 - 7,000)}{5 \text{ years}} = \$10,600 \text{ per annum}$$

The carrying value of the non-current asset would be:

	After 1 year $	After 2 years $	After 3 years $	After 4 years $	After 5 years $
Cost of the asset	60,000	60,000	60,000	60,000	60,000
Accumulated depreciation	10,600	21,200	31,800	42,400	53,000
Carrying value	49,400	38,800	28,200	17,600	7,000 *

* ie its estimated residual value.

Since the depreciation charge per annum is the same amount every year with the straight line method, it is often convenient to state that depreciation is charged at the rate of x per cent per annum on the cost of the asset. In the example in Paragraph 3.3(a) above, the depreciation charge per annum is 10% of cost (ie 10% of $20,000 = $2,000).

Examination questions often describe straight line depreciation in this way.

The straight line method of depreciation is a fair allocation of the total depreciable amount between the different accounting periods, *provided that* it is reasonable to assume that the business enjoys equal benefits from the use of the asset in every period throughout its life. An example of this could be shelving (fixtures and fittings) in the accounts department.

3.4 Assets acquired in the middle of an accounting period

A business can purchase new non-current assets at any time during the course of an accounting period. It might seem fair to charge an amount for depreciation, in the period when the purchase occurs, which reflects the limited use the business has had from the asset in that period.

3.5 Example: Assets acquired in the middle of an accounting period

A business which has an accounting year which runs from 1 January to 31 December purchases a new non-current asset on 1 April 20X1, at a cost of $24,000. The expected life of the asset is 4 years, and its residual value is nil. What should be the depreciation charge for 20X1?

Solution

The annual depreciation charge will be $\dfrac{\$24,000}{4 \text{ years}}$ = $6,000 per annum

However, since the asset was acquired on 1 April 20X1, the business has only benefited from the use of the asset for 9 months instead of a full 12 months. It would therefore seem fair to charge depreciation in 20X1 of only:

$\dfrac{9}{12}$ × $6,000 = $4,500

Exam focus point

> If an examination question gives you the purchase date of a non-current asset, which is in the middle of an accounting period, you should generally assume that depreciation should be calculated in this way as a 'part-year' amount.

In practice, many businesses ignore the niceties of part-year depreciation, and charge a full year's depreciation on non-current assets in the year of their purchase, regardless of the time of year they were acquired.

3.6 The reducing balance method

The **reducing balance method** of depreciation calculates the annual depreciation charge as a fixed percentage of the carrying value of the asset, as at the end of the previous accounting period.

For example, a business purchases a non-current asset at a cost of $10,000. Its expected useful life is 3 years and its estimated residual value is $2,160. The business wishes to use the reducing balance method to depreciate the asset, and calculates that the rate of depreciation should be 40% of the reducing (carrying) value of the asset. (The method of deciding that 40% is a suitable annual percentage is a problem of mathematics, not financial accounting, and is not described here.)

The total depreciable amount is $(10,000 – 2,160) = $7,840.

The depreciation charge per annum and the carrying value of the asset as at the end of each year will be as follows.

	$	Accumulated depreciation $	
Asset at cost	10,000		
Depreciation in year 1 (40%)	4,000	4,000	
Carrying value at end of year 1	6,000		
Depreciation in year 2			
(40% of reducing balance)	2,400	6,400	(4,000 + 2,400)
Carrying value at end of year 2	3,600		
Depreciation in year 3 (40%)	1,440	7,840	(6,400 + 1,440)
Carrying value at end of year 3	2,160		

You should note that with the reducing balance method, the annual charge for depreciation is higher in the earlier years of the asset's life, and lower in the later years. In the example above, the annual charges for years 1, 2 and 3 are $4,000, $2,400 and $1,440 respectively.

The reducing balance method might therefore be used when it is considered fair to allocate a greater proportion of the total depreciable amount to the earlier years and a lower proportion to later years, on the assumption that the benefits obtained by the business from using the asset decline over time. An example of this could be machinery in a factory, where productivity falls as the machine gets older.

3.7 Applying a depreciation method consistently

It is up to the business concerned to decide which method of depreciation to apply to its non-current assets. Once that decision has been made, however, it should not be changed; the chosen method of depreciation should be applied **consistently from year to year**. This is an instance of the fundamental accounting assumption of consistency, which we looked at in Chapter 3.

Similarly, it is up to the business to decide what a sensible life span for a non-current asset should be. Again, once that life span has been chosen, it should not be changed unless something unexpected happens to the asset.

It is permissible for a business to depreciate different categories of non-current assets in different ways. For example, if a business owns three cars, then each car would normally be depreciated in the same way (eg by the straight line method); but another category of non-current asset, say, photocopiers, might be depreciated using a different method (eg by the reducing balance method).

Question	Depreciation methods

A lorry bought for a business cost $17,000. It is expected to last for five years and then be sold for scrap for $2,000.

Required

Work out the depreciation to be charged each year under:

(a) The straight line method
(b) The reducing balance method (using a rate of 35%)

Answer

(a) Under the straight line method, depreciation for each of the five years is:

$$\text{Annual depreciation} = \frac{\$(17,000 - 2,000)}{5} = \$3,000$$

(b) Under the reducing balance method, depreciation for each of the five years is:

Year	Depreciation		
1	35% × $17,000	=	$5,950
2	35% × ($17,000 − $5,950) = 35% × $11,050	=	$3,868
3	35% × ($11,050 − $3,868) = 35% × $7,182	=	$2,514
4	35% × ($7,182 − $2,514) = 35% × $4,668	=	$1,634
5	Balance to bring book value down to $2,000 = $4,668 − $1,634 − $2,000	=	$1,034

3.8 Change in method of depreciation

Having made the above comments about consistency, the depreciation method should be reviewed for appropriateness. If there are any changes in the expected pattern of use of the asset (and hence economic benefit), then the method used should be changed. In such cases, the remaining carrying value is depreciated under the new method, ie only current and future periods are affected; the change is not retrospective.

3.9 Example: Change in method of depreciation

Jakob Co purchased an asset for $100,000 on 1.1.X1. It had an estimated useful life of 5 years and it was depreciated using the reducing balance method at a rate of 40%. On 1.1.X3 it was decided to change the method to straight line.

Show the depreciation charge for each year (to 31 December) of the asset's life.

Solution

Year		Depreciation charge $	Aggregate depreciation $
20X1	$100,000 × 40%	40,000	40,000
20X2	$60,000 × 40%	24,000	64,000
20X3	$\dfrac{\$100,000 - \$64,000}{3}$	12,000	76,000
20X4		12,000	88,000
20X5		12,000	100,000

3.10 A fall in the value of a non-current asset

When the 'market' value of a non-current asset falls so that it is worth less than the amount of its carrying value, **and the fall in value is expected to be permanent**, the asset should be **written down to its new low market value**. The charge in the income statement for the diminution in the value of the asset during the accounting period should then be:

	$
Carrying value at the beginning of the period	X
Less new reduced value	(X)
Equals the charge for the diminution in the asset's value in the period.	X

3.11 Example: Fall in asset value

A business purchased a building on 1 January 20X1 at a cost of $100,000. The building has a 20 year life. After 5 years' use, on 1 January 20X6, the business decides that since property prices have fallen sharply, the building is now worth only $60,000, and that the value of the asset should be reduced in the accounts of the business.

The building was being depreciated at the rate of 5% per annum on cost.

Before the asset is reduced in value, the annual depreciation charge is:

$$\frac{\$100,000}{20 \text{ years}} = \$5,000 \text{ per annum } (= 5\% \text{ of } \$100,000)$$

After 5 years, the accumulated depreciation would be $25,000 and the carrying value of the building $75,000, which is $15,000 more than the new asset value. This $15,000 should be written off as a charge for depreciation (or fall in the asset's value) in year 5, so that the total charge in year 5 is:

	$
Carrying value of the leasehold after 4 years $(100,000 – 20,000)	80,000
Revised asset value at end of year 5	60,000
Charge against profit in year 5	20,000

An alternative method of calculation is:

	$
'Normal' depreciation charge per annum	5,000
Further fall in value, from carrying value at end of year 5 to revised value	15,000
Charge against profit in year 5	20,000

The building has a further life of 15 years, and its value is now $60,000. From year 6 to year 20, the annual charge for depreciation will be:

$$\frac{\$60,000}{15 \text{ years}} = \$4,000 \text{ per annum}$$

3.12 Change in expected useful life or residual value of an asset

The depreciation charge on a non-current asset depends not only on the cost (or value) of the asset and its estimated residual value, but also on its **estimated useful life**.

A business purchased a non-current asset costing $12,000 with an estimated life of four years and no residual value. If it used the straight line method of depreciation, it would make an annual provision of 25% of $12,000 = $3,000.

Now what would happen if the business decided after two years that the useful life of the asset has been underestimated, and it still had five more years in use to come (making its total life seven years)?

For the first two years, the asset would have been depreciated by $3,000 per annum, so that its carrying value after two years would be $(12,000 − 6,000) = $6,000. If the remaining life of the asset is now revised to five more years, the remaining amount to be depreciated (here $6,000) should be spread over the remaining life, giving an annual depreciation charge for the final five years of:

$$\frac{\text{Net book value at time of life readjustment, minus residual value}}{\text{New estimate of remaining useful life}} = \frac{\$6,000}{5\text{ years}} = \$1,200\text{ per year}$$

Formula to learn

$$\text{New depreciation} = \frac{\text{NBV less residual value}}{\text{Revised useful life}}$$

Similar adjustments are made when there is a change in the expected residual value of the asset.

3.13 Depreciation is not a cash expense

Depreciation spreads the cost of a non-current asset (less its estimated residual value) over the asset's life. The cash payment for the non-current asset will be made when, or soon after, the asset is purchased. Annual depreciation of the asset in subsequent years is not a cash expense – rather it allocates costs to those later years for a cash payment that has occurred previously.

For example, a business purchased some shop fittings for $6,000 on 1 July 20X5 and paid for them in cash on that date.

Subsequently, depreciation may be charged at $600 every year for ten years. So each year $600 is deducted from profits and the carrying value of the fittings goes down, but no actual cash is being paid. The cash was all paid on 1 July 20X5. So annual depreciation is not a cash expense, but rather an allocation of the original cost to later years.

Question
Depreciation

(a)   What are the purposes of providing for depreciation?

(b)   In what circumstances is the reducing balance method more appropriate than the straight-line method? Give reasons for your answer.

Answer

(a)   The accounts of a business try to recognise that the cost of a non-current asset is gradually consumed as the asset wears out. This is done by gradually writing off the asset's cost in the income statement over several accounting periods. This process is known as depreciation, and is an example of the accrual assumption. IAS 16 *Property, plant and equipment* requires that depreciation should be allocated on a systematic basis to each accounting period during the useful life of the asset.

With regard to the accrual principle, it is fair that the profits should be reduced by the depreciation charge; this is not an arbitrary exercise. Depreciation is not, as is sometime supposed, an attempt to set aside funds to purchase new non-current assets when required. Depreciation is not generally provided on freehold land because it does not 'wear out' (unless it is held for mining etc).

(b)   The reducing balance method of depreciation is used instead of the straight line method when it is considered fair to allocate a greater proportion of the total depreciable amount to the earlier years and a lower proportion to the later years, on the assumption that the benefits obtained by the business from using the asset decline over time.

In favour of this method it may be argued that it links the depreciation charge to the costs of maintaining and running the asset. In the early years these costs are low and the depreciation charge is high, while in later years this is reversed.

3.14 Accumulated depreciation

Key term

> **Accumulated depreciation** is the amount set aside as a charge for the wearing out of non-current assets.

There are two basic aspects of accumulated depreciation to remember.

(a)   A depreciation charge is made in the income statement in each accounting period for every depreciable non-current asset. Nearly all non-current assets are depreciable, the most important exceptions being freehold land and non-current investments.

(b)   The total accumulated depreciation on a non-current asset builds up as the asset gets older. The total accumulated depreciation is always getting larger, until the non-current asset is fully depreciated.

The ledger accounting entries for depreciation are as follows.

(a)   There is an accumulated depreciation account for each separate category of non-current assets, for example, plant and machinery, land and buildings, fixtures and fittings.

(b)   The depreciation charge for an accounting period is a charge against profit. It is accounted for as follows.

DEBIT   Income statement (depreciation expense)
CREDIT   Accumulated depreciation account (statement of financial position)

with the depreciation charge for the period.

(c)   The balance on the statement of financial position depreciation account is the total accumulated depreciation. This is always a credit balance brought forward in the ledger account for depreciation.

(d)   The non-current asset accounts are unaffected by depreciation. Non-current assets are recorded in these accounts at cost (or, if they are revalued, at their revalued amount).

(e)   In the statement of financial position of the business, the total balance on the accumulated depreciation account is set against the value of non-current asset accounts (ie non-current assets at cost or revalued amount) to derive the carrying value of the non-current assets.

This is how the non-current asset accounts might appear in a trial balance:

	DR	CR
Freehold building – cost	2,000,000	
Freehold building – accumulated depreciation		500,000
Motor vehicles – cost	70,000	
Motor vehicles – accumulated depreciation		40,000
Office equipment – cost	25,000	
Office equipment – accumulated depreciation		15,000

And this is how they would be shown in the statement of financial position:

Non current assets	
Freehold building	1,500,000
Motor vehicles	30,000
Office equipment	10,000

3.15 Example: Depreciation

Brian Box set up his own computer software business on 1 March 20X6. He purchased a computer system on credit from a manufacturer, at a cost of $16,000. The system has an expected life of three years and a residual value of $2,500. Using the straight line method of depreciation, the non-current asset account, accumulated depreciation account and I & E account (extract) and statement of financial position (extract) would be as follows, for each of the next three years, 28 February 20X7, 20X8 and 20X9.

NON-CURRENT ASSET: COMPUTER EQUIPMENT

	Date		$	Date		$
(a)	1.3.X6	Accounts payable	16,000	28.2.X7	Balance c/d	16,000
(b)	1.3.X7	Balance b/d	16,000	28.2.X8	Balance c/d	16,000
(c)	1.3.X8	Balance b/d	16,000	28.2.X9	Balance c/d	16,000
(d)	1.3.X9	Balance b/d	16,000			

In theory, the non-current asset has now lasted out its expected useful life. However, until it is sold off or scrapped, the asset will still appear in the statement of financial position at cost (less accumulated depreciation) and it should remain in the ledger account for computer equipment until it is eventually disposed of.

ACCUMULATED DEPRECIATION

	Date		$	Date		$
(a)	28.2.X7	Balance c/d	4,500	28.2.X7	I & E account	4,500
(b)	28.2.X8	Balance c/d	9,000	1.3.X7	Balance b/d	4,500
				28.2.X8	I & E account	4,500
			9,000			9,000
(c)	28.2.X9	Balance c/d	13,500	1.3.X8	Balance b/d	9,000
				28.2.X9	I & E account	4,500
			13,500			13,500
				1.3.X9 Balance b/d		13,500

The annual depreciation charge is $\dfrac{\$(16,000 - 2,500)}{3\ \text{years}} = \$4,500\ \text{pa}$

At the end of three years, the asset is fully depreciated down to its residual value (16,000 – 13,500 = 2,500). If it continues to be used by Brian Box, it will not be depreciated any further (unless its estimated residual value is reduced).

INCOME STATEMENT (EXTRACT)

	Date		$
	Date		
(a)	28 Feb 20X7	Depreciation	4,500
(b)	28 Feb 20X8	Depreciation	4,500
(c)	28 Feb 20X9	Depreciation	4,500

STATEMENT OF FINANCIAL POSITION (EXTRACT) AS AT 28 FEBRUARY

	20X7	20X8	20X9
	$	$	$
Computer equipment at cost	16,000	16,000	16,000
Less accumulated depreciation	4,500	9,000	13,500
Carrying value	11,500	7,000	2,500

3.16 Example: Allowance for depreciation with assets acquired part-way through the year

Brian Box prospers in his computer software business, and before long he purchases a car for himself, and later for his chief assistant Bill Ockhead. Relevant data is as follows.

	Date of purchase	Cost	Estimated life	Estimated residual value
Brian Box car	1 June 20X6	$20,000	3 years	$2,000
Bill Ockhead car	1 June 20X7	$8,000	3 years	$2,000

The straight line method of depreciation is to be used.

Prepare the motor vehicles account and motor vehicle depreciation account for the years to 28 February 20X7 and 20X8. (You should allow for the part-year's use of a car in computing the annual charge for depreciation.)

Calculate the carrying value of the motor vehicles as at 28 February 20X8.

Solution

(a) (i) Brian Box car   Annual depreciation $\dfrac{\$(20,000-2,000)}{3\text{ years}}=$ $6,000 pa

Monthly depreciation = $500

Depreciation	1 June-20X6 – 28 February 20X7 (9 months)	$4,500
	1 March 20X7 – 28 February 20X8	$6,000

(ii) Bill Ockhead car   Annual depreciation $\dfrac{\$(8,000-2,000)}{3\text{ years}}=$ $2,000 pa

Depreciation	1 June 20X7 – 28 February 20X8 (9 months)	$1,500

(b)

MOTOR VEHICLES

Date		$	Date		$
1 Jun 20X6	Payables (or cash) (car purchase)	20,000	28 Feb 20X7	Balance c/d	20,000
1 Mar 20X7	Balance b/d	20,000			
1 Jun 20X7	Payables (or cash) (car purchase)	8,000	28 Feb 20X8	Balance c/d	28,000
		28,000			28,000
1 Mar 20X8	Balance b/d	28,000			

MOTOR VEHICLES – ACCUMULATED DEPRECIATION

Date		$	Date		$
28 Feb 20X7	Balance c/d	4,500	28 Feb 20X7	I & E account	4,500
			1 Mar 20X7	Balance b/d	4,500
28 Feb 20X8	Balance c/d	12,000	28 Feb 20X8	I & E account (6,000+1,500)	7,500
		12,000			12,000
			1 Mar 20X8	Balance b/d	12,000

STATEMENT OF FINANCIAL POSITION (WORKINGS) AS AT 28 FEBRUARY 20X8

	Brian Box car $	$	Bill Ockhead car $	$	Total $
Asset at cost		20,000		8,000	28,000
Accumulated depreciation					
Year to 28 Feb 20X7	4,500		–		
Year to 28 Feb 20X8	6,000		1,500		
		10,500		1,500	12,000
Carrying value		9,500		6,500	16,000

4 Revaluation of non-current assets

When a non-current asset is **revalued**, depreciation is charged on the **revalued amount**.

Largely because of inflation, it is now quite common for the market value of certain non-current assets to **go up, in spite of getting older**. The most obvious example of rising market values is land and buildings.

A business which owns non-current assets which are rising in value is not obliged to revalue those assets in its statement of financial position. However, in order to give a more 'true and fair view' of the position of the business, it might be decided that some non-current assets should be revalued upwards; otherwise the total value of the assets of the business might seem unrealistically low. When non-current assets are revalued, depreciation should be charged on the *revalued amount*.

4.1 Example: The revaluation of non-current assets

When Ira Vann commenced trading as a car hire dealer on 1 January 20X1, he purchased business premises at a cost of $50,000.

For the purpose of accounting for depreciation, he decided the following.

(a)   The land part of the business premises was worth $20,000; this would not be depreciated.

(b)   The building part of the business premises was worth the remaining $30,000. This would be depreciated by the straight-line method to a nil residual value over 30 years.

After five years of trading on 1 January 20X6, Ira decides that his business premises are now worth $150,000, divided into:

	$
Land	75,000
Building	75,000
	150,000

He estimates that the building still has a further 25 years of useful life remaining.

Calculate the annual charge for depreciation in each of the 30 years of its life, and the statement of financial position value of the land and building as at the end of each year.

Solution

Before the revaluation, the annual depreciation charge is $1,000 per annum on the building. This charge is made in each of the first five years of the asset's life.

The carrying value of the asset will decline by $1,000 per annum, to:

(a) $49,000 as at 31.12.X1
(b) $48,000 as at 31.12.X2
(c) $47,000 as at 31.12.X3
(d) $46,000 as at 31.12.X4
(e) $45,000 as at 31.12.X5

When the revaluation takes place, the amount of the revaluation is:

	$
New asset value (to be shown in statement of financial position)	150,000
Carrying value as at end of 20X5 ($20,000 + ($30,000 − $5,000))	45,000
Amount of revaluation	105,000

The asset will be revalued by $105,000 to $150,000. If you remember the accounting equation, that the total value of assets must be equalled by the total value of capital and liabilities, you should recognise that if assets go up in value by $105,000, capital or liabilities must also go up by the same amount. Since the increased value benefits the owners of the business, the amount of the revaluation is added to capital.

However, the gain on revaluation cannot go to the income statement, as it has not been realised. Instead it is recognised in the statement of comprehensive income (see Chapter 21). From here, the 'gain' is transferred to a **revaluation reserve**.

This treatment may surprise you at first. However remember the prudence concept, which states that a profit can not be anticipated before it is realised. Therefore the 'profit' can not be dealt with as income in the income statement. **If the building were to be subsequently sold for the revalued amount, the profit would be realised and could be taken to the income statement.**

4.2 Accounting entries

The accounting treatment for the revaluation above will be:

DEBIT	Building	– cost ($75,000 – $30,000)	$45,000	
	Building	– accumulated depreciation	$5,000	
	Land	– cost ($75,000 – $20,000)	$55,000	
CREDIT	Revaluation reserve			$105,000

The effect of these entries is as follows:

BUILDING – COST

	$		$
Bal b/f	30,000	Bal c/f	75,000
Revaluation reserve	45,000		
	75,000		75,000

BUILDING – ACCUMULATED DEPRECIATION

	$		$
Revaluation reserve	5,000	Bal b/f	5,000
Bal c/f	-		
	5,000		5,000

LAND – COST

	$		$
Bal b/f	20,000	Bal c/f	75,000
Revaluation reserve	55,000		
	75,000		75,000

REVALUATION RESERVE

	$		$
Bal c/f	105,000	Building – cost	45,000
		Building – acc dep'n	5,000
		Land – cost	55,000
	105,000		105,000

4.3 Depreciation on revalued assets

After the revaluation, depreciation will be charged on the building at a new rate of:

$$\frac{\text{Revalued amount}}{\text{Remaining useful life}}$$

$$\frac{\$75,000}{25 \text{ years}} = \$3,000 \text{ per year}$$

The carrying value of the property will then fall by $3,000 per year over 25 years, from $150,000 as at 1 January 20X6 to only $75,000 at the end of the 25 years, ie the building part of the property value will have been fully depreciated.

The consequence of a revaluation is therefore a higher annual depreciation charge.

4.4 Revaluation downwards

After some years, it may become apparent that the building is overvalued and needs to be revalued downwards

Using the example above five years later, the land is still valued at $75,000 but the building is now valued at $25,000.

BUILDING COST

	$		£
Balance b/f	75,000	Revaluation reserve	50,000
		Bal c/d	25,000

BUILDING-ACCUMULATED DEPRECIATION

	$		$
Revaluation reserve	15,000	Balance b/f (5 × $3,000)	15,000

LAND COST

	$		$
Balance b/f	75,000	Balance c/f	75,000

REVALUATION RESERVE

	$		$
Cost	50,000	Balance b/f	105,000
Bal c/f	70,000	Excess depreciation	15,000
	120,000	(accumulated depreciation)	120,000

5 Non-current asset disposals

When a non-current asset is **sold**, there is likely to be a **profit or loss on disposal**. This is the difference between the net sale price of the asset and its carrying value at the time of disposal.

5.1 The disposal of non-current assets

Non-current assets are not purchased by a business with the intention of reselling them in the normal course of trade. However, they might be sold off at some stage during their life, either when their useful life is over or before then. A business might decide to sell off a non-current asset long before its useful life has ended.

Whenever a business sells something, it will make a profit or a loss. When non-current assets are disposed of, there will be a profit or loss on disposal. As it is a capital item being sold, the profit or loss will be a capital gain or a capital loss. These gains or losses are reported in the income and expenses part of the income statement of the business (not as a trading profit in the trading account). They are commonly referred to as '**profit on disposal of non-current assets**' or '**loss on disposal**'.

Examination questions on the disposal of non-current assets are likely to ask for ledger accounts to be prepared, showing the entries in the accounts to record the disposal. But before we look at the ledger accounting for disposing of assets, we had better look at the principles behind calculating the profit (or loss) on disposing of assets.

5.2 The principles behind calculating the profit or loss on disposal

The profit or loss on the disposal of a non-current asset is the difference between (a) and (b) below.

(a)   The carrying value of the asset at the time of its sale.
(b)   Its net sale price, which is the price minus any costs of making the sale.

A profit is made when the sale price exceeds the carrying value, and a loss is made when the sale price is less than the carrying value.

5.3 Example: Disposal of a non-current asset

A business purchased a non-current asset on 1 January 20X1 for $25,000. It had an estimated life of six years and an estimated residual value of $7,000. The asset was eventually sold after three years on 1 January 20X4 to another trader who paid $17,500 for it.

What was the profit or loss on disposal, assuming that the business uses the straight line method for depreciation?

Solution

$$\text{Annual depreciation} = \frac{\$(25,000 - 7,000)}{6 \text{ years}} = \$3,000 \text{ per annum}$$

	$
Cost of asset	25,000
Less accumulated depreciation (three years)	9,000
Carrying value at date of disposal	16,000
Sale price	17,500
Profit on disposal	1,500

This profit will be shown in the income statement of the business where it will be an item of other income added to the gross profit brought down from the trading account.

5.4 Second example: Disposal of a non-current asset

A business purchased a machine on 1 July 20X1 at a cost of $35,000. The machine had an estimated residual value of $3,000 and a life of eight years. The machine was sold for $18,600 on 31 December 20X4, the last day of the accounting year of the business. To make the sale, the business had to incur dismantling costs and costs of transporting the machine to the buyer's premises. These amounted to $1,200.

The business uses the straight line method of depreciation. What was the profit or loss on disposal of the machine?

Solution

$$\text{Annual depreciation} \frac{\$(35,000 - 3,000)}{8 \text{ years}} = \$4,000 \text{ per annum}$$

It is assumed that in 20X1 only one-half year's depreciation was charged, because the asset was purchased six months into the year.

	$	$
Non-current asset at cost		35,000
Depreciation in 20X1 (½ year)	2,000	
20X2, 20X3 and 20X4	12,000	
Accumulated depreciation		14,000
Carrying value at date of disposal		21,000
Sale price	18,600	
Costs incurred in making the sale	(1,200)	
Net sale price		17,400
Loss on disposal		(3,600)

This loss will be shown as an expense in the income statement of the business. It is a capital loss, not a trading loss, and it should not therefore be shown in the trading account.

5.5 The disposal of non-current assets: ledger accounting entries

We have already seen how the profit or loss on disposal of a non-current asset should be computed. A profit on disposal is an item of 'other income' in the income statement, and a loss on disposal is an item of expense in the income statement

It is customary in ledger accounting to record the disposal of non-current assets in a **disposal of non-current assets account**.

(a)   The profit or loss on disposal is the difference between:

(i)   the sale price of the asset (if any); and
(ii)   the carrying value of the asset at the time of sale.

(b)   The following items must appear in the disposal of non-current assets account:

(i)   The value of the asset (at cost, or revalued amount*)
(ii)   The accumulated depreciation up to the date of sale
(iii)   The sale price of the asset

*To simplify the explanation of the rules, we will assume now that the non-current assets disposed of are valued at cost.

(c)   The ledger accounting entries are as follows.

(i)   DEBIT   Disposal of non-current asset account
         CREDIT   Non-current asset account

with the cost of the asset disposed of.

(ii)   DEBIT   Accumulated depreciation account
         CREDIT   Disposal of non-current asset account

with the accumulated depreciation on the asset as at the date of sale.

(iii)   DEBIT   Receivable account or cash book
         CREDIT   Disposal of non-current asset account

with the sale price of the asset. The sale is therefore not recorded in a sales account, but in the disposal of non-current asset account itself. You will notice that the effect of these entries is to remove the asset, and its accumulated depreciation, from the statement of financial position.

The balance on the disposal account is the profit or loss on disposal and the corresponding double entry is recorded in the I & E account itself.

5.6 Example: Disposal of assets: Ledger accounting entries

A business has $110,000 worth of machinery at cost. Its policy is to make a provision for depreciation at 20% per annum straight line. The total provision now stands at $70,000. The business sells for $19,000 a machine which it purchased exactly two years ago for $30,000.

Show the relevant ledger entries.

Solution

PLANT AND MACHINERY ACCOUNT

	$		$
Balance b/d	110,000	Plant disposals account	30,000
		Balance c/d	80,000
	110,000		110,000
Balance b/d	80,000		

PLANT AND MACHINERY ACCUMULATED DEPRECIATION

	$		$
Plant disposals (20% of $30,000 for 2 years)	12,000	Balance b/d	70,000
Balance c/d	58,000		
	70,000		70,000
		Balance b/d	58,000

PLANT DISPOSALS

	$		$
Plant and machinery account	30,000	Accumulated depreciation	12,000
I & E a/c (profit on sale)	1,000	Cash	19,000
	31,000		31,000

Check

	$
Asset at cost	30,000
Accumulated depreciation at time of sale	12,000
Carrying value at time of sale	18,000
Sale price	19,000
Profit on sale	1,000

5.7 Example continued: Part exchange

Taking the example above assume that, instead of the machine being sold for $19,000, it was exchanged for a new machine costing $60,000, a credit of $19,000 being received upon exchange. In other words $19,000 is the trade-in price of the old machine. Now what are the relevant ledger account entries?

Solution

PLANT AND MACHINERY ACCOUNT

	$		$
Balance b/d	110,000	Plant disposal	30,000
Cash $(60,000 – 19,000)	41,000	Balance c/d	140,000
Plant disposals	19,000		
	170,000		170,000
Balance b/d	140,000		

The new asset is recorded in the non-current asset account at cost $(41,000 + 19,000) = $60,000.

PLANT AND MACHINERY ACCUMULATED DEPRECIATION

	$		$
Plant disposals (20% of $30,000 for 2 years)	12,000	Balance b/d	70,000
Balance c/d	58,000		
	70,000		70,000
		Balance b/d	58,000

PLANT DISPOSALS

	$		$
Plant and machinery	30,000	Accumulated depreciation	12,000
Profit transferred to I & E	1,000	Plant and machinery-part exchange	19,000
	31,000		31,000

A business purchased two rivet-making machines on 1 January 20X5 at a cost of $15,000 each. Each had an estimated life of five years and a nil residual value. The straight line method of depreciation is used.

Owing to an unforeseen slump in market demand for rivets, the business decided to reduce its output of rivets, and switch to making other products instead. On 31 March 20X7, one rivet-making machine was sold (on credit) to a buyer for $8,000.

Later in the year, however, it was decided to abandon production of rivets altogether, and the second machine was sold on 1 December 20X7 for $2,500 cash.

Prepare the machinery account, depreciation of machinery account and disposal of machinery account for the accounting year to 31 December 20X7.

Answer

MACHINERY ACCOUNT

		$				$
20X7			*20X7*			
1 Jan	Balance b/f	30,000	31 Mar	Disposal of machinery account		15,000
			1 Dec	Disposal of machinery account		15,000
		30,000				30,000

MACHINERY – ACCUMULATED DEPRECIATION

		$				$
20X7			*20X7*			
31 Mar	Disposal of machinery account*	6,750	1 Jan	Balance b/f		12,000
1 Dec	Disposal of machinery account**	8,750	31 Dec	I & E account***		3,500
		15,500				15,500

*	Depreciation at date of disposal = $6,000 + $750
**	Depreciation at date of disposal = $6,000 + $2,750
***	Depreciation charge for the year = $750 + $2,750

DISPOSAL OF MACHINERY

		$			$
20X7			*20X7*		
31 Mar	Machinery account	15,000	31 Mar	Account receivable (sale price)	8,000
			31 Mar	Accumulated depreciation	6,750
1 Dec	Machinery	15,000	1 Dec	Cash (sale price)	2,500
			1 Dec	Accumulated depreciation	8,750
			31 Dec	I & E a/c (loss on disposal)	4,000
		30,000			30,000

You should be able to calculate that there was a loss on the first disposal of $250, and on the second disposal of $3,750, giving a total loss of $4,000.

Workings

1   At 1 January 20X7, accumulated depreciation on the machines will be:

$$2 \text{ machines} \times 2 \text{ years} \times \frac{\$15,000}{5} \text{ per machine pa} = \$12,000, \text{ or } \$6,000 \text{ per machine}$$

2   Monthly depreciation is $\dfrac{\$3,000}{12}$ = $250 per machine per month

3   The machines are disposed of in 20X7.

    (a)   On 31 March – after 3 months of the year.
            Depreciation for the year on the machine = 3 months × $250 = $750.

    (b)   On 1 December – after 11 months of the year.
            Depreciation for the year on the machine = 11 months × $250 = $2,750

5.8 Example: disposal of a revalued asset

Returning to the case of the revalued asset in Sections 4.2 and 4.3, suppose that two years later the land and property is sold for $200,000. What is the profit on disposal?

BUILDING – COST

	$		$
Bal b/f	75,000	Disposal account	75,000

BUILDING – ACCUMULATED DEPRECIATION

	$		$
Disposal account	6,000	Bal b/f ($2,000 × 2)	6,000

LAND – COST

	$		$
Bal b/f	75,000	Disposal account	75,000

REVALUATION RESERVE

	$		$
Disposal account	105,000	Bal b/f	105,000

DISPOSAL ACCOUNT

	$		$
Building – cost	75,000	Cash	200,000
Land – cost	75,000	Building – acc dep'n	6,000
Profit on disposal	161,000	Revaluation reserve	105,000
	311,000		311,000

Ignoring the revaluation:

	$
Original cost of building	30,000
Original cost of land	20,000
	50,000
Depreciation ($5,000 + $6,000)	(11,000)
Carrying value	39,000
Sale proceeds	200,000
Profit on sale	161,000

6 IAS 16 Property, plant and equipment

IAS 16 covers all aspects of accounting for property, plant and equipment. This represents the bulk of items which are **'tangible' non-current assets**.

6.1 Scope

IAS 16 should be followed when accounting for property, plant and equipment *unless* another international accounting standard requires a **different treatment**.

IAS 16 **does not apply** to the following.

(a)   Forests and other regenerative natural resources

(b)   Mineral rights, exploration for and extraction of minerals, oil, gas and other non-regenerative resources.

6.2 Definitions

The standard gives a large number of definitions.

Key terms

> - **Property, plant and equipment** are tangible assets that:
>
>   - Are held by an entity for use in the production or supply of goods or services, for rental to others, or for administrative purposes; and
>   - Are expected to be used during more than on period.
>
> - **Cost** is the amount of cash or cash equivalents paid or the fair value of the other consideration given to acquire an asset at the time of its acquisition or construction.
>
> - **Residual value** is the estimated amount that an entity would currently obtain from disposal of the asset, after deducting the estimated costs of disposal, if the asset were already of the age and in the conditions expected at the end of its useful life.
>
> - **Fair value** is the amount for which an asset could be exchanged between knowledgeable, willing parties in an arm's length transaction.
>
> - **Carrying amount** is the amount at which an asset is recognised after deducting any accumulated depreciation and impairment losses.
>
> - **Recoverable amount** is the amount which the entity expects to recover from the future use of an asset, including its residual value on disposal. This is the higher of net selling price or value in use.
>
>   *(IAS 16)*

6.3 Recognition

In this context, recognition simply means incorporation of the item in the business's accounts, in this case as a non-current asset. The recognition of property, plant and equipment depends on two criteria.

(a)   It is probable that **future economic benefits** associated with the asset will flow to the entity.

(b)   The cost of the asset to the entity can be **measured reliably**.

Property, plant and equipment can amount to **substantial amounts** in financial statements, affecting both the presentation of the company's statement of financial position and the profitability of the entity as shown in the income statement. Smaller items such as tools are often written off as expenses of the period. Most companies have their own policy on this – items below a certain value are charged as expenses.

6.4 Initial measurement

Once an item of property, plant and equipment qualifies for recognition as an asset, it will initially be **measured at cost**.

Exam focus point

> From your studies of double entry in Chapter 5, you should remember that the entries to record an acquisition are:
>
> | | | | |
> |---|---|---|---|
> | DEBIT | Non-current asset – cost | X | |
> | CREDIT | Cash (or payable if credit transaction) | | X |

6.4.1 Components of cost

The standard lists the components of the cost of an item of property, plant and equipment.

- **Purchase price**, less any trade discount or rebate

- **Initial estimate of the costs of dismantling and removing the item and restoring the site on which it is located**

- **Directly attributable costs** of bringing the asset to working condition for its intended use, eg:

    - The cost of site preparation
    - Initial delivery and handling costs
    - Installation costs
    - Professional fees (architects, engineers)

The following costs **will not be part of the cost** of property, plant or equipment unless they can be attributed directly to the asset's acquisition, or bringing it into its working condition.

- Expenses of operations that are incidental to the construction or development of the item
- Administration and other general overhead costs
- Start-up and similar pre-production costs
- Initial operating losses before the asset reaches planned performances

All of these will be recognised as an **expense** rather than an asset.

6.4.2 Exchanges of assets

Exchange or part exchange of assets occurs frequently for items of property, plant and equipment. IAS 16 states that the cost of an item obtained through (part)exchange is the **fair value of the asset received (unless this cannot be measured reliably)**.

6.5 Subsequent expenditure

How should we treat any subsequent expenditure on long-term assets, after their purchase and recognition? **Subsequent expenditure is added to the carrying amount** of the asset, but only when it is probable that future economic benefits, in excess of the originally assessed standard of performance of the existing asset, will flow to the enterprise. All other subsequent expenditure is simply recognised as an expense in the period in which it is incurred.

The important point here is whether any subsequent expenditure on an asset **improves** the condition of the asset beyond the previous performance. The standard gives the following examples of such improvements.

(a)   **Modification** of an item of plant to extend its useful life, including increased capacity
(b)   **Upgrade** of machine parts to improve the quality of output
(c)   Adoption of a **new production process** leading to large reductions in operating costs

Normal repairs and maintenance on property, plant and equipment items merely maintain or restore value, they do *not* improve or increase it, so such costs are recognised as an expense when incurred.

6.6 Measurement subsequent to initial recognition

The standard offers two possible treatments here, essentially a choice between keeping an asset recorded at **cost** or revaluing it to **fair value**.

(a)   **Cost model.** Carry the asset at its cost less accumulated depreciation and any accumulated impairment losses.

(b)   **Revaluation model.** Carry the asset at a revalued amount, being its fair value at the date of the revaluation less any subsequent accumulated depreciation and any accumulated impairment losses. Revaluations should be made regularly enough so that the carrying amount approximates to fair value at the reporting date. The revaluation model is only available if the item can be measured reliably.

6.6.1 Revaluations

The **market value** of land and buildings usually represents fair value, assuming existing use and line of business. Such valuations are usually carried out by professionally qualified valuers.

In the case of **plant and equipment**, fair value can also be taken as **market value**. Where a market value is not available, however, depreciated replacement cost should be used. There may be no market value where types of plant and equipment are sold only rarely or because of their specialised nature (ie they would normally only be sold as part of an ongoing business).

The frequency of valuation depends on the **volatility of the fair values** of individual items of property, plant and equipment. The more volatile the fair value, the more frequently revaluations should be carried out. Where the current fair value is very different from the carrying value then a revaluation should be carried out.

Most importantly, when an item of property, plant and equipment is revalued, **the whole class of assets to which it belongs should be revalued.**

All the items within a class should be **revalued at the same time**, to prevent selective revaluation of certain assets and to avoid disclosing a mixture of costs and values from different dates in the financial statements. A rolling basis of revaluation is allowed if the revaluations are kept up to date and the revaluation of the whole class is completed in a short period of time.

How should any **increase in value** be treated when a revaluation takes place? The debit will be the increase in value in the statement of financial position, but what about the credit? IAS 16 requires the increase to be credited to a **revaluation surplus** (ie part of owners' equity), *unless* the increase is reversing a previous decrease which was recognised as an expense. To the extent that this offset is made, the increase is recognised as income; any excess is then taken to the revaluation reserve.

IAS 16 makes further statements about revaluation, but these are beyond the scope of your syllabus.

6.7 Depreciation

The standard reflects the following approach to depreciation.

- The **depreciable amount** of an item of property, plant and equipment should be allocated on a systematic basis over its useful life.
- The **depreciation method** used should reflect the pattern in which the asset's economic benefits are consumed by the entity.
- The **depreciation charge** for each period would be recognised as an expense unless it is included in the carrying amount of another asset.

Most of the comments on depreciation in IAS 16 are dealt with in Section 1.

Land and buildings are dealt with separately even when they are acquired together because land normally has an unlimited life and is therefore not depreciated. In contrast buildings do have a limited life and must be depreciated. Any increase in the value of land on which a building is standing will have no impact on the determination of the building's useful life.

Depreciation is usually treated as an **expense**, but not where it is absorbed by the entity in the process of producing other assets. For example, depreciation of plant and machinery is incurred in the production of goods for sale (inventory items). In such circumstances, the depreciation is included in the cost of the new assets produced.

6.7.1 Review of useful life

A review of the **useful life** of property, plant and equipment should be carried out at least **annually** and the depreciation charge for the current and future periods should be adjusted if expectations have changed significantly from previous estimates.

6.7.2 Review of depreciation method

The **depreciation method** should also be reviewed **periodically** and, if there has been a significant change in the expected pattern of economic benefits from those assets, the method should be changed to suit this changed pattern. When such a change in depreciation method takes place the change should be accounted for as a **change in accounting estimate** and the depreciation charge for the current and future periods should be adjusted.

6.7.3 Impairment of asset values

The **carrying amount** of an item or group of identical items of property, plant and equipment should also be reviewed **periodically**. This is to assess whether the recoverable amount has declined below the carrying amount. When there has been such a decline, the carrying amount should be reduced to the **recoverable amount**.

Recoverable amounts should be considered on an **individual asset basis** or for **groups of identical assets**.

6.8 Retirements and disposals

When an asset is permanently **withdrawn from use, or sold or scrapped**, and no future economic benefits are expected from its disposal, it should be withdrawn from the statement of financial position.

Gains or losses are the difference between the estimated net disposal proceeds and the carrying amount of the asset. They should be recognised as income or expense in the income statement.

6.9 Disclosure

The standard has a long list of disclosure requirements, only some of which are relevant to your syllabus.

- **Measurement bases** for determining the gross carrying amount (if more than one, the gross carrying amount for that basis in each category)
- **Depreciation methods** used
- **Useful lives** or depreciation rates used
- **Gross carrying amount** and accumulated depreciation at the beginning and end of the period
- **Reconciliation** of the carrying amount at the beginning and end of the period showing:
  - Additions
  - Disposals
  - Increases/decreases from revaluations
  - Reductions in carrying amount
  - Depreciation
  - Any other movements.

The financial statements should also disclose the following.

- Existence and amounts of **restrictions on title**, and items pledged as security for liabilities
- Accounting policy for **restoration costs**
- Amount of expenditures on account of **items in the course of construction**
- Amount of commitments to **acquisitions**

Revalued assets require further disclosures.

- **Basis** used to revalue the assets
- **Effective date** of the revaluation
- Whether an **independent valuer** was involved
- Nature of any **indices** used to determine replacement cost
- **Carrying amount** of each class of property, plant and equipment that would have been included in the financial statements had the assets been carried at cost less depreciation

- **Revaluation surplus**, indicating the movement for the period and any restrictions on the distribution of the balance to shareholders.

The standard also **encourages disclosure** of additional information, which the users of financial statements may find useful.

- The carrying amount of temporarily idle property, plant and equipment
- The gross carrying amount of any fully depreciated property, plant and equipment that is still in use
- The carrying amount of property, plant and equipment retired from active use and held for disposal
- When the benchmark treatment is used, the fair value of property, plant and equipment when this is materially different from the carrying amount

The following format (with notional figures) is commonly used to disclose non-current assets movements.

	Total $	Land and buildings $	Plant and equipment $
Cost or valuation			
At 1 January 20X4	50,000	40,000	10,000
Revaluation surplus	12,000	12,000	–
Additions in year	4,000	–	4,000
Disposals in year	(1,000)	–	(1,000)
At 31 December 20X4	65,000	52,000	13,000
Depreciation			
At 1 January 20X4	16,000	10,000	6,000
Charge for year	4,000	1,000	3,000
Eliminated on disposals	(500)	–	(500)
At 31 December 20X4	19,500	11,000	8,500
Carrying value			
At 31 December 20X4	45,500	41,000	4,500
At 1 January 20X4	34,000	30,000	4,000

Note that this format is only required for company accounts.

Question

Net book value

(a) In a statement of financial position prepared in accordance with IAS 16, what does the carrying value (net book value) represent?

(b) In a set of financial statements prepared in accordance with IAS 16, is it correct to say that the carrying value (net book value) figure in a statement of financial position cannot be greater than the market (net realisable) value of the partially used asset as at the reporting date? Explain your reasons for your answer.

Answer

(a) In simple terms the carrying value of an asset is the cost of an asset less the 'accumulated depreciation', that is all depreciation charged so far. It should be emphasised that the main purpose of charging depreciation is to ensure that profits are fairly reported. Thus depreciation is concerned with the income statement rather than the statement of financial position. In consequence the carrying value figure in the statement of financial position can be quite arbitrary. In particular, it does not necessarily bear any relation to the market value of an asset and is of little use for planning and decision making.

An obvious example of the disparity between carrying value and market value is found in the case of buildings, which may be worth more than ten times as much as their carrying value.

(b)   Carrying value can in some circumstances be higher than market value (net realisable value). IAS 16 *Property, plant and equipment* states that the value of an asset cannot be greater than its 'recoverable amount'. However 'recoverable amount' as defined in IAS 16 is the amount recoverable from further use. This may be higher than the market value.

This makes sense if you think of a specialised machine which could not fetch much on the secondhand market but which will produce goods which can be sold at a profit for many years.

Exam focus point

Student Accountant contains a two part article on *Property, plant and equipment and tangible fixed assets* in its 30 May 2007 and 1 August 2007 editions. These are worth reading.

7 The asset register

FAST FORWARD

An **asset register** is used to record all non-current assets and is an **internal check** on the accuracy of the nominal ledger.

Nearly all organisations keep an asset register. This is a listing of all non-current assets owned by the organisation, broken down perhaps by department, location or asset type.

An asset register is maintained primarily for internal purposes. It shows an organisation's investment in capital equipment. The register is also part of the **internal control system**. The asset registers are sometimes called **real accounts**.

7.1 Data kept in an asset register

Details about each non-current asset include the following.

*   The internal reference number (for physical identification purposes)
*   Manufacturer's serial number (for maintenance purposes)
*   Description of asset
*   Location of asset
*   Department which 'owns' asset
*   Purchase date (for calculation of depreciation)
*   Cost
*   Depreciation method and estimated useful life (for calculation of depreciation)
*   Carrying value (or written down value or net book value)

7.2 Use of asset register

From time to time, the asset register should be checked to the accounting records. Any discrepancies must be investigated and the records corrected. For example, an asset may have been scrapped and the asset register updated, but the asset had not yet been written off in the accounting records.

Periodically, all physical non-current assets should be checked to the current register. This helps to deter theft.

8 Worked example

You have already had practice at preparing an income statement and statement of financial position from a simple trial balance. Now see if you can do the same thing but at a more advanced level, taking account of adjustments for depreciation and inventory. Have a go at the following question.

Exam focus point

At the 2009 ACCA Teachers' Conference, the examiner recommended working full length questions not only to become familiar with the techniques involved, but also as a good grounding for future studies at F7.

 **Final accounts**

The following list of account balances was extracted from the ledger of Kevin Webster, a sole trader, as at 31 May 20X1, the end of his financial year.

KEVIN WEBSTER
TRIAL BALANCE AS AT 31 MAY 20X1

	Dr $	Cr $
Property, at cost	120,000	
Equipment, at cost	80,000	
Accumulated depreciation (as at 1 June 20X0)		
– on property		20,000
– on equipment		38,000
Purchases	250,000	
Sales		402,200
Inventory, as at 1 June 20X0	50,000	
Returns out (purchase returns)		15,000
Wages and salaries	58,800	
Selling expenses	22,600	
Loan interest	5,100	
Other operating expenses	17,700	
Trade accounts payable		36,000
Trade accounts receivable	38,000	
Cash in hand	300	
Bank	1,300	
Drawings	24,000	
17% long-term loan		30,000
Capital, as at 1 June 20X0		126,600
	667,800	667,800

The following additional information as at 31 May 20X1 is available.

(a)   Inventory as at the close of business has been valued at cost at $42,000.

(b)   Depreciation for the year ended 31 May 20X1 has still to be charged as follows:

Property: 1.5% per annum using the straight line method
Equipment: 25% per annum using the reducing balance method

Required

Prepare Kevin Webster's income statement for the year ended 31 May 20X1 and his statement of financial position as at that date.

KEVIN WEBSTER
INCOME STATEMENT
FOR THE YEAR ENDED 31 MAY 20X1

	$	$
Sales		402,200
Cost of sales		
Opening inventory	50,000	
Purchases	250,000	
Purchases returns	(15,000)	
	285,000	
Closing inventory	42,000	
		243,000
Gross profit		159,200
Expenses		
Wages and salaries	58,800	
Selling expenses	22,600	
Loan interest	5,100	
Depreciation (W1)	12,300	
Other operating expenses	17,700	
		116,500
Net profit for the year		42,700

KEVIN WEBSTER
STATEMENT OF FINANCIAL POSITION AS AT 31 MAY 20X1

	$	$
Assets		
Non-current assets		
Property: cost	120,000	
accumulated depreciation (W1)	21,800	
		98,200
Equipment: cost	80,000	
accumulated depreciation (W1)	48,500	
		31,500
Current assets		
Inventory	42,000	
Trade accounts receivable	38,000	
Bank	1,300	
Cash in hand	300	
		81,600
Total assets		211,300
	$	$
Capital and liabilities		
Capital		
Balance at 1 June 20X0	126,600	
Net profit for the year	42,700	
Drawings	(24,000)	
Balance at 31 May 20X1		145,300
Non-current liabilities		
17% loan		30,000
Current liabilities		
Trade accounts payable		36,000
Total capital and liabilities		211,300

Working

1   *Depreciation*

		$
Property		
Opening balance		20,000
Charge for the year (1.5% × 120,000)		1,800
Closing balance		21,800
Equipment		
Opening balance		38,000
Charge for the year (25% × 42,000)		10,500
Closing balance		48,500
Depreciation charge in income statement (1,800 + 10,500)		12,300

Chapter Roundup

- **Capital expenditure** is expenditure which results in the **acquisition of non-current assets**.

  Revenue expenditure is expenditure incurred for the **purpose of the trade** or to **maintain non current assets**.

- The **cost** of a non-current asset, less its estimated residual value, is **allocated fairly** between accounting periods by means of **depreciation**. Depreciation is both:

  – **Charged against profit**; and
  – **Deducted from the value of the non-current asset in the statement of financial position**.

- Two methods of depreciation are specified in your syllabus:

  – The straight line method
  – The reducing balance method

- When a non-current asset is **revalued, depreciation is charged on the revalued amount**.

- When a non-current asset is **sold**, there is likely to be a **profit or loss on disposal**. This is the difference between the net sale price of the asset and its carrying value at the time of disposal.

- IAS 16 covers all aspects of accounting for property, plant and equipment. This represents the bulk of items which are '**tangible non-current assets**'.

- An **asset register** is used to record all non-current assets and is an **internal check** on the accuracy of the nominal ledger.

Quick Quiz

1   Which of the following statements regarding non-current asset accounting is correct?

A   All non-current assets should be revalued each year.

B   Non-current assets may be revalued at the discretion of management. Once revaluation has occurred it must be repeated regularly for all non-current assets in a class.

C   Management can choose which non-current assets in a class of non-current assets should be revalued.

D   Non-current assets should be revalued to reflect rising prices.

2   Which of the following statements regarding depreciation is correct?

A   All non-current assets must be depreciated.

B   Straight line depreciation is usually the most appropriate method of depreciation.

C   A change in the chosen depreciation method is a change in accounting policy which should be disclosed.

D   Depreciation charges must be based upon the carrying value of an asset (less residual value if appropriate).

3   What is an asset's carrying value?

   A   Its cost less annual depreciation
   B   Its cost less accumulated depreciation
   C   Its net realisable value
   D   Its replacement value

4   Give two common depreciation methods.

5   A non-current asset (cost $10,000, depreciation $7,500) is given in part exchange for a new asset costing $20,500. The agreed trade-in value was $3,500. The income statement will include?

   A   A loss on disposal $1,000
   B   A profit on disposal $1,000
   C   A loss on purchase of a new asset $3,500
   D   A profit on disposal $3,500

6   What details about a non-current asset might be included in an assets register?

7   Why might the assets register not reconcile with the non-current assets?

   A   Asset stolen or damaged
   B   New asset, not yet recorded in the register
   C   Errors in the register
   D   All of the above

Answers to Quick Quiz

1   B   Correct.
     A   Non-current assets may be revalued, there is no requirement to do so in IAS 16.
     C   Incorrect, all non-current assets in a class must be revalued.
     D   Incorrect, non-current assets may be reduced in value as well as being increased.

2   D   Correct, carrying value is another name for net book value.
     A   Incorrect, some non-current assets are not depreciated eg land.
     B   Incorrect, management should choose the most appropriate method.
     C   Incorrect, a method change is not a change in accounting policy.

3   B   Its cost less accumulated depreciation.

4   Straight-line and reducing balance.

5   B

	$
Carrying value at disposal (10,000 – 7,500)	2,500
Trade-in allowance	3,500
Profit	1,000

6   • Date of purchase
     • Description
     • Original cost
     • Depreciation rate and method
     • Accumulated depreciation to date
     • Date and amount of any revaluation

7   D   Other reasons include an asset that is obsolete and so scrapped or improvements not yet recorded in the register.

Now try the questions below from the Exam Question Bank

Number	Level	Marks	Time
Q14	Examination	2	2 mins
Q15	Examination	2	2 mins
Q16	Examination	2	2 mins
Q17	Examination	1	1 min

Intangible non-current assets

Topic list	Syllabus reference
1 Intangible assets	D6(a)-(b)
2 Research and development costs	D6(c) –(f)

Introduction

Intangible non-current assets are long-term assets which have a value to the business because they have been paid for, but which do not have any physical substance. The most significant of such intangible assets are research and deferred development costs.

In many companies, especially those which produce food or 'scientific' products such as medicines or 'high technology' products, the expenditure on **research and development** is considerable. When R & D is a large item of cost its accounting treatment may have a significant influence on the profits of a business and its statement of financial position valuation. Because of this attempts have been made to standardise the treatment, and these are discussed in this chapter.

Study guide

		Intellectual level
D6	**Intangible non-current assets and amortisation**	
(a)	Recognise the difference between tangible and intangible non-current assets	1
(b)	Identify types of intangible assets	1
(c)	Identify the definition and treatment of 'research costs' and 'development costs' in accordance with IFRSs.	1
(d)	Calculate amounts to be capitalised as development expenditure or to be expensed from given information	1
(e)	Explain the purpose of amortisation	1
(f)	Calculate and account for the charge for amortisation	1

Exam guide

Calculations of R & D expenses are highly likely to be examined. Be prepared for a question asking you to apply the standard to a given situation.

Exam focus point

> At the 2009 ACCA Teachers' Conference, the examiner highlighted intangible non-current assets as one of the areas that are consistently answered badly in the exam.

1 Intangible assets

1.1 Intangible assets

'Intangible assets' means assets that literally cannot be touched, as opposed to tangible assets (such as plant and machinery) which have a physical existence. Intangible assets include goodwill (which we will meet in Chapter 19), intellectual rights (eg patents, performing rights and authorship rights), as well as research and development costs.

1.2 Accounting treatment

Intangible assets are usually capitalised in the accounts and amortised (another word for depreciation but referring specifically to intangible assets). Amortisation is intended to write off the asset over its economic life (under the accruals concept).

1.3 Example: patent

A business buys a patent for $50,000. It expects to use the patent for the next ten years, after which it will be valueless. Amortisation is calculated in the same way as for tangible assets:

$$\frac{\text{Cost} - \text{residual value}}{\text{Estimated useful life}}$$

In this case, amortisation will be $5,000 per annum (50,000/10).

2 Research and development costs

FAST FORWARD

Expenditure on **research** must always be written off in the period in which it is incurred.

Development costs are also usually written off. However, if the criteria laid down by IAS 38 are satisfied, development expenditure can be capitalised as an **intangible asset**. If it has a **finite useful life**, it should then be amortised over that life.

2.1 Introduction to R & D

Large companies may spend significant amounts of money on research and development (R & D) activities. Obviously, any amounts so expended must be credited to cash and debited to an account for research and development expenditure. The accounting problem is **how to treat the debit balance on R & D account** at the reporting date.

There are two possibilities.

(a) The debit balance may be classified as an **expense** and transferred to the income statement. This is referred to as 'writing off' the expenditure. The argument here is that it is an expense just like rent or wages and its accounting treatment should be the same.

(b) The debit balance may be classified as an **asset** and included in the statement of financial position. This is referred to as 'capitalising' or 'carrying forward' or 'deferring' the expenditure. This argument is based on the accrual assumption. If R & D activity eventually leads to new or improved products which generate revenue, the costs should be carried forward to be matched against that revenue in future accounting periods.

So the main question surrounding research and development (R & D) costs is whether they should be treated as an expense or capitalised as an asset. This question is dealt with in IAS 38 *Intangible assets*.

2.2 Definitions

The following definitions are given by the standard.

Key terms

- An **intangible asset** is an identifiable non-monetary asset without physical substance . The asset must be:
  - controlled by the entity as a result of events in the past; and
  - something from which the entity expects future economic benefits to flow

- **Research** is original and planned investigation undertaken with the prospect of gaining new scientific or technical knowledge and understanding.

- **Development** is the application of research findings or other knowledge to a plan or design for the production of new or substantially improved materials, devices, products, processes, systems or services prior to the commencement of commercial production or use.

- **Amortisation** is the systematic allocation of the depreciable amount of an intangible asset over its useful life. Amortisation period and amortisation method should be reviewed at each financial year end.

- **Depreciable amount** is the cost of an asset, or other amount substituted for cost, less its residual value.

- **Useful life** is:
  (a) the period over which an asset is expected to be available for use by an entity; or
  (b) the number of production or similar units expected to be obtained from the asset by an entity.
  IAS 38 (revised)

Although these definitions are usually well-understood, **in practice** it may not be so easy to identify the activities encompassed by R & D and the dividing line between the categories may be indistinct. Identification often depends on the type of business involved, the projects it undertakes and how it is organised.

The standard gives examples of activities which might be included in either research or development, or which are neither but may be closely associated with both.

- **Research**
    - Activities aimed at obtaining new knowledge
    - The search for applications of research findings or other knowledge
    - The search for product or process alternatives
    - The formulation and design of possible new or improved product or process alternatives

- **Development**
    - The design, construction and testing of pre-production prototypes and models
    - The design of tools, jigs, moulds and dies involving new technology
    - The design, construction and operation of a pilot plant that is not of a scale economically feasible for commercial production
    - The design construction and testing of a chosen alternative for new/improved materials

2.3 Components of research and development costs

Research and development costs will include all costs that are **directly attributable** to research and development activities, or that can be **allocated on a reasonable basis.**

The standard lists the costs which may be included in R & D, where applicable (note that **selling costs are excluded**).

- **Salaries, wages** and other employment related costs of personnel engaged in R & D activities
- Costs of **materials and services** consumed in R & D activities
- **Depreciation** of property, plant and equipment to the extent that these assets are used for R & D activities
- **Overhead costs**, other than general administrative costs, related to R & D activities; these cost are allocated on bases similar to those used in allocating overhead costs to inventories (see IAS 2 *Inventories*)
- **Other costs**, such as the amortisation of patents and licences, to the extent that these assets are used for R & D activities

2.4 Recognition of R & D costs

The relationship between the R & D costs and the **economic benefit** expected to derive from then will determine the allocation of those costs to different periods. Recognition of the costs as an asset will only occur where it is probable that the cost will produce future economic benefits for the entity and where the costs can be measured reliably.

(a) In the case of **research costs**, this will not be the case due to uncertainty about the resulting benefit from them; and so they should be expensed in the period in which they arose.

(b) **Development activities** tend to be much further advanced than the research stage and so it may be possible to determine the likelihood of future economic benefit. Where this can be determined, the development costs should be carried forward as an asset.

2.4.1 Research costs

Research costs should be recognised as an **expense in the period in which they are incurred**. They should not be recognised as an asset in a later period.

2.4.2 Development costs

Alternative treatments are given for development costs, the use of which depends on the situation. Most of the time, development costs will be recognised as an **expense in the period in which they are incurred** unless the criteria for asset recognition identified below are met. Development costs initially recognised as an expense should not be recognised as an asset in a later period.

Development expenditure should be recognised as an asset only when the business can demonstrate **all** of the following. Where the criteria are met, development expenditure *must* be capitalised.

- The technical feasibility of **completing** the intangible asset so that it will be available for use or sale
- Its intention to complete the intangible asset and **use or sell** it
- Its **ability** to use or sell the intangible asset
- How the intangible asset will generate probable **future economic benefits**. Among other things, the entity should demonstrate the existence of a market for the output of the intangible asset itself or, if it is to be used internally, the usefulness of the intangible asset
- The availability of adequate technical, financial and other **resources** to complete the development and to use or sell the intangible asset
- Its ability to **measure reliably** the expenditure attributable to the intangible asset during its development

There is also an important point about the carrying amount of the asset and recoverability. The development costs of a project recognised as an asset should not exceed the amount that it is probable will be **recovered from related future economic benefits**, after deducting further development costs, related production costs, and selling and administrative costs directly incurred in marketing the product.

2.5 Amortisation of development costs

Once capitalised as an asset, development costs must be **amortised** and recognised as an expense to match the costs with the related revenue or cost savings. This must be done on a systematic basis, so as to reflect the pattern in which the related economic benefits are recognised.

It is unlikely to be possible to **match exactly** the economic benefits obtained with the costs which are held as an asset simply because of the nature of development activities. The entity should consider either:

(a)   The revenue or other benefits from the sale/use of the product/process
(b)   The period of time over which the product/process is expected to be sold/used

Point to note

> If the pattern cannot be determined reliably, the straight-line method should be used.

The amortisation will begin when the **asset is available for use**.

If the intangible asset is considered to have an *indefinite* useful life, it should not be amortised but should be subjected to an annual impairment review.

2.6 Impairment of development costs

As with all assets, impairment (fall in value of an asset) is a possibility, but perhaps even more so in cases such as this. The development costs should be **written down** to the extent that the unamortised balance (taken together with further development costs, related production costs, and selling and administrative costs directly incurred in marketing the product) is no longer probable of being recovered from the expected future economic benefit.

2.7 Disclosure

The standard has fairly extensive disclosure requirements for intangible assets. The financial statements should disclose the **accounting policies** for intangible assets that have been adopted.

For **each class of intangible assets** (including development costs), disclosure is required of the following.

- The **method of amortisation** used
- The **useful life** of the assets or the amortisation rate used
- The **gross carrying amount**, the **accumulated amortisation** and the **accumulated impairment losses** as at the beginning and the end of the period
- A **reconciliation of the carrying amount** as at the beginning and at the end of the period (additions, retirements/disposals, revaluations, impairment losses, impairment losses reversed, amortisation charge for the period, net exchange differences, other movements)
- The carrying amount of **internally-generated intangible assets**

Y Co is a research company which specialises in developing new materials and manufacturing processes for the furniture industry. The company receives payments from a variety of manufacturers, which pay for the right to use the company's patented fabrics and processes.

Research and development costs for the year ended 30 September 20X5 can be analysed as follows.

	$
Expenditure on continuing research projects	1,420,000
Amortisation of development expenditure capitalised in earlier years	240,000

New projects started during the year:

Project A   280,000

New flame-proof padding. Expected to cost a total of $800,000 to develop. Expected total revenue $2,000,000 once work completed - probably late 20X6

Project B   150,000

New colour-fast dye. Expected to cost a total of $3,000,000 to complete. Future revenues are likely to exceed $5,000,000. The completion date is uncertain because external funding will have to be obtained before research work can be completed.

Project C   110,000

Investigation of new adhesive recently developed in aerospace industry. If this proves effective then Y Co may well generate significant income because it will be used in place of existing adhesives.

	2,200,000

The company has a policy of capitalising all development expenditure where permitted by IAS 38.

Explain how the three research projects A, B and C will be dealt with in Y Co's income statement and statement of financial position.

In each case, explain your proposed treatment in terms of IAS 38 *Intangible assets* and, where relevant, in terms of the fundamental accounting assumptions of going concern and accruals, and the prudence concept.

Answer

Project A

This project meets the criteria in IAS 38 for development expenditure to be recognised as an asset. These are as follows.

(a)   The product or process is clearly defined and the costs attributable to the product or process can be separately identified and measured reliably.

(b)   The technical feasibility of the product or process can be demonstrated.

(c)   The entity intends to produce and market, or use, the product or process and has the ability to do so.

(d)   The existence of a market for the product or process or, if it is to be used internally rather than sold, its usefulness to the enterprise, can be demonstrated.

(e)   Adequate resources exist, or their availability can be demonstrated, to complete the project and market or use the product or process.

The capitalisation development costs in a company which is a going concern means that these are accrued in order that they can be matched against the income they are expected to generate.

Hence the costs of $280,000 incurred to date should be transferred from research and development costs to capitalised development expenditure and carried forward until revenues are generated; they should then be matched with those revenues.

Project B

Whilst this project meets most of the criteria discussed above which would enable the costs to be carried forward it fails on the requirements that 'adequate resources exist, or their availability can be demonstrated, to complete the project'.

Hence it would be prudent to write off these costs. Once funding is obtained the situation can then be reassessed and future costs may be capitalised.

Project C

This is a research project according to IAS 38, ie original and planned investigation undertaken with the prospect of gaining new scientific or technical knowledge or understanding.

There is no certainty as to its ultimate success or commercial viability and therefore it cannot be considered to be a development project. IAS 38 therefore requires that costs be written off as incurred.

Question
Y Co (2)

Show how the research and development costs in the previous question will be disclosed in the accounts of Y Co. Assume the cost of capitalised development expenditure brought forward is $1,480,000, and that accumulated amortisation of $240,000 was brought forward at the beginning of the year.

(a) Income statement
(b) Statement of financial position
(c) Notes to the accounts

Answer

(a) INCOME STATEMENT (EXTRACT)

	$
Research expenditure (Project C + 1,420,000)	1,530,000
Development costs (Project B)	150,000
Amortisation of capitalised development costs	240,000

(b) STATEMENT OF FINANCIAL POSITION (EXTRACT)

	$
Non current assets	
Intangible assets	
Deferred development costs	1,280,000

(c) NOTE TO ACCOUNTS

Deferred development costs

	$
Cost	
Balance b/f	1,480,000
Additions during year (Project A)	280,000
Balance c/f	1,760,000
Amortisation	
Balance b/f	240,000
Charge during year	240,000
Balance c/f	480,000
Net book value at 30 September 20X5	1,280,000
Net book value at 30 September 20X4	1,240,000

Exam focus point

There is an article on research and development in the *Student Accountant* dated 7 September 2007. You are recommended to read this article.

Chapter Roundup

- Expenditure on **research** must always be written off in the period in which it is incurred.

  Development costs are also usually written off. However, if the criteria laid down by IAS 38 are satisfied, development expenditure can be capitalised as an **intangible asset**. If it has a **finite useful life**, it should then be amortised over that life.

Quick Quiz

1   What is the required accounting treatment for expenditure on research?

    A   Write off as an expense in the period it is incurred

    B   Capitalise and carry forward as an asset

2   Which of the following items is an intangible asset?

    A   Land

    B   Patents

    C   Buildings

    D   Van

3   Research expenditure is incurred in the application of knowledge for the production of new products.

Is this statement

    A   True

    B   False

4   XY Co has development expenditure of $500,000. Its policy is to amortise development expenditure at 2% per annum. Accumulated amortisation brought forward is $20,000. What is the charge in the income statement for the year's amortisation?

    A $10,000

    B $400

    C $20,000

    D $9,600

5   Given the facts in 4 above, what is the amount shown in the statement of financial position for development expenditure?

    A $500,000

    B $480,000

    C $470,000

    D $490,000

Answers to Quick Quiz

1   A   Research expenditure is always written off as it is incurred.

2   B   All the others are tangible assets.

3   B   False. This is a definition of development expenditure.

4   A   2% × $500,000 = $10,000.

5   C   Deferred development expenditure b/f is $480,000 (cost $500,000 – accumulated depreciation $20,000), then deduct annual depreciation of $10,000 to give figure c/f of $470,000.

Now try the question below from the Exam Question Bank

Number	Level	Marks	Time
Q18	Examination	2	2 mins

11

Accruals and prepayments

Topic list	Syllabus reference
1 Accruals and prepayments	D7(a)–(e)

Introduction

In Chapter 8, we looked at the adjustments needed for inventory in cost of sales. This chapter deals with the adjustments which may need to be made to the **expenses** in the income statement.

Study guide

		Intellectual level
D7	**Accruals and prepayments**	
(a)	Understand how the matching concept applies to accruals and prepayments	1
(b)	Identify and calculate the adjustments needed for accruals and prepayments in preparing financial statements	1
(c)	Illustrate the process of adjusting for accruals and prepayments in preparing financial statements	1
(d)	Prepare the journal entries and ledger entries for the creation of an accrual or prepayment	1
(e)	Understand and identify the impact on profit and net assets of accruals and prepayments	1

Exam guide

These topics are very important and you are bound to have a question including accruals and prepayments.

1 Accruals and prepayments

FAST FORWARD

Accrued expenses (accruals) are expenses which relate to an accounting period but have not been paid for. They are shown in the statement of financial position as a liability.

Prepaid expenses (prepayments) are expenses which have already been paid but relate to a future accounting period. They are shown in the statement of financial position as an asset.

1.1 Introduction

We have already seen that the gross profit for a period should be calculated by **matching** sales and the cost of goods sold. In the same way, the net profit for a period should be calculated by charging the expenses which relate to that period. For example, in preparing the income statement of a business for a period of, say, six months, it would be appropriate to charge six months' expenses for rent and local taxes, insurance costs and telephone costs, etc.

Expenses might not be paid for during the period to which they relate. For example, a business rents a shop for $20,000 per annum and pays the full annual rent on 1 April each year. If we calculate the profit of the business for the first six months of the year 20X7, the correct charge for rent in the income statement is $10,000, even though the rent paid is $20,000 in that period. Similarly, the rent charge in the income statement for the second six months of the year is $10,000, even though no rent was actually paid in that period.

Key terms

Accruals or accrued expenses are expenses which are charged against the profit for a particular period, even though they have not yet been paid for.

Prepayments are payments which have been made in one accounting period, but should not be charged against profit until a later period, because they relate to that later period.

Accruals and prepayments might seem difficult at first, but the following examples should help to clarify the principle involved, that expenses should be matched against the period to which they relate. We can regard accruals and prepayments as the means by which we move charges into the correct accounting period. If we pay in this period for something which relates to the next accounting period, we use a prepayment to transfer that charge forward to the next period. If we have incurred an expense in this period which will not be paid for until next period, we use an accrual to bring the charge back into this period.

1.2 Example: Accruals

Horace Goodrunning, trading as Goodrunning Motor Spares, ends his financial year on 28 February each year. His telephone was installed on 1 April 20X6 and he receives his telephone account quarterly at the end of each quarter. On the basis of the following data, you are required to calculate the telephone expense to be charged to the income statement for the year ended 28 February 20X7.

Goodrunning Motor Spares – telephone expense for the three months ended:

	$
30.6.20X6	23.50
30.9.20X6	27.20
31.12.20X6	33.40
31.3.20X7	36.00

Solution

The telephone expenses for the year ended 28 February 20X7 are:

	$
1 March – 31 March 20X6 (no telephone)	0.00
1 April – 30 June 20X6	23.50
1 July – 30 September 20X6	27.20
1 October – 31 December 20X6	33.40
1 January – 28 February 20X7 (two months)	24.00
	108.10

The charge for the period 1 January – 28 February 20X7 is two-thirds of the quarterly bill received on 31 March. As at 28 February 20X7, no telephone bill has been received because it is not due for another month. However, it is inappropriate to ignore the telephone expenses for January and February, and so an accrued charge of $24 is made, being two-thirds of the quarter's bill of $36.

The accrued charge will also appear in the statement of financial position of the business as at 28 February 20X7, as a current liability.

1.3 Example: Accrual

Cleverley started in business as a paper plate and cup manufacturer on 1 January 20X2, making up accounts to 31 December 20X2. Electricity bills received were as follows.

	20X2	20X3	20X4
	$	$	$
31 January	–	6,491.52	6,753.24
30 April	5,279.47	5,400.93	6,192.82
31 July	4,663.80	4,700.94	5,007.62
31 October	4,117.28	4,620.00	5,156.40

What should the electricity charge be for the year ended 31 December 20X2?

Solution

The three invoices received during 20X2 totalled $14,060.55, but this is not the full charge for the year: the November and December electricity charge was not invoiced until the end of January. To show the correct charge for the year, it is necessary to **accrue** the charge for November and December based on January's bill. The charge for 20X2 is:

	$
Paid in year	14,060.55
Accrual ($^2/_3 \times$ $6,491.52)	4,327.68
	18,388.23

The double entry for the accrual (using the **journal**) will be:

DEBIT	Electricity account	$4,327.68
CREDIT	Accruals (liability)	$4,327.68

1.4 Example: Prepayment

A business opens on 1 January 20X4 in a shop which is on a 20 year lease. The rent is $20,000 per year and is payable quarterly in advance. Payments were made on what are known as the 'quarter-days' (except the first payment) as follows.

	$
1 January 20X4	5,000.00
25 March 20X4	5,000.00
24 June 20X4	5,000.00
29 September 20X4	5,000.00
25 December 20X4	5,000.00

What will the rental charge be for the year ended 31 December 20X4?

Solution

The total amount paid in the year is $25,000. The yearly rental, however, is only $20,000. The last payment was almost entirely a prepayment (give or take a few days) as it is payment in advance for the first three months of 20X5. The charge for 20X4 is therefore:

	$
Paid in year	25,000.00
Prepayment	(5,000.00)
	20,000.00

The double entry for this prepayment is:

DEBIT	Prepayments (asset)	$5,000.00
CREDIT	Rent account	$5,000.00

1.5 Double entry for accruals and prepayments

You can see from the double entry shown for both these examples that the other side of the entry is taken to an asset or a liability account.

- **Prepayments** are included in **receivables** in current assets in the statement of financial position. They are **assets** as they represent money that has been paid out in advance of the expense being incurred.
- **Accruals** are included in **payables** in **current liabilities** as they represent liabilities which have been incurred but for which no invoice has yet been received.

Transaction	DR	CR	Description
Accrual	Expense	Liability	Expense incurred in period, not recorded
Prepayment	Asset	(Reduction in) expense	Expense recorded in period, not incurred until next period

1.5.1 Reversing accruals and prepayments in subsequent periods

In each of the above examples, as with all prepayments and accruals, the double entry will be **reversed** in the following period, otherwise the organisation will charge itself twice for the same expense (accruals) *or* will never charge itself (prepayments). It may help to see the accounts in question.

ELECTRICITY ACCOUNT

20X2		$	20X2		$
30.4	Cash	5,279.47	31.12	Income statement	18,388.23
31.7	Cash	4,663.80			
31.10	Cash	4,117.28			
31.12	Balance c/d (accrual)	4,327.68			
		18,388.23			18,388.23
20X3			20X3		
31.1	Cash	6,491.52	1.1	Balance b/d	
30.4	Cash	5,400.93		(accrual reversed)	4,327.68
31.7	Cash	4,700.94	31.12	Income statement	21,387.87
31.10	Cash	4,620.00			
31.12	Balance c/d (accrual)	4,502.16			
		25,715.55			25,715.55

The income statement charge and accrual for 20X3 can be checked as follows.

Invoice paid		Proportion charged in 20X3	$
31.1.X3	6,491.52	1/3	2,163.84
30.4.X3	5,400.94	all	5,400.93
31.7.X3	4,700.94	all	4,700.94
31.10.X3	4,620.00	all	4,620.00
31.1.X4	6,753.24	2/3	4,502.16
Charge to income statement in 20X3			21,387.87

It should be clear to you here that the $5,000 rent prepaid in 20X2 will be added to by the payments in 20X3, and then reduced at the end of 20X3 in the same way.

Question

Accruals

Ratsnuffer is a business dealing in pest control. Its owner, Roy Dent, employs a team of eight who were paid $12,000 per annum each in the year to 31 December 20X5. At the start of 20X6 he raised salaries by 10% to $13,200 per annum each.

On 1 July 20X6, he hired a trainee at a salary of $8,400 per annum.

He pays his work force on the first working day of every month, one month in arrears, so that his employees receive their salary for January on the first working day in February, etc.

Required

(a) Calculate the cost of salaries which would be charged in the income statement of Ratsnuffer for the year ended 31 December 20X6.

(b) Calculate the amount actually paid in salaries during the year (ie the amount of cash received by the work force).

(c) State the amount of accrued charges for salaries which would appear in the statement of financial position of Ratsnuffer as at 31 December 20X6.

Answer

(a) Salaries cost in the income statement

	$
Cost of 8 employees for a full year at $13,200 each	105,600
Cost of trainee for a half year	4,200
	109,800

(b) *Salaries actually paid in 20X6*

	$
December 20X5 salaries paid in January (8 employees × $1,000 per month)	8,000
Salaries of 8 employees for January – November 20X6 paid in February – December (8 employees × $1,100 per month × 11 months)	96,800
Salaries of trainee (for July – November paid in August – December 20X6: 5 months × $700 per month)	3,500
Salaries actually paid	108,300

(c) *Accrued salaries costs as at 31 December 20X6*
(ie costs charged in the Income statement, but not yet paid)

	$
8 employees x 1 month x $1,100 per month	8,800
1 trainee x 1 month x $700 per month	700
	9,500

(d) *Summary*

	$
Accrued wages costs as at 31 December 20X5	8,000
Add salaries cost for 20X6 (Income statement)	109,800
	117,800
Less salaries paid	108,300
Equals accrued wages costs as at 31 December 20X6 (liability)	9,500

1.6 Example: Prepayments

The Square Wheels Garage pays fire insurance annually in advance on 1 June each year. The firm's financial year end is 28 February. From the following record of insurance payments you are required to calculate the charge to income statement for the financial year to 28 February 20X8.

Insurance paid

	$
1.6.20X6	600
1.6.20X7	700

Insurance cost for:

		$
(a)	The 3 months, 1 March – 31 May 20X7 (3/12 × $600)	150
(b)	The 9 months, 1 June 20X7 – 28 February 20X8 (9/12 × $700)	525
Insurance cost for the year, charged to the income statement		675

At 28 February 20X8 there is a prepayment for fire insurance, covering the period 1 March – 31 May 20X8. This insurance premium was paid on 1 June 20X7, but only nine months worth of the full annual cost is chargeable to the accounting period ended 28 February 20X8. The prepayment of (3/12 × $700) $175 as at 28 February 20X8 will appear as a current asset in the statement of financial position of the Square Wheels Garage as at that date.

In the same way, there was a prepayment of (3/12 × $600) $150 in the statement of financial position one year earlier as at 28 February 20X7.

Summary

	$
Prepaid insurance premiums as at 28 February 20X7	150
Add insurance premiums paid 1 June 20X7	700
	850
Less insurance costs charged to the income statement for the year ended 28 February 20X8	675
Equals prepaid insurance premiums as at 28 February 20X8 (asset)	175

Question

The Batley Print Shop rents a photocopying machine from a supplier for which it makes a quarterly payment as follows:

(a) Three months rental in advance
(b) A further charge of 2 pence per copy made during the quarter just ended

The rental agreement began on 1 August 20X4 and the first six quarterly bills were as follows.

Bills dated and received	Rental	Costs of copies taken	Total
	$	$	$
1 August 20X4	2,100	0	2,100
1 November 20X4	2,100	1,500	3,600
1 February 20X5	2,100	1,400	3,500
1 May 20X5	2,100	1,800	3,900
1 August 20X5	2,700	1,650	4,350
1 November 20X5	2,700	1,950	4,650

The bills are paid promptly, as soon as they are received.

(a) Calculate the charge for photocopying expenses for the year to 31 August 20X4 and the amount of prepayments and/or accrued charges as at that date.

(b) Calculate the charge for photocopying expenses for the following year to 31 August 20X5, and the amount of prepayments and/or accrued charges as at that date.

Answer

(a) *Year to 31 August 20X4* $

One months' rental (1/3 × $2,100) *	700
Accrued copying charges (1/3 × $1,500) **	500
Photocopying expense (Income statement)	1,200

*   From the quarterly bill dated 1 August 20X4
**   From the quarterly bill dated 1 November 20X4

There is a prepayment for 2 months' rental ($1,400) as at 31 August 20X4.

(b) *Year to 31 August 20X5*

	$	$
Rental from 1 September 20X4 – 31 July 20X5 (11 months at		
$2,100 per quarter or $700 per month)		7,700
Rental from 1 August – 31 August 20X5 (1/3 × $2,700)		900
Rental charge for the year		8,600
Copying charges:		
1 September – 31 October 20X4 (2/3 × $1,500)	1,000	
1 November 20X4 – 31 January 20X5	1,400	
1 February – 30 April 20X5	1,800	
1 May – 31 July 20X5	1,650	
Accrued charges for August 20X5 (1/3 × $1,950)	650	
		6,500
Total photocopying expenses (Income statement)		15,100

There is a prepayment for 2 months' rental ($1,800) as at 31 August 20X5.

	Rental charges	Copying costs
	$	$
Prepayments as at 31.8.20X4	1,400	
Accrued charges as at 31.8.20X4		(500)
Bills received during the year		
1 November 20X4	2,100	1,500
1 February 20X5	2,100	1,400
1 May 20X5	2,100	1,800
1 August 20X5	2,700	1,650
Prepayment as at 31.8.20X5	(1,800)	
Accrued charges as at 31.8.20X5		650
Charge to the income statement for the year	8,600	6,500
Financial position items as at 31 August 20X5		
Prepaid rental (current asset)	1,800	
Accrued copying charges (current liability)		650

1.7 Further example: Accruals

Willie Woggle opens a shop on 1 May 20X6 to sell hiking and camping equipment. The rent of the shop is $12,000 per annum, payable quarterly in arrears (with the first payment on 31 July 20X6). Willie decides that his accounting period should end on 31 December each year.

The rent account as at 31 December 20X6 will record only two rental payments (on 31 July and 31 October) and there will be two months' accrued rental expenses for November and December 20X6 ($2,000), since the next rental payment is not due until 31 January 20X7.

The charge to the income statement for the period to 31 December 20X6 will be for 8 months' rent (May-December inclusive) and so it follows that the total rental cost should be $8,000.

So far, the rent account appears as follows.

RENT ACCOUNT

		$			$
20X6			*20X6*		
31 July	Cash	3,000			
31 Oct	Cash	3,000	31 Dec	Income statement	8,000

2.21   To complete the picture, the accrual of $2,000 has to be put in, to bring the balance on the account up to the full charge for the year. At the beginning of the next year the accrual is reversed.

RENT ACCOUNT

		$			$
20X6			*20X6*		
31 July	Cash *	3,000			
31 Oct	Cash *	3,000			
31 Dec	Balance c/d (accruals)	2,000	31 Dec	Income statement	8,000
		8,000			8,000
			20X7		
			1 Jan	Balance b/d (accrual reversed)	2,000

* The corresponding credit entry would be cash if rent is paid without the need for an invoice – eg with payment by standing order or direct debit at the bank. If there is always an invoice where rent becomes payable, the double entry would be:

DEBIT	Rent account	$2,000	
CREDIT	Payables		$2,000

Then when the rent is paid, the ledger entries would be:

DEBIT	Payables	$2,000	
CREDIT	Bank		$2,000

The rent account for the *next* year to 31 December 20X7, assuming no increase in rent in that year, would be as follows.

RENT ACCOUNT

		$			$
20X7			*20X7*		
31 Jan	Cash	3,000	1 Jan	Balance b/d	
30 Apr	Cash	3,000		(accrual reversed)	2,000
31 Jul	Cash	3,000			
31 Oct	Cash	3,000			
31 Dec	Balance c/d (accruals)	2,000	31 Dec	Income statement	12,000
		14,000			14,000
			20X8		
			1 Jan	Balance b/d	
				(accrual reversed)	2,000

A full twelve months' rental charges are taken as an expense to the income statement.

1.8 Further example: Prepayments of income

Terry Trunk commences business as a landscape gardener on 1 September 20X5. He immediately decides to join his local trade association, the Confederation of Luton Gardeners, for which the annual membership subscription is $180, payable annually in advance. He paid this amount on 1 September. The Confederation makes up its accounts to 30 June each year.

In the first period to 30 June 20X6, Terry has paid a full year's membership, but only ten twelfths of the subscription should be charged to the period (ie $10/12 \times \$180 = \$150$). There is a prepayment of two months of membership subscription (ie $2/12 \times \$180 = \$30$).

The prepayment is recognised in the Confederation's ledger account for subscriptions. For simplicity, only Terry's subscription is shown. This is done in much the same way as accounting for accruals, by using the balance carried down/brought down technique.

DEBIT	Subscriptions account with prepayment as a balance c/d	$30	
CREDIT	Subscriptions account with the same balance b/d		$30

Remember that the prepaid subscription is a liability because, theoretically, this amount could be repaid to Terry.

The remaining expenses in the subscriptions account should then be taken to the income statement. The balance on the account will appear as a current liability (prepaid subscriptions) in the statement of financial position as at 30 June 20X6.

SUBSCRIPTIONS ACCOUNT

		$			$
20X6			*20X5*		
30 Jun	Income statement	150	1 Sept	Cash	180
30 Jun	Balance c/d				
	(prepayment)	30			
		180			180
			20X6		
			1 Jul	Balance b/d	
				(prepayment reversed)	30

The subscription account for the next year, assuming no increase in the annual charge, will be:

SUBSCRIPTIONS ACCOUNT

		$			$
20X7			**20X6**		
30 Jun	Income statement	180	1 Jul	Balance b/d	30
30 Jun	Balance c/d		1 Sep	Cash	180
	(prepayment)	30			
		210			210
			20X67		
			1 Jul	Balance b/d	
				(prepayment reversed)	30

Again, the charge to the income statement is for a full year's subscriptions. Remember that the prepaid subscription b/d is, theoretically, repayable if Terry ceases to be a member. Therefore it is a liability.

1.9 Effect on profit and net assets

You may find the following table a useful summary of the effects of accruals and prepayments.

	Effect on income/expenses	Effect on profit	Effect on assets/liabilities
Accruals	Increases expenses	Reduces profit	Increases liabilities
Prepayments	Reduces expenses	Increases profit	Increases assets
Prepayments of income	Reduces income	Reduces profit	Increases liabilities

Question   Income statement and statement of financial position

The Umbrella Shop has the following trial balance as at 30 September 20X8.

	$	$
Sales		156,000
Purchases	65,000	
Land & buildings – net book value at 30.9.X8	125,000	
Plant & machinery – net book value at 30.9.X8	75,000	
Inventory at 1.10.X7	10,000	
Cash at bank	12,000	
Trade accounts receivable	54,000	
Trade accounts payable		40,000
Selling expenses	10,000	
Cash in hand	2,000	
Administration expenses	15,000	
Finance expenses	5,000	
Carriage inwards	1,000	
Carriage outwards	2,000	
Capital account at 1.10.X7		180,000
	376,000	376,000

The following information is available:

(a)   Closing inventory at 30.9.X8 is $13,000, after writing off damaged goods of $2,000.

(b)   Included in administration expenses is machinery rental of $6,000 covering the year to 31 December 20X8.

(c)   A late invoice for $12,000 covering rent for the year ended 30 June 20X9 has not been included in the trial balance.

Prepare an income statement and statement of financial position for the year ended 30 September 20X8.

THE UMBRELLA SHOP
INCOME STATEMENT FOR THE YEAR END 30 SEPTEMBER 20X8

	$	$
Sales		156,000
Opening inventory	10,000	
Purchases	65,000	
Carriage inwards	1,000	
	76,000	
Closing inventory (W1)	13,000	
Cost of goods sold		63,000
Gross profit		93,000
Selling expenses	10,000	
Carriage outwards	2,000	
Administration expenses (W2)	16,500	
Finance expenses	5,000	
		33,500
Net profit for the period		59,500

THE UMBRELLA SHOP
STATEMENT OF FINANCIAL POSITION AS AT 30 SEPTEMBER 20X8

	$	$
Assets		
Non-current assets		
Land & buildings		125,000
Plant & machinery		75,000
		200,000
Current assets		
Inventory (W1)	13,000	
Trade accounts receivable	54,000	
Prepayments (W4)	1,500	
Cash at bank and in hand	14,000	
		82,500
		282,500
Capital and liabilities		
Proprietor's capital		
Balance brought forward	180,000	
Profit for the period	59,500	
		239,500
Current liabilities		
Trade account payable	40,000	
Accruals (W3)	3,000	
		43,000
		282,500

Workings

1   *Closing inventory*

As the figure of $13,000 is **after** writing off damaged goods, no further adjustments are necessary. Remember that you are effectively crediting closing inventory to the trading account of the income statement and the corresponding debit is to the statement of financial position.

2   Administration expenses

	$
Per trial balance	15,000
Add: accrual (W3)	3,000
	18,000
Less: prepayment (W4)	(1,500)
	16,500

3   Accrual

	$
Rent for year to 30 June 20X9	12,000
Accrual for period to 30 September 20X8 ($^{3}/_{12} \times \$12,000$)	3,000

4   Prepayment

	$
Machinery rental for the year to 31 December 20X8	6,000
Prepayment for period 1 October to 31 December 20X8 ($^{3}/_{12} \times \$6,000$)	1,500

Chapter Roundup

- **Accrued expenses (accruals)** are expenses which relate to an accounting period but have not yet been paid for. They are shown in the statement of financial position as a **liability**.

- **Prepaid expenses (prepayments)** are expenses which have already been paid but relate to a future accounting period. They are shown in the statement of financial position as an **asset**.

1   How is the cost of goods sold calculated?

    A   Opening inventory + purchases + closing inventory

    B   Opening inventory + closing inventory – purchases

    C   Opening inventory + purchases – closing inventory

    D   Closing inventory + purchases – closing inventory

2   Electricity paid during the year is $14,000. There was an opening accrual b/f of $500. A bill for the quarter ended 31 January 20X7 was $900. What is the electricity charge in the income statement for the year ended 31 December 20X6?

    A $14,000

    B $14,100

    C $13,900

    D $14,400

3   If a business has paid rent of $1,000 for the year to 31 March 20X9, what is the prepayment in the accounts for the year to 31 December 20X8?

    A $250

    B $750

4   What is the correct journal for an electricity prepayment of $500?

A	Debit:	prepayment	$500	
	Credit:	expense		$500
B	Debit:	expense	$500	
	Credit:	prepayment		$500

5   An accrual is an expense charged against profit for a period, even though it has not yet been paid or invoiced.

    Is this statement:

    A   True

    B   False

Answers to Quick Quiz

1   C

2   B

ELECTRICITY

	$		$
Cash	14,800	Accrual b/f	500
Accrual c/f (2/3 × 900)	600	Income statement	14,100
	14,600		14,600

3   A $^3/_{12} \times \$1,000 = \$250$

4   A   A prepayment needs to reduce the expense and set up an asset in the statement of financial position.

5   A   True.

Now try the questions below from the Exam Question Bank

Number	Level	Marks	Time
Q19	Examination	2	2 mins
Q20	Examination	2	2 mins

Irrecoverable debts and allowances

12

Topic list	Syllabus reference
1 Irrecoverable debts	D8(b)–(g)
2 Allowances for receivables	D8(h)–(i)
3 Accounting for irrecoverable debts and receivables allowances	D8(e)–(i)

Introduction

In this chapter we move even closer to our goal of preparing the financial statements. We look at two types of adjustment which need to be made in respect of credit sales.

- Irrecoverable debts
- Allowance for receivables

Important note:

In past exam papers you will see reference to 'allowance for doubtful receivables'. ACCA announced that this terminology would no longer be used, starting from the December 2005 sitting. The December 2005 exam referred to 'receivables allowances' or 'allowance for receivables' and that is the terminology used in this text.

In addition, 'bad debts' are now usually referred to as 'irrecoverable debts' (although you may see both terms used in the exam).

Study guide

		Intellectual level
D8	**Receivables and payables**	
(b)	Identify the benefits and costs of offering credit facilities to customers	1
(c)	Understand the purpose of an aged receivables analysis	1
(d)	Understand the purpose of credit limits	1
(e)	Prepare the bookkeeping entries to write off a bad (irrecoverable) debt	1
(f)	Record a bad (irrecoverable) debt recovered	1
(g)	Identify the impact of bad (irrecoverable) debts on the income statement and statement of financial position	1
(h)	Prepare the bookkeeping entries to create and adjust an allowance for receivables	1
(i)	Illustrate how to include movements in the allowable for receivables in the income statement and how the closing balance of the allowance should appear in the statement of financial position	1

Exam guide

This topic lends itself particularly well to MCQs. Such questions will often involve an adjustment for irrecoverable debts and receivables allowances.

1 Irrecoverable debts

FAST FORWARD

Irrecoverable debts are specific debts owed to a business which it decides are never going to be paid. They are written off as an expense in the income statement.

1.1 Introduction

Very few businesses expect to be paid immediately in cash, unless they are retail businesses on the high street. Most businesses buy and sell to one another on credit terms. This has the **benefit** of allowing businesses to keep trading without having to provide cash 'up front'. So a business will allow credit terms to customers and receive credit terms from its suppliers. Ideally a business wants to receive money from its customers as quickly as possible, but delay paying its suppliers for as long as possible. This can lead to problems.

Most businesses aim to control such problems by means of **credit control**. A customer will be given a **credit limit**, which cannot be exceeded (compare an overdraft limit or a credit card limit). If an order would take the account over its credit limit, it will not be filled until a payment is received.

Another tool in **credit control** is the **aged receivables analysis**. This shows how long invoices have been outstanding and may indicate that a customer is unable to pay. Most credit controllers will have a system of chasing up payment for long outstanding invoices.

Customers might fail to pay, perhaps out of dishonesty or because they have gone bankrupt and cannot pay. Customers in another country might be prevented from paying by the unexpected introduction of foreign exchange control restrictions by their country's government during the credit period. Therefore, the **costs** of offering credit facilities to customers can include:

(a)   Interest costs of an overdraft, if customers do not pay promptly.
(b)   Costs of trying to obtain payment.
(c)   Court costs.

For one reason or another, a business might decide to give up expecting payment and to write the debt off.

> An **irrecoverable debt** is a debt which is not expected to be paid.

1.2 Writing off irrecoverable debts

When a business decides that a particular debt is unlikely to be paid, the amount of the debt is **'written off'** as an expense in the income statement:

DR   IRRECOVERABLE DEBTS

CR   RECEIVABLES CONTROL ACCOUNT

Alfred's Mini-Cab Service sends an invoice for $300 to a customer who subsequently does a 'moonlight flit' from his office premises, never to be seen or heard of again. The debt of $300 must be written off. It might seem sensible to record the business transaction as:

Sales $(300 − 300) = $0.

However, irrecoverable debts written off are accounted for as follows.

(a)   **Sales** are shown at their invoice value in the **income statement**. The sale has been made, and gross profit should be earned. The subsequent failure to collect the debt is a separate matter, which is reported in the income statement under expenses.

(b)   **Irrecoverable debts** written off are shown as an **expense in the income and expense account**.

(c)   The credit entry removes the receivable from the receivables account. (We also need to update the personal account in the receivables ledger.)

In our example of Alfred's Mini-Cab Service:

	$
Sale (in the income statement)	300
Irrecoverable debt written off (expense in the I & E account)	300
Net profit on this transaction	0

Obviously, when a debt is written off, the value of the receivable as a current asset falls to zero. If the debt is expected to be uncollectable, its **'net realisable value'** is nil, and so it has a zero value in the statement of financial position.

1.3 Irrecoverable debts written off and subsequently paid

An irrecoverable debt which has been written off might occasionally be unexpectedly paid. Regardless of when the payment is received, the account entries are as follows.

DR   Cash account

CR   Irrecoverable debts expense

For example, an income statement for the Blacksmith's Forge for the year to 31 December 20X5 could be prepared as shown below from the following information.

	$
Inventory, 1 January 20X5	6,000
Purchases of goods	122,000
Inventory, 31 December 20X5	8,000
Cash sales	100,000
Credit sales	70,000
Irrecoverable debts written off	9,000
Debts paid in 20X5 which were previously written off as irrecoverable in 20X4	2,000
Other expenses	31,800

BLACKSMITH'S FORGE
INCOME STATEMENT FOR THE YEAR ENDED 31.12.20X5

	$	$
Sales		170,000
Opening inventory	6,000	
Purchases	122,000	
	128,000	
Less closing inventory	8,000	
Cost of goods sold		120,000
Gross profit		50,000
Expenses		
Irrecoverable debts written off (9,000 – 2,000)	7,000	
Other expenses	31,800	
		38,800
Net profit		11,200

2 Allowances for receivables

Allowances for receivables may be **specific** (an allowance against a particular receivable) or simply a percentage allowance based on past experience of irrecoverable debts. An increase in the allowance for receivables is shown as an expense in the income statement.

Trade receivables in the statement of financial position are shown **net** of any receivables allowance.

When irrecoverable debts are written off, specific debts owed to the business are identified as unlikely ever to be collected.

However, because of the risks involved in selling goods on credit, it might be accepted that a certain percentage of outstanding debts at any time are unlikely to be collected. But although it might be estimated that, say, 5% of debts will prove irrecoverable, the business will not know until later which specific debts are irrecoverable.

A business commences operations on 1 July 20X4, and in the twelve months to 30 June 20X5 makes sales of $300,000 (all on credit) and writes off irrecoverable debts amounting to $6,000. Cash received from customers during the year is $244,000, so that at 30 June 20X5, the business has outstanding receivables of $50,000.

	$
Credit sales during the year	300,000
Add receivables at 1 July 20X4	0
Total debts owed to the business	300,000
Less cash received from credit customers	244,000
	56,000
Less bad debts written off	6,000
Trade receivables outstanding at 30 June 20X5	50,000

Now, some of these outstanding debts might turn out to be bad. The business does not know on 30 June 20X5 which specific debts in the total $50,000 owed will be bad, but it might guess (from experience perhaps) that 5% of debts will eventually be found to be irrecoverable.

When a business expects irrecoverable debts amongst its current receivables, but does not yet know which specific debts will be irrecoverable, it can make an **allowance for receivables**.

Key term

An **allowance for receivables** is an estimate of the percentage of debts which are not expected to be paid.

An allowance for receivables provides for future irrecoverable debts, as a prudent precaution by the business. The business will be more likely to avoid claiming profits which subsequently fail to materialise because some debts turn out to be irrecoverable.

(a) When an allowance is first made, the amount of this initial allowance is charged as an expense in the income statement, for the period in which the allowance is created.

(b) When an allowance already exists, but is subsequently increased in size, the amount of the **increase** in allowance is charged as an **expense** in the income statement for the period in which the increased allowance is made.

(c) When an allowance already exists, but is subsequently reduced in size, the amount of the **decrease** in allowance is credited back to the income statement for the period in which the reduction in allowance is made.

Exam focus point

In an exam you may well be required to calculate the increase or decrease in the allowance for receivables.

The statement of financial position, as well as the income statement of a business, must be adjusted to show the allowance.

Important!

The value of trade accounts receivable in the statement of financial position must be shown after deducting the allowance for receivables.

This is because the net realisable value of all the receivables of the business is estimated to be less than their 'sales value'. After all, this is the reason for making the allowance in the first place. The net realisable value of trade accounts receivable is the total value of receivables minus receivables allowance. Such an allowance is an example of the **prudence concept**, discussed in detail in Chapter 3.

In the example above the newly created allowance for receivables at 30 June 20X5 will be 5% of $50,000 = $2,500. This means that although total trade accounts receivable are $50,000, eventual payment of only $47,500 is expected.

(a) In the income statement, the newly created allowance of $2,500 will be shown as an expense.

(b) In the statement of financial position, trade accounts receivable will be shown as:

	$
Total receivables at 30 June 20X5	50,000
Less allowance for receivables	2,500
	47,500

2.1 Example: Allowance for receivables

Corin Flakes owns and runs the Aerobic Health Foods Shop in Dundee. He commenced trading on 1 January 20X1, selling health foods to customers, most of whom make use of a credit facility that Corin offers. (Customers are allowed to purchase up to $200 of goods on credit but must repay a certain proportion of their outstanding debt every month.)

This credit system gives rise to a large number of irrecoverable debts, and Corin Flake's results for his first three years of operations are as follows.

Year to 31 December 20X1

Gross profit	$27,000
Irrecoverable debts written off	$8,000
Debts owed by customers as at 31 December 20X1	$40,000
Allowance for receivables	2½% of outstanding receivables
Other expenses	$20,000

Year to 31 December 20X2

Gross profit	$45,000
Irrecoverable debts written off	$10,000
Debts owed by customers as at 31 December 20X2	$50,000
Allowance for receivables	2½% of outstanding receivables
Other expenses	$28,750

Year to 31 December 20X3

Gross profit	$60,000
Irrecoverable debts written off	$11,000
Debts owed by customers as at 31 December 20X3	$30,000
Allowance for receivables	3% of outstanding receivables
Other expenses	$32,850

Required

For each of these three years, prepare the income statement of the business, and state the value of trade accounts receivable appearing in the statement of financial position as at 31 December.

Solution

AEROBIC HEALTH FOOD SHOP
INCOME STATEMENT FOR THE YEARS ENDED 31 DECEMBER

	20X1		*20X2*		*20X3*	
	$	$	$	$	$	$
Gross profit		27,000		45,000		60,000
Expenses:						
Irrecoverable debts written off	8,000		10,000		11,000	
Increase/decrease in allowance for receivables*	1,000		250		(350)	
Other expenses	20,000		28,750		32,850	
		29,000		39,000		43,500
Net profit/(loss)		(2,000)		6,000		16,500

*At 1 January 20X1 when Corin began trading the allowance for receivables was nil. At 31 December 20X1 the allowance required was 2½% of $40,000 = $1,000. The increase in the allowance is therefore $1,000. At 31 December 20X2 the allowance required was 2½% of $50,000 = $1,250. The 20X1 allowance must therefore be increased by $250. At 31 December 20X3 the allowance required is 3% × $30,000 = $900. The 20X2 allowance is therefore reduced by $350.

VALUE OF TRADE ACCOUNTS RECEIVABLE IN THE STATEMENT OF FINANCIAL POSITION

	As at 31.12.20X1	*As at 31.12.20X2*	*As at 31.12.20X3*
	$	$	$
Total value of receivables	40,000	50,000	30,000
Less allowance for receivables	1,000	1,250	900
Statement of financial position value	39,000	48,750	29,100

You should now try to use what you have learned to attempt a solution to the following exercise, which involves preparing an income statement and statement of financial position.

The financial affairs of Newbegin Tools prior to the commencement of trading were as follows.

NEWBEGIN TOOLS
STATEMENT OF FINANCIAL POSITION AS AT 1 AUGUST 20X5

	$	$
Assets		
Non-current assets		
Motor vehicle	2,000	
Shop fittings	3,000	
		5,000
Current assets		
Inventories	12,000	
Cash	1,000	
		13,000
		18,000
Equity and liabilities		
Equity		12,000
Current liabilities		
Bank overdraft	2,000	
Trade payables	4,000	
		6,000
Total capital and liabilities		18,000

At the end of six months the business had made the following transactions.

(a) Goods were purchased on credit at a gross amount of $10,000.

(b) Closing inventories were valued at $5,450.

(c) Cash sales and credit sales together totalled $27,250.

(d) Outstanding trade accounts receivable balances at 31 January 20X6 amounted to $3,250 of which $250 were to be written off.

(e) A further allowance for receivables is to be made amounting to 2% of the remaining outstanding receivables.

(f) Cash payments were made in respect of the following expenses.

		$
(i)	Stationery, postage and wrapping	500
(ii)	Telephone charges	200
(iii)	Electricity	600
(iv)	Cleaning and refreshments	150
(v)	Suppliers	8,000

(g) Cash drawings by the proprietor, Alf Newbegin, amounted to $6,000.

(h) The outstanding overdraft balance as at 1 August 20X5 was paid off. Interest charges and bank charges on the overdraft amounted to $40.

Alf Newbegin knew the balance of cash on hand at 31 January 20X6 but he wanted to know if the business had made a profit for the six months that it had been trading, and so he asked his friend, Harry Oldhand, if he could tell him.

Prepare the income statement of Newbegin Tools for the six months to 31 January 20X6 and a statement of financial position as at that date.

The income statement should be fairly straightforward.

NEWBEGIN TOOLS
INCOME STATEMENT FOR THE SIX MONTHS ENDED 31 JANUARY 20X6

	$	$
Sales		27,250
Opening inventories	12,000	
Purchases	10,000	
	22,000	
Less closing inventories	5,450	
Cost of goods sold		16,650
Gross profit		10,700
Electricity (note (a))	600	
Stationery, postage and wrapping	500	
Irrecoverable debts written off	250	
Allowance for receivables (note (b))	60	
Telephone charges	200	
Cleaning and refreshments	150	
Interest and bank charges	40	
		1,800
Net profit		8,900

Notes

(a) Expenses are grouped into sales and distribution expenses (here assumed to be electricity, stationery and postage, irrecoverable debts and allowance for receivables) administration expenses (here assumed to be telephone charges and cleaning) and finance charges.

(b) 2% of $3,000 = $60.

The preparation of a statement of financial position is not so easy, because we must calculate the value of trade accounts payable and cash in hand.

(a) *Trade accounts payable as at 31 January 20X6*

The amount owing on trade accounts is the sum of the amount owing at the beginning of the period, plus the cost of purchases during the period (net of all discounts), less the payments already made for purchases. If you think carefully about this, you might see that this calculation is logical. What is still owed is the total amount of costs incurred less payments already made.

	$
Accounts payable as at 1 August 20X5	4,000
Add purchases during the period	10,000
	14,000
Less payments to suppliers accounts during the period	(8,000)
	6,000

(b) *Cash at bank and in hand at 31 January 20X6*

This too requires a fairly lengthy calculation. You need to identify cash payments received and cash payments made.

(i) Cash received from sales

	$
Total sales in the period	27,250
Add trade accounts receivable as at 1 August 20X5	0
	27,250
Less unpaid debts as at 31 January 20X6	3,250
Cash received	24,000

(ii)   *Cash paid*

	$
Trade accounts payable	8,000
Stationery, postage and wrapping	500
Telephone charges	200
Electricity	600
Cleaning and refreshments	150
Bank charges and interest	40
Bank overdraft repaid	2,000
Drawings by proprietor	6,000
	17,490

Note. It is easy to forget some of these payments, especially drawings.

		$
(iii)	Cash in hand at 1 August 20X5	1,000
	Cash received in the period	24,000
		25,000
	Cash paid in the period	(17,490)
	Cash at bank and in hand as at 31 January 20X6	7,510

(c)   When irrecoverable debts are written off, the value of outstanding receivables must be reduced by the amount written off. This is because the customers are no longer expected to pay, and it would be misleading to show them in the statement of financial position as current assets of the business for which cash payment is expected within one year. Receivables will be valued at $3,000 less the allowance for receivables of $60 – ie at $2,940.

NEWBEGIN TOOLS
STATEMENT OF FINANCIAL POSITION AS AT 31 JANUARY 20X6

	$	$
Assets		
Non-current assets		
Motor vehicles	2,000	
Shop fittings	3,000	
		5,000
Current assets		
Inventory	5,450	
Trade accounts receivable	2,940	
Cash	7,510	
		15,900
		20,900
Equity and liabilities		
Equity		
Capital at 1 August 20X5	12,000	
Net profit for the period	8,900	
Less drawings	(6,000)	
Capital at 31 January 20X6		14,900
Current liabilities		
Trade accounts payable		6,000
Total capital and liabilities		20,900

The bank overdraft has now been repaid and is therefore not shown.

3 Accounting for irrecoverable debts and receivables allowances

3.1 Irrecoverable debts written off: ledger accounting entries

For irrecoverable debts written off, there is an irrecoverable debts account. The double-entry bookkeeping is fairly straightforward, but there are two separate transactions to record.

(a)   When it is decided that a particular debt will not be paid, the customer is no longer called an outstanding receivable, and becomes a irrecoverable debt.

   DEBIT   Irrecoverable debts account (expense)
   CREDIT   Trade accounts receivable

(b)   At the end of the accounting period, the balance on the irrecoverable debts account is transferred to the I & E ledger account (like all other expense accounts).

   DEBIT   I & E account
   CREDIT   Irrecoverable debts account.

However, where an irrecoverable debt is subsequently recovered, the accounting entries will be as follows.

   DEBIT   Cash account
   CREDIT   Irrecoverable debts account (expense)

3.2 Example: Irrecoverable debts written off

At 1 October 20X5 a business had total outstanding debts of $8,600. During the year to 30 September 20X6 the following transaction took place.

(a)   Credit sales amounted to $44,000.
(b)   Payments from various customers (accounts receivable) amounted to $49,000.
(c)   Two debts, for $180 and $420, were declared irrecoverable and the customers are no longer purchasing goods from the company. These are to be written off.

Required

Prepare the trade accounts receivable account and the irrecoverable debts account for the year.

Solution

TRADE ACCOUNTS RECEIVABLE

	$		$
Opening balance b/f	8,600	Cash	49,000
Sales	44,000	Irrecoverable debts	180
		Irrecoverable debts	420
		Closing balance c/d	3,000
	52,600		52,600
Opening balance b/d	3,000		

IRRECOVERABLE DEBTS

	$		$
Receivables	180	I & E a/c: irrecoverable debts written off	600
Receivables	420		
	600		600

In the receivables ledger, personal accounts of the customers whose debts are irrecoverable will be taken off the ledger. The business should then take steps to ensure that it does not sell goods on credit to those customers again.

3.3 Allowance for receivables: ledger accounting entries

FAST FORWARD Only **movement** on the receivables allowance is debited or credited to irrecoverable debts in the income statement.

A business might know from past experience that, say 2% of receivables balances are unlikely to be collected. It would then be considered prudent to make a general allowance of 2%. It may be that no particular customers are regarded as suspect and so it is not possible to write off any individual customer balances as irrecoverable debts. The procedure is then to leave the total receivables balances completely untouched, but to open up an allowance account by the following entries:

DEBIT   Irrecoverable debts account (expense)
CREDIT   Allowance for receivables

Important!

When preparing a statement of financial position, the credit balance on the allowance account is deducted from the total debit balances in the receivables ledger.

In subsequent years, adjustments may be needed to the amount of the allowance. The procedure to be followed then is as follows.

(a)   Calculate the new allowance required.

(b)   Compare it with the existing balance on the allowance account (ie the balance b/f from the previous accounting period).

(c)   Calculate increase or decrease required.

(i)   If a higher allowance is required now:

CREDIT   Allowance for receivables
DEBIT   Irrecoverable debts expense

with the amount of the increase.

(ii)   If a lower allowance is needed now than before:

DEBIT   Allowance for receivables
CREDIT   Irrecoverable debts expense

with the amount of the decrease.

3.4 Example: Accounting entries for allowance for receivables

Alex Gullible has total receivables outstanding at 31 December 20X2 of $28,000. He believes that about 1% of these balances will not be collected and wishes to make an appropriate allowance. Before now, he has not made any allowance for receivables at all.

On 31 December 20X3 his trade accounts receivable amount to $40,000. His experience during the year has convinced him that an allowance of 5% should be made.

What accounting entries should Alex make on 31 December 20X2 and 31 December 20X3, and what figures for trade accounts receivable will appear in his statements of financial position as at those dates?

Solution

At 31 December 20X2

Allowance required   = 1% × $28,000
                               = $280

Alex will make the following entries:

DEBIT	Irrecoverable debts expense	$280
CREDIT	Allowance for receivables	$280

Receivables will appear as follows under current assets.

	$
Receivables ledger balances	28,000
Less allowance for receivables	280
	27,720

At 31 December 20X3

Following the procedure described above, Alex will calculate as follows.

	$
Allowance required now (5% × $40,000)	2,000
Existing allowance	(280)
∴ Additional allowance required	1,720

He will make the following entries:

DEBIT	Irrecoverable debts expense	$1,720	
CREDIT	Allowance for receivables		$1,720

The allowance account will by now appear as follows.

ALLOWANCE FOR RECEIVABLES

20X2		$	20X2		$
31 Dec	Balance c/d	280	31 Dec	I & E account	280
20X3			20X3		
31 Dec	Balance c/d	2,000	1 Jan	Balance b/d	280
			31 Dec	I & E account	1,720
		2,000			2,000
			20X4		
			1 Jan	Balance b/d	2,000

Trade accounts receivable will be valued as follows.

	$
Receivables ledger balances	40,000
Less allowance for receivables	2,000
	38,000

In practice, it is unnecessary to show the total receivables balances and the allowance as separate items in the statement of financial position. Normally it shows only the net figure ($27,720 in 20X2, $38,000 in 20X3).

Now try the following question on allowance for receivables for yourself.

Question

Receivables allowance

Horace Goodrunning fears that his business will suffer an increase in defaulting receivables in the future and so he decides to make an allowance for receivables of 2% of outstanding trade receivables at the reporting date from 28 February 20X6. On 28 February 20X8, Horace decides that the allowance has been over-estimated and he reduces it to 1% of outstanding trade receivables. Outstanding receivables balances at the various reporting dates are as follows.

	$
28.2.20X6	15,200
28.2.20X7	17,100
28.2.20X8	21,400

You are required to show extracts from the following accounts for each of the three years above.

(a) Trade accounts receivable
(b) Allowance for receivables
(c) Income and expense account

Show how receivables would appear in the statement of financial position at the end of each year.

The entries for the three years are denoted by (a), (b) and (c) in each account.

TRADE ACCOUNTS RECEIVABLE (EXTRACT)

			$		$
(a)	28.2.20X6	Balance	15, 200		
(b)	28.2.20X7	Balance	17,100		
(c)	28.2.20X8	Balance	21,400		

ALLOWANCE FOR RECEIVABLES

			$			$
(a)	28.2.20X6	Balance c/d (2% of 15,200)	304	28.2.20X6	I & E account	304
			304			304
(b)	28.2.20X7	Balance c/d (2% of 17,100)	342	1.3.20X6	Balance b/d	304
				28.2.20X7	I & E account (note (i))	38
			342			342
(c)	28.2.20X8	I & E account (note (ii))	128	1.3.20X7	Balance b/d	342
	28.2.20X8	Balance c/d (1% of 21,400)	214			
			342			342
				1.3.20X8	Balance b/d	214

INCOME AND EXPENSE (EXTRACT)

		$			$
28.2.20X6	Allowance for receivables	304			
28.2.20X7	Allowance for receivables	38			
			28.2.20X8	Allowance for receivables	128

Notes

(i)   The increase in the allowance is $(342 – 304) = $38

(ii) The decrease in the allowance is $(342 – 214) = $128

(iii) We calculate the net receivables figure for inclusion in the statement of financial position as follows.

	20X6	20X7	20X8
	$	$	$
Current assets			
Trade accounts receivable	15,200	17,100	21,400
Less allowance for receivables	304	342	214
	14,896	16,758	21,186

Exam focus point

There was a question on irrecoverable debts and the allowance for receivables in the December 2008 exam. The examiner commented that this was one of the questions that was answered particularly badly. A similar question is shown below to demonstrate the correct technique.

3.5 Example: combined entries

Fatima's receivables at 31 May 20X7 were $723,800. The balance on the allowance for receivables account at 1 June 20X6 was $15,250. Fatima has decided to change the allowance for receivables to 1.5% of receivables at 31 May 20X7.

On 14 May 20X7 Fatima received $540 in final settlement of an amount written off during the year ended 31 May 20X6.

What total amount should be recognised for receivables in the income statement for the year ended 31 May 20X7?

The exam question gave four options for 2 marks. However we will concentrate on calculating the correct answer.

Solution

First, note the requirement's wording 'recognised for receivables in the income statement'. This means that the examiner wants to know the total charge (or recovery) in respect of irrecoverable debts and the allowance for receivables.

Secondly, consider the allowance for receivables.

	$
Closing provision required (723,800 × 1.5%)	10,857
Opening provision	(15,250)
Reduction needed	(4,393)

Thirdly, the amount received of $540 had already been written off the previous year and now needs to be credited to irrecoverable debts.

Total credit to I/S = 540 + 4,393

= 4,933

Chapter Roundup

- Irrecoverable debts are specific debts owed to a business which it decides are never going to be paid. They are written off as an expense in the income statement.

- Allowances for receivables may be **specific** (an allowance against a particular receivable) or simply a percentage allowance based on past experience of irrecoverable debts. An increase in the allowance for receivables is shown as an expense in the income statement.

  Trade receivables in the statement of financial position are shown **net** of any receivables allowance.

- Only **movement** on the receivables allowance is debited or credited to irrecoverable debts in the income statement.

Quick Quiz

1　An irrecoverable debt arises in which of the following situations?

   A   A customer pays part of the account

   B   An invoice is in dispute

   C   The customer goes bankrupt

   D   The invoice is not yet due for payment

2　Irrecoverable debts are $5,000. Trade accounts receivable at the year end are $120,000. If an allowance for receivables of 5% is required, what is the entry for irrecoverable debts and allowance for receivables in the income statement?

   A $5,000

   B $11,000

   C $6,000

   D $10,750

3　An allowance for receivables of 2% is required. Trade accounts receivable at the period end are $200,000 and the allowable for receivables brought forward from the previous period is $2,000. What movement is required this year?

   A   Increase by $4,000

   B   Decrease by $4,000

   C   Increase by $2,000

   D   Decrease by $2,000

4　If a receivables allowance is increased, what is the effect on the income statement?

   A   Reduction in expenses

   B   Increase in expenses

5　What is the double entry to record an irrecoverable debt written off?

   A   Debit: expenses   Credit: trade account receivable

   B   Debit: trade account receivable   Credit: expenses

Answers to Quick Quiz

1   C

2   B $5,000 + (5% × 120,000)

3   C   2% of $200,000 = $4,000. Therefore the allowable needs to be increased by $2,000.

4   B   The increase in the allowance is charged as an expense in the income statement.

5   A   DEBIT   Irrecoverable debts account (expenses)
               CREDIT   Trade accounts receivable

Now try the question below from the Exam Question Bank

Number	Level	Marks	Time
Q21	Examination	2	2 mins

Provisions and contingencies

Topic list	Syllabus reference
1 Provisions and contingencies (IAS 37)	D9(a)–(f)

Introduction

You are required here to consider accounting issues which are the subject of an international accounting standard (IAS 37).

IAS 37 is important standard that you will meet again later in your studies. At this stage, you need to understand the basic definitions and whether an item needs to be disclosed in the financial statements.

Study guide

		Intellectual level
D9	**Provisions and contingencies**	
(a)	Understand the definition of 'provision', 'contingent liability' and 'contingent asset'	1
(b)	Distinguish between and classify items as provisions, contingent liabilities or contingent assets	1
(c)	Identify and illustrate the different methods of accounting for provisions, contingent liabilities and contingent assets	1
(d)	Calculate provisions and changes in provisions	1
(e)	Account for the movement in provisions	1
(f)	Report provisions in the final accounts	1

Exam guide

These are extremely important topics that will feature in your future studies and so are highly likely to be examined.

Exam focus point

At the 2009 ACCA Teachers' Conference, the examiner highlighted areas that are consistently answered badly in the exam. Provisions are one of these areas, so make sure you study this chapter closely.

1 Provisions and contingencies (IAS 37)

1.1 Provisions

FAST FORWARD

A **provision** should be recognised

- When an entity has incurred a **present obligation**
- When it is **probable** that a **transfer of economics benefits** will be required to settle it
- When a **reliable estimate** can be made of the amount involved

IAS 37 views a provision as a liability.

Key terms

A **provision** is a **liability** of uncertain timing or amount.

A **liability** is an obligation of an entity to transfer economic benefits as a result of past transactions or events. *(IAS 37)*

The IAS distinguishes provisions from other liabilities such as trade payables and accruals. This is on the basis that for a provision there is **uncertainty** about the timing or amount of the future expenditure. Whilst uncertainty is clearly present in the case of certain accruals the uncertainty is generally much less than for provisions.

Rule of thumb

A provision is made for something which will *probably* happen. It should be recognised when it is probable that a transfer of economic events will take place and when its amount can be estimated reliably.

A provision is accounted for as follows:

DEBIT Expense account (I/S)
CREDIT Provision account (SOFP)

1.2 Example of provisions

A business has been told by its lawyers that it is likely to have to pay $10,000 damages for a product that failed. The business duly set up a provision at 31 December 20X7. However, the following year, the lawyers found that damages were more likely to be $50,000. How is the provision treated in the accounts at:

(a)   31 December 20X7?
(b)   31 December 20X8?

Solution

(a)   The business needs to set up a provision as follows:

DEBIT	Damages (I/S)	$10,000	
CREDIT	Provision (SOFP)		$10,000

EXTRACT FROM INCOME STATEMENT

	$
Expenses:	
:	
:	
Provision for damages	10,000

EXTRACT FROM STATEMENT OF FINANCIAL POSITION

	$
Non-current liabilities	
Provision for damages	10,000

(b)   The business needs to increase the provision.

DEBIT	Damages (I/S)	$40,000	
CREDIT	Provision (SOFP)		$40,000

Do not forget that the provision account has already got a balance brought forward of $10,000, so that we only need to account for the **increase** in the provision.

EXTRACT FROM INCOME STATEMENT

	$
Expenses:	
:	
:	
Provision for damages	40,000

EXTRACT FROM STATEMENT OF FINANCIAL POSITION

	$
Non-current liabilities	
Provision for damages (10,000 + 40,000)	50,000

1.3 Legal and constructive obligation

A provision is set up when there is a legal and constructive obligation. This means that the business is obliged to pay an amount as a result of this obligation. Examples include warranties, guarantees and sales returns.

Warranties are given on new items , for example cars, that they will be repaired free of charge if something goes wrong during an initial period of ownership, for example two years. Extended warranties may be granted on payment of a premium.

Guarantees may be given to a bank to help another company in a group to obtain a loan.

Sales returns may arise on a regular basis and it may be prudent to make a provision to cover these.

1.4 Example of sales returns

Apple Co has noticed that sales returns average 5% of sales during a year. It has decided to make a provision for these sales returns. During the year ended 30 April 20X8, sales are $500,000 and sales for the year ended 30 April 20X9 are projected to be $750,000. Set up a provision as at 30 April 20X8.

Solution

The provision is to be set up to meet **future** liabilities. It is likely that any returns for the year ended 30 April 20X8 have already been made. Therefore the provision must be based on projected sales for the following year ie 5% × $750,000 ($37,500).

1.5 Contingent liabilities

An entity should not recognise a **contingent asset or liability** but they should be disclosed.

Contingent liabilities are defined as follows.

Key term

IAS 37 defines a **contingent liability** as:

- A possible obligation that arises from past events and whose existence will be confirmed only by the occurrence or non-occurrence of one or more uncertain future events not wholly within the entity's control; or
- A present obligation that arises from past events but is not recognised because:
    - It is not probable that a transfer of economic benefits will be required to settle the obligation; or
    - The amount of the obligation cannot be measured with sufficient reliability.

As a rule of thumb, probable means more than 50% likely. **If an obligation is probable, it is not a contingent liability** – instead, a **provision is needed**.

1.6 Treatment of contingent liabilities

Contingent liabilities **should not be recognised in financial statements** but they **should be disclosed**. The required disclosures are:

- A brief description of the nature of the contingent liability
- An estimate of its financial effect
- An indication of the uncertainties that exist
- The possibility of any reimbursement

1.7 Contingent assets

Key term

IAS 37 defines a **contingent asset** as:

A possible asset that arises from past events and whose existence will be confirmed by the occurrence of one or more uncertain future events not wholly within the enterprise's control.

A contingent asset must not be recognised. Only when the realisation of the related economic benefits is **virtually certain** should recognition take place. At that point, **the asset is no longer a contingent asset!**

1.7.1 Disclosure: contingent liabilities

A **brief description** must be provided of all material contingent liabilities unless they are likely to be remote. In addition, provide

- An estimate of their **financial effect**
- Details of **any uncertainties**

1.7.2 Disclosure: contingent assets

Contingent assets must only be disclosed in the notes if they are **probable**. In that case a brief description of the contingent asset should be provided along with an estimate of its likely financial effect.

You must practise the questions below to get the hang of the IAS 37 rules on contingencies. But first, study the flow chart, taken from IAS 37, which is a good summary of its requirements.

Exam focus point

If you learn this flow chart you should be able to deal with most questions you are likely to meet in an exam.

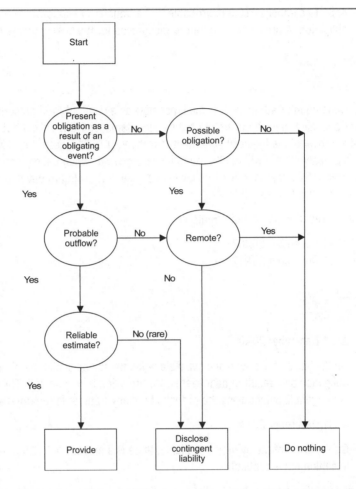

 Question   **Contingencies 1**

During 20X9 Smack Co gives a guarantee of certain borrowings of Pony Co, whose financial condition at that time is sound. During 20Y0, the financial condition of Pony Co deteriorates and at 30 June 20Y0 Pony Co files for protection from its creditors.

What accounting treatment is required:

(a)   at 31 December 20X9?
(b)   at 31 December 20Y0?

Answer

(a)   At 31 December 20X9

There is a present obligation as a result of a past obligating event. The obligating event is the giving of the guarantee, which gives rise to a legal obligation. However, at 31 December 20X9 no transfer of economic benefits is probable in settlement of the obligation.

No provision is recognised. The guarantee is disclosed as a contingent liability unless the probability of any transfer is regarded as remote.

An appropriate note to the accounts would be as follows.

Contingent liability

The company has given a guarantee in respect of the bank borrowings (currently $500,000) of Pony Co. At the reporting date, Pony Co was sound and it is unlikely that the company will be required to fulfil its guarantee.

(b) At 31 December 20Y0

As above, there is a present obligation as a result of a past obligating event, namely the giving of the guarantee.

At 31 December 20Y0 it is probable that a transfer of economic events will be required to settle the obligation. A provision is therefore recognised for the best estimate of the obligation.

Question

After a wedding in 20X0 ten people died, possibly as a result of food poisoning from products sold by Callow Co. Legal proceedings are started seeking damages from Callow but it disputes liability. Up to the date of approval of the financial statements for the year to 31 December 20X0, Callow's lawyers advise that it is probable that it will not be found liable. However, when Callow prepares the financial statements for the year to 31 December 20X1 its lawyers advise that, owing to developments in the case, it is probable that it will be found liable.

What is the required accounting treatment:

(a) At 31 December 20X0?
(b) At 31 December 20X1?

Answer

(a) At 31 December 20X0

On the basis of the evidence available when the financial statements were approved, there is no obligation as a result of past events. No provision is recognised. The matter is disclosed as a contingent liability unless the probability of any transfer is regarded as remote.

(b) At 31 December 20X1

On the basis of the evidence available, there is a present obligation. A transfer of economic benefits in settlement is probable.

A provision is recognised for the best estimate of the amount needed to settle the present obligation.

Question

An oil company causes environmental contamination in the course of its operations, but cleans up only when required to do so under the laws of the country in which it is operating. One country in which it has been operating for several years has up to now had no legislation requiring cleaning up. However, there is now an environmental lobby in this country. At the date of the company's year end, it is virtually certain that a draft law requiring clean up of contaminated land will be enacted very shortly. The oil company will then be obliged to deal with the contamination it has caused over the past several years.

What accounting treatment is required at the year end?

226   **13: Provisions and contingencies** │ Part D Recording transactions and events

At the year end there is a **present obligation** as a result of a **past obligating event**. Because the passage of the Act is 'virtually certain', the past contamination becomes an obligating event. It is highly probable that an **outflow of economic resources** will be required to settle this. A provision should therefore be made of the best estimate of the costs involved.

Chapter Roundup

- A **provision** should be recognised

    - When an entity has a **present obligation**
    - It is **probable** that a **transfer of economic benefits** will be required to settle it
    - A **reliable estimate** can be made of its amount

- An entity **should not recognise a contingent asset or liability**, but they **should be disclosed**.

Quick Quiz

1   A company is being sued for $10,000 by a customer. The company's lawyers reckon that it is likely that the claim will be upheld. Legal fees are currently $5,000.

How should the company account for this?

A   Provision
B   Contingent liability

2   Given the facts in 1 above, how much of a provision should be made if further legal fees of $2,000 are likely to be incurred?

A $10,000
B $5,000
C $15,000
D $12,000

3   A company has a provision for warranty claims b/f of $50,000. It does a review and decides that the provision needed in future should be $45,000. What is the effect on the financial statements?

	Income statement	Statement of financial position
A	Increase expenses by $5,000	Provision $50,000
B	Increases expenses by $5,000	Provision $45,000
C	Decrease expenses by $5,000	Provision $50,000
D	Decrease expenses by $5,000	Provision $45,000

4   A contingent liability is always disclosed on the face of the statement of financial position.

Is this statement

A   True
B   False

5   How does a company account for a contingent asset that is not probable?

A   By way of note
B   As an asset in the statement of financial position
C   It does nothing

Answers to Quick Quiz

1   A
2   D   The legal fees currently incurred of $5,000 is a current liability and should already be included in the accounts. The provision is for the claim of $10,000 plus the additional legal fees of $2,000.
3   D

PROVISION ACCOUNT

	$		$
I&E account	5,000	Bal b/f	50,000
Bal c/f	45,000		
	50,000		50,000

Note. We are debiting provision account $5,000 and so crediting income statement $5,000. Therefore, we are **decreasing** expenses.

4   B   False. A contingent liability is disclosed by way of notes to the statements.
5   C

Now try the question below from the Exam Question Bank

Number	Level	Marks	Time
Q22	Examination	1	1 min

Preparing a trial balance

Control accounts

14

Topic list	Syllabus reference
1 What are control accounts?	E3(b)
2 Discounts	D1(e), D8(k)
3 The operation of control accounts	D8(j), E3(c)
4 The purpose of control accounts	E3(a), (d)–(f)

Introduction

So far in this text we have assumed that the bookkeeping and double entry (and subsequent preparation of financial accounts) has been carried out by a business without any mistakes. This is not likely to be the case in real life: even the bookkeeper of a very small business with hardly any accounting entries to make will be prone to human error. If a debit is written as $123 and the corresponding credit as $321, then the books of the business are immediately out of balance by $198.

Once an error has been detected, it has to be corrected.

In this chapter and in the following two chapters we explain how errors can be **detected**, what kinds of error might **exist**, and how to post **corrections** and adjustments to produce final accounts.

Study guide

		Intellectual level
D1	**Sales and purchases**	
(e)	Account for discounts allowed and discounts received	1
D8	**Receivables and payables**	
(j)	Account for contras between trade receivables and payables	1
(k)	Prepare, reconcile and understand the purpose of supplier statements	1
E3	**Control accounts and reconciliations**	
(a)	Understand the purpose of control accounts for accounts receivable and payable	1
(b)	Understand how control accounts relate to the double entry system	1
(c)	Prepare ledger control accounts from given information	1
(d)	Perform control account reconciliations for accounts receivable and payable	1
(e)	Identify errors which would be highlighted by performing a control account reconciliation	1
(f)	Identify and correct errors in control accounts and ledger accounts	1

Exam guide

These are important topics. You are likely to find questions on control accounts in the exam. The questions will mainly be computational, although you could be asked to explain the reasons for keeping a control account.

1 What are control accounts?

FAST FORWARD

> A control account keeps a total record of a number of individual items. It is an **impersonal** account which is part of the double entry system.

Key terms

A **control account** is an account in the nominal ledger in which a record is kept of the total value of a number of similar but individual items. Control accounts are used chiefly for trade receivables and payables.

- A **receivables control account** is an account in which records are kept of transactions involving all receivables in total. The balance on the receivables control account at any time will be the total amount due to the business at that time from its receivables.
- A **payables control account** is an account in which records are kept of transactions involving all payables in total, and the balance on this account at any time will be the total amount owed by the business at that time to its payables.

Although control accounts are used mainly in accounting for receivables and payables, they can also be kept for other items, such as inventories, wages and salaries, and cash. The first important idea to remember, however, is that a control account is an account which keeps a total record for a collective item (eg receivables), which in reality consists of many individual items (eg individual trade accounts receivable).

A control account is an (impersonal) ledger account which will appear in the nominal ledger.

1.1 Control accounts and personal accounts

The personal accounts of individual customers of the business are kept in the receivables ledger, and the amount owed by each receivable will be a balance on his personal account. The amount owed by all the receivables together (ie all the trade account receivables) will be a balance on the receivables control account.

At any time the balance on the receivables control account should be equal to the sum of the individual balances on the personal accounts in the receivables ledger.

For example, a business has three trade accounts receivable: A Arnold owes $80, B Bagshaw owes $310 and C Cloning owes $200. The debit balances on the various accounts would be:

Receivables ledger (personal accounts)

	$
A Arnold	80
B Bagshaw	310
C Cloning	200
	590
Nominal ledger: receivables control account	590

What has happened here is that the three entries of $80, $310 and $200 were first entered into the sales day book. They were also recorded in the three personal accounts of Arnold, Bagshaw and Cloning in the receivables ledger – but remember that this is not part of the double entry system.

Later, the **total** of $590 is posted from the sales day book by a debit into the receivables (control) account and a credit to sales. If you add up all the debit figures on the personal accounts, they also total $590, as shown above.

2 Discounts

FAST FORWARD

Discounts can be defined as follows:

- **Trade discount** is a reduction in the list price of an article, given by a wholesaler or manufacturer to a retailer. It is often given in return for bulk purchase orders.

- **Cash discount** is a reduction in the amount payable in return for payment in cash, or within an agreed period

Before looking at control accounts for accounts receivable and payable, we need to consider the accounting treatment for discounts.

2.1 Types of discount

A discount is a reduction in the price of goods below the amount at which those goods would normally be sold to other customers. There are two types of discount.

- **Trade** discount
- **Cash discount**

Key term

> **Trade discount** is a reduction in the cost of goods owing to the nature of the trading transaction. It usually results from buying goods in bulk.

2.1.1 Examples of trade discount

(a)   A customer is quoted a price of $1 per unit for a particular item, but a lower price of 95 cents per unit if the item is bought in quantities of 100 units or more at a time.

(b)   An important customer or a regular customer is offered a discount on all the goods he buys, regardless of the size of each individual order, because the total volume of his purchases over time is so large.

Cash discount is a reduction in the amount payable to the supplier, in return for immediate payment in cash, rather than purchase on credit, or for payment within an agreed period.

For example, a supplier charges $1,000 for goods, but offers a discount of 5% if the goods are paid for immediately in cash.

For example, a supplier charges $1,000 to a credit customer for goods purchased, but offers a discount of 5% for payment within so many days of the invoice date.

2.2 Accounting for trade discounts

Trade discounts received are deducted from the cost of purchases. **Cash discounts received** are included as 'other income' of the period. **Trade discounts allowed** are deducted from sales and **cash discounts allowed** are shown as expenses of the period.

A trade discount is a reduction in the amount of money demanded from a customer.

(a)   If a trade discount is received by a business for goods purchased from a supplier, the amount of money demanded from the business by the supplier will be net of discount (ie it will be the normal sales value less the discount).

(b)   Similarly, if a trade discount is given by a business for goods sold to a customer, the amount of money demanded by the business will be after deduction of the discount.

Trade discounts should therefore be accounted for as follows.

(a)   **Trade discounts received** should be deducted from the gross cost of purchases. In other words, the cost of purchases in the trading account will be stated at gross cost minus discount (ie it will be stated at the invoiced amount).

(b)   **Trade discounts allowed** should be deducted from the gross sales price, so that sales for the period will be reported in the trading account at their invoice value.

2.3 Cash discounts received

When a business is given the opportunity to take advantage of a cash discount or a settlement discount for prompt payment, the decision as to whether or not to take the discount is a matter of financing policy, not of trading policy.

2.4 Example: Cash discounts received

A buys goods from B, on the understanding that A will be allowed a period of credit before having to pay for the goods. The terms of the transaction are as follows.

(a)   Date of sale: 1 July 20X6
(b)   Credit period allowed: 30 days
(c)   Invoice price of the goods: $2,000
(d)   Cash discount offered: 4% discount for prompt payment

A has the following choices.

(a)   Holding on to his money for 30 days and then paying the full $2,000.
(b)   Paying $2,000 less 4% – ie $1,920 now.

This is a financing decision about whether it is worthwhile for A to save $80 by paying its debts sooner, or whether it can employ its cash more usefully for 30 days, and pay the debt at the latest acceptable moment.

If A decides to take the cash discount, he will pay $1,920, instead of the invoiced amount of $2,000. The cash discount received ($80) will be accounted for in the books of A as follows.

(a)   In the purchases account, the cost of purchases will be at the invoiced price (or 'full trade' price) of $2,000. When the invoice for $2,000 is received by A, it will be recorded in his books of account at that price, and the subsequent financing decision about accepting the cash discount is ignored.

(b)   In the income and expense part of the income statement (which determines net profit or loss), the cash discount received is shown as though it were income received. There is no expense in the income statement from which the cash discount can be deducted, and so there is no alternative other than to show the discount received as income.

In our example

	$
Cost of purchase from B by A	2,000
Discount received (income in the I & E account)	(80)
Net cost	1,920

Question	Discounts

Soft Supplies Co recently purchased from Hard Imports Co 10 printers originally priced at $200 each. A 10% trade discount was negotiated together with a 5% cash discount if payment was made within 14 days. Calculate the following.

(a)   The total of the trade discount
(b)   The total of the cash discount

Answer

(a) $200 ($200 × 10 × 10%)
(b) $90 ($200 × 10 × 90% × 5%)

2.5 Cash discounts allowed

The same principle is applied in accounting for cash discounts or settlement discounts allowed to customers. Goods are sold at a trade price, and the offer of a discount on that price is a matter of financing policy for the business and not a matter of trading policy.

2.6 Example: Cash discounts allowed

X sells goods to Y at a price of $5,000. Y is allowed 60 days' credit before payment, but is also offered a discount of 2% for payment within 10 days of the invoice date.

X will issue an invoice to Y for $5,000 when the goods are sold. X has no idea whether or not Y will take advantage of the discount. In trading terms, and in terms of the amount charged in the invoice to Y, Y is a debtor for $5,000.

If Y subsequently decides to take the discount, he will pay $5,000 less 2% – ie $4,900 – ten days later. The discount allowed ($100) will be accounted for by X as follows.

(a)   In the trading account, sales will be valued at their full invoice price, $5,000.
(b)   In the income and expense account, the discount allowed will be shown as an expense.

In our example

	$
Sales	5,000
Discounts allowed (I & E account)	(100)
Net sales	4,900

You are required to prepare the income statement of Seesaw Timber Merchants for the year ended 31 March 20X6, given the following information.

	$
Purchases at gross cost	120,000
Trade discounts received	4,000
Cash discounts received	1,500
Cash sales	34,000
Credit sales at invoice price	150,000
Cash discounts allowed	8,000
Selling expenses	32,000
Administrative expenses	40,000
Drawings by proprietor, Tim Burr	22,000

Answer

SEESAW TIMBER MERCHANTS
INCOME STATEMENT
FOR THE YEAR ENDED 31 MARCH 20X6

	$	$
Sales (note 1)		184,000
Purchases (note 2)		116,000
Gross profit		68,000
Discounts received		1,500
		69,500
Expenses		
Selling expenses	32,000	
Administrative expenses	40,000	
Discounts allowed	8,000	
		80,000
Net loss transferred to statement of financial position		(10,500)

Notes

1 $(34,000 + 150,000)
2 $(120,000 – 4,000)
3 Drawings are not an expense, but an appropriation of profit.

Exam focus point

The June 2008 exam included a question on recording discounts allowed. Remember that only **cash discounts** are recorded in the books, sales and purchases are recorded **net of trade discounts**. This question included both cash and trade discounts, and the examiner commented that students showed a 'lack of knowledge in the treatment of discounts'.

2.7 Supplier statements

A supplier will usually send a monthly statement showing invoices issued, credit notes, payments received and discounts given. It is **vitally important** that these statements are compared to the supplier's personal account in the payables ledger. Any discrepancies need to be identified and any errors corrected.

A statement of account is reproduced below.

STATEMENT OF ACCOUNT

Pickett (Handling Equipment) Co
Unit 7, Western Industrial Estate
Dunford DN2 7RJ

Tel: (01990) 72101   Fax: (01990) 72980   VAT Reg No 982 7213 49

Accounts Department
Finstar Co
67 Laker Avenue
Dunford DN4 5PS

RECEIVED
1 JUN X1

Date: 31 May 20X1

A/c No: F023

Date	Details	Debit $	c	Credit $	c	Balance $	c
30/4/X1	Balance brought forward from previous statement					492	22
3/5/X1	Invoice no. 34207	129	40√			621	62
4/5/X1	Invoice no. 34242	22	72√			644	34
5/5/X1	Payment received - thank you			412	17√	232	17
17/5/X1	Invoice no. 34327	394	95√			627	12
18/5/X1	Credit note no. 00192			64	40√	562	72
21/5/X1	Invoice no. 34392	392	78			955	50
28/5/X1	Credit note no. 00199			107	64√	847	86

Amount now due						$	847	86

Terms: 30 days net, 1% discount for payment in 7 days. E & OE

Registered office: 4 Arkwright Road, London E16 4PQ Registered in England No 2182417

The statement is received on 1 June 20X1 and is passed to Linda Kelly who is the purchase ledger clerk at Finstar Co. Linda obtains a printout of the transactions with Pickett (Handling Equipment) Co from Finstar's purchase ledger system. (The reason why Linda has made ticks on the statement and on the printout which follows will be explained below.)

FINSTAR CO		**PURCHASE LEDGER**
ACCOUNT NAME:	PICKETT (HANDLING EQUIPMENT) CO	
ACCOUNT REF:	PO42	
DATE OF REPORT:	1 JUNE 20X1	

Date	Transaction	(Debit)/Credit $
16.03.X1	Invoice 33004	350.70
20.03.X1	Invoice 33060	61.47
06.04.X1	Invoice 34114	80.05
03.05.X1	Invoice 34207	129.40 ✓
04.05.X1	Payment	(412.17) ✓
06.05.X1	Invoice 34242	22.72 ✓
19.05.X1	Invoice 34327	394.95 ✓
19.05.X1	Credit note 00192	(64.40) ✓
28.05.X1	Payment	(117.77)
30.05.X1	Credit note 00199	(107.64) ✓
	Balance	337.31

The purchase ledger of Finstar shows a balance due to Pickett of $337.31, while Pickett's statement shows a balance due of $847.86.

2.7.1 Supplier statement reconciliations

Linda wants to be sure that her purchase ledger record for Pickett is correct and so she prepares a **supplier statement reconciliation**.

These are the steps to follow.

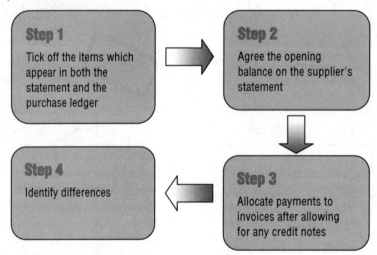

Step 1
Tick off the items which appear in both the statement and the purchase ledger

Step 2
Agree the opening balance on the supplier's statement

Step 3
Allocate payments to invoices after allowing for any credit notes

Step 4
Identify differences

2.7.2 Example: Supplier reconciliation

Linda applies the above steps to Pickett's statement.

Step 1   The common items have been ticked off on the statement and purchase ledger above.

Step 2   The balance brought forward at 30.4.X1 consists of three invoices.

	$
33004	350.70
33060	61.47
34114	80.05
	492.22

Step 3   Invoices 33004 and 33060 were paid on 4 May and 34114 was part of the payment on 28 May.

Step 4   Pickett's statement does not show the payment of $117.77 made on 28 May. However this is reasonable, as the cheque was probably still in the post. The statement also shows an invoice 34392 dated 21 May, which is not in the purchase ledger. This is surprising. Finstar needs to check if the invoice has been received (using the purchase day book), if so has it been posted to the wrong account? If it has not been received, Linda will need to contact Pickett and ask for a duplicate.

SUPPLIER STATEMENT RECONCILIATION
ACCOUNT: PICKETT (HANDLING EQUIPMENT) CO (PO42)

	$
Balance per supplier's statement	847.86
Less: Payment (28 May) not on statement	(117.77)
Invoice (supplier no 34392) on statement, not on purchase ledger	(392.78)
Balance per purchase ledger	337.31

2.7.3 The reasons for reconciling items

Reconciling items may occur as a result of the following items.

Reconciling item	Effect	Status
Payments in transit	A payment will go in the purchase ledger when the cheque is issued or when a bank transfer instruction is made. There will be delay (postal, processing) before this payment is entered in the records of the supplier. Any statement of account received by post will also be out of date by the length of time taken to deliver it.	Timing difference
Omitted invoices and credit notes	Invoices or credit notes may appear in the ledger of one business but not in that of the other due to error or omission. However, the most common reason will be a timing difference in recording the items in the different ledgers.	Error or omission or timing difference
Other errors	Addition errors can occur, particularly if a statement of account is prepared manually. Invoice, credit note or payment amounts can be misposted. Regular reconciliation of supplier statements will minimise the possibility of missing such errors.	Error

3 The operation of control accounts

FAST FORWARD

The two most important **control accounts** are those for **receivables** and **payables**. They are part of the double entry system.

3.1 Example: accounting for receivables

You might still be uncertain why we need to have control accounts at all. Before turning our attention to this question, it will be useful first of all to see how transactions involving receivables are accounted for by means of an illustrative example. Reference numbers are shown in the accounts to illustrate the cross-referencing that is needed, and in the example reference numbers beginning:

(a)   SDB, refer to a page in the sales day book
(b)   RL, refer to a particular account in the receivables ledger
(c)   NL, refer to a particular account in the nominal ledger
(d)   CB, refer to a page in the cash book

At 1 July 20X2, the Outer Business Company had no trade accounts receivable. During July, the following transactions affecting credit sales and customers occurred.

(a)   July 3: invoiced A Arnold for the sale on credit of hardware goods: $100

(b)   July 11: invoiced B Bagshaw for the sale on credit of electrical goods: $150

(c)   July 15: invoiced C Cloning for the sale on credit of hardware goods: $250

(d)   July 10: received payment from A Arnold of $90, in settlement of his debt in full, having taken a permitted discount of $10 for payment within seven days

(e)   July 18: received a payment of $72 from B Bagshaw in part settlement of $80 of his debt; a discount of $8 was allowed for payment within seven days of invoice

(f)   July 28: received a payment of $120 from C Cloning, who was unable to claim any discount

Account numbers are as follows:

RL 4 Personal account: A Arnold
RL 9 Personal account: B Bagshaw
RL 13 Personal account: C Cloning
NL 6 Receivables control account
NL 7 Discounts allowed
NL 21 Sales: hardware
NL 22 Sales: electrical
NL 1 Cash at bank

The accounting entries would be as follows.

SALES DAY BOOK

SDB 35

Date 20X2	Name	Ref.	Total $	Hardware $	Electrical $
July 3	A Arnold	RL 4 Dr	100.00	100.00	
11	B Bagshaw	RL 9 Dr	150.00		150.00
15	C Cloning	RL 13 Dr	250.00	250.00	
			500.00	350.00	150.00
			NL 6 Dr	NL 21 Cr	NL 22 Cr

Note. The personal accounts in the receivables ledger are debited on the day the invoices are sent out. The double entry in the ledger accounts might be made at the end of each day, week or month; here it is made at the end of the month, by posting from the sales day book as follows.

			$	$
DEBIT	NL 6	Receivables control account	500	
CREDIT	NL 21	Sales: hardware		350
	NL 22	Sales: electrical		150

CASH BOOK EXTRACT
RECEIPTS – JULY 20X2

CB 23

Date 20X2	Narrative	Ref.	Total $	Discount allowed $	Accounts receivable $
July 10	A Arnold	RL 4 Cr	90.00	10.00	100.00
18	B Bagshaw	RL 9 Cr	72.00	8.00	80.00
28	C Cloning	RL 13 Cr	120.00	–	120.00
			282.00	18.00	300.00
			NL 1 Dr	NL 7 Dr	NL 6 Cr

At the end of July, the cash book is posted to the nominal ledger.

		$	$
DEBIT	Cash at bank	282.00	
	Discount allowed	18.00	
CREDIT	Receivables control account		300.00

The personal accounts in the receivables ledger are memorandum accounts, because they are not a part of the double entry system.

MEMORANDUM RECEIVABLES LEDGER
ARNOLD

A/c no: RL 4

Date 20X2	Narrative	Ref.	$	Date 20X2	Narrative	Ref.	$
July 3	Sales	SDB 35	100.00	July 10	Cash	CB 23	90.00
					Discount	CB 23	10.00
			100.00				100.00

B BAGSHAW — A/c no: RL 9

Date 20X2	Narrative	Ref.	$	Date 20X2	Narrative	Ref.	$
July 11	Sales	SDB 35	150.00	July 18	Cash	CB 23	72.00
					Discount	CB 23	8.00
				July 31	Balance	c/d	70.00
			150.00				150.00
Aug 1	Balance	b/d	70.00				

C CLONING — A/c no: RL 13

Date 20X2	Narrative	Ref.	$	Date 20X2	Narrative	Ref.	$
July 15	Sales	SDB 35	250.00	July 28	Cash	CB 23	120.00
				July 31	Balance	c/d	130.00
			250.00				250.00
Aug 1	Balance	b/d	130.00				

In the nominal ledger, the accounting entries are made from the books of prime entry to the ledger accounts, in this example at the end of the month.

NOMINAL LEDGER (EXTRACT)
RECEIVABLES LEDGER CONTROL ACCOUNT — A/c no: NL 6

Date 20X2	Narrative	Ref.	$	Date 20X2	Narrative	Ref.	$
July 31	Sales	SDB 35	500.00	July 31	Cash and discount	CB 23	300.00
				July 31	Balance	c/d	200.00
			500.00				500.00
Aug 1	Balance	b/d	200.00				

Note. At 31 July the closing balance on the receivables control account ($200) is the same as the total of the individual balances on the personal accounts in the receivables ledger ($0 + $70 + $130).

DISCOUNT ALLOWED — A/c no: NL 7

Date 20X2	Narrative	Ref.	$	Date	Narrative	Ref.	$
July 31	Receivables	CB 23	18.00				

CASH CONTROL ACCOUNT — A/c no: NL 1

Date 20X2	Narrative	Ref.	$	Date	Narrative	Ref.	$
July 31	Cash received	CB 23	282.00				

SALES: HARDWARE — A/c no: NL 21

Date	Narrative	Ref.	$	Date 20X2	Narrative	Ref.	$
				July 31	Receivables	SDB 35	350.00

SALES: ELECTRICAL — A/c no: NL 22

Date	Narrative	Ref.	$	Date 20X2	Narrative	Ref.	$
				July 31	Receivables	SDB 35	150.00

If we take the balance on the accounts shown in this example as at 31 July 20X2, the trial balance is as follows.

	Debit	Credit
	$	$
Cash (all receipts)	282	
Receivables	200	
Discount allowed	18	
Sales: hardware		350
Sales: electrical		150
	500	500

The trial balance is shown here to emphasise the point that a trial balance includes the balances on control accounts, but excludes the balances on the personal accounts in the receivables ledger and payables ledger.

3.2 Accounting for payables

If you are able to follow the example above dealing with the receivables control account, you should have no difficulty in dealing with similar examples relating to purchases/payables. If necessary refer back to revise the entries made in the purchase day book and purchase ledger personal accounts.

3.3 Entries in control accounts

Typical entries in the control accounts are listed below. Reference 'Jnl' indicates that the transaction is first lodged in the journal before posting to the control account and other accounts indicated. References SRDB and PRDB are to sales returns and purchase returns day books.

RECEIVABLES CONTROL ACCOUNT

	Ref.	$		Ref.	$
Opening debit balances	b/d	7,000	Opening credit balances		
Sales	SDB	52,390	(if any)	b/d	200
Dishonoured bills or	Jnl	1,000	Cash received	CB	52,250
Cheques			Discounts allowed	CB	1,250
Cash paid to clear credit			Returns inwards from		
balances	CB	110	customers	SRDB	800
Interest changed on late					
paid accounts	Jnl	30	Irrecoverable debts	Jnl	300
Closing credit balances	c/d	90	Closing debit balances	C/d	5,820
		60,620			60,620
Debit balances b/d		5,820	Credit balances b/d		90

Note. Opening credit balances are unusual in the receivables control account. They represent debtors to whom the business owes money, probably as a result of the over-payment of debts or for advance payments of debts for which no invoices have yet been sent.

PAYABLES CONTROL ACCOUNT

	Ref.	$		Ref.	$
Opening debit balances			Opening credit balances	b/d	8,300
(if any)	b/d	70	Purchases	PDB	31,000
Cash paid	CB	29,840	Interest paid on overdue		
			accounts	CB	35
Discounts received	CB	35	Cash received clearing		
Returns outwards to	PRDB		debit balances	CB	25
suppliers		60	Closing debit balances		
Closing credit balances	c/d	9,400	(if any)	c/d	45
		39,405			39,405
Debit balances	b/d	45	Credit balances	b/d	9,400

Note. Opening debit balances in the payables control account would represent suppliers who owe the business money, perhaps because the business has overpaid or because a credit note is awaited for returned goods.

Posting from the journal to the memorandum receivables or payables ledgers and to the nominal ledger may be effected at the same time; as in the following example, where C Cloning has returned goods with a sales value of $50.

Journal entry	Ref.	Dr $	Cr $
Sales	NL 21	50	
To receivables control	NL 6		50
To C Cloning (memorandum)	RL 13	–	50
Return of electrical goods inwards			

3.4 Contra entries

Sometimes the same business may be both a receivable and a payable. For example, C Cloning buys hardware from you and you buy stationery from C Cloning. In the receivables ledger, C Cloning owes you $130. However, you owe C Cloning $250. You may reach an agreement to offset the balances receivable and payable. This is known as a 'contra'. The double entry is as follows:

DEBIT	Payables control	$130	
CREDIT	Receivables control		$130

You will also need to make the appropriate entries in the memorandum receivables and payables ledger. After this, C Cloning will owe you nothing and you will owe C Cloning $120 ($250 – $130).

Question	Payables control account

A payables control account contains the following entries:

	$
Bank	79,500
Credit purchases	83,200
Discounts received	3,750
Contra with receivables control account	4,000
Balance c/f at 31 December 20X8	12,920

There are no other entries in the account. What was the opening balance brought forward at 1 January 20X8?

Answer

PAYABLES CONTROL

	$		$
Bank payments	79,500	Balance b/f (balancing figure)	16,970
Discounts received	3,750	Purchases	83,200
Contra with receivables	4,000		
Balance c/f	12,920		
	100,170		100,170

Question

The total of the balances in a company's receivables ledger is $800 more than the debit balance on its receivables control account. Which one of the following errors could by itself account for the discrepancy?

A   The sales day book has been undercast by $800
B   Settlement discounts totalling $800 have been omitted from the nominal ledger
C   One receivables ledger account with a credit balance of $800 has been treated as a debit balance
D   The cash receipts book has been undercast by $800

Answer

A   The total of sales invoices in the day book is debited to the control account. If the total is understated by $800, the debits in the control account will also be understated by $800. Options B and D would have the opposite effect: credit entries in the control account would be understated. Option C would lead to a discrepancy of 2 × $800 = $1,600.

3.5 Summary of entries

It may help you to see how the receivables ledger and receivables control account are used, by means of a flowchart.

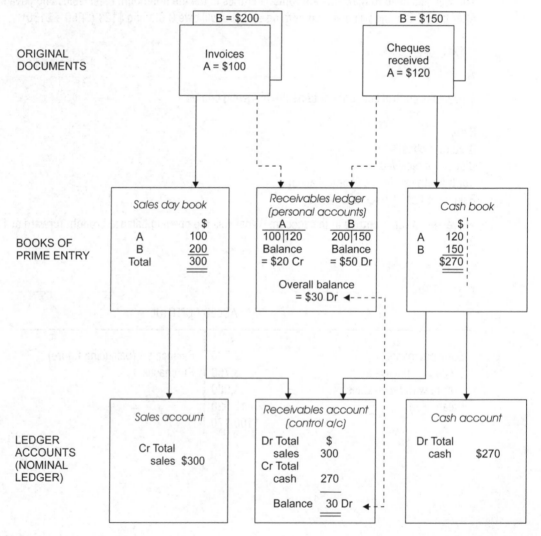

Notes

(a) The receivables ledger is not part of the double entry system (it is not used to post the ledger accounts).

(b) Nevertheless, the total balance on the receivables ledger (ie all the personal account balances added up) should equal the balance on the receivables control account.

Attention!

> The diagram shows the personal accounts being written up from the original documents. An alternative way is to transfer the information from the books of prime entry. The system shown has the advantage of helping to reduce errors (as an error made in the books of prime entry will not be transferred to the personal accounts and so will be spotted in the control account reconciliation).

See now whether you can do the following question yourself.

Question   Receivables and payables control accounts

On examining the books of Exports Co, you ascertain that on 1 October 20X8 the receivables ledger balances were $8,024 debit and $57 credit, and the payables ledger balances on the same date $6,235 credit and $105 debit.

For the year ended 30 September 20X9 the following particulars are available.

	$
Sales	63,728
Purchases	39,974
Cash from trade accounts receivable	55,212
Cash to trade accounts payable	37,307
Discount received	1,475
Discount allowed	2,328
Returns inwards	1,002
Returns outwards	535
Irrecoverable debts written off	326
Cash received in respect of debit balances in payables ledger	105
Amount due from customer as shown by receivables ledger, offset against amount due to the same firm as shown by payables ledger (settlement by contra)	434
Allowances to customers on goods damaged in transit	212

On 30 September 20X9 there were no credit balances in the receivables ledger except those outstanding on 1 October 20X8, and no debit balances in the payables ledger.

You are required to write up the following accounts recording the above transactions bringing down the balances as on 30 September 20X9:

(a) Receivables control account
(b) Payables control account

(a)

RECEIVABLES CONTROL ACCOUNT

20X8		$	20X8		$
Oct 1	Balances b/f	8,024	Oct 1	Balances b/f	57
20X9			20X9		
Sept 30	Sales	63,728	Sept 30	Cash received from	
				credit customers	55,212
	Balances c/f	57		Discount allowed	2,328
				Returns	1,002
				Irrecoverable debts	
				written off	326
				Contra payables	
				control account	434
				Allowances on goods	
				damaged	212
				Balances c/f	12,238
		71,809			71,809

(b)

PAYABLES CONTROL ACCOUNT

20X8		$	20X8		$
Oct 1	Balances b/f	105	Oct 1	Balances b/f	6,235
20X9			20X9		
Sept 30	Cash paid to credit		Sept 30	Purchases	39,974
	suppliers	37,307		Cash	105
	Discount received	1,475			
	Returns outwards	535			
	Contra receivables				
	control account	434			
	Balances c/f	6,458			
		46,314			46,314

4 The purpose of control accounts

FAST FORWARD

Cash books and day books are totalled periodically and the totals posted to the control accounts. At suitable intervals, the balances on the personal accounts are extracted and totalled. These balance totals should agree to the balance on the control account. In this way, errors can be located and corrected.

4.1 Reasons for having control accounts

The reasons for having control accounts are as follows.

(a) They provide a **check on the accuracy** of entries made in the personal accounts in the receivables ledger and payables ledger. It is very easy to make a mistake in posting entries, because there might be hundreds of entries to make. Figures can get transposed. Some entries might be omitted altogether, so that an invoice or a payment transaction does not appear in a personal account as it should. By comparing (i) and (ii) below, it is possible to identify that fact that errors have been made.

   (i) The total balance on the receivables control account with the total of individual balances on the personal accounts in the receivables ledger.

   (ii) The total balance on the payables control account with the total of individual balances on the personal accounts in the payables ledger.

(b) The control accounts also assist in the **location of errors**, where postings to the control accounts are made daily or weekly, or even monthly. If a clerk fails to record an invoice or a payment in a personal account, or makes a transposition error, it would be a formidable task to locate the error or errors at the end of a year, say, given the number of transactions. By using the control account, a comparison with the individual balances in the receivables or payables ledger can be made for every week or day of the month, and the error found much more quickly than if control accounts did not exist.

(c) Where there is a separation of clerical (bookkeeping) duties, the control account provides an **internal check**. The person posting entries to the control accounts will act as a check on a different person(s) whose job it is to post entries to the receivables and payables ledger accounts.

(d) To provide total receivables and payables balances more quickly for producing a trial balance or statement of financial position. A single balance on a control account is obviously **extracted more simply and quickly** than many individual balances in the receivables or payables ledger. This means also that the number of accounts in the double entry bookkeeping system can be kept down to a manageable size, since the personal accounts are memorandum accounts only.

However, particularly in computerised systems, it may be feasible to use receivables and payables ledgers without the need for operating separate control accounts. In such a system, the receivables or payables ledger printouts produced by the computer constitute the list of individual balances as well as providing a total balance which represents the control account balance.

4.2 Balancing and agreeing control accounts with receivables and payables ledgers

The control accounts should be **balanced regularly** (at least monthly), and the balance on the account agreed with the sum of the individual debtors' or suppliers balances extracted from the receivables or payables ledgers respectively. It is one of the sad facts of an accountant's life that more often than not the balance on the control account does not agree with the sum of balances extracted, for one or more of the following reasons.

(a) An **incorrect amount** may be **posted** to the control account because of a **miscast** of the total in the book of original entry (ie adding up incorrectly the total value of invoices or payments). The nominal ledger debit and credit postings will then balance, but the control account balance will not agree with the sum of individual balances extracted from the (memorandum) receivables ledger or payables ledger. A journal entry must then be made in the nominal ledger to correct the control account and the corresponding sales or expense account.

(b) A **transposition error** may occur in posting an individual's balance from the book of prime entry to the memorandum ledger, eg a sale to C Cloning of $250 might be posted to his account as $520. This means that the sum of balances extracted from the memorandum ledger must be corrected. No accounting entry would be required to do this, except to alter the figure in C Cloning's account.

(c) A transaction may be **recorded in the control account** and *not* **in the memorandum ledger**, or vice versa. This requires an entry in the ledger that has been missed out which means a double posting if the control account has to be corrected, and a single posting if it is the individual's balance in the memorandum ledger that is at fault.

(d) The sum of balances extracted from the memorandum ledger may be **incorrectly extracted or miscast**. This would involve simply correcting the total of the balances.

4.3 Example: Agreeing control account balances with the receivables and payables ledgers

Reconciling the control account balance with the sum of the balances extracted from the (memorandum) receivables ledger or payables ledger should be done in two stages.

(a) Correct the total of the balances extracted from the memorandum ledger. (The errors must be located first of course.)

	$	$
Receivables ledger total		
Original total extracted		15,320
Add difference arising from transposition error ($95 written as $59)		36
		15,356
Less		
Credit balance of $60 extracted as a debit balance ($60 × 2)	120	
Overcast of list of balances	90	
		210
		15,146

(b) Bring down the balance before adjustments on the control account, and adjust or post the account with correcting entries.

RECEIVABLES CONTROL ACCOUNT

	$		$
Balance before adjustments	15,091	Petty cash: posting omitted	10
		Returns inwards: individual posting omitted from control Account	35
		Balance c/d (now in agreement	
Undercast of total invoices issued		with the corrected total of	
in sales day book	100	individual balances in (a))	15,146
	15,191		15,191
Balance b/d	15,146		

 Question

April Showers sells goods on credit to most of its customers. In order to control its receivables collection system, the company maintains a receivables control account. In preparing the accounts for the year to 30 October 20X3 the accountant discovers that the total of all the personal accounts in the receivables ledger amounts to $12,802, whereas the balance on the receivables control account is $12,550.

Upon investigating the matter, the following errors were discovered.

(a) Sales for the week ending 27 March 20X3 amounting to $850 had been omitted from the control account.

(b) A customer's account balance of $300 had not been included in the list of balances.

(c) Cash received of $750 had been entered in a personal account as $570.

(d) Discounts allowed totalling $100 had not been entered in the control account.

(e) A personal account balance had been undercast by $200

(f) A contra item of $400 with the payables ledger had not been entered in the control account.

(g) An irrecoverable debt of $500 had not been entered in the control account.

(h) Cash received of $250 had been debited to a personal account.

(i) Discounts received of $50 had been debited to Bell's receivables ledger account.

(j) Returns inwards valued at $200 had not been included in the control account.

(k) Cash received of $80 had been credited to a personal account as $8.

(l) A cheque for $300 received from a customer had been dishonoured by the bank, but no adjustment had been made in the control account.

Required

(a) Prepare a corrected receivables control account, bringing down the amended balance as at 1 November 20X3.

(b)   Prepare a statement showing the adjustments that are necessary to the list of personal account
balances so that it reconciles with the amended receivables control account balance.

Answer

(a)   RECEIVABLES CONTROL ACCOUNT

	$		$
Uncorrected balance b/f	12,550	Discounts omitted (d)	100
Sales omitted (a)	850	Contra entry omitted (f)	400
Bank: cheque dishonoured (l)	300	Irrecoverable debt omitted (g)	500
		Returns inwards omitted (j)	200
		Amended balance c/d	12,500
	13,700		13,700
Balance b/d	12,500		

Note. Items (b), (c), (e), (h), (i) and (k) are matters affecting the personal accounts of customers.
They have no effect on the control account.

(b)   STATEMENT OF ADJUSTMENTS TO LIST OF PERSONAL ACCOUNT BALANCES

	$	$
Original total of list of balances		12,802
Add: debit balance omitted (b)	300	
debit balance understated (e)	200	
		500
		13,302
Less: transposition error (c): understatement of cash received	180	
cash debited instead of credited (2 × $250) (h)	500	
discounts received wrongly debited to Bell (i)	50	
understatement of cash received (k)	72	
		802
		12,500

Question   Payables control account

ABC has a payables control account balance of $12,500 at 31 December 20X6. However the extract of
balances from the payables ledger totals $12,800. Investigation finds the following errors: purchases for
week 52 of $1,200 had been omitted form the control account; a supplier account of $900 had been
omitted form the list of balances.

What is the correct payables balance at 31 December 20X6?

A $12,500
B $13,400
C $12,800
D $13,700

Answer

D   PAYABLES CONTROL

	$		$
		Bal b/f	12,500
Bal c/f	13,700	Purchases – week 52	1,200
	13,700		13,700

Corrected list of balances:

	$
Original	12,800
Omitted account	900
	13,700

- A control account keeps a total record of a number of individual items. It is an **impersonal** account which is part of the double entry system.

- Discounts can be defined as follows:

    - **Trade discount** is a reduction in the list price of an article, given by a wholesaler or manufacturer to a retailer. It is often given in return for bulk purchase orders.

    - **Cash discounts** is a reduction in the amount payable for the purchase of goods or services in return for payment in cash, or within an agreed period.

- **Trade discounts received** are deducted from the cost of purchases. **Cash discounts received** are included as 'other income' of the period in the income statement. **Trade discounts allowed** are deducted from sales and **cash discounts allowed** are shown as expenses of the period.

- The two most important **control accounts** are those for **receivables** and **payables**. They are part of the double entry system.

- Cash books and day books are totalled periodically and the totals posted to the control accounts. At suitable intervals, the balances on the personal accounts are extracted and totalled. These balance totals should agree to the balance on the control account. In this way, errors can be located and corrected.

Quick Quiz

1   Which of the following accounting items may have control accounts in the nominal ledger?
    (i)   Receivables and payables
    (ii)   Inventories
    (iii)   Cash
    (iv)   Salaries and wages
    A   (i) and (ii)
    B   (i), (ii) and (iv)
    C   (i), (ii) and (iii)
    D   (i), (ii), (iii) and (iv)

2   Sales of $4,000 have been omitted from the receivables control account. What is the entry to correct this?
    A   Debit RCA $4,000
    B   Credit RCA $4,000

3   During a period, A Co has the following transactions on receivables control account. Sales $125,000, cash received $50,000, discounts allowed $2,000. The balance carried forward is $95,000. What was the opening balance at the beginning of the period?
    A $22,000 debit
    B $22,000 credit
    C $18,000 debit
    D $20,000 debit

4   An invoice amount has been incorrectly posted to the sales day book. The memorandum accounts are posted direct from the invoices. A receivables control account reconciliation will reveal this error. True or false?

5   A transaction for $10,000 of sales offers 2% trade discount and 5% cash discount. If both discounts are claimed, how much is posted to discounts allowed?
    A $490
    B $690

Answers to Quick Quiz

1   D

2   A

3   A
RECEIVABLES CONTROL

	$		$
Bal b/f (bal figure)	22,000	Cash	50,000
Sales	125,000	Discounts allowed	2,000
		Bal c/f	95,000
	147,000		147,000

If you had answer B, you reversed the double entry and so produced a payables control account. In answer D, you omitted the discounts allowed figure; while in answer C you put discounts allowed on the debit instead of the credit side of the control account.

4   True.   However, if the memorandum accounts were posted from the sales day book, then the answer would be false.

5   A   The sale is recorded as $9,800 ($10,000 – $200 trade discount).
Discount allowed is then 5% × $9,800 = $490.

Now try the questions below from the Exam Question Bank

Number	Level	Marks	Time
Q23	Examination	2	2 mins
Q24	Examination	2	2 mins
Q25	Examination	2	2 mins
Q26	Examination	2	2 mins

15

Bank reconciliations

Topic list	Syllabus reference
1 Bank statement and cash book	E4(b)
2 The bank reconciliation	E4(a), (c)–(f)
3 Worked examples	E4(c)–(f)

Introduction

It is very likely that you will have had to do bank reconciliation at work. If not, you will probably have done one on your own bank account without even being aware of it.

The first two sections of this chapter explain why we need a bank reconciliation, and the sort of differences that need to be reconciled.
The third section takes you through some examples of increasing complexity.

Study guide

		Intellectual level
E4	**Bank reconciliations**	
(a)	Understand the purpose of bank reconciliations	1
(b)	Identify the main reasons for differences between the cash book and the bank statement	1
(c)	Correct cash book errors and/or omissions	1
(d)	Prepare bank reconciliation statements	1
(e)	Derive bank statements and cash bank balances from given information	1
(f)	Identify the bank balance to be reported in the final accounts	1

Exam guide

You are extremely likely to have a bank reconciliation question in the exam.

1 Bank statement and cash book

FAST FORWARD

In theory, the entries appearing on a business's **bank statement** should be exactly the same as those in the business cash book. The balance shown by the bank statement should be the same as the **cash book** balance on the same date.

The cash book of a business is the record of **how much cash the business believes** that it **has in the bank**. In the same way, you might keep a private record of how much you think you have in your own bank account, perhaps by making a note in your cheque book of income received and the cheques you write. If you do keep such a record, you will probably agree that your bank statement balance is rarely exactly the same as your own figure.

Why might your own estimate of your bank balance be different from the amount shown on your bank statement? There are three common explanations.

(a) **Error**. Errors in calculation, or recording income and payments, are more likely to have been made by you than by the bank, but it is conceivable that the bank has made a mistake too.

(b) **Bank charges or bank interest**. The bank might deduct charges for interest on an overdraft or for its services, which you are not informed about until you receive the bank statement.

(c) **Time differences**

   (i) There might be some cheques that you have received and paid into the bank, but which have not yet been 'cleared' and added to your account. So although your own records show that some cash has been added to your account, it has not yet been acknowledged by the bank – although it will be soon once the cheque has cleared.

   (ii) Similarly, you might have made some payments by cheque, and reduced the balance in your account in the record that you keep, but the person who receives the cheque might not bank it for a while. Even when it is banked, it takes a day or two for the banks to process it and for the money to be deducted from your account.

If you do keep a personal record of your cash position at the bank, and if you do check your periodic bank statements against what you think you should have in your account, you will be doing a bank reconciliation.

> A **bank reconciliation** is a comparison of a bank statement (sent monthly, weekly or even daily by the bank) with the cash book. Differences between the balance on the bank statement and the balance in the cash book will be errors or timing differences, and they should be identified and satisfactorily explained.

2 The bank reconciliation

FAST FORWARD

Differences between the cash book and the bank statement arise for three reasons:

- Errors – usually in the cash book
- Omissions – such as bank charges not posted in the cash book
- Timing differences – such as unpresented cheques

2.1 The bank statement

It is a common practice for a business to issue a monthly statement to each credit customer, itemising:

(a)   The **balance** owed at the **beginning** of the month
(b)   **New debts** incurred during the month
(c)   **Payments** made during the month
(d)   The **balance** owed at the **end** of the month

In the same way, a bank statement is sent by a bank to its short-term receivables and payables – ie customers with bank overdrafts and customers with money in their account – itemising the balance on the account at the beginning of the period, receipts into the account and payments from the account during the period, and the balance at the end of the period.

It is necessary to remember, however, that if a customer has money in his account, the bank owes him that money, and the customer is therefore a **payable** of the bank (hence the phrase 'to be in credit' means to have money in your account). This means that if a business has $8,000 cash in the bank, it will have a debit balance in its own cash book, but the bank statement, if it reconciles exactly with the cash book, will state that there is a credit balance of $8,000. *(The bank's records are a 'mirror image' of the customer's own records, with debits and credits reversed.)*

2.2 Why is a bank reconciliation necessary?

A bank reconciliation is needed to identify and account for the differences between the cash book and the bank statement.

Question

Differences

These differences fall into three categories. What are they?

Answer

Look back to the beginning of this section.

2.3 What to look for when doing a bank reconciliation

The cash book and bank statement will rarely agree at a given date. If you are doing a bank reconciliation, you may have to look for the following items.

(a)   **Corrections and adjustments to the cash book**

   (i)   Payments made into the account or from the account by way of standing order, which have not yet been entered in the cash book.

(ii)   Dividends received (on investments held by the business), paid direct into the bank account but not yet entered in the cash book.

(iii)   Bank interest and bank charges, not yet entered in the cash book.

(b)   **Items reconciling the correct cash book balance to the bank statement**

(i)   Cheques drawn (ie paid) by the business and credited in the cash book, which have not yet been presented to the bank, or 'cleared', and so do not yet appear on the bank statement.

(ii)   Cheques received by the business, paid into the bank and debited in the cash book, but which have not yet been cleared and entered in the account by the bank, and so do not yet appear on the bank statement.

Exam focus point

You are likely to have a bank reconciliation question. You may have to adjust the cash book, the bank balance or both.

3 Worked examples

FAST FORWARD

When the differences between the bank statement and the cash book are identified, the cash book must be corrected for any errors or omissions. Any remaining difference can then be shown to be due to timing differences.

3.1 Example: Bank reconciliation

At 30 September 20X6, the balance in the cash book of Wordsworth Co was $805.15 debit. A bank statement on 30 September 20X6 showed Wordsworth Co to be in credit by $1,112.30.

On investigation of the difference between the two sums, it was established that:

(a)   The cash book had been undercast by $90.00 on the debit side*.

(b)   Cheques paid in not yet credited by the bank amounted to $208.20, called outstanding lodgements.

(c)   Cheques drawn not yet presented to the bank amounted to $425.35 called unpresented cheques.

* Note. 'Casting' is an accountant's term for adding up.

Required

(a)   Show the correction to the cash book.

(b)   Prepare a statement reconciling the balance per bank statement to the balance per cash book.

Solution

(a)

	$
Cash book balance brought forward	805.15
Add	
Correction of undercast	90.00
Corrected balance	895.15

(b)

	$
Balance per bank statement	1,112.30
Add	
Outstanding lodgements	208.20
	1,320.50
Less	
Unpresented cheques	(425.35)
Balance per cash book	895.15

Question

On 31 January 20X8 a company's cash book showed a credit balance of $150 on its current account which did not agree with the bank statement balance. In performing the reconciliation the following points come to light.

	$
Not recorded in the cash book	
Bank charges	36
Transfer from deposit account to current account	500
Not recorded on the bank statement	
Unpresented cheques	116
Outstanding lodgements	630

It was also discovered that the bank had debited the company's account with a cheque for $400 in error. What was the original balance on the bank statement?

Answer

CASH ACCOUNT

	$		$
		Balance b/d	150
Transfer from deposit a/c	500	Charges	36
		Balance c/d	314
	500		500

	$
Balance per cash book	314
Add unpresented cheques	116
Less outstanding lodgements	(630)
Less error by bank*	(400)
Balance per bank statement	(600)

*Note that, on the bank statement, a debit is a payment out of the account.

Exam focus point

You may well be asked to reconstruct opening figures in the exam. If so, then you may need to reverse the usual workings, as illustrated in the example above.

Question

A company's bank statement shows $715 direct debits and $353 investment income not recorded in the cash book. The bank statement does not show a customer's cheque for $875 entered in the cash book on the last day of the accounting period. If the cash book shows a credit balance of $610 what balance appears on the bank statement?

A $1,847 debit
B $1,847 credit
C $972 credit
D $972 debit

A

	$	$
Balance per cash book		(610)
Items on statement, not in cash book		
Direct debits	(715)	
Investment income	353	
		(362)
Corrected balance per cash book		(972)
Item in cash book not on statement:		
Customer's cheque		(875)
Balance per bank statement		(1,847)

As the balance is overdrawn, this is a debit on the bank statement.

Question
Bank balance

Given the facts in the question above, what is the figure for the bank balance to be reported in the final accounts?

A $1,847 credit
B $972 credit
C $972 debit
D $1,847 debit

Answer

B   The figure to go in the statement of financial position is the corrected cash book figure. This is $972 credit (or overdrawn). So the bank figure will appear in liabilities.

3.2 Example: More complicated bank reconciliation

On 30 June 20X0, Cook's cash book showed that he had an overdraft of $300 on his current account at the bank. A bank statement as at the end of June 20X0 showed that Cook was in credit with the bank by $65.

On checking the cash book with the bank statement you find the following.

(a)   Cheques drawn, amounting to $500, had been entered in the cash book but had not been presented.

(b)   Cheques received, amounting to $400, had been entered in the cash book, but had not been credited by the bank.

(c)   On instructions from Cook the bank had transferred interest received on his deposit account amounting to $60 to his current account, recording the transfer on 5 July 20X0. This amount had, however, been credited in the cash book as on 30 June 20X0.

(d)   Bank charges of $35 shown in the bank statement had not been entered in the cash book.

(e)   The payments side of the cash book had been undercast by $10.

(f)   Dividends received amounting to $200 had been paid direct to the bank and not entered in the cash book.

(g)   A cheque for $50 drawn on deposit account had been shown in the cash book as drawn on current account.

(h)   A cheque issued to Jones for $25 was replaced when out of date. It was entered again in the cash book, no other entry being made. Both cheques were included in the total of unpresented cheques shown above.

Required

(a) Indicate the appropriate adjustments in the cash book.

(b) Prepare a statement reconciling the amended balance with that shown in the bank statement.

Solution

(a) The errors to correct are given in notes (c) (e) (f) (g) and (h) of the problem. Bank charges (note (d)) also call for an adjustment.

(Note that debit entries add to the cash balance and credit entries are deductions from the cash balance)

		Adjustments in cash book	
		Debit	Credit
		$	$
Item			
(c)	Cash book incorrectly credited with interest on 30 June It should have been debited with the receipt	60	
(c)	Debit cash book (current a/c) with transfer of interest from deposit a/c (note 1)	60	
(d)	Bank charges		35
(e)	Undercast on payments (credit) side of cash book		10
(f)	Dividends received should be debited in the cash book	200	
(g)	Cheque drawn on deposit account, not current account. Add cash back to current account	50	
(h)	Cheque paid to Jones is out of date and so cancelled. Cash book should now be debited, since previous credit entry is no longer valid (note 2)	25	
		395	45

	$	$
Cash book: balance on current account as at 30 June 20X0		(300)
Adjustments and corrections:		
Debit entries (adding to cash)	395	
Credit entries (reducing cash balance)	(45)	
Net adjustments		350
Corrected balance in the cash book		50

Notes

1 Item (c) is rather complicated. The transfer of interest from the deposit to the current account was presumably given as an instruction to the bank on or before 30 June 20X0. Since the correct entry is to debit the current account (and credit the deposit account) the correction in the cash book should be to debit the current account with $2 \times \$60 = \$120$ – ie to cancel out the incorrect credit entry in the cash book and then to make the correct debit entry. However, the bank does not record the transfer until 5 July, and so it will not appear in the bank statement.

2 Item (h). Two cheques have been paid to Jones, but one is now cancelled. Since the cash book is credited whenever a cheque is paid, it should be debited whenever a cheque is cancelled. The amount of cheques paid but not yet presented should be reduced by the amount of the cancelled cheque.

(b)   BANK RECONCILIATION STATEMENT AT 30 JUNE 20X0

	$	$
Balance per bank statement		65
Add: outstanding lodgements	400	
deposit interest not yet credited	60	
		460
		525
Less: unpresented cheques	500	
less cheque to Jones cancelled	(25)	
		475
Balance per corrected cash book		50

Notice that in preparing a bank reconciliation it is good practice to begin with the balance shown by the bank statement and end with the balance shown by the cash book. It is this corrected cash book balance which will appear in the statement of financial position as 'cash at bank'. However examination questions sometimes ask for the reverse order: as always, read the question carefully.

You might be interested to see the adjustments to the cash book in part (a) of the problem presented in the 'T' account format, as follows:

CASH BOOK

20X0		$	20X0		$
Jun 30	Bank interest – reversal of		Jun 30	Balance brought down	300
	incorrect entry	60		Bank charges	35
	Bank interest account	60		Correction of undercast	10
	Dividends paid direct to bank	200		Balance carried down	50
	Cheque drawn on deposit				
	account written back	50			
	Cheque issued to Jones				
	cancelled	25			
		395			395

Question   Bank reconciliation

From the information given below relating to PWW Co you are required:

(a)   to make such additional entries in the cash at bank account of PWW Co as you consider necessary to show the correct balance at 31 October 20X2.

(b)   to prepare a statement reconciling the correct balance in the cash at bank account as shown in (a) above with the balance at 31 October 20X2 that is shown on the bank statement from Z Bank Co.

CASH AT BANK ACCOUNT IN THE LEDGER OF PWW CO

20X2 October		$	20X2 October		$
1	Balance b/f	274	1	Wages	3,146
8	Q Manufacturing	3,443	1	Petty Cash	55
8	R Cement	1,146	8	Wages	3,106
11	S Co	638	8	Petty Cash	39
11	T & Sons	512	15	Wages	3,029
11	U & Co	4,174	15	Petty Cash	78
15	V Co	1,426	22	A & Sons	929
15	W Electrical	887	22	B Co	134
22	X and Associates	1,202	22	C & Company	77
26	Y Co	2,875	22	D & E	263
26	Z Co	982	22	F Co	1,782
29	ABC Co	1,003	22	G Associates	230
29	DEE Corporation	722	22	Wages	3,217
29	GHI Co	2,461	22	Petty Cash	91
31	Balance c/f	14	25	H & Partners	26
			26	J Sons & Co	868
			26	K & Co	107
			26	L, M & N	666
			28	O Co	112
			29	Wages	3,191
			29	Petty Cash	52
			29	P & Sons	561
		21,759			21,759

Z BANK CO – STATEMENT OF ACCOUNT WITH PWW CO

20X2 October		Payments $	Receipts $		Balance $
1					1,135
1	cheque	55			
1	cheque	3,146			
1	cheque	421		O/D	2,487
2	cheque	73			
2	cheque	155		O/D	2,715
6	cheque	212		O/D	2,927
8	sundry credit		4,589		
8	cheque	3,106			
8	cheque	39		O/D	1,483
11	sundry credit		5,324		3,841
15	sundry credit		2,313		
15	cheque	78			
15	cheque	3,029			3,047
22	sundry credit		1,202		
22	cheque	3,217			
22	cheque	91			941
25	cheque	1,782			
25	cheque	134		O/D	975
26	cheque	929			
26	sundry credit		3,857		
26	cheque	230			1,723
27	cheque	263			
27	cheque	77			1,383
29	sundry credit		4,186		
29	cheque	52			

20X2 October		Payments $	Receipts $	Balance $
29	cheque	3,191		
29	cheque	26		
29	dividends on investments		2,728	
29	cheque	666		4,362
31	bank charges	936		3,426

Answer

(a)

CASH BOOK

		$			$
31 Oct	Dividends received	2,728	31 Oct	Unadjusted balance b/f (overdraft)	14
			31 Oct	Bank charges	936
			31 Oct	Adjusted balance c/f	1,778
		2,728			2,728

(b) **BANK RECONCILIATION STATEMENT AT 31 OCTOBER 20X2**

	$	$
Corrected balance as per cash book		1,778
Cheques paid out but not yet presented	1,648	
Cheques paid in but not yet cleared by bank	0	
		1,648
Balance as per bank statement		3,426

Workings

1 Payments shown on bank statement but not in cash book*
  $(421 + 73 + 155 + 212) $861

  * Presumably recorded in cash book before 1 October 20X2 but not yet presented for payment as at 30 September 20X2

2 Payments in the cash book and on the bank statement
  $(3,146 + 55 + 3,106 + 39 + 78 + 3,029 + 3,217 + 91 + 1,782 + 134 + 929 + 230 + 263 + 77 + 52 + 3,191 + 26 + 666) $20,111

3 Payments in the cash book but not on the bank statement = Total payments in cash book $21,759 minus $20,111 = $1,648

		$
(Alternatively	J & Sons	868
	K & Co	107
	O Co	112
	P & Sons	561
		1,648)

4 Bank charges, not in the cash book $936

5 Receipts recorded by bank statement but not in cash book: dividends on investments $2,728

6 Receipts in the cash book and also bank statement $21,471
  (8 Oct $4,589; 11 Oct $5,324; 15 Oct $2,313; 22 Oct $1,202; 26 Oct $3,857; 29 Oct $4,186)

7 Receipts recorded in cash book but not bank statement   None

Chapter Roundup

- In theory, the entries appearing on a business's **bank statement** should be exactly the same as those in the business **cash book**. The balance shown by the bank statement as on a particular date should be the same as the cash book balance at the same date.

- Differences between the cash book and the bank statement arise for three reasons:
  - Errors – usually in the cash book
  - Omissions – such as bank charges not posted in the cash book
  - Timing differences – such as unpresented cheques

- When the differences between the bank statement and the cash book are identified, the cash book must be corrected for any errors or omissions. Any remaining difference can then be shown to be due to timing differences.

Quick Quiz

1   Which of the following are common reasons for differences between the cash book and the bank statements?
    (i)   Timing differences
    (ii)   Errors
    (iii)   Omissions
    (iv)   Contra entries
    A   (i) and (ii)
    B   (i) and (iv)
    C   (ii), (iii) and (iv)
    D   (i), (ii) and (iii)

2   A cash book and a bank statement will never agree.
    Is this statement?
    A   True
    B   False

3   A bank statement shows a balance of $1,200 in credit. An examination of the statement shows a $500 cheque paid in per the cash book but not yet on the bank statement and a $1,250 cheque paid out but not yet on the statement. In addition the cash book shows deposit interest received of $50 but this is not yet on the statement. What is the balance per the cash book?
    A $1,900 overdrawn
    B $500 overdrawn
    C $1,900 in hand
    D $500 in hand

4   Comparing the cash book with the bank statement is called a .... (complete the blanks).

5   Why is it necessary to compare the cash book and bank statement?

Answers to Quick Quiz

1　D　Contra entries only occur between the receivables and payables control account.

2　B　False. In very small businesses, with few transactions, the cash book and bank statement could well agree.

3　D

	$	$
Balance per bank statement		1,200
Add: outstanding lodgements	500	
deposit interest not yet credited	50	550
	1,750	
Less: unpresented cheques		(1,250)
Balance per cash book		500

4　Bank reconciliation.

5　It highlights errors and omissions in the cash book and helps to prevent fraud. It also checks the bank figure and helps to spot any bank errors.

Now try the questions below from the Exam Question Bank

Number	Level	Marks	Time
Q27	Examination	2	2 mins
Q28	Examination	2	2 mins

Correction of errors

Topic list	Syllabus reference
1 Types of error in accounting	E2(a), (b)
2 The correction of errors	E2(d)–(e), E5(a)–(d)
3 Material errors (IAS 8)	E2(c)

Introduction

This chapter continues the subject of errors in accounts. You have already
learned about errors which arise in the context of the cash book or the
receivables and payables ledgers and control accounts.

Here we deal with errors that may be corrected by means of the journal or
a suspense account. Finally we look at the correction of material errors from a
prior period in IAS 8.

By the end of this chapter you should be able to prepare a set of final accounts
for a sole trader from a trial balance after incorporating adjustments to profits
for errors.

Study guide

		Intellectual level
E2	**Correction of errors**	
(a)	Identify the types of error which may occur in bookkeeping systems	1
(b)	Identify errors which would be highlighted by the extraction of a trial balance	1
(c)	Understand the provision of IFRSs governing financial statements regarding material errors which result in prior year adjustment	1
(d)	Prepare journal entries to correct errors	1
(e)	Calculate and understand the impact of errors on the income statement, statement of comprehensive income and statement of financial position	1
E5	**Suspense accounts**	
(a)	Understand the purpose of a suspense account	1
(b)	Identify errors leading to the creation of suspense account	1
(c)	Record entries in a suspense account	1
(d)	Make journal entries to clear a suspense account	1

Exam guide

Be prepared for theoretical questions on errors as well as questions asking you to correct errors.

Exam focus point

At the 2009 ACCA Teachers' Conference, the examiner highlighted suspense accounts and errors as areas that are consistently answered badly in the exam.

1 Types of error in accounting

FAST FORWARD

There are five main types of error. Some can be corrected by journal entry, some require the use of a suspense account.

It is not really possible to draw up a complete list of all the errors which might be made by bookkeepers and accountants. Even if you tried, it is more than likely that as soon as you finished, someone would commit a completely new error that you had never even dreamed of! However, it is possible to describe **five types of error** which cover most of the errors which might occur. They are as follows.

- Errors of **transposition**
- Errors of **omission**
- Errors of **principle**
- Errors of **commission**
- **Compensating errors**

Once an error has been detected, it needs to be put right.

- If the correction **involves a double entry** in the ledger accounts, then it is done by using a **journal entry** in the journal.
- When the error **breaks the rule of double entry**, then it is corrected by the use of a **suspense account** as well as a journal entry.

Topics covered in this chapter

- The five common types of error
- Review journal entries (which we briefly looked at earlier in this text)
- Define a **suspense account**, and describe how it is used

1.1 Errors of transposition

An **error of transposition** is when two digits in an amount are accidentally recorded the wrong way round.

For example, suppose that a sale is recorded in the sales account as $6,843, but it has been incorrectly recorded in the total receivables account as $6,483. The error is the transposition of the 4 and the 8. The consequence is that total debits will not be equal to total credits. You can often detect a transposition error by checking whether the difference between debits and credits can be divided exactly by 9. For example, $6,843 − $6,483 = $360; $360 ÷ 9 = 40.

1.2 Errors of omission

An **error of omission** means failing to record a transaction at all, or making a debit or credit entry, but not the corresponding double entry.

Here is an example.

(a)   If a business receives an invoice from a supplier for $250, the transaction might be omitted from the books entirely. As a result, both the total debits and the total credits of the business will be out by $250.

(b)   If a business receives an invoice from a supplier for $300, the payables control account might be credited, but the debit entry in the purchases account might be omitted. In this case, the total credits would not equal total debits (because total debits are $300 less than they ought to be).

1.3 Errors of principle

An **error of principle** involves making a double entry in the belief that the transaction is being entered in the correct accounts, but subsequently finding out that the accounting entry breaks the 'rules' of an accounting principle or concept.

A typical example of such an error is to treat certain revenue expenditure incorrectly as capital expenditure.

(a)   For example, repairs to a machine costing $150 should be treated as revenue expenditure, and debited to a repairs account. If, instead, the repair costs are added to the cost of the non-current asset (capital expenditure) an error of principle would have occurred. As a result, although total debits still equal total credits, the repairs account is $150 less than it should be and the cost of the non-current asset is $150 greater than it should be.

(b)   Similarly, suppose that the proprietor of the business sometimes takes cash out of the till for his personal use and during a certain year these withdrawals on account of profit amount to $280. The book-keeper states that he has reduced cash sales by $280 so that the cash book could be made to balance. This would be an error of principle, and the result of it would be that the withdrawal account is understated by $280, and so is the total value of sales in the sales account.

1.4 Errors of commission

Errors of commission are where the bookkeeper makes a mistake in carrying out his or her task of recording transactions in the accounts.

Here are two common types of errors of commission.

(a)   **Putting a debit entry or a credit entry in the wrong account**. For example, if telephone expenses of $540 are debited to the electricity expenses account, an error of commission would have occurred. The result is that although total debits and total credits balance, telephone expenses are understated by $540 and electricity expenses are overstated by the same amount.

(b)   **Errors of casting (adding up).** The total daily credit sales in the sales day book should be $28,425, but are incorrectly added up as $28,825. The total sales in the sales day book are then used to credit total sales and debit total receivables in the ledger accounts. Although total debits and total credits are still equal, they are incorrect by $400.

1.5 Compensating errors

> **Compensating errors** are errors which are, coincidentally, equal and opposite to one another.

For example, two transposition errors of $540 might occur in extracting ledger balances, one on each side of the double entry. In the administration expenses account, $2,282 might be written instead of $2,822, while in the sundry income account, $8,391 might be written instead of $8,931. Both the debits and the credits would be $540 too low, and the mistake would not be apparent when the trial balance is cast. Consequently, compensating errors hide the fact that there are errors in the trial balance.

1.6 Summary: errors that can be detected by a trial balance

- Errors of transposition
- Errors of omission (if the omission is one-sided)
- Errors of commission (if one-sided, or two debit entries are made, for example)

Other errors will not be detected by extracting a trial balance, but may be spotted by other controls (such as bank or control account reconciliations).

2 The correction of errors

> Errors which leave total debits and credits in the ledger accounts in balance can be corrected by using **journal entries**. Otherwise a suspense account has to be opened first, and later cleared by a journal entry.

2.1 Journal entries

Some errors can be corrected by journal entries. To remind you, the format of a journal entry is:

Date	Debit $	Credit $
Account to be debited	X	
Account to be credited		X
(Narrative to explain the transaction)		

> As already indicated, in the exam you are often required to select answers in the form of journal entries.

The journal requires a debit and an equal credit entry for each 'transaction', ie for each correction. This means that if total debits equal total credits before a journal entry is made then they will still be equal after the journal entry is made. This would be the case if, for example, the original error was a debit wrongly posted as a credit and vice versa.

Similarly, if total debits and total credits are unequal before a journal entry is made, then they will still be unequal (by the same amount) after it is made.

For example, a bookkeeper accidentally posts a bill for $40 to the local taxes account instead of to the electricity account. A trial balance is drawn up, and total debits are $40,000 and total credits are $40,000. A journal entry is made to correct the misposting error as follows.

1.7.20X7

DEBIT	Electricity account	$40	
CREDIT	Local taxes account		$40

To correct a misposting of $40 from the local taxes account to electricity account

After the journal has been posted, total debits will still be $40,000 and total credits will be $40,000. Total debits and totals credits are still equal.

Now suppose that, because of some error which has not yet been detected, total debits were originally $40,000 but total credits were $39,900. If the same journal correcting the $40 is put through, total debits will remain $40,000 and total credits will remain $39,900. Total debits were different by $100 **before** the journal, and they are still different by $100 **after** the journal.

This means that journals can only be used to correct errors which require both a credit and (an equal) debit adjustment.

2.2 Example: Journal entries

Listed below are five errors which were used as examples earlier in this chapter. Write out the journal entries which would correct these errors.

(a)   A business receives an invoice for $250 from a supplier which was omitted from the books entirely.

(b)   Repairs worth $150 were incorrectly debited to the non-current asset (machinery) account instead of the repairs account.

(c)   The bookkeeper of a business reduces cash sales by $280 because he was not sure what the $280 represented. In fact, it was a withdrawal on account of profit.

(d)   Telephone expenses of $540 are incorrectly debited to the electricity account.

(e)   A page in the sales day book has been added up to $28,425 instead of $28,825.

Solution

(a)   DEBIT   Purchases $250
      CREDIT   Trade accounts payable $250
      A transaction previously omitted

(b)   DEBIT   Repairs account $150
      CREDIT   Non-current asset (machinery) a/c $150
      The correction of an error of principle: Repairs costs incorrectly added to non-current asset costs

(c)   DEBIT   Withdrawals on account $280
      CREDIT   Sales $280
      An error of principle, in which sales were reduced to compensate for cash withdrawals not accounted for

(d)   DEBIT   Telephone expenses $540
      CREDIT   Electricity expenses $540
      Correction of an error of commission: telephone expenses wrongly charged to the electricity account

(e)   DEBIT   Trade accounts receivable $400
      CREDIT   Sales $400
      The correction of a casting error in the sales day book
      ($28,825 – $28,425 = $400)

2.3 Use of journal entries in examinations

Occasionally an examination question might ask you to 'journalise' a transaction (ie select one of two, three or four journal entries), even though the transaction is perfectly normal and nothing to do with an error. This is just the examiner's way of finding out whether you know your debits and credits. For example:

Question

A business sells $500 of goods on credit. What is the correct journal to reflect this transaction?

A   Debit sales $500, credit trade accounts receivable $500

B   Debit trade accounts receivable $500, credit sales $500

Answer

B	DEBIT	Trade accounts receivable	$500	
	CREDIT	Sales		$500

No error has occurred here, just a normal credit sale of $500. By asking you to select a journal, the examiner can see that you understand the double-entry bookkeeping.

2.4 Suspense accounts

FAST FORWARD

Suspense accounts, as well as being used to correct some errors, are also opened when it is not known immediately where to post an amount. When the mystery is solved, the suspense account is closed and the amount correctly posted using a journal entry.

Key term

A **suspense account** is an account showing a balance equal to the difference in a trial balance.

A suspense account is a **temporary** account which can be opened for a number of reasons. The most common reasons are as follows.

(a)   A trial balance is drawn up which does not balance (ie total debits do not equal total credits).

(b)   The bookkeeper of a business knows where to post the credit side of a transaction, but does not know where to post the debit (or vice versa). For example, a cash payment might be made and must obviously be credited to cash. But the bookkeeper may not know what the payment is for, and so will not know which account to debit.

In both these cases, a temporary suspense account is opened up until the problem is sorted out. The next few paragraphs explain exactly how this works.

2.5 Use of suspense account: when the trial balance does not balance

When an error has occurred which results in an imbalance between total debits and total credits in the ledger accounts, the first step is to open a suspense account. For example, an accountant draws up a trial balance and finds that total debits exceed total credits by $162.

He knows that there is an error somewhere, but for the time being he opens a suspense account and enters a credit of $162 in it. This serves two purposes.

(a)   As the suspense account now exists, the accountant will not forget that there is an error (of $162) to be sorted out.

(b)   Now that there is a credit of $162 in the suspense account, the trial balance balances.

When the cause of the $162 discrepancy is tracked down, it is corrected by means of a journal entry. For example, the credit of $162 should be to purchases. The journal entry would be:

DEBIT	Suspense a/c	$162	
CREDIT	Purchases		$162

To close off suspense a/c and correct error

Whenever an error occurs which results in total debits not being equal to total credits, the first step an accountant makes is to open up a suspense account. Three more examples are given below.

2.6 Example: Transposition error

The bookkeeper of Mixem Gladly Co made a transposition error when entering an amount for sales in the sales account. Instead of entering the correct amount of $37,453.60 he entered $37,543.60, transposing the 4 and 5. The trade accounts receivable were posted correctly, and so when total debits and credits on the ledger accounts were compared, it was found that credits exceeded debits by $(37,543.60 – 37,453.60) = $90.

The initial step is to equalise the total debits and credits by posting a debit of $90 to a suspense account.

When the cause of the error is discovered, the double entry to correct it should be logged in the journal as:

DEBIT	Sales	$90	
CREDIT	Suspense a/c		$90

To close off suspense a/c and correct transposition error

2.7 Example: Error of omission

When Guttersnipe Builders paid the monthly salary cheques to its office staff, the payment of $5,250 was correctly entered in the cash account, but the bookkeeper omitted to debit the office salaries account. As a consequence, the total debit and credit balances on the ledger accounts were not equal, and credits exceeded debits by $5,250.

The initial step in correcting the situation is to debit $5,250 to a suspense account, to equalise the total debits and total credits.

When the cause of the error is discovered, the double entry to correct it should be logged in the journal as:

DEBIT	Office salaries account	$5,250	
CREDIT	Suspense a/c		$5,250

To close off suspense account and correct error of omission

2.8 Example: Error of commission

A bookkeeper might make a mistake by entering what should be a debit entry as a credit, or vice versa. For example, a credit customer pays $460 of the $660 he owes to Ashdown Tree Felling Contractors, but Ashdown's bookkeeper debits $460 on the receivables account in the nominal ledger by mistake instead of crediting the payment received.

The total debit balances in Ashdown's ledger accounts would now exceed the total credits by $2 \times \$460 = \$920$. The initial step in correcting the error would be to make a credit entry of $920 in a suspense account. When the cause of the error is discovered, it should be corrected as follows.

DEBIT	Suspense a/c	$920	
CREDIT	Trade accounts receivable		$920

To close off suspense account and correct error of commission

In the receivables control account in the nominal ledger, the correction would appear therefore as follows.

RECEIVABLES CONTROL ACCOUNT

	$		$
Balance b/f	660	Suspense a/c: error corrected	920
Payment incorrectly debited	460	Balance c/f	200
	1,120		1,120

2.9 Use of suspense account: not knowing where to post a transaction

Another use of suspense accounts occurs when a bookkeeper does not know where to post one side of a transaction. Until the mystery is sorted out, the entry can be recorded in a suspense account. A typical example is when the business receives cash through the post from a source which cannot be determined. The double entry in the accounts would be a debit in the cash book, and a credit to a suspense account.

2.10 Example: Not knowing where to post a transaction

Windfall Garments received a cheque in the post for $620. The name on the cheque is R J Beasley, but Windfall Garments have no idea who this person is, nor why he should be sending $620. The bookkeeper decides to open a suspense account, so that the double entry for the transaction is:

DEBIT	Cash	$620	
CREDIT	Suspense a/c		$620

Eventually, it transpires that the cheque was in payment for a debt owed by the Haute Couture Corner Shop and paid out of the proprietor's personal bank account. The suspense account can now be cleared, as follows.

DEBIT	Suspense a/c	$620	
CREDIT	Trade accounts receivable		$620

2.11 Suspense accounts might contain several items

If more than one error or unidentifiable posting to a ledger account arises during an accounting period, they will all be merged together in the same suspense account. Indeed, until the causes of the errors are discovered, the bookkeepers are unlikely to know exactly how many errors there are. An examination question might give you a balance on a suspense account, together with enough information to make the necessary corrections, leaving a nil balance on the suspense account and correct balances on various other accounts. In practice, of course, finding these errors is far from easy!

2.12 Suspense accounts are temporary

Suspense accounts are only temporary. None should exist when it comes to drawing up the financial statements at the end of the accounting period.

It must be stressed that a **suspense account can only be temporary**. Postings to a suspense account are only made when the bookkeeper doesn't know yet what to do, or when an error has occurred. Mysteries must be solved, and errors must be corrected. **Under no circumstances should there still be a suspense account when it comes to preparing the statement of financial position of a business. The suspense account must be cleared and all the correcting entries made before the final accounts are drawn up.**

This question is quite comprehensive. See if you can tackle it.

Question

Errors

At the year end of T Down & Co, an imbalance in the trial balance was revealed which resulted in the creation of a suspense account with a credit balance of $1,040.

Investigations revealed the following errors.

(i)   A sale of goods on credit for $1,000 had been omitted from the sales account.

(ii)   Delivery and installation costs of $240 on a new item of plant had been recorded as a revenue expense.

(iii)   Cash discount of $150 on paying a supplier, JW, had been taken, even though the payment was made outside the time limit.

(iv)   Inventory of stationery at the end of the period of $240 had been ignored.

(v)   A purchase of raw materials of $350 had been recorded in the purchases account as $850.

(vi)   The purchase returns day book included a sales credit note for $230 which had been entered correctly in the account of the customer concerned, but included with purchase returns in the nominal ledger.

Required

(a)   Prepare journal entries to correct *each* of the above errors. Narratives are *not* required.

(b)   Open a suspense account and show the corrections to be made.

(c)   Prior to the discovery of the errors, T Down & Co's gross profit for the year was calculated at
        $35,750 and the net profit for the year at $18,500.

Calculate the revised gross and net profit figures after the correction of the errors.

(a)

				Dr $	Cr $
(i)	DEBIT	Suspense a/c		1,000	
	CREDIT	Sales			1,000
(ii)	DEBIT	Plant		240	
	CREDIT	Delivery cost			240
(iii)	DEBIT	Cash discount received		150	
	CREDIT	JW a/c			150
(iv)	DEBIT	Inventory of stationery		240	
	CREDIT	Stationery expense			240
(v)	DEBIT	Suspense a/c		500	
	CREDIT	Purchases			500
(vi)	DEBIT	Purchase returns		230	
	DEBIT	Sales returns		230	
	CREDIT	Suspense a/c			460

(b)

SUSPENSE A/C

		$			$
(i)	Sales	1,000		End of year balance	1,040
(v)	Purchases	500	(vi)	Purchase returns/sales returns	460
		1,500			1,500

(c)

	$
Gross profit originally reported	35,750
Sales omitted	1,000
Plant costs wrongly allocated	240
Incorrect recording of purchases	500
Sales credit note wrongly allocated	(460)
Adjusted gross profit	37,030
Net profit originally reported	18,500
Adjustments to gross profit $(37,030 − 35,750)	1,280
Cash discount incorrectly taken	(150)
Stationery inventory	240
Adjusted net profit	19,870

Note. It has been assumed that the delivery and installation costs on plant have been included in purchases.

Exam focus point

There was a question in the December 2007 exam on suspense accounts that the examiner highlighted as being badly answered. You were asked to calculate the balance remaining on the suspense account after certain errors had been adjusted. The key to the question was recognising which errors affected the suspense account, then putting the adjustments through correctly, as in the above example.

3 Material errors (IAS 8)

IAS 8 *Accounting policies, changes in accounting estimates and errors* is an important standard. You should be able to define and deal with:

- errors

IAS 8 lays down the criteria for selecting and changing accounting policies and specifies the accounting treatment and disclosure of changes in accounting policies, changes in accounting estimates, and errors.

3.1 Definitions

The following definitions are given in the standard.

Key terms

- **Accounting policies** are the specific principles, bases, conventions, rules and practices applied by an entity in preparing and presenting financial statements.

- A **change in accounting estimate** is an adjustment of the carrying amount of an asset or a liability, or the amount of the periodic consumption of an asset.

- **Material**: Omissions or misstatements of items are material if they could, individually or collectively, influence the economic decisions of users taken on the basis of the financial statements.

- **Prior period errors** are omissions from, and misstatements in, the entity's financial statements for one or more prior periods.

- **Impracticable**: Applying a requirement is impracticable when the entity cannot apply it after making every reasonable effort to do so.

3.2 Errors

Errors discovered during a current period which **relate to a prior period** may arise through:

(a) Mathematical mistakes
(b) Mistakes in the application of accounting policies
(c) Misinterpretation of facts
(d) Oversights
(e) Fraud

Most of the time these errors can be **corrected through net profit or loss for the current period**. Where they fulfil the definition of material errors (given above), however, this is not appropriate.

As laid down in IAS 8 the amount of the correction of a material error that relates to prior periods should be reported by **adjusting the opening balance of retained earnings**. Comparative information should be restated (unless this is impracticable).

This treatment means that the financial statements appear as if the material error had been **corrected in the period it was made**. Financial statements include comparatives for the previous period, so any amount relating to the previous period immediately prior to the current one will be included in the net profit or loss for that period. Amounts relating to periods before that will be used to adjust the opening reserves figure of the previous period shown.

Various **disclosures** are required:

(a) **Nature** of the material error
(b) **Amount of the correction** for the current period and for each prior period presented
(c) Amount of the correction relating to periods prior to those included in the **comparative** information
(d) The fact that comparative information has been **restated** or that it is impracticable to do so

Question

During 20X7 Lubi Co discovered that certain items had been included in inventory at 31 December 20X6, valued at $4.2m, which had in fact been sold before the year end. The following figures for 20X6 (as reported) and 20X7 (draft) are available.

	20X6	20X7 (draft)
	$'000	$'000
Sales	47,400	67,200
Cost of goods sold	(34,570)	(55,800)
Profit before taxation	12,830	11,400
Income taxes	(3,880)	(3,400)
Net profit	8,950	8,000

Reserves at 1 January 20X6 were $13m. The cost of goods sold for 20X7 includes the $4.2m error in opening inventory. The income tax rate was 30% for 20X6 and 20X7.

Required

Show the income statement for 20X7, with the 20X6 comparative, and the adjusted retained earnings.

Answer

INCOME STATEMENT

	20X6	20X7
	$'000	$'000
Sales	47,400	67,200
Cost of goods sold (W1)	(38,770)	(51,600)
Profit before tax	8,630	15,600
Income tax (W2)	(2,620)	(4,660)
Net profit	6,010	10,940

RETAINED EARNINGS

Opening retained earnings		
As previously reported	13,000	21,950
Correction of prior period error (4,200 – 1,260)	–	(2,940)
As restated	13,000	19,010
Net profit for year	6,010	10,940
Closing retained earnings	19,010	29,950

Working

1   *Cost of goods sold*

	20X6	20X7
	$'000	$'000
As stated in question	34,570	55,800
inventory adjustment	4,200	(4,200)
	38,770	51,600

2   *Income tax*

	20X6	20X7
	$'000	$'000
As stated in question	3,880	3,400
Inventory adjustment (4,200 × 30%)	1,260	1,260
	2,620	4,660

Chapter Roundup

- There are five main types of error. Some can be corrected by journal entry, some require the use of a suspense account.

- Errors which leave total debits and credits in the ledger accounts in balance can be corrected by using **journal entries**. Otherwise a suspense account has to be opened first, and later cleared by a journal entry.

- **Suspense accounts**, as well as being used to correct some errors, are also opened when it is not known immediately where to post an amount. When the mystery is solved, the suspense account is closed and the amount correctly posted using a journal entry.

- **Suspense accounts are only temporary**. None should exist when it comes to drawing up the financial statements at the end of the accounting period.

- IAS 8 *Accountancy policies, changes in accounting estimates and errors* is an important standard. You should be able to define and deal with errors.

Quick Quiz

1   List five types of error made in accounting.

2   What is a journal used for?

    A   To correct errors

    B   To correct errors and post unusual transactions

    C   To correct errors and clear suspense account

    D   To make adjustments to the double entry

3   A suspense account is a temporary account to make the trial balance balance.

    Is this statement

    A   True

    B   False

4   What must be done with a suspense account before preparing a statement of financial position?

    A   Include in assets

    B   Clear it to nil

    C   Include in liabilities

    D   Write it off to capital

5   Sales returns of $460 have inadvertently been posted to the purchase returns, although the correct entry has been made to the accounts receivable control. A suspense account needs to be set up for how much?

    A $460 debit

    B $460 credit

    C $920 debit

    D $920 credit

Answers to Quick Quiz

1   Transposition, omission, principle, commission and compensating errors.
2   D   Although A, B and C are correct as far as they go, they don't cover everything. Selection D is the most comprehensive answer.
3   A
4   B   All errors must be identified and the suspense account cleared to nil.
5   C   The sales returns of $460 have been credited to accounts receivable and also $460 has been credited to purchase returns. Therefore the trial balance needs a debit of 2 × $460 = $920 to balance.

Now try the questions below from the Exam Question Bank

Number	Level	Marks	Time
Q29	Examination	2	2 mins
Q30	Examination	2	2 mins
Q31	Examination	2	2 mins
Q32	Examination	2	2 mins

Preparation of financial statements for sole traders

17

Topic list	Syllabus reference
1 Preparation of final accounts	F1(d), F2(a)

Introduction

We have now reached our goal of preparing of the final accounts of a sole trader!

We will deal with the case of a trial balance and then making adjustments to produce final accounts.

This chapter also acts as a revision of what we have covered to date. Use this period to review all the work covered to date. If you have any problems with the examples and questions, thoroughly revise the appropriate chapter before proceeding to the next part.

Study guide

		Intellectual level
F1	**Statements of financial position**	
(d)	Prepare extracts of a statement of financial position from given information	1
F2	**Income statements and statements of comprehensive income**	
(a)	Prepare extracts of an income statement from given information	1

Exam guide

This chapter covers a lot of ground, all of which is examinable. Use it as useful revision of what you have learned to date.

Exam focus point

> At the 2009 ACCA Teachers' Conference, the examiner emphasised the need to practise full questions particularly in certain key areas. One of these key areas was accounts preparation. Therefore do not neglect this chapter. It will also serve as a good foundation for your later studies at F7.

1 Preparation of final accounts

FAST FORWARD

> You should now be able to prepare a set of final accounts for a sole trader from a trial balance after incorporating period end adjustments for depreciation, inventory, prepayments, accruals, irrecoverable debts, and allowances for receivables.

1.1 Adjustments to accounts

You should now use what you have learned to produce a solution to the following exercise, which involves preparing an income statement and statement of financial position. We have met Newbegin Tools before, but now we add a lot more information.

Question   Adjustment to accounts

The financial affairs of Newbegin Tools prior to the commencement of trading were as follows.

NEWBEGIN TOOLS
STATEMENT OF FINANCIAL POSITION AS AT 1 AUGUST 20X5

	$	$
Non-current assets		
Motor vehicle		2,000
Shop fittings		3,000
		5,000
Current assets		
Inventories		12,000
Cash		1,000
		18,000
Capital		12,000
Current liabilities		
Bank overdraft	2,000	
Trade payables	4,000	
		6,000
		18,000

At the end of six months the business had made the following transactions.

(a) Goods were purchased on credit at a list price of $10,000.

(b) Trade discount received was 2% on list price and there was a settlement discount received of 5% on settling debts to suppliers of $8,000. These were the only payments to suppliers in the period.

(c) Closing inventories of goods were valued at $5,450.

(d) All sales were on credit and amounted to $27,250.

(e) Outstanding receivables balances at 31 January 20X6 amounted to $3,250 of which $250 were to be written off. An allowance for receivables is to be made amounting to 2% of the remaining outstanding receivables.

(f) Cash payments were made in respect of the following expenses.

		$
(i)	Stationery, postage and wrapping	500
(ii)	Telephone charges	200
(iii)	Electricity	600
(iv)	Cleaning and refreshments	150

(g) Cash drawings by the proprietor, Alf Newbegin, amounted to $6,000.

(h) The outstanding overdraft balance as at 1 August 20X5 was paid off. Interest charges and bank charges on the overdraft amounted to $40.

Prepare the income statement of Newbegin Tools for the six months to 31 January 20X6 and a statement of financial position as at that date. Ignore depreciation.

Answer

INCOME STATEMENT
FOR THE SIX MONTHS ENDED 31 JANUARY 20X6

	$	$
Sales		27,250
Opening inventories	12,000	
Purchases (note (a))	9,800	
	21,800	
Less closing inventories	5,450	
Cost of goods sold		16,350
Gross profit		10,900
Discounts received (note (b))		400
		11,300
Electricity (note (c))	600	
Stationery, postage and wrapping	500	
Irrecoverable debts written off	250	
Allowance for receivables (note (d))	60	
Telephone charges	200	
Cleaning and refreshments	150	
Interest and bank charges	40	
		1,800
Net profit		9,500

Notes

(a) Purchases at cost $10,000 less 2% trade discount.

(b) 5% of $8,000 = $400.

(c) Expenses are grouped into sales and distribution expenses (here assumed to be electricity, stationery and postage, bad debts and allowance for receivables) administration expenses (here assumed to be telephone charges and cleaning) and finance charges.

(d) 2% of $3,000 = $60.

The preparation of a statement of financial position is not so easy, because we must calculate the value of payables and cash in hand.

(a) Payables as at 31 January 20X6

The amount owing to payables is the sum of the amount owing at the beginning of the period, plus the cost of purchases during the period (net of all discounts), less the payments already made for purchases.

	$
Payables as at 1 August 20X5	4,000
Add purchases during the period, net of trade discount	9,800
	13,800
Less settlement discounts received	(400)
	13,400
Less payments to payables during the period*	(7,600)
	5,800

* $8,000 less cash discount of $400.

(b) Cash at bank and in hand at 31 January 20X6

You need to identify cash payments received and cash payments made.

	$
(i) *Cash received from sales*	
Total sales in the period	27,250
Add receivables as at 1 August 20X5	0
	27,250
Less unpaid debts as at 31 January 20X6	3,250
Cash received	24,000

	$
(ii) *Cash paid*	
Trade payables (see (a))	7,600
Stationery, postage and wrapping	500
Telephone charges	200
Electricity	600
Cleaning and refreshments	150
Bank charges and interest	40
Bank overdraft repaid	2,000
Drawings by proprietor	6,000
	17,090

Note. It is easy to forget some of these payments, especially drawings.

	$
(iii) Cash in hand at 1 August 20X5	1,000
Cash received in the period	24,000
	25,000
Cash paid in the period	(17,090)
Cash at bank and in hand as at 31 January 20X6	7,910

(c) When irrecoverable debts are written off, the value of outstanding receivables must be reduced by the amount written off. Receivables will be valued at $3,250 less bad debts $250 and the allowance for receivables of $60 – ie at $2,940.

(d) Non-current assets should be depreciated. However, in this exercise depreciation has been ignored.

NEWBEGIN TOOLS
STATEMENT OF FINANCIAL POSITION AS AT 31 JANUARY 20X6

	$	$
Non-current assets		
Motor vehicles	2,000	
Shop fittings	3,000	
		5,000
Current assets		
Inventories	5,450	
Receivables, less allowance for receivables	2,940	
Cash	7,910	
		16,300
		21,300
Capital		
Capital at 1 August 20X5		12,000
Net profit for the period		9,500
		21,500
Less drawings		6,000
Capital at 31 January 20X6		15,500
Current liabilities		
Trade payables		5,800
		21,300

The opening bank overdraft was repaid during the year and is therefore not shown at the year end.

Exam focus point

Although your exam is all MCQs, you might be given a lot of information and asked to calculate a figure to go in the income statement and/or statement of financial position. Therefore calculating account balances and preparing financial statements must become second nature to you.

1.2 Example: accounts preparation from a trial balance

The following trial balance was extracted from the ledger of Stephen Chee, a sole trader, as at 31 May 20X1 – the end of his financial year.

STEPHEN CHEE
TRIAL BALANCE AS AT 31 MAY 20X1

	Dr $	Cr $
Property, at cost	120,000	
Equipment, at cost	80,000	
Provisions for depreciation (as at 1 June 20X0)		
– on property		20,000
– on equipment		38,000
Purchases	250,000	
Sales		402,200
Inventory, as at 1 June 20X0	50,000	
Discounts allowed	18,000	
Discounts received		4,800
Returns out		15,000
Wages and salaries	58,800	
Irrecoverable debts	4,600	
Loan interest	5,100	
Other operating expenses	17,700	
Trade payables		36,000
Trade receivables	38,000	
Cash in hand	300	
Bank	1,300	
Drawings	24,000	
Allowance for receivables		500
17% long term loan		30,000
Capital, as at 1 June 20X0		121,300
	667,800	667,800

The following additional information as at 31 May 20X1 is available.

(a)   Inventory as at the close of business has been valued at cost at $42,000.

(b)   Wages and salaries need to be accrued by $800.

(c)   Other operating expenses are prepaid by $300.

(d)   The allowance for receivables is to be adjusted so that it is 2% of trade receivables.

(e)   Depreciation for the year ended 31 May 20X1 has still to be provided for as follows.
        Property: 1.5% per annum using the straight line method; and
        Equipment: 25% per annum using the reducing balance method.

Required

Prepare Stephen Chee's income statement for the year ended 31 May 20X1 and his statement of financial position as at that date.

Tutorial note. Again you have met a simplified form of Stephen Chee before. However, this version contains a lot more information for you to deal with before you can prepare the accounts.

Solution

STEPHEN CHEE
INCOME STATEMENT
FOR THE YEAR ENDED 31 MAY 20X1

	$	$
Sales		402,200
Cost of sales		
Opening inventory	50,000	
Purchases	250,000	
Purchases returns	(15,000)	
	285,000	
Closing inventory	42,000	
		243,000
Gross profit		159,200
Other income – discounts received		4,800
		164,000
Expenses		
Operating expenses		
Wages and salaries ($58,800 + $800)	59,600	
Discounts allowed	18,000	
Irrecoverable debts (W1)	4,860	
Loan interest	5,100	
Depreciation (W2)	12,300	
Other operating expenses ($17,700 – $300)	17,400	
		117,260
Net profit for the year		46,740

STEPHEN CHEE
STATEMENT OF FINANCIAL POSITION AS AT 31 MAY 20X0

	Cost $	Accumulated depn. $	Net book value $
Non-current assets			
Property	120,000	21,800	98,200
Equipment	80,000	48,500	31,500
	200,000	70,300	129,700
Current assets			
Inventory		42,000	
Trade receivables net of allowance for receivables ($38,000 – 760 (W1))		37,240	
Prepayments		300	
Bank		1,300	
Cash in hand		300	
			81,140
			210,840
Capital			
Balance at 1 June 20X0			121,300
Net profit for the year			46,740
			168,040
Drawings			24,000
			144,040
Non-current liabilities			
17% loan			30,000
Current liabilities			
Trade payables		36,000	
Accruals		800	
			36,800
			210,840

Workings

		$
1	*Irrecoverable debts*	
	Previous allowance	500
	New allowance (2% × 38,000)	760
	Increase	260
	Per trial balance	4,600
	Income statement	4,860
2	*Depreciation*	
	Property	
	Opening provision	20,000
	Provision for the year (1.5% × 120,000)	1,800
	Closing provision	21,800
	Equipment	
	Opening provision	38,000
	Provision for the year (25% × 42,000)	10,500
	Closing provision	48,500
	Total charge in I/S	12,300

Question
Final accounts

Donald Brown, a sole trader, extracted the following trial balance on 31 December 20X0.

TRIAL BALANCE AS AT 31 DECEMBER 20X0

	Debit $	Credit $
Capital at 1 January 20X0		26,094
Receivables	42,737	
Cash in hand	1,411	
Payables		35,404
Fixtures and fittings at cost	42,200	
Discounts allowed	1,304	
Discounts received		1,175
Inventory at 1 January 20X0	18,460	
Sales		491,620
Purchases	387,936	
Motor vehicles at cost	45,730	
Lighting and heating	6,184	
Motor expenses	2,862	
Rent	8,841	
General expenses	7,413	
Bank overdraft		19,861
Provision for depreciation		
Fixtures and fittings		2,200
Motor vehicles		15,292
Drawings	26,568	
	591,646	591,646

The following information as at 31 December is also available.

(a) $218 is owing for motor expenses.

(b) $680 has been prepaid for rent.

(c) Depreciation is to be provided of the year as follows.

Motor vehicles: 20% on cost
Fixtures and fittings: 10% reducing balance method

(d) Inventory at the close of business was valued at $19,926.

Required

Prepare Donald Brown's income statement for the year ended 31 December 20X0 and his statement of financial position at that date.

Answer

Tutorial note. You should note these points.

(a) Discounts allowed are an expense of the business and should be shown as a deduction from gross profit. Similarly, discounts received is a revenue item and should be added to gross profit.

(b) The figure for depreciation in the trial balance represents accumulated depreciation up to and including 20W9. You have to calculate the charge for the year 20X0 for the income statement and add this to the trial balance figure to arrive at the accumulated depreciation figure to be included in the statement of financial position.

DONALD BROWN
INCOME STATEMENT
FOR THE YEAR ENDED 31 DECEMBER 20X0

	$	$
Sales		491,620
Less cost of sales		
Opening inventory	18,460	
Purchases	387,936	
	406,396	
Closing inventory	19,926	
		386,470
Gross profit		105,150
Discounts received		1,175
		106,325
Less expenses:		
discounts allowed	1,304	
lighting and heating	6,184	
motor expenses (2,862 + 218)	3,080	
rent (8,841 – 680)	8,161	
general expenses	7,413	
depreciation (W)	13,146	
		39,288
Net profit		67,037

Working: depreciation charge

Motor vehicles: $45,730 × 20% = $9,146
Fixtures and fittings: 10% × $(42,200 – 2,200) = $4,000
Total: $4,000 + $9,146 = $13,146.

DONALD BROWN
STATEMENT OF FINANCIAL POSITION AS AT 31 DECEMBER 20X0

	Cost $	Depreciation $	Net $
Non-current assets			
Fixtures and fittings	42,200	6,200	36,000
Motor vehicles	45,730	24,438	21,292
	87,930	30,638	57,292
Current assets			
Inventory		19,926	
Receivables		42,737	
Prepayments		680	
Cash in hand		1,411	
			64,754
			122,046

	$	$
Capital		
Balance b/f		26,094
Net profit for year		67,037
		93,131
Less drawings		26,568
		66,563
Current liabilities		
Payables	35,404	
Accruals	218	
Bank overdraft	19,861	
		55,483
		122,046

Exam focus point

In the June 2008 exam, there was a question giving a number of adjustments and asking for the effect on profit. The examiner commented that only 30% of students got this right. You need to follow the procedure shown in the question below.

Question

Effect on profit

Given the facts in Final accounts (Donald Brown) above, what is the net effect on profit of the adjustments in (a) to (c)?

Answer

(a) Motor expenses accrual – $218 additional expense, so reduction in profit.

(b) Rent prepayment – $680 reduction in expense, so increase in profit.

(c) Depreciation – total charge $13,146 additional expense, so reduction in profit.

Total effect on net profit = + 680 – 218 – 13,146
= 12,684 reduction

Chapter Roundup

- You should now be able to prepare a set of final accounts for a sole trader from a trial balance after incorporating period end adjustments for depreciation, inventory, prepayments, accruals, irrecoverable debts, and allowances for receivables.

Quick Quiz

1 Which of the following is the correct formula for cost of sales?

    A   Opening inventory – purchases + closing inventory.

    B   Purchases – closing inventory + sales.

    C   Opening inventory – closing inventory + purchases.

    D   Opening inventory + closing inventory – purchases.

2 If an owner takes goods out of inventory for his own use, how is this dealt with?

    A   Credited to drawings at cost

    B   Credited to drawings at selling price

    C   Debited to drawings at cost

    D   Debited to drawings at selling price

3 A business starts trading on 1 September 20X0. During the year, it has sales of $500,000, purchases of $250,000 and closing inventory of $75,000. What is the gross profit for the year?

    A $175,000

    B $675,000

    C $325,000

    D $250,000

4 Mario's trial balance includes the following items: non-current assets $50,000, inventory $15,000, payables $10,000, receivables $5,000, bank $110,000, allowance for receivables $1,000.

What is the figure for current assets?

    A $180,000

    B $170,000

    C $129,000

    D $134,000

5 Using the information in Question 4 above, what is the figure for total assets?

    A $184,000

    B $179,000

Answers to Quick Quiz

1   C   Correct, this is a version of the more normal formula: opening inventory + purchases – closing inventory.

    A   Incorrect.

    B   Incorrect. Sales should never form part of cost of sales.

    C   Incorrect.

2   C   Although we have not specifically covered this point, you should have realised that goods for own use must be treated as drawings (and so debited to drawings). Thinking about prudence, if the goods were transferred at selling price, the business would show a profit on the sale of the goods that it has not made. So the transaction must be shown at cost. (Now think about where the credit entry goes before trying the question from the EQB.)

3   C

	$
Sales	500,000
Purchases	250,000
Closing inventory	(75,000)
Cost of sales	175,000
Gross profit	325,000

4   C

		$
Current assets		
Inventory		15,000
Receivables (5,000 – 1,000)		4,000
Bank		110,000
		129,000

5   B   Trial assets = non-current assets + current assets
                           = 50,000 + 129,000
                           = 179,000

Now try the question below from the Exam Question Bank

Number	Level	Marks	Time
Q33	Examination	1	1 min

Preparing basic financial statements

Incomplete records

Introduction

So far in your work on preparing the final accounts for a sole trader we have assumed that a full set of records are kept. In practice many sole traders do not keep a full set of records and you must apply certain techniques to arrive at the necessary figures.

Incomplete records questions are a very good test of your understanding of the way in which a set of accounts is built up.

In most countries, limited liability companies are obliged by national laws to keep proper accounting records.

Study guide

		Intellectual level
F6	**Incomplete records**	
(a)	Understand and apply techniques used in incomplete record situations	1
	(i) Use of accounting equation	
	(ii) Use of ledger accounts to calculate missing figures	
	(iii) Use of cash and/or bank summaries	
	(iv) Use of profit percentages to calculate missing figures	

Exam guide

Incomplete records questions are likely to appear regularly. Learn the tricks presented in this chapter and you should be able to tackle anything the examiner throws at you. Make sure you understand the difference between **margin** and **mark-up**.

1 Incomplete records questions

FAST FORWARD

Incomplete records questions may test your ability to prepare accounts in the following situations.

- A trader **does not maintain a ledger** and therefore has no continuous double entry record of transactions.

- Accounting records are **destroyed** by accident, such as fire

- Some essential figure is **unknown** and must be calculated as a balancing figure. This may occur as a result of inventory being damaged or destroyed, or because of misappropriation of assets.

Incomplete records problems occur when a business does not have a full set of accounting records, for one of the following reasons.

- The proprietor of the business does not keep a full set of accounts.
- Some of the business accounts are accidentally lost or destroyed.

The problem for the accountant is to prepare a set of year-end accounts for the business; ie an income statement and a statement of financial position. Since the business does not have a full set of accounts, preparing the final accounts is not a simple matter of closing off accounts and transferring balances to the trading, income and expense account, or showing outstanding balances in the statement of financial position. The task of preparing the final accounts involves the following.

(a)   Establishing the **cost of purchases** and other expenses

(b)   Establishing the **total amount of sales**

(c)   Establishing the amount of **accounts payable, accruals, accounts receivable and prepayments** at the end of the year

Examination questions often take incomplete records problems a stage further, by introducing an 'incident', such as fire or burglary which leaves the owner of the business uncertain about how much inventory has been destroyed or stolen.

The great merit of incomplete records problems is that they focus attention on the relationship between cash received and paid, sales and accounts receivable, purchases and accounts payable, and inventory, as well as calling for the preparation of final accounts from basic principles.

To understand what incomplete records are about, it will obviously be useful now to look at what exactly might be incomplete. The items we shall consider in turn are:

(a)   The opening position

(b)   Credit sales and trade accounts receivable

(c) Purchases and trade accounts payable
(d) Purchases, inventory and the cost of sales
(e) Stolen goods or goods destroyed
(f) The cash book
(g) Accruals and prepayments
(h) Drawings

2 The opening position

In practice there should not be any missing item in the opening statement of financial position of the business, because it should be available from the preparation of the previous year's final accounts. However, an examination problem might provide information about the assets and liabilities of the business at the beginning of the period under review, but then leave the balancing figure (ie the proprietor's business capital) unspecified. If you remember the accounting equation (A = C + L), the problem is quite straightforward.

2.1 Example: Opening statement of financial position

Suppose Joe Han's business has the following assets and liabilities as at 1 January 20X3.

	$
Fixtures and fittings at cost	7,000
Provision for depreciation, fixtures and fittings	4,000
Motor vehicles at cost	12,000
Provision for depreciation, motor vehicles	6,800
Inventory	4,500
Trade accounts receivable	5,200
Cash at bank and in hand	1,230
Trade accounts payable	3,700
Prepayment	450
Accrued rent	2,000

You are required to prepare a statement of financial position for the business, inserting a balancing figure for proprietor's capital.

Solution

STATEMENT OF FINANCIAL POSITION AS AT 1 JANUARY 20X3

	$	$
Assets		
Non-current assets		
Fixtures and fittings at cost	7,000	
Less accumulated depreciation	4,000	
		3,000
Motor vehicles at cost	12,000	
Less accumulated depreciation	6,800	
		5,200
Current assets		
Inventory	4,500	
Trade accounts receivable	5,200	
Prepayment	450	
Cash	1,230	
		11,380
Total assets		19,580

	$	$
Capital and liabilities		
Proprietor's capital as at 1 January 20X3 (balancing figure)		13,880
Current liabilities		
Trade accounts payable	3,700	
Accrual	2,000	
		5,700
Total capital and liabilities		19,580

3 Credit sales and trade accounts receivable

The approach to incomplete records questions is to build up the information given so as to complete the necessary **double entry**. This may involve reconstructing **control accounts** for:

- cash and bank
- trade accounts receivable and payable

If a business does not keep a record of its sales on credit, the value of these sales can be derived from the opening balance of trade accounts receivable, the closing balance of trade accounts receivable, and the payments received from customers during the period.

Formula to learn: credit sales

	$
Payments from trade accounts receivable	X
Plus closing balance of trade accounts receivable (since these represent sales in the current period for which cash payment has not yet been received)	X
Less opening balance of trade accounts receivable (these represent credit sales in a previous period)	(X)
Credit sales in the period	X

For example, suppose that Joe Han's business had trade accounts receivable of $1,750 on 1 April 20X4 and trade accounts receivable of $3,140 on 31 March 20X5. If payments received from receivables during the year to 31 March 20X5 were $28,490, and if there are no bad debts, then credit sales for the period would be:

	$
Cash from receivables	28,490
Plus closing receivables	3,140
Less opening receivables	(1,750)
Credit sales	29,880

If there are irrecoverable debts during the period, the value of sales will be increased by the amount of irrecoverable debts written off, no matter whether they relate to opening receivables or credit sales during the current period.

Question

Calculating sales

The calculation above could be made in a T-account, with credit sales being the balancing figure to complete the account. Prepare the T-account.

Answer

TRADE ACCOUNTS RECEIVABLE

	$		$
Opening balance b/f	1,750	Cash received	28,490
Credit sales (balancing fig)	29,880	Closing balance c/f	3,140
	31,630		31,630

The same interrelationship between credit sales, cash from receivables, and opening and closing receivables balances can be used to derive a missing figure for cash from receivables, or opening or closing receivables, given the values for the three other items. For example, if we know that opening receivables are $6,700, closing receivables are $3,200 and credit sales for the period are $69,400, then cash from receivables during the period would be as follows.

TRADE ACCOUNTS RECEIVABLE

	$		$
Opening balance	6,700	Cash received (balancing figure)	72,900
Sales (on credit)	69,400	Closing balance c/f	3,200
	76,100		76,100

An alternative way of presenting the same calculation would be:

	$
Opening balance of accounts receivable	6,700
Credit sales during the period	69,400
Total money owed to the business	76,100
Less closing balance of accounts receivable	(3,200)
Equals cash received during the period	72,900

4 Purchases and trade accounts payable

A similar relationship exists between purchases of inventory during a period, the opening and closing balances for trade accounts payable, and amounts paid to suppliers during the period.

If we wish to calculate an unknown amount for purchases, the amount would be derived as follows.

Formula to learn: purchases

	$
Payments to trade accounts payable during the period	X
Plus closing balance of trade accounts payable (since these represent purchases in the current period for which payment has not yet been made)	X
Less opening balance of trade accounts payable (these debts, paid in the current period, relate to purchases in a previous period)	(X)
Purchases during the period	X

For example, suppose that Joe Han's business had trade payables of $3,728 on 1 October 20X5 and trade payables of $2,645 on 30 September 20X6. If payments to trade payables during the year to 30 September 20X6 were $31,479, then purchases during the year would be:

	$
Payments to trade accounts payable	31,479
Plus closing balance of trade accounts payable	2,645
Less opening balance of trade accounts payable	(3,728)
Purchases	30,396

Question   **Calculating purchases 1**

Again, the calculation above could be made in a T-account, with purchases being the balancing figure to complete the account. Prepare the T-account.

Answer

TRADE ACCOUNTS PAYABLE

	$		$
Cash payments	31,479	Opening balance b/f	3,728
Closing balance c/f	2,645	Purchases (balancing figure)	30,396
	34,124		34,124

Mr Harmon does not keep full accounting records, but the following information is available in respect of his accounting year ended 31 December 20X9.

	$
Cash purchases in year	3,900
Cash paid for goods supplied on credit	27,850
Trade accounts payable at 1 January 20X9	970
Trade accounts payable at 31 December 20X9	720

In his trading account for 20X9, what will be Harmon's figure for purchases?

Answer

Credit purchases = $(27,850 + 720 − 970) = $27,600. Therefore total purchases = $(27,600 + 3,900) = $31,500.

5 Establishing cost of sales

FAST FORWARD

Where inventory, sales or purchases is the unknown figure it will be necessary to use information on **gross profit percentages** to construct a working for gross profit in which the unknown figure can be inserted as a balance.

When the value of purchases is not known, a different approach might be required to find out what they were, depending on the nature of the information given to you.

One approach would be to use information about the cost of sales, and opening and closing inventory rather than trade accounts payable to find the cost of purchases.

Formula to learn

		$
Since	opening inventory	X
	plus purchases	X
	less closing inventory	(X)
	equals the cost of goods sold	X
then	the cost of goods sold	X
	plus closing inventory	X
	less opening inventory	(X)
	equals purchases	X

Suppose that the inventory of Joe Han's business on 1 July 20X6 has a value of $8,400, and an inventory count at 30 June 20X7 showed inventory to be valued at $9,350. Sales for the year to 30 June 20X7 are $80,000, and the business makes a mark-up of $33^1/3\%$ on cost for all the items that it sells. What were the purchases during the year?

The cost of goods sold can be derived from the value of sales, as follows.

		$
Sales	$(133^1/3\%)$	80,000
Gross profit (mark-up)	$(33^1/3\%)$	20,000
Cost of goods sold	(100%)	60,000

The cost of goods sold is 75% of sales value.

	$
Cost of goods sold	60,000
Plus closing inventory	9,350
Less opening inventory	(8,400)
Purchases	60,950

It is worth mentioning here that two different terms may be given to you in the exam for the calculation of profit.

Key terms

- **Mark-up** is the profit as a percentage of **cost**.
- **Gross profit** is the profit as a percentage of **sales**.

Looking at the above example:

(a) The mark-up on cost is $33^1/_3\%$

(b) The gross profit percentage is 25% (ie $33^1/_3 / 133^1/_3 \times 100\%$)

Question
Calculating purchases 3

Harry has budgeted sales for the coming year of $175,000. He achieves a constant gross mark-up of 40% on cost. He plans to reduce his inventory level by $13,000 over the year.

What will Harry's purchases be for the year?

Answer

Cost of sales   = 100/140 × $175,000
                 = $125,000

Since the inventory level is being allowed to fall, it means that purchases will be $13,000 less than $125,000 = $112,000.

Question
Calculating purchases 4

Using the same facts as in the question above, calculate Harry's purchases for the year if he achieves a constant **margin** of 40% on sales.

Answer

Gross profit = 40% of sales, so cost of sales = 60% of sales.

$$\text{Cost of sales} = \frac{60}{100} \times \$175,000$$

$$= \$105,000$$

Since the inventory level is being allowed to fall, it means purchases will be $13,000 less than $105,000 = $92,000.

6 Stolen goods or goods destroyed

A similar type of calculation might be required to derive the value of goods stolen or destroyed. When an unknown quantity of goods is lost, whether they are stolen, destroyed in a fire, or lost in any other way such that the quantity lost cannot be counted, then the cost of the goods lost is the difference between (a) and (b).

(a)   The **cost of goods sold**

(b)   **Opening inventory of the goods** (at cost) plus **purchases** less **closing inventory of the goods** (at cost)

In theory (a) and (b) should be the same. However, if (b) is a larger amount than (a), it follows that the difference must be the cost of the goods purchased and neither sold nor remaining in inventory, ie the cost of the goods lost.

6.1 Example: Cost of goods destroyed

Orlean Flames is a shop which sells fashion clothes. On 1 January 20X5, it had trade inventory which cost $7,345. During the 9 months to 30 September 20X5, the business purchased goods from suppliers costing $106,420. Sales during the same period were $154,000. The shop makes a gross profit of 40% on cost for everything it sells. On 30 September 20X5, there was a fire in the shop which destroyed most of the inventory in it. Only a small amount of inventory, known to have cost $350, was undamaged and still fit for sale.

How much of the inventory was lost in the fire?

Solution

(a)

	$
Sales (140%)	154,000
Gross profit (40%)	44,000
Cost of goods sold (100%)	110,000

(b)

	$
Opening inventory, at cost	7,345
Plus purchases	106,420
	113,765
Less closing inventory, at cost	350
Equals cost of goods sold and goods lost	113,415

(c)

	$
Cost of goods sold and lost	113,415
Cost of goods sold	110,000
Cost of goods lost	3,415

6.2 Example: Cost of goods stolen

Beau Gullard runs a jewellery shop in the High Street. On 1 January 20X9, his trade inventory, at cost, amounted to $4,700 and his trade payables were $3,950.

During the six months to 30 June 20X9, sales were $42,000. Beau Gullard makes a gross profit of $33^{1}/3\%$ on the sales value of everything he sells.

On 30 June, there was a burglary at the shop, and all the inventory was stolen.

In trying to establish how much inventory had been taken, Beau Gullard was only able to say that:

(a)   He knew from his bank statements that he had paid $28,400 to trade account payables in the 6 month period to 30 June 20X9.

(b)   He currently had payables due of $5,550.

Required

(a)   Calculate the amount of inventory stolen.

(b)   Calculate gross profit for the 6 months to 30 June 20X9.

Solution

Step 1 The first 'unknown' is the amount of purchases during the period. This is established by the method previously described in this chapter.

TRADE ACCOUNTS PAYABLE

	$		$
Payments to trade accounts payable	28,400	Opening balance b/f	3,950
		Purchases (balancing figure)	30,000
Closing balance c/f	5,550		
	33,950		33,950

Step 2 The cost of goods sold is also unknown, but this can be established from the gross profit margin and the sales for the period.

		$
Sales	(100%)	42,000
Gross profit	($33\frac{1}{3}$%)	14,000
Cost of goods sold	($66\frac{2}{3}$%)	28,000

Step 3 The cost of the goods stolen is:

	$
Opening inventory at cost	4,700
Purchases	30,000
	34,700
Less closing inventory (after burglary)	0
Cost of goods sold and goods stolen	34,700
Cost of goods sold (see (b) above)	28,000
Cost of goods stolen	6,700

Step 4 The cost of the goods stolen will not be included in cost of sales, and so the gross profit for the period is as follows.

BEAU GULLARD
GROSS PROFIT FOR THE SIX MONTHS TO 30 JUNE 20X9

	$	$
Sales		42,000
Less cost of goods sold		
Opening inventory	4,700	
Purchases	30,000	
	34,700	
Less inventory stolen	6,700	
		28,000
Gross profit		14,000

6.3 Accounting for inventory destroyed, stolen or otherwise lost

When inventory is stolen, destroyed or otherwise lost, the loss must be accounted for somehow. The procedure was described briefly in the earlier chapter on inventory accounting. Since the loss is not a trading loss, the cost of the goods lost is not included in the cost of sales, as the previous example showed. The accounting double entry is therefore

DEBIT   See below
CREDIT   Cost of sales

The account that is to be debited is one of two possibilities, depending on whether or not the lost goods were insured against the loss.

(a)   If the lost goods were not insured, the business must bear the loss, and the loss is shown in the net profit (income and expenses) part of the income statement; ie

DEBIT   I & E a/c
CREDIT   Cost of sales

(b)   If the lost goods were insured, the business will not suffer a loss, because the insurance will pay back the cost of the lost goods. This means that there is no charge at all in the income statement, and the appropriate double entry is:

DEBIT   Insurance claim account (receivable account)
CREDIT   Cost of sales

with the cost of the loss. The insurance claim will then be a current asset, and shown in the statement of financial position of the business as such. When the claim is paid, the account is then closed by:

DEBIT   Cash
CREDIT   Insurance claim account

7 The cash book

FAST FORWARD

The construction of a cash book, largely from bank statements showing receipts and payments of a business during a given period, is often an important feature of incomplete records problems.

Exam focus point

In an examination, the purpose of an incomplete records question is largely to test the understanding of candidates about how various items of receipts or payments relate to the preparation of a final set of accounts for a business.

We have already seen in this chapter that information about cash receipts or payments might be needed to establish:

(a)   The amount of purchases during a period
(b)   The amount of credit sales during a period

Other items of receipts or payments might be relevant to establishing:

(a)   The amount of cash sales
(b)   The amount of certain expenses in the income statement
(c)   The amount of withdrawals on account of profit by the business proprietor

It might therefore be helpful, if a business does not keep a cash book day-to-day, to construct a cash book at the end of an accounting period. A business which typically might not keep a day-to-day cash book is a shop.

(a)   Many sales, if not all sales, are cash sales (ie with payment by notes and coins, cheques, or credit cards at the time of sale).
(b)   Some payments are made in notes and coins out of the till rather than by payment out of the business bank account by cheque.

Where there appears to be a sizeable volume of receipts and payments in cash (ie notes and coins), then it is also helpful to construct a two column cash book.

Key term

A **two column cash book** is a cash book with one column for receipts and payments, and one column for money paid into and out of the business bank account.

An example will illustrate the technique and the purpose of a two column cash book.

7.1 Example: Two column cash book

Jonathan Slugg owns and runs a shop selling fishing tackle, making a gross profit of 25% on the cost of everything he sells. He does not keep a cash book.

On 1 January 20X7 the statement of financial position of his business was as follows.

	$	$
Current assets		
Inventory	10,000	
Cash in the bank	3,000	
Cash in the till	200	
		13,200
Net long-term assets		20,000
		33,200
Trade accounts payable		1,200
Proprietor's capital		32,000
		33,200

In the year to 31 December 20X7:

(a) There were no sales on credit.

(b) $41,750 in receipts were banked.

(c) The bank statements of the period show the payments:

		$
(i)	to trade accounts payable	36,000
(ii)	sundry expenses	5,600
(iii)	to drawings	4,400

(d) Payments were also made in cash out of the till:

		$
(i)	for trade accounts payable	800
(ii)	sundry expenses	1,500
(iii)	to drawings	3,700

At 31 December 20X7, the business had cash in the till of $450 and trade accounts payable of $1,400. The cash balance in the bank was not known and the value of closing inventory has not yet been calculated. There were no accruals or prepayments. No further long-term assets were purchased during the year. The depreciation charge for the year is $900.

Required

(a) Prepare a two column cash book for the period.

(b) Prepare the income statement for the year to 31 December 20X7 and the statement of financial position as at 31 December 20X7.

7.2 Discussion and solution

A two column cash book is completed as follows.

Step 1 Enter the opening cash balances.

Step 2 Enter the information given about cash payments (and any cash receipts, if there had been any such items given in the problem).

Step 3 The cash receipts banked are a 'contra' entry, being both a debit (bank column) and a credit (cash in hand column) in the same account.

Step 4 Enter the closing cash in hand (cash in the bank at the end of the period is not known).

CASH BOOK

	Cash in hand $	Bank $		Cash in hand $	Bank $
Balance b/f	200	3,000	Trade accounts		
Cash receipts			payable	800	36,000
banked (contra)		41,750	Sundry expenses	1,500	5,600
Sales*	48,000		Drawings	3,700	4,400
			Cash receipts		
			banked (contra)	41,750	
Balance c/f		*1,250	Balance c/f	450	
	48,200	46,000		48,200	46,000

* Balancing figure

Step 5   The closing balance of money in the bank is a balancing figure.

Step 6   Since all sales are for cash, a balancing figure that can be entered in the cash book is sales, in the cash in hand (debit) column.

It is important to notice that since not all receipts from cash sales are banked, the value of cash sales during the period is:

	$
Receipts banked	41,750
Plus expenses and withdrawals paid out of the till in cash	
$(800 + 1,500 + 3,700)$	6,000
Plus any cash stolen (here there is none)	0
Plus the closing balance of cash in hand	450
	48,200
Less the opening balance of cash in hand	(200)
Equals cash sales	48,000

The cash book constructed in this way has enabled us to establish both the closing balance for cash in the bank and also the volume of cash sales. The income statement and the statement of financial position can also be prepared, once a value for purchases has been calculated.

TRADE ACCOUNTS PAYABLE

	$		$
Cash book: payments from bank	36,000	Balance b/f	1,200
Cash book: payments in cash	800	Purchases (balancing figure)	37,000
Balance c/f	1,400		
	38,200		38,200

The gross profit margin of 25% on cost indicates that the cost of the goods sold is $38,400, ie:

	$
Sales (125%)	48,000
Gross profit (25%)	9,600
Cost of goods sold (100%)	38,400

The closing inventory is now a balancing figure in the trading account.

JONATHAN SLUGG
INCOME STATEMENT
FOR THE YEAR ENDED 31 DECEMBER 20X7

	$	$
Sales		48,000
Less cost of goods sold		
Opening inventory	10,000	
Purchases	37,000	
	47,000	
Less closing inventory (balancing figure)	8,600	
		38,400
Gross profit (25/125 × $48,000)		9,600
Expenses		
Sundry $(1,500 + 5,600)	7,100	
Depreciation	900	
		8,000
Net profit		1,600

JONATHAN SLUGG
STATEMENT OF FINANCIAL POSITION AS AT 31 DECEMBER 20X7

	$	$
Assets		
Current assets		
Inventory	8,600	
Cash in the till	450	
		9,050
Net long-term assets $(20,000 – 900)		19,100
Total assets		28,150
Capital and liabilities		
Proprietor's capital		
Balance b/f	32,000	
Net profit for the year	1,600	
Withdrawals on account $(3,700 + 4,400)	(8,100)	
Balance c/f		25,500
Current liabilities		
Bank overdraft	1,250	
Trade payables	1,400	
		2,650
Total capital and liabilities		28,150

7.3 Theft of cash from the till

When cash is stolen from the till, the amount stolen will be a credit entry in the cash book, and a debit in either the net profit section (income and expenses account) of the income statement or insurance claim account, depending on whether the business is insured. The missing figure for cash sales, if this has to be calculated, must not ignore cash received but later stolen – see above.

8 Accruals and prepayments

Where there is an accrued expense or a prepayment, the charge to be made in the income statement for the item concerned should be found from the opening balance b/f, the closing balance c/f, and cash payments for the item during the period. The charge in the income statement is perhaps most easily found as the balancing figure in a T-account.

For example, suppose that on 1 April 20X6 a business had prepaid rent of $700 which relates to the next accounting period. During the year to 31 March 20X7 it pays $9,300 in rent, and at 31 March 20X7 the prepayment of rent is $1,000. The cost of rent in the I&E account for the year to 31 March 20X7 would be the balancing figure in the following T-account. (Remember that a prepayment is a current asset, and so is a debit balance b/f.)

RENT

	$		$
Prepayment: balance b/f	700	I & E a/c (balancing figure)	9,000
Cash	9,300	Prepayment: balance c/f	1,000
	10,000		10,000
Balance b/f	1,000		

Similarly, if a business has accrued telephone expenses as at 1 July 20X6 of $850, pays $6,720 in telephone bills during the year to 30 June 20X7, and has accrued telephone expenses of $1,140 as at 30 June 20X7, then the telephone expense to be shown in the income statement for the year to 30 June 20X7 is the balancing figure in the following T-account. (Remember that an accrual is a current liability, and so is a credit balance b/f.)

TELEPHONE EXPENSES

	$		$
Cash	6,720	Balance b/f (accrual)	850
Balance c/f (accrual)	1,140	I & E a/c (balancing figure)	7,010
	7,860		7,860
		Balance b/f	1,140

9 Drawings

FAST FORWARD

Drawings often feature as the missing item in an incomplete records problem. The trader has been drawing money but does not know how much.

Drawings would normally represent no particular problem at all in preparing a set of final accounts from incomplete records, but it is not unusual for examination questions to contain complicating situations.

(a) The business owner may pay income into his bank account which has nothing whatever to do with the business operations. For example, the owner might pay dividend income, or other income from investments into the bank, from stocks and shares which he owns personally, separate from the business itself. (In other words, there are no investments in the business statement of financial position, and so income from investments cannot possibly be income of the business.) These amounts will be credited to his drawings.

(b) The business owner may pay money out of the business bank account for items which are not business expenses, such as life insurance premiums or a payment for his family's holidays etc. These will be treated as drawings.

Where such **personal items of receipts or payments** are made the following adjustments should be made.

(a) Receipts should be set off against drawings. For example, if a business owner receives $600 in dividend income and pays it into his business bank account, although the dividends are from investments not owned by the business, then the accounting entry is:

DEBIT	Cash
CREDIT	Drawings

(b) Payments should be charged to drawings on account; ie:

DEBIT	Drawings
CREDIT	Cash

9.1 Beware of the wording in an examination question

You should note that:

(a) If a question states that a proprietor's drawings during a given year are 'approximately $40 per week' then you should assume that drawings for the year are $40 × 52 weeks = $2,080.

(b) However, if a question states that drawings in the year are 'between $35 and $45 per week', do not assume that the drawings average $40 per week and so amount to $2,080 for the year. You could not be certain that the actual withdrawals did average $40, and so you should treat the withdrawals figure as a missing item that needs to be calculated.

10 The business equation

Where no trading records have been kept, profit can be derived from opening and closing net assets by use of the **business equation.**

The most obvious incomplete records situation is that of a sole trader who has kept no trading records. It may not be possible to reconstruct his whole income statement, but it will be possible to compute his profit for the year using the **business equation.**

Here is the basic statement of financial position format:

Assets		XX
Capital	X	
Liabilities	X	XX

This can be rearranged as:

Assets	XX	
Liabilities	(X)	X
Capital		X

So this gives us a figure for capital – assets less liabilities, or **net assets**.

What will increase or decrease capital?

Capital is changed by:

(a) Money paid in by the trader
(b) Drawings by the trader
(c) Profits or losses

So, if we are able to establish the traders net assets at the beginnings and end of the period, we can compute profits as follows:

Profit (loss) = movement in net assets – capital introduced + drawings

We want to eliminate any movement caused by money paid in or taken out for personal use by the trader. So we take out capital introduced and add back in drawings.

10.1 Example: Business equation

Joe starts up his camera shop on 1 January 20X1, from rented premises, with $5,000 inventory and $3,000 in the bank. All of his sales are for cash. He keeps no record of his takings.

At the end of the year he has inventory worth $6,600 and $15,000 in the bank. He owes $3,000 to suppliers. He had paid in $5,000 he won on the lottery and drawn out $2,000 to buy himself a motorbike. The motorbike is not used in the business. He has been taking drawings of $100 per week. What is his profit at 31 December 20X1?

Solution

Opening net assets	$
Inventory	5,000
Cash	3,000
	8,000

Closing net assets	
Inventory	6,600
Cash	15,000
Payables	(3,000)
	18,600

Movement in capital (net assets)	10,600
Less capital paid in	(5,000)
Plus drawings ((100 × 52) + 2000)	7,200
Profit	12,800

11 Comprehensive worked examples

A suggested approach to dealing with incomplete records problems brings together the various points described so far in this chapter. The nature of the 'incompleteness' in the records will vary from problem to problem, but the approach, suitably applied, should be successful in arriving at the final accounts whatever the particular characteristics of the problem might be.

The approach is as follows.

Step 1 If possible, and if it is not already known, establish the opening statement of financial position and the proprietor's interest.

Step 2 Open up four accounts.

- Income and expense account
- A cash book, with two columns if cash sales are significant and there are payments in cash out of the till
- A trade receivables account
- A trade payables account

Step 3 Enter the opening balances in these accounts.

Step 4 Work through the information you are given line by line; and each item should be entered into the appropriate account if it is relevant to one or more of these four accounts.

You should also try to recognise each item as an 'income or expense item' or a 'closing statement of financial position item'.

It may be necessary to calculate an amount for withdrawals on account and an amount for non-current asset depreciation.

Step 5 Look for the balancing figures in your accounts. In particular you might be looking for a value for credit sales, cash sales, purchases, the cost of goods sold, the cost of goods stolen or destroyed, or the closing bank balance. Calculate these missing figures, and make any necessary double entry (eg to the trading account from trade accounts payable for purchases, to the trading account from the cash book for cash sales, and to the trading account from trade accounts receivable for credit sales).

Step 6 Now complete the income statement and statement of financial position. Working T-accounts might be needed where there are accruals or prepayments.

The business equation [Profit = increase in net assets − capital introduced + drawings] may be useful as a check on the profit figure or to calculate it in a MCQ.

An example will illustrate this approach.

11.1 Example: An incomplete records problem

John Snow is the sole distribution agent in the Branton area for Diamond floor tiles. Under an agreement with the manufacturers, John Snow purchases the Diamond floor tiles at a trade discount of 20% off list price and annually in May receives an agency commission of 1% of his purchases for the year ended on the previous 31 March.

For several years, John Snow has obtained a gross profit of 40% on all sales. In a burglary in January 20X1 John Snow lost inventory costing $4,000 as well as many of his accounting records. However, after careful investigations, the following information has been obtained covering the year ended 31 March 20X1.

(a)   Assets and liabilities at 31 March 20X0 were as follows.

		$
Buildings:	at cost	10,000
	accumulated depreciation	6,000
Motor vehicles:	at cost	5,000
	accumulated depreciation	2,000
Inventory: at cost		3,200
Trade accounts receivable (for sales)		6,300
Agency commission due		300
Prepayments (trade expenses)		120
Balance at bank		4,310
Trade accounts payable		4,200
Accrued vehicle expenses		230

(b)   John Snow has been notified that he will receive an agency commission of $440 on 1 May 20X1.

(c)   Inventory, at cost, at 31 March 20X1 was valued at an amount $3,000 more than a year previously.

(d)   In October 20X0 inventory costing $1,000 was damaged by dampness and had to be scrapped as worthless.

(e)   Trade accounts payable at 31 March 20X1 related entirely to goods received whose list prices totalled $9,500.

(f)   Discounts allowed amounted to $1,620 whilst discounts received were $1,200.

(g)   Trade expenses prepaid at 31 March 20X1 totalled $80.

(h)   Vehicle expenses for the year ended 31 March 20X1 amounted to $7,020.

(i)   Trade accounts receivable (for sales) at 31 March 20X1 were $6,700.

(j)   All receipts are passed through the bank account.

(k)   Depreciation is charged annually at the following rates.

Buildings 5% on cost
Motor vehicles 20% on cost.

(l)   Commissions received are paid directly to the bank account.

(m)   In addition to the payments for purchases, the bank payments were:

	$
Vehicle expenses	6,720
Drawings	4,300
Trade expenses	7,360

(n)   John Snow is not insured against loss of inventory owing to burglary or damage to inventory caused by damp.

Required

Prepare John Snow's income statement for the year ended 31 March 20X1 and a statement of financial position on that date.

11.2 Discussion and solution

This is an incomplete records problem because we are told that John Snow has lost many of his accounting records. In particular we do not know sales for the year, purchases during the year, or all the cash receipts and payments.

The first step is to find the opening statement of financial position, if possible. In this case, it is. The proprietor's capital is the balancing figure.

JOHN SNOW
STATEMENT OF FINANCIAL POSITION AS AT 31 MARCH 20X0

		$	$
Assets			
Non-current assets			
Buildings:	cost	10,000	
	accumulated deprecation	6,000	
			4,000
Motor vehicles:	cost	5,000	
	accumulated depreciation	2,000	
			3,000
Current assets			
Inventory		3,200	
Trade accounts receivable		6,300	
Commission due		300	
Prepayments		120	
Balance of cash at hand		4,310	
			14,230
Total assets			21,230
Capital and liabilities			
Proprietor's capital (balance)			16,800
Current liabilities			
Trade payables		4,200	
Accrued expenses		230	
			4,430
Total capital and liabilities			21,230

The next step is to open up an income and expense account, cash book, trade receivables account and trade payables account and to insert the opening balances, if known. Cash sales and payments in cash are not a feature of the problem, and so a single column cash book is sufficient.

The problem should then be read line by line, identifying any transactions affecting those accounts.

I & E ACCOUNT

	$	$
Sales (note (f))		60,000
Opening inventory	3,200	
Purchases (note (a))	44,000	
	47,200	
Less: damaged inventory written off (note (c))	(1,000)	
inventory stolen (note (e))	(4,000)	
	42,200	
Less closing inventory (note (b))	(6,200)	
Cost of goods sold		36,000
Gross profit (note (f))		24,000

CASH BOOK

	$		$
Opening balance	4,310	Trade accounts payable	
Trade accounts receivable (see below)	57,980	(see trade accounts payable)	39,400
Agency commission (note (g))	300	Trade expenses	7,360
		Vehicle expenses	6,720
		Drawings	4,300
		Balance c/f	4,810
	62,590		62,590

TRADE ACCOUNTS RECEIVABLE

	$		$
Opening balance b/f	6,300	Discounts allowed (note (d))	1,620
Sales (note (f))	60,000	Cash received (balancing figure)	57,980
		Closing balance c/f	6,700
	66,300		66,300

TRADE ACCOUNTS PAYABLE

	$		$
Discounts received (note (d))	1,200	Opening balance b/f	4,200
Cash paid (balancing figure)	39,400	Purchases (note (a))	44,000
Closing balance c/f	7,600		
	48,200		48,200

VEHICLE EXPENSES

	$		$
Cash	6,720	Accrual b/f	230
Accrual c/f (balancing figure)	530	I & E account	7,020
	7,250		7,250

The trading account is complete already, but now the income statement and statement of financial position can be prepared. Remember not to forget items such as the inventory losses, commission earned on purchases, discounts allowed and discounts received.

JOHN SNOW
INCOME STATEMENT FOR THE YEAR ENDED 31 MARCH 20X1

	$	$
Sales (note (f))		60,000
Opening stock	3,200	
Purchases (note (a))	44,000	
	47,200	
Less: damaged inventory written off (note (c))	(1,000)	
inventory stolen	(4,000)	
	42,200	
Less closing inventory (note (b))	6,200	
Cost of goods sold		36,000
Gross profit (note (f))		24,000
Add: commission on purchases		440
discounts received		1,200
		25,640
Expenses		
Trade expenses (note (h))	7,400	
Inventory damaged	1,000	
Inventory stolen	4,000	
Vehicle expenses	7,020	
Discounts allowed	1,620	
Depreciation		
Buildings	500	
Motor vehicles	1,000	
		22,540
Net profit (to capital account)		3,100

JOHN SNOW
STATEMENT OF FINANCIAL POSITION AS AT 31 MARCH 20X1

		$	$
Assets			
Non-current assets			
Buildings:	cost	10,000	
	accumulated depreciation	6,500	
			3,500
Motor vehicles:	cost	5,000	
	accumulated depreciation	3,000	
			2,000
Current assets			
Inventory		6,200	
Trade accounts receivable		6,700	
Commission due		440	
Prepayments (trade expenses)		80	
Balance at bank		4,810	
			18,230
Total assets			23,730
Capital and liabilities			
Proprietor's capital			
As at 31 March 20X0		16,800	
Net profit for year to 31 March 20X0		3,100	
Less drawings		(4,300)	
As at 31 March 20X0			15,600
Current liabilities			
Trade accounts payable		7,600	
Accrued expenses		530	
			8,130
Total capital and liabilities			23,730

Notes

(a)   The agency commission due on 1 May 20X1 indicates that purchases for the year to 31 March 20X1 were:

100%/1% × $440 = $44,000

(b)   Closing inventory at cost on 31 March 20X1 was $(3,200 + 3,000) = $6,200.

(c)   Inventory scrapped ($1,000) is accounted for by:

CREDIT   Cost of sales
DEBIT   I & E account

(d)   Discounts allowed are accounted for by:

DEBIT   Discounts allowed account
CREDIT   Trade accounts receivable

Similarly, discounts received are:

DEBIT   Trade accounts payable
CREDIT   Discounts received

Note. Discounts received represents settlement discounts, not *trade* discounts, which are not usually accounted for as they are given automatically at source.

(e)   Inventory lost in the burglary is accounted for by:

CREDIT   Cost of sales
DEBIT   I & E account

(f)   The trade discount of 20% has already been deducted in arriving at the value of the purchases. The gross profit is 40% on sales, so with cost of sales = $36,000

			$
Cost	(60%)		36,000
Profit	(40%)		24,000
Sales	(100%)		60,000

(It is assumed that trade expenses are not included in the cost of sales, and so should be ignored in this calculation.)

(g) The agency commission of $300 due on 1 May 20X0 would have been paid to John Snow at that date.

(h) The I & E account expenditure for trade expenses and closing balance on vehicle expenses account are as follows.

TRADE EXPENSES

	$		$
Prepayment	120	I & E account (balancing figure)	7,400
Cash	7,360	Prepayment c/f	80
	7,480		7,480

11.3 Using trade accounts receivable to calculate both cash sales and credit sales

A final point which needs to be considered is how a missing value can be found for cash sales and credit sales, when a business has both, but takings banked by the business are not divided between takings from cash sales and takings from credit sales.

11.4 Example: Using trade accounts receivable

Suppose, for example, that a business had, on 1 January 20X8, trade accounts receivable of $2,000, cash in the bank of $3,000, and cash in hand of $300.

During the year to 31 December 20X8 the business banked $95,000 in takings.

It also paid out the following expenses in cash from the till:

Drawings	$1,200
Sundry expenses	$800

On 29 August 20X8 a thief broke into the shop and stole $400 from the till.

At 31 December 20X8 trade accounts receivable amounted to $3,500, cash in the bank $2,500 and cash in the till $150.

What was the value of sales during the year?

Solution

If we tried to prepare a trade accounts receivable account and a two column cash book, we would have insufficient information, in particular about whether the takings which were banked related to cash sales or credit sales.

TRADE ACCOUNTS RECEIVABLE

	$		$
Balance b/f	2,000	Cash from receivables	
		(credit sales)	Unknown
Credit sales	Unknown		
		Balance c/f	3,500

CASH BOOK

	Cash	Bank		Cash	Bank
	$	$		$	$
Balance b/f	300	3,000	Drawings	1,200	
			Sundry expenses	800	
Cash from receivables		Unknown	Cash stolen	400	
Cash sales	Unknown		Balance c/f	150	2,500

All we do know is that the combined sums from trade accounts receivable and cash takings banked is $95,000.

The value of sales can be found instead by using the trade receivables account, which should be used to record cash takings banked as well as payments from receivables. The balancing figure in the receivables account will then be a combination of credit sales and some cash sales. The cash book only needs to be a single column.

TRADE ACCOUNTS RECEIVABLE

	$		$
Balance b/f	2,000	Cash banked	95,000
Sales: to trading account	96,500	Balance c/f	3,500
	98,500		98,500

CASH (EXTRACT)

	$		$
Balance in hand b/f	300	*Payments in cash*	
Balance in bank b/f	3,000	Drawings	1,200
Trade receivables a/c	95,000	Expenses	800
		Other payments	?
		Cash stolen	400
		Balance in hand c/f	150
		Balance in bank c/f	2,500

The remaining 'undiscovered' amount of cash sales is now found as follows.

	$	$
Payments in cash out of the till		
Drawings	1,200	
Expenses	800	
		2,000
Cash stolen		400
Closing balance of cash in hand		150
		2,550
Less opening balance of cash in hand		(300)
Further cash sales		2,250

(This calculation is similar to the one described above for calculating cash sales.)

Total sales for the year are:

	$
From trade receivables	96,500
From cash book	2,250
Total sales	98,750

 Question

Incomplete records

Mary Grimes, wholesale fruit and vegetable merchant, does not keep a full set of accounting records. However, the following information has been produced from the business's records.

(a)   *Summary of the bank account for the year ended 31 August 20X8*

	$		$
1 Sept 20X7 balance b/f	1,970	Payments to suppliers	72,000
Cash from trade receivables	96,000	Purchase of motor van (E471 KBR)	13,000
Sale of private yacht	20,000	Rent and local taxes	2,600
Sale of motor van (A123 BWA)	2,100	Wages	15,100
		Motor vehicle expenses	3,350
		Postages and stationery	1,360
		Drawings	9,200
		Repairs and renewals	650
		Insurances	800
		31 August 20X8 balance c/f	2,010
	120,070		120,070
1 Sept 20X8 balance b/f	2,010		

(b)   *Assets and liabilities, other than balance at bank*

		1 Sept 20X7	31 Aug 20X8
		$	$
Trade accounts payable		4,700	2,590
Trade accounts receivable		7,320	9,500
Rent and local taxes accrued		200	260
Motor vans:			
A123 BWA:	At cost	10,000	–
	Accumulated depreciation	8,000	–
E471 KBR:	At cost	–	13,000
	Accumulated depreciation	–	To be determined
Inventory		4,900	5,900
Insurance prepaid		160	200

(c)   All receipts are banked and all payments are made from the business bank account.

(d)   A trade debt of $300 owing by John Blunt and included in the trade accounts receivable at 31 August 20X8 (see (b) above), is to be written off as an irrecoverable debt.

(e)   It is Mary Grimes' policy to provide depreciation at the rate of 20% on the cost of motor vans held at the end of each financial year; no depreciation is provided in the year of sale or disposal of a motor van.

(f)   Discounts received during the year ended 31 August 20X8 from trade accounts payable amounted to $1,100.

Required

(a)   Prepare Mary Grimes' income statement for the year ended 31 August 20X8.
(b)   Prepare Mary Grimes' statement of financial position as at 31 August 20X8.

(a) INCOME STATEMENT
FOR THE YEAR ENDED 31 AUGUST 20X8

	$	$
Sales (W1)		98,180
Opening inventory	4,900	
Purchases (W2)	70,990	
	75,890	
Less closing inventory	5,900	
		69,990
Gross profit		28,190
Discounts received		1,100
Profit on sale of motor vehicle ($2,100 – $(10,000 – 8,000))		100
		29,390
Rent and local taxes (W3)	2,660	
Wages	15,100	
Motor vehicle expenses	3,350	
Postages and stationery	1,360	
Repairs and renewals	650	
Insurances (W4)	760	
Irrecoverable debt	300	
Depreciation of van (20% × $13,000)	2,600	
		26,780
		2,610

(b) STATEMENT OF FINANCIAL POSITION AS AT 31 AUGUST 20X8

	$	$
Assets		
Non-current assets		
Motor van: cost	13,000	
Depreciation	2,600	
		10,400
Current assets		
Inventory	5,900	
Trade accounts receivable ($9,500 – $300 irrecoverable debt)	9,200	
Prepayment	200	
Cash at bank	2,010	
		17,310
Total assets		27,710
Capital and liabilities		
Capital account		
Balance at 1 September 20X7 (W5)	11,450	
Additional capital: proceeds on sale of yacht	20,000	
Net profit for the year	2,610	
Less drawings	(9,200)	
Balance at 31 August 20X8		24,860
Current liabilities		
Trade accounts payable	2,590	
Accrual	260	
		2,850
Total capital and liabilities		27,710

Workings

1   *Sales*

		$
Cash received from customers		96,000
Add trade accounts receivable at 31 August 20X8		9,500
		105,500
Less trade accounts receivable at 1 September 20X7		7,320
Sales in year		98,180

2   *Purchases*

	$	$
Payments to suppliers		72,000
Add: trade accounts payable at 31 August 20X8	2,590	
discounts granted by suppliers	1,100	
		3,690
		75,690
Less trade accounts payable at 1 September 20X7		4,700
		70,990

3   *Rent and local taxes*

	$
Cash paid in year	2,600
Add accrual at 31 August 20X8	260
	2,860
Less accrual at 1 September 20X7	200
Charge for the year	2,660

4   *Insurances*

	$
Cash paid in year	800
Add prepayment at 1 September 20X7	160
	960
Less prepayment at 31 August 20X8	200
	760

Workings 1-4 could also be presented in ledger account format as follows.

TRADE ACCOUNTS RECEIVABLE

	$		$
Balance b/f	7,320	Bank	96,000
∴ Sales	98,180	Balance c/f	9,500
	105,500		105,500

TRADE ACCOUNTS PAYABLE

	$		$
Bank	72,000	Balance b/f	4,700
Discounts received	1,100	∴ Purchases	70,990
Balance c/f	2,590		
	75,690		75,690

RENT AND LOCAL TAXES

	$		$
Bank	2,600	Balance b/f	200
Balance c/f	260	∴ I & E charge	2,660
	2,860		2,860

INSURANCES

	$		$
Balance b/f	160	∴ I & E charge	760
Bank	800	Balance c/f	200
	960		960

5   *Capital at 1 September 20X7*

	$	$
Assets		
Bank balance		1,970
Trade accounts receivable		7,320
Motor van $(10,000 – 8,000)		2,000
Inventory		4,900
Prepayment		160
		16,350
Liabilities		
Trade accounts payable	4,700	
Accrual	200	
		4,900
		11,450

Exam focus point

> You will NOT be asked to prepare a full set of accounts in the exam. However, it is essential that you practise on full questions, so that you can easily calculate any missing figure that you need in the exam.

Chapter Roundup

- **Incomplete records** questions may test your ability to prepare accounts in the following situations.

    - A trader **does not maintain a ledger** and therefore has no continuous double entry record of transactions.

    - Accounting records are **destroyed** by accident, such as fire.

    - Some essential figure is **unknown** and must be calculated as a balancing figure. This may occur as a result of inventory being damaged or destroyed, or because of misappropriation of assets.

- The approach to incomplete records questions is to build up the information given so as to complete the necessary **double entry**. This may involve reconstructing **control accounts** for:

    - cash and bank
    - trade accounts receivable and payable.

- Where inventory, sales or purchases is the unknown figure it will be necessary to use information on **gross profit percentages** so as to construct a working for gross profit in which the unknown figure can be inserted as a balance.

- The construction of a cashbook, largely from bank statements, showing receipts and payments during the period, is often an important feature of incomplete records problems.

- **Drawings** often feature as the missing item in an incomplete records problem. The trader has been drawing money but does not know how much.

- Where no trading records have been kept, profit can be derived from opening and closing net assets by use of the **business equation**.

Quick Quiz

1   In the absence of a sales account or sales day book, how can a figure of sales for the year be computed?

2   A business has opening payables of $75,000 and closing payables of $65,000. Cash paid to suppliers was $65,000 and discounts received $3,000. What is the figure for purchase?

    A $58,000
    B $78,000
    C $52,000
    D $55,000

3   What is the difference between 'mark-up' and 'gross profit percentage'?

4   What is the accounting double entry to record the loss of inventory by fire or burglary?

    A   DR I&E, CR sales
    B   DR sales, CR I&E

5   In what circumstances is a two-column cash book useful?

6   If a business proprietor pays his personal income into the business bank account, what is the accounting double entry to record the transaction?

    A   DR drawings, CR cash
    B   DR cash, CR drawings

7   A business has net assets of $70,000 at the beginning of the year and $80,000 at the end of the year. Drawings were $25,000 and a lottery win of $5,000 was paid into the business during the year. What was the profit for the year?

    A $10,000 loss
    B $30,000 profit
    C $10,000 profit
    D $30,000 loss

8   A business usually has a mark-up of 20% on cost of sales. During a year, its sales were $90,000. What was cost of sales?

    A $15,000
    B $72,000
    C $18,000
    D $75,000

Answers to Quick Quiz

1   By using the trade accounts receivable control account to calculate sales as a balancing figure.

2   A

	PAYABLES CONTROL		
	$		$
Bank	65,000	Opening payables	75,000
Discounts received	3,000	Purchases (bal fig)	58,000
Closing payables	65,000		
	133,000		133,000

3   •   Mark-up is the profit as a percentage of cost.
     •   Gross profit percentage is the profit as a percentage of sales.

4   A   DEBIT   I & E a/c
               CREDIT   Cost of sales

     Assuming that the goods were not insured.

5   Where a large amount of receipts and payments are made in cash.

6   B   DEBIT   Cash
           CREDIT   Drawings

7   B   Profit = movement in net assets − capital introduced + drawings
                  = (80,000 − 70,000) − 5,000 + 25,000
                  = 30,000

8   D

	$
Sales	90,000
Cost of sales (bal fig)	75,000
Profit $\left(\dfrac{20}{120} \times 90,000 \right)$	15,000

Now try the questions below from the Exam Question Bank

Number	Level	Marks	Time
Q34	Examination	2	2 mins
Q35	Examination	2	2 mins
Q36	Examination	2	2 mins
Q37	Examination	2	2 mins

19

Partnerships

Topic list	Syllabus reference
1 The characteristics of partnerships	F4(a), (c)
2 Preparing partnership accounts	F4(b)-(n)

Introduction

So far we have considered businesses owned by one person: sole traders. Now we will consider how we can account for businesses owned by more than one person. This chapter will examine how we can account for partnerships and the next two chapters will examine how we can account for companies.

Study guide

		Intellectual level
F4	**Accounting for partnerships**	
(a)	Understand and identify the typical content of a partnership agreement, including profit-sharing terms	1
(b)	Understand the nature of:	1
	(i) Capital account	
	(ii) Current accounts	
	(iii) Division of profits	
(c)	Calculate and record the partners' shares of profits/losses	1
(d)	Account for guaranteed minimum profit shares	1
(e)	Calculate and record partners' drawings	1
(f)	Calculate and record interest on drawings	1
(g)	Calculate and record interest on capital	1
(h)	Calculate and record partner salaries	1
(i)	Prepare an extract of a current account	1
(j)	Prepare an extract of a capital account	1
(k)	Prepare extracts of the income statement, including division of profit, and statement of financial position of a partnership	1
(l)	Define goodwill, in relation to partnership accounts	1
(m)	Identify the factors leading to the creation of goodwill in relation to partnership accounts	1
(n)	Calculate the value of goodwill from given information	1

Note. Questions on partnerships may include the effect of admission of new partners.

Exam guide

This is an important topic and it is almost certain to appear in the exam.

Exam focus point

At the 2009 ACCA Teachers' Conference, the examiner highlighted partnership accounts as an area consistently answered badly in the exam. She also emphasised the need to practise full questions on this topic as a good foundation for future studies.

1 The characteristics of partnerships

Try this exercise to get you thinking.

Question   Partnership

Try to think of reasons why a business should be conducted as a partnership, rather than:

(a)   As a sole trader
(b)   As a limited liability company

(a) The main problems with trading as a sole trader is the limitation on resources it implies. As the business grows, there will be a need for the following.

    (i) **Additional capital:** although some capital may be provided by a bank, it would not be desirable to have the business entirely dependent on borrowing.

    (ii) **Additional expertise:** a sole trader technically competent in his own field may not have, for example, the financial skills that would be needed in a larger business.

    (iii) **Additional management time:** once a business grows to a certain point, it becomes impossible for one person to look after all aspects of it without help.

(b) The main **disadvantage** of incorporating is the **regulatory burden** faced by limited liability companies in most countries. In addition, there are certain 'businesses' which are not allowed to enjoy limited liability; you may have read about the Lloyd's 'names' who face personal bankruptcy because the option of limited liability was not available to them.

There are also tax factors to consider, but these are beyond the scope of this book.

Key term

> **Partnership** can be defined as the relationship which exists between persons carrying on a business in common with a view of profit.

In other words, a partnership is an arrangement between two or more individuals in which they undertake to share the risks and rewards of a joint business operation.

It is usual for a partnership to be established formally by means of a *partnership agreement*. However, if individuals act as though they are in partnership even if no written agreement exists, then it will be presumed that a partnership does exist and that its terms of agreement are reflected in the way the partners conduct the business, ie the way profits have been divided in the past, etc. In some countries legislation may exist which governs partnerships.

1.1 The partnership agreement

FAST FORWARD

> The terms under which the partnership operates are set out in the **partnership agreement**. The initial capital put into the business by each partner is shown by means of a **capital account** for each partner. The net profit of the partnership is **appropriated** by the partners according to a previously agreed ratio. Each partner also has a current account to which their drawings are charged. Partners may be charged **interest** on their **drawings** and may receive **interest on capital**.

The partnership agreement is a written agreement in which the terms of the partnership are set out, and in particular the financial arrangements as between partners. The items it should cover include the following.

(a) **Capital**. Each partner puts in a share of the business capital. If there is to be an agreement on how much each partner should put in and keep in the business, as a minimum fixed amount, this should be stated.

(b) **Profit-sharing ratio**. Partners can agree to share profits in any way they choose. For example, if there are three partners in a business, they might agree to share profits equally but on the other hand, if one partner does a greater share of the work, or has more experience and ability, or puts in more capital, the ratio of profit sharing might be different.

(c) **Interest on capital**. Partners might agree to pay themselves interest on the capital they put into the business. If they do so, the agreement will state what rate of interest is to be applied.

(d) **Partners' salaries**. Partners might also agree to pay themselves salaries. These are not salaries in the same way that an employee of the business will be paid a wage or salary, because partners' salaries are an appropriation of profit, and not an expense in the income statement of the business.

The purpose of paying salaries is to give each partner a satisfactory basic income before the residual profits are shared out.

(e) **Drawings.** Partners may draw out their share of profits from the business. However, they might agree to put a limit on how much they should draw out in any period. If so, this limit should be specified in the partnership agreement. To encourage partners to delay making withdrawals from the business until the financial year has ended, the agreement might also be that partners should be charged interest on their drawings during the year.

1.2 Example: Partners' salaries and profit-sharing

Bill and Ben are partners sharing profit in the ratio 2:1 and that they agree to pay themselves a salary of $10,000 each. If profits before deducting salaries are $26,000, how much income would each partner receive?

Solution

First, the two salaries are deducted from profit, leaving $6,000 ($26,000 – $20,000).

This $6,000 has to be distributed between Bill and Ben in the ratio 2:1. In other words, Bill will receive twice as much as Ben. You can probably work this out in your head and see that Bill will get $4,000 and Ben $2,000, but we had better see how this is calculated properly.

Add the 'parts' of the ratio together. For our example, 2 + 1 = 3. Divide this total into whatever it is that has to be shared out. In our example, $6,000 ÷ 3 = $2,000. Each 'part' is worth $2,000, so Bill receives 2 × $2,000 = $4,000 and Ben will receive 1 × $2,000 = $2,000.

So the final answer to the question is that Bill receives his salary plus $4,000 and Ben his salary plus $2,000. This could be laid out as follows:

	Bill	Ben	Total
	$	$	$
Salary	10,000	10,000	20,000
Share of residual profits (ratio 2:1)	4,000	2,000	6,000
	14,000	12,000	26,000

Question	Profitshare

Suppose Tom, Dick and Harry want to share out $150 in the ratio 7:3:5. How much would each get?

Answer

The sum of the ratio 'parts' is 7 + 3 + 5 = 15. Each part is therefore worth $150 ÷ 15 = $10. So the $150 would be shared as follows.

			$
(a)	Tom:	7 × $10 =	70
(b)	Dick:	3 × $10 =	30
(c)	Harry:	5 × $10 =	50
			150

1.3 Advantages and disadvantages of trading as a partnership

Operating as a partnership entails certain advantages and disadvantages when compared with both sole traders and limited liability companies.

1.3.1 Partnership v sole trader

The advantages of operating as a partnership rather than as a sole trader are practical rather than legal. They include the following.

(a) Risks are spread across a larger number of people.
(b) The trader will have access to a wider network of contacts through the other partners.
(c) Partners should bring to the business not only capital but skills and experience.
(d) It may well be easier to raise finance from external sources such as banks.

Possible disadvantages include the following.

(a) While the risk is spread over a larger number of people, so are the profits!
(b) By bringing in more people the former sole trader dilutes control over his business.
(c) There may be disputes between the partners.

1.3.2 Partnership v limited liability company

Limited liability companies (covered in detail in the next chapter) offer limited liability to their owners. This means that the maximum amount that an owner stands to lose in the event that the company becomes insolvent and must pay off its debts is the capital in the business. In the case of partnerships (and sole traders), liability for the debts of the business is unlimited, which means that if the business runs up debts and is unable to pay, the proprietors will become personally liable for the unpaid debts and would be required, if necessary, to sell their private possessions in order to pay for them.

Limited liability is clearly a significant incentive for a partnership to incorporate (become a company). Other advantages of incorporation are that it is easier to raise capital and that the retirement or death of one of its members does not necessitate dissolution and re-formation of the firm.

In practice, however, particularly for small firms, these advantages are more apparent than real. Banks will normally seek personal guarantees from shareholders before making loans or granting an overdraft facility and so the advantage of limited liability is lost to a small owner managed business.

In addition, a company faces a greater administrative and financial burden.

(a) Compliance with national company legislation, notably in having to prepare annual accounts and have them audited, file annual returns and keep statutory books.
(b) Compliance with national accounting standards and/or IFRSs.
(c) Formation and annual registration costs.

2 Preparing partnership accounts

If a partner makes a **loan** to the business, he will receive interest on it in the normal way. Loan interest due, interest on capital and partners salaries are deducted and the remaining net profit is apportioned according to the profit sharing ratio.

2.1 How does accounting for partnerships differ from accounting for sole traders?

Partnership accounts are identical in many respects to the accounts of sole traders.

(a) The assets of a partnership are like the assets of any other business, and are accounted for in the same way. The assets side of a partnership statement of financial position is no different from what has been shown in earlier chapters of this Study Text.
(b) The net profit of a partnership is calculated in the same way as the net profit of a sole trader. The only minor difference is that if a partner makes a loan to the business (as distinct from capital contribution) then interest on the loan will be an expense in the income statement, in the same way as interest on any other loan from a person or organisation who is not a partner. We will return to partner loans later in the chapter.

There are two respects in which partnership accounts are different, however.

(a) The funds put into the business by each partner are shown differently.

(b) The net profit must be **appropriated** by the partners, ie shared out according to the partnership agreement. This appropriation of profits must be shown in the partnership accounts.

Appropriation of profit means sharing out profits in accordance with the partnership agreement.

2.2 Funds employed

When a partnership is formed, each partner puts in some capital to the business. These initial capital contributions are recorded in a series of *capital accounts*, one for each partner. (Since each partner is ultimately entitled to repayment of his capital it is clearly vital to keep a record of how much is owed to whom.) The precise amount of initial capital contributed by each partner is a matter for general agreement and there is no question of each partner necessarily contributing the same amount, although this does sometimes happen.

The balance for the capital account will always be a brought forward credit entry in the partnership accounts, because the capital contributed by proprietors is a liability of the business.

In addition to a capital account, each partner normally has the following accounts.

(a) A **current account**

(b) A **withdrawals account**

A **current account** is used to record the **profits retained in the business** by the partner.

The current account is a sort of capital account, which increases in value when the partnership makes profits, and falls in value when the partner whose current account it is makes drawings out of the business.

The main differences between the capital and current account in accounting for partnerships are as follows.

(a) (i) The balance on the capital account remains static from year to year (with one or two exceptions).

(ii) The current account is continually fluctuating up and down, as the partnership makes profits which are shared out between the partners, and as each partner makes drawings.

(b) A further difference is that when the partnership agreement provides for interest on capital, partners receive interest on the balance in their capital account, but *not on the balance in their current account*.

The drawings accounts serve exactly the same purpose as the drawings account for a sole trader. Each partner's drawings are recorded in a separate account. At the end of an accounting period, each partner's drawings are cleared to his current account.

DEBIT   Current account of partner
CREDIT   Drawings account of partner

(If the amount of the drawings exceeds the balance on a partner's current account, the current account will show a debit balance. However, in normal circumstances, we should expect to find a credit balance on the current accounts.)

The partnership statement of financial position will therefore consist of:

(a) the capital accounts of each partner; and

(b) the current accounts of each partner, net of drawings.

This will be illustrated in an example later.

2.3 Loans by partners

In addition, it is sometimes the case that an existing or previous partner will make a loan to the partnership in which case he becomes a creditor of the partnership. On the statement of financial position, such a loan is not included as partners' funds, but is shown separately as a long-term liability (unless repayable within twelve months in which case it is a current liability). This is the case whether or not the loan creditor is also an existing partner.

However, **interest on such loans will be credited to the partner's current account**. This is administratively more convenient, especially when the partner does not particularly want to be paid the loan interest in cash immediately it becomes due. You should bear in mind the following.

(a) Interest on loans from a partner is accounted for as an expense in the income statement, and not as an appropriation of profit, even though the interest is added to the current account of the partners.

(b) If there is no interest rate specified, national legislation *may* provide for interest to be paid at a specified percentage on loans by partners.

2.4 Appropriation of net profits

The net profit of a partnership is shared out between them according to the terms of their agreement. This sharing out is shown in an **appropriation account**, which follows on from the income statement.

The accounting entries are:

(a) DEBIT   Income and expense account with net profit c/d
CREDIT   Appropriation account with net profit b/d

(b) DEBIT   Appropriation account
CREDIT   Current accounts of each partner

with an individual share of profits for each partner.

The way in which profit is shared out depends on the terms of the partnership agreement. The steps to take are as follows.

(a) Establish how much the net profit is.

(b) Appropriate interest on capital and salaries first. Both of these items are an appropriation of profit and are not expenses in the income statement.

(c) If partners agree to pay interest on their drawings during the year:

DEBIT   Current accounts
CREDIT   Appropriation of profit account

(d) *Residual profits*: the difference between net profits (plus any interest charged on drawings) and appropriations for interest on capital and salaries is the residual profit. This is shared out between partners in the profit-sharing ratio.

(e) Each partner's share of profits is credited to his current account.

(f) The balance on each partner's drawings account is debited to his current account.

In practice each partner's capital account will occupy a separate ledger account, as will his current account etc. The examples which follow in this text use the columnar form; they might also ignore the breakdown of net assets employed (non-current assets, current assets, etc) to help to clarify and simplify the illustrations.

2.4.1 Guaranteed minimum profit share

The partnership agreement may provide that one partner has a guaranteed minimum profit share.

Example:

Tony, John and Gordon are in business sharing profits 4:3:3 after allowing salaries of $30,000 for Tony and John. Tony also has a guaranteed minimum profit share of $120,000. Profit for the year is $260,000. Show the appropriation.

Solution

	Tony $	John $	Gordon $	Total $
Salaries	30,000	30,000	–	60,000
Residual profit share	80,000	60,000	60,000	200,000
4:3:3	110,000	90,000	60,000	260,000
Adjustment to allow for guaranteed minimum profit share	10,000	(5,000)	(5,000)	–
	120,000	85,000	55,000	260,000

> For examination purposes it is customary to represent the details of these accounts side by side, in columnar form, to save time.

2.5 Example: Partnership accounts

Locke, Niece and Munster are in partnership with an agreement to share profits in the ratio 3:2:1. They also agree the following terms.

(a)   All three should receive interest at 12% on capital.

(b)   Munster should receive a salary of $6,000 per annum.

(c)   Interest will be charged on drawings at the rate of 5% (charged on the end of year drawings balances).

(d)   The interest rate on the loan by Locke is 5%.

The statement of financial position of the partnership as at 31 December 20X5 revealed the following.

	$	$
Capital accounts		
Locke	20,000	
Niece	8,000	
Munster	6,000	
		34,000
Current accounts		
Locke	3,500	
Niece	(700)	
Munster	1,800	
		4,600
Loan account (Locke)		6,000
Capital employed to finance net long-term assets and working capital		44,600

Drawings made during the year to 31 December 20X6 were as follows.

	$
Locke	6,000
Niece	4,000
Munster	7,000

The net profit for the year to 31 December 20X6 was $24,530 before deducting loan interest.

Required

Prepare the appropriation account for the year to 31 December 20X6, and the partners' capital accounts, and current accounts.

Solution

The interest payable by each partner on their drawings during the year is:

		$
Locke	5% of $6,000	300
Niece	5% of $4,000	200
Munster	5% of $7,000	350
		850

These payments are debited to the current accounts and credited to the *appropriation* account.

The interest payable to Locke on his loan is:

5% of $6,000 = $300

We can now begin to work out the appropriation of profits.

		$	$
Net profit, less loan interest (deducted in I & E a/c $24,530 – $300)			24,230
Add interest on drawings			850
			25,080
Less Munster salary			6,000
			19,080
Less interest on capital			
Locke	(12% of $20,000)	2,400	
Niece	(12% of $ 8,000)	960	
Munster	(12% of $ 6,000)	720	
			4,080
			15,000
Residual profits			
Locke	(3)	7,500	
Niece	(2)	5,000	
Munster	(1)	2,500	
			15,000

Make sure you remember what the various interest figures represent and that you understand exactly what has been calculated here.

(a) The partners can take drawings out of the business, but if they do they will be charged interest on it.

(b) The partners have capital tied up in the business (of course, otherwise there would be no business) and they have agreed to pay themselves interest on whatever capital each has put in.

(c) Once all the necessary adjustments have been made to net profit, $15,000 remains and is divided up between the partners in the ratio 3:2:1.

Now the financial statements for the partnership can be prepared.

LOCKE NIECE MUNSTER
APPROPRIATION ACCOUNT
FOR THE YEAR ENDED 31 DECEMBER 20X6

	$	$		$	$
			Net profit b/d		24,230
Salaries: Munster		6,000	Interest on drawings		
Interest on capital			Locke	300	
Locke	2,400		Niece	200	
Niece	960		Munster	350	
Munster	720				850
		4,080			
Residual profits					
Locke	7,500				
Niece	5,000				
Munster	2,500				
		15,000			
		25,080			25,080

PARTNERS' CURRENT ACCOUNTS

	Locke $	Niece $	Munster $		Locke $	Niece $	Munster $
Balance b/f		700		Balance b/f	3,500		1,800
Interest on drawings	300	200	350	Loan interest	300		
Drawings	6,000	4,000	7,000	Interest on capital	2,400	960	720
Balance c/f	7,400	1,060	3,670	Salary			6,000
				Residual profits	7,500	5,000	2,500
	13,700	5,960	11,020		13,700	5,960	11,020
				Balance b/f	7,400	1,060	3,670

PARTNERS' CAPITAL ACCOUNTS

	Locke $	Niece $	Munster $
Balance b/f	20,000	8,000	6,000

The statement of financial position of the partners as at 31 December 20X6 would be as follows.

	$	$
Capital accounts		
Locke	20,000	
Niece	8,000	
Munster	6,000	
		34,000
Current accounts		
Locke	7,400	
Niece	1,060	
Munster	3,670	
		12,130
Loan account (Locke)		6,000
		52,130
Net assets		
As at 31 December 20X5		44,600
Added during the year (applying the business equation, this is the		
difference between net profits and drawings = $24,230 – $17,000)		7,230
Add loan interest added to Locke's current account and not paid out		300
As at 31 December 20X6		52,130

Again, make sure you understand what has happened here.

(a) The partners' *capital* accounts have not changed. They were brought forward at $20,000, $8,000 and $6,000, and they are just the same in the new statement of financial position.

(b) The partners' *current* accounts have changed. The balances brought forward from last year's statement of financial position of $3,500, ($700) and $1,800 have become $7,400, $1,060 and $3,670 in the new statement of financial position. How this came about is shown in the partners' current (ledger) accounts.

(c) The events recorded in the current accounts are a reflection of how the partnership has distributed its profit, and this was shown in the appropriation account.

Question	Partnership accounts

Ganatri and Lucifer are in partnership sharing profits and losses in the ratio 7:3 respectively.

The following information has been taken from the partnership records for the financial year ended 31 May 20X9.

Partners' capital account balances:

Ganatri $200,000
Lucifer $140,000

Partners' current accounts, balances as at 1 June 20X8:

Ganatri $15,000 Cr
Lucifer $13,000 Cr

During the year ended 31 May 20X9 the partners made the following withdrawals from the partnership bank account.

Ganatri $10,000   on 31 August 20X8
            $10,000   on 30 November 20X8
            $10,000   on 28 February 20X9
            $10,000   on 31 May 20X9
Lucifer $7,000   on 31 August 20X8
            $7,000   on 30 November 20X8
            $7,000   on 28 February 20X9
            $7,000   on 31 May 20X9

Interest is to be charged on drawings at the rate of 12% per annum. Interest is allowed on capital accounts and credit balances on current accounts at the rate of 12% per annum.

Lucifer is to be allowed a salary of $15,000 per annum.

The net profit of the partnership for the year ended 31 May 20X9 is $102,940.

Required

(a) Calculate of the amount of interest chargeable on each partner's drawings for the year ended 31 May 20X9.

(b) Produce the partnership appropriation account for the year ended 31 May 20X9.

(c) Calculate the balance on each partner's current account as at 31 May 20X9.

(a) *Interest on partners' drawings for the year ended 31 May 20X9*

			$
Ganatri			
31.8.X8	$10,000 × 12% × $\frac{9}{12}$		900
30.11.X8	$10,000 × 12% × $\frac{6}{12}$		600
28.2.X9	$10,000 × 12% × $\frac{3}{12}$		300
			1,800
Lucifer			
31.8.X8	$7,000 × 12% × $\frac{9}{12}$		630
30.11.X8	$7,000 × 12% × $\frac{6}{12}$		420
28.2.X9	$7,000 × 12% × $\frac{3}{12}$		210
			1,260
Total			3,060

(b) **GANATRI AND LUCIFER**
APPROPRIATION ACCOUNT
FOR THE YEAR ENDED 31 MAY 20X9

	$	$
Net profit b/d		102,940
Add: interest on drawings paid to partnership		3,060
		106,000
Less salary: Lucifer		15,000
Less interest on capital and current accounts		
Ganatri (12% × $215,000)	25,800	
Lucifer (12% × $153,000)	18,360	
		44,160
		46,840
Profit share		
Ganatri (7/10)	32,788	
Lucifer (3/10)	14,052	
		46,840

(c) **PARTNERS' CURRENT ACCOUNTS**

	Ganatri $	Lucifer $		Ganatri $	Lucifer $
Drawings	40,000	28,000	Balances b/d	15,000	13,000
Interest on drawings	1,800	1,260	Salary	–	15,000
Balances c/d	31,788	31,152	Interest on capital		
			and current accounts	25,800	18,360
			Profit share	32,788	14,052
	73,588	60,412		73,588	60,412

Exam focus point

In the December 2007 exam, there was a question asking for the net increase in a partner's current account during the year. The examiner commented that most students chose the option giving the closing balance. Remember to read the requirement carefully and to answer the question actually asked.

In the question above, Lucifer's closing balance is $31,152 but the net increase in his account is $18,152 (15,000 + 18,360 + 14,052 – 28,000 – 1,260).

One of the competences you require to fulfil performance objective 5 of the PER is the ability to communicate effectively. Your examination is a means of demonstrating this competence by answering the question set.

2.6 Changes in the partnership

Another aspect to consider is how changes in the partnership will affect the profit sharing arrangements. When a partner retires or a new partner is taken on during the year, the profit for that year will have to be apportioned into the periods before and after the change and the two or more sets of profit sharing arrangements applied. Unless told otherwise, assume that profits were earned evenly throughout the year.

2.7 Example: Profit share

Hook and Line have been in partnership for many years, sharing profits equally. On 1 October 20X8, Floater is admitted to the partnership and it is decided that Hook, Line and Floater will now share profits 4:4:2. The net profit for the year to 31 December 20X8 is $150,000. Show how this will be split between the partners.

Solution

There are two distinct periods here – 9 months of Hook and Line and 3 months of Hook, Line and Floater. Profits average $12,500 per month. So we apportion as follows:

	Hook	Line	Floater	Total
Jan-Sept 20X8				
112,000/5:5	56,250	56,250		112,500
Oct-Dec 20X8				
37,500/4:4:2	15,000	15,000	7,500	37,500
	71,250	71,250	7,500	150,000

2.8 Goodwill

When a partner retires or a new partner is admitted, it is usual to calculate the 'goodwill' in the business.

Goodwill arises because an existing, thriving business is usually worth more than the value of the net assets in the statement of financial position. Customer 'goodwill' means that customers will return because of the good service given. Supplier 'goodwill' can also arise if there are good relationships with suppliers, so that suppliers trust the business. Goodwill is an example of an intangible asset. Goodwill is allocated to the partners before the change in the old PSR. After the change, goodwill is then written back to all the new partners in the new PSR.

Exam focus point

Goodwill should not be left in the statement of financial position.

2.9 Example: goodwill

In the case of Hook, Line and Floater in 2.7 above, assume that the business had goodwill of $300,000 at 1 October 20X8.

The partners request that goodwill is created and then reversed on each change.

Solution

CURRENT ACCOUNTS

	Hook $	Line $	Floater $			Hook $	Line $	Floater $
1/10/X8				1/10/X8				
Goodwill reversed	120,000	120,000	60,000	Goodwill created	150,000	150,000	–

GOODWILL

		$			$
1/10/X8	Current accounts	300,000	1/10/X8	Current accounts	300,000

Notice the effect that this has on the partners' current accounts. Although goodwill does not remain in the books, when Floater is admitted, he effectively pays for his share of the goodwill because Hook and Line's shares have been diminished on his admission.

2.10 Calculation of goodwill

You may have wondered how the goodwill in Section 2.9 was calculated. In real life, the calculation of goodwill can be extremely complex and this is outside the scope of your syllabus.

In the exam, you are only likely to be asked to calculate goodwill using the following formula.

Formula to learn

> Goodwill = value of business – net asset value.

Question

Calculation of goodwill

Hook, Line and Floater have continued trading for a further year and they are considering admitting Sinker on 31 December 20X9. For the purposes of calculating goodwill, the partners obtain a valuation of the business as if it were to be sold on 31 December 20X9. This valuation is $750,000. The statement of financial position at 31 December 20X9 shows net assets of $375,000. Calculate goodwill.

Answer

Goodwill = value of business – net assets value
= 750,000 – 375,000
= $375,000

Chapter Roundup

- The terms under which the partnership operates are set out in the **partnership agreement**. The initial capital put into the business by each partner is shown by means of a **capital account** for each partner. The net profit of the partnership is **appropriated** by the partners according to a previously agreed ratio. Each partner also has a current account to which their drawings are charged. Partners may be charged **interest** on their **drawings** and may receive **interest on capital**.

- If a partner makes a **loan** to the business, he will receive interest on it in the normal way. Loan interest due, interest on capital and partners salaries are deducted and the remaining net profit is apportioned according to the profit sharing ratio.

Quick Quiz

1 What is a partnership?

2 A partner's salary is an expense of the partnership. Is this statement:

   A   True
   B   False

3 Why might a sole trader take on a partner?

4 What is the difference between a partner's capital account and a partner's current account?

5 How is profit shared between partners?

6 A, B and C are in partnership with a profit sharing ratio of 3:2:1. For the year ended 31.12.X9, the partnership profits are $18,000. What is B's share of the profits?

   A $3,000
   B $6,000
   C $9,000
   D $18,000

7 X, Y and Z are in partnership. X receives a salary of $14,000. If the profits for the year are $80,000 and the partners share profits equally, what is Y's share of the profits?

   A $14,000
   B $22,000
   C $26,000
   D $26,667

8 Profits for the year are $75,000. A, B and C share profits in the ratio 4:3:3. Opening balances on their current accounts were $10,000, $12,000 and $15,000 respectively. If each partner had drawings of $20,000, what is the closing balance on B's account?

   A $17,500
   B $20,000
   C $14,500
   D $22,500

9 Goodwill is brought into the partnership accounts in the old PSR and written off in the new PSR. Is this statement:

   A   True
   B   False

Answers to Quick Quiz

1. An arrangement between two or more individuals to carry on the risks and rewards of a business together.
2. B   False. It is an appropriation of profit.
3. See 1.3.
4. The capital account reflects the amount of money invested in the business by each partner. The current account reflects each partner's share of the profits less drawings.
5. According to the terms of the partnership agreements. This may allow interest on capital accounts, charge interest on drawings, allow salaries and then divide the residual profits according to the profit sharing ratio.
6. B   Each 'share' is worth $\frac{\$18,000}{6}$ ($3,000). B's share is, therefore, $6,000.
7. B

	$
Appropriation account	
Profits	80,000
X's salary	(14,000)
	66,000

Shared equally:		
X	22,000	
Y	22,000	
Z	22,000	66,000

So Y's share of the profits is $22,000.

8. C

CURRENT ACCOUNTS

	A $	B $	C $		A $	B $	C $
Drawings	20,000	20,000	20,000	Opening balance	10,000	12,000	15,000
Closing balance	20,000	14,500	17,500	Profits (4:3:3)	30,000	22,500	22,500
	40,000	24,500	37,500		40,000	34,500	37,500

9. A   True.

Now try the questions below from the Exam Question Bank

Number	Level	Marks	Time
Q38	Examination	2	2 mins
Q39	Examination	1	1 min
Q40	Examination	2	2 mins

Introduction to company accounting

Topic list	Syllabus reference
1 Limited liability and accounting records	D10(a)
2 Share capital	D10(a)
3 Reserves	D10(b), (c), (j), F1(b), F1(c)
4 Bonus and rights issues	D10(d)–(g)
5 Ledger accounts and limited liability companies	D10(h)–(i)

Introduction

We begin this chapter by considering the **status of limited** liability companies and the type of accounting records they maintain in order to prepare financial statements.

Then we will look at those accounting entries unique to limited liability companies: share capital, reserves, and bonus and rights issues.

This chapter provides the grounding for Chapter 21, where you will learn to prepare company financial statements.

Study guide

		Intellectual level
D10	**Capital structure and finance costs**	
(a)	Understand the capital structure of a limited liability company including:	1
	(i) Ordinary shares	
	(ii) Preference shares (redeemable and irredeemable)	
	(iii) Loan notes	
(b)	Record movements in the share capital and share premium accounts	1
(c)	Identify and record the other reserves which may appear in the company statement of financial position	1
(d)	Define a bonus (capitalisation) issue and its advantages and disadvantages	1
(e)	Define a rights issue and its advantages and disadvantages	1
(f)	Record and show the effects of a bonus (capitalisation) issue in the statement of financial position	1
(g)	Record and show the effects of a right issue in the statement of financial position	1
(h)	Record dividends in ledger accounts and the financial statements	1
(i)	Calculate and record finance costs in ledger accounts and the financial statements	1
(j)	Identify the components of the statement of changes in equity	1
F1	**Statements of financial position**	
(b)	Understand the nature of reserves	1
(c)	Identify and report reserves in a company statement of financial position	1

Exam guide

This is the most important topic studied so far. It will form the foundation for all your future studies. You will be examined on it!

1 Limited liability and accounting records

There are some important differences between the accounts of a **limited liability company** and those of sole traders or partnerships.

So far, this Study Text has dealt mainly with the accounts of businesses in general. In this chapter we shall turn our attention to the accounts of limited liability companies. As we should expect, the accounting rules and conventions for recording the business transactions of limited liability companies and then preparing their final accounts are much the same as for sole traders. For example, companies will have a cash book, sales day book, purchase day book, journal, sales ledger, purchase ledger and nominal ledger. They will also prepare an income statement annually and a statement of financial position at the end of the accounting year.

There are, however, some **fundamental differences** in the accounts of limited liability companies, of which the following are perhaps the most significant.

(a) The **national legislation** governing the activities of limited liability companies tends to be very extensive. Amongst other things such legislation may define certain minimum accounting records which must be maintained by companies; they may specify that the annual accounts of a company must be filed with a government bureau and so available for public inspection; and they often contain detailed requirements on the minimum information which must be disclosed in a company's accounts. Businesses which are not limited liability companies (non-incorporated businesses) often enjoy comparative freedom from statutory regulation.

(b)   The **owners of a company** (its **members** or **shareholders**) may be **very numerous**. Their capital is shown differently from that of a sole trader; and similarly the 'appropriation account' of a company is different.

1.1 Limited liability

> **Unlimited liability** means that if the business runs up debts that it is unable to pay, the proprietors will become personally liable for the unpaid debts and would be required, if necessary, to sell their private possessions to repay them.

It is worth recapping on the relative **advantages and disadvantages** of limited liability (which we have mentioned in earlier parts of the text). Sole traders and partnerships are, with some significant exceptions, generally fairly small concerns. The amount of capital involved may be modest, and the proprietors of the business usually participate in managing it. Their liability for the debts of the business is unlimited, which means that if the business runs up debts that it is unable to pay, the proprietors will become personally liable for the unpaid debts, and would be required, if necessary, to sell their private possessions in order to repay them. For example, if a sole trader has some capital in his business, but the business now owes $40,000 which it cannot repay, the trader might have to sell his house to raise the money to pay off his business debts.

Limited liability companies offer limited liability to their owners.

> **Limited liability** means that the maximum amount that an owner stands to lose in the event that the company becomes insolvent and cannot pay off its debts, is his share of the capital in the business.

Thus limited liability is a **major advantage** of turning a business into a limited liability company. However, in practice, banks will normally seek personal guarantees from shareholders before making loans or granting an overdraft facility and so the advantage of limited liability is lost to a small owner managed business.

1.1.1 Disadvantages

(a)   Compliance with national legislation
(b)   Compliance with national accounting standards and/or IFRSs
(c)   Any formation and annual registration costs

These are needed to avoid the privilege of limited liability being abused.

As a business grows, it needs **more capital** to finance its operations, and significantly more than the people currently managing the business can provide themselves. One way of obtaining more capital is to invite investors from outside the business to invest in the ownership or equity of the business. These new co-owners would not usually be expected to help with managing the business. To such investors, limited liability is very attractive.

Investments are always risky undertakings, but with limited liability the investor knows the maximum amount that he stands to lose when he puts some capital into a company.

1.2 The accounting records of limited companies

There is almost always a **national legal requirement** for companies to keep accounting records which are sufficient to show and explain the company's transactions. The records will probably have the following qualities.

(a)   Disclose the company's current financial position at any time.

(b)   Contain:

    (i)   day-to-day entries of money received and spent.

    (ii)   a record of the company's assets and liabilities.

    (iii)   where the company deals in goods:

        (1)   a statement of inventories held at the year end, and supporting inventory count records.

        (2)   with the exception of retail sales, statements of goods bought and sold which identify the sellers and buyers of those goods.

(c)   Enable the managers of the company to ensure that the final accounts of the company give a true and fair view of the company's profit or loss and statement of financial position.

The detailed requirements of accounting records which must be maintained will vary from country to country.

Question	Companies

How are limited liability companies regulated in your country?

2 Share Capital

FAST FORWARD

In preparing a statement of financial position you must be able to deal with:

- Ordinary and preference share capital
- Reserves
- Loan stock

2.1 The capital of limited liability companies

The proprietors' capital in a limited liability company consists of **share capital**. When a company is set up for the first time, it issues shares, which are paid for by investors, who then become shareholders of the company. Shares are denominated in units of 25 cents, 50 cents, $1 or whatever seems appropriate. The 'face value' of the shares is called their **par value** or **legal value** (or sometimes the **nominal value**).

For example, when a company is set up with a share capital of, say, $100,000, it may be decided to issue:

(a)   100,000 shares of $1 each par value; or
(b)   200,000 shares of 50c each; or
(c)   400,000 shares of 25c each; or
(d)   250,000 shares of 40c each, etc.

The amount at which the shares are issued may exceed their par value. For example, a company might issue 100,000 $1 shares at a price of $1.20 each. Subscribers will then pay a total of $120,000. The issued share capital of the company would be shown in its accounts at par value, $100,000; the excess of $20,000 is described not as share capital, but as **share premium** or **capital paid-up in excess of par value.**

2.2 Authorised, issued, called-up and paid-up share capital

A distinction must be made between authorised, issued, called-up and paid-up share capital.

(a) **Authorised (or legal) capital** is the maximum amount of share capital that a company is empowered to issue. The amount of authorised share capital varies from company to company, and can change by agreement.

For example, a company's authorised share capital might be 5,000,000 ordinary shares of $1 each. This would then be the maximum number of shares it could issue, unless the maximum were to be changed by agreement.

(b) **Issued capital** is the par amount of share capital that has been issued to shareholders. The amount of issued capital cannot exceed the amount of authorised capital.

Continuing the example above, the company with authorised share capital of 5,000,000 ordinary shares of $1 might have issued 4,000,000 shares. This would leave it the option to issue 1,000,000 more shares at some time in the future.

When share capital is issued, shares are allotted to shareholders. The term 'allotted' share capital means the same thing as issued share capital.

(c) **Called-up capital**. When shares are issued or allotted, a company does not always expect to be paid the full amount for the shares at once. It might instead call up only a part of the issue price, and wait until a later time before it calls up the remainder.

For example, if a company allots 400,000 ordinary shares of $1, it might call up only, say, 75 cents per share. The issued share capital would be $400,000, but the called-up share capital would only be $300,000.

(d) **Paid-up capital**. Like everyone else, investors are not always prompt or reliable payers. When capital is called up, some shareholders might delay their payment (or even default on payment). Paid-up capital is the amount of called-up capital that has been paid.

For example, if a company issues 400,000 ordinary shares of $1 each, calls up 75 cents per share, and receives payments of $290,000, we would have:

	$
Allotted or issued capital	400,000
Called-up capital	300,000
Paid-up capital	290,000
Capital not yet paid-up	10,000

The statement of financial position of the company would appear as follows.

	$
Assets	
Called-up capital not paid	10,000
Cash (called-up capital paid)	290,000
	300,000
Equity	
Called-up share capital	
(400,000 ordinary shares of $1, with 75c per share called up)	300,000

Notice that in a limited liability company's statement of financial position the owners' capital is called **equity**. In your reading, you may find that shares are called **equities**.

2.3 Ordinary shares and preference (preferred) shares

At this stage it is relevant to distinguish between the two types of shares most often encountered: **preference shares** and **ordinary shares**.

2.3.1 Preference shares

Key term

> **Preference shares** are shares which confer certain preferential rights on their holder.

Preference shares carry the right to a final dividend which is expressed as a percentage of their par value: eg a 6% $1 preference share carries a right to an annual dividend of 6c. Preference dividends have priority over ordinary dividends; in other words, if the managers of a company wish to pay a dividend (which they are not obliged to do) they must pay any preference dividend first. Otherwise, no ordinary dividend may be paid.

The rights attaching to preference shares are set out in the company's constitution. They may vary from company to company and country to country, but typically:

(a) Preference shareholders have a **priority right** over ordinary shareholders to a return of their capital if the company goes into liquidation.

(b) Preference shares do not **carry a right to vote**.

(c) If the preference shares are **cumulative**, it means that before a company can pay an ordinary dividend it must not only pay the current year's preference dividend, but must also make good any arrears of preference dividends unpaid in previous years.

2.3.2 Classification of preference shares

Preference shares may be classified in one of two ways.

- Redeemable
- Irredeemable

Redeemable preference shares mean that the company will redeem (repay) the nominal value of those shares at a later date. For example, 'redeemable 5% $1 preference shares 20X9' means that the company will pay these shareholders $1 for every share they hold on a certain date in 20X9. The shares will then be cancelled and no further dividends paid. Redeemable preference shares are treated like loans and are included as non-current liabilities in the statement of financial position. Remember to reclassify as current liabilities if the redemption is due within 12 months. Dividends paid on redeemable preference shares are treated like interest paid on loans and are included in financial costs in the income statement.

Irredeemable preference shares are treated just like other shares. They form part of equity and their dividends are treated as appropriations of profit.

> In the exam, the question will specifically state whether the shares are redeemable or irredeemable preference shares.

2.3.3 Ordinary shares

Ordinary shares are by far the most common. They carry no right to a fixed dividend but are entitled to all profits left after payment of any preference dividend. Generally, however, only a part of such remaining profits is distributed, the rest being kept in reserve (see below).

Key term

> **Ordinary shares** are shares which are not preferred with regard to dividend payments. Thus a holder only receives a dividend after fixed dividends have been paid to preference shareholders.

The amount of ordinary dividends fluctuates although there is a general expectation that it will increase from year to year. Should the company be wound up, any surplus not distributed is shared between the ordinary shareholders. Ordinary shares normally carry voting rights.

Ordinary shareholders are thus the effective **owners** of a company. They own the 'equity' of the business, and any reserves of the business (described later) belong to them. Ordinary shareholders are sometimes referred to as **equity shareholders**. Preference shareholders are in many ways more like payables of the company (although legally they are members, not payables). It should be emphasised, however, that the precise rights attached to preference and ordinary shares may vary; the distinctions noted above are generalisations.

2.4 Example: Dividends on ordinary shares and preference shares

Garden Gloves Co has issued 50,000 ordinary shares of 50 cents each and 20,000 7% preference shares of $1 each. Its profits after taxation for the year to 30 September 20X5 were $8,400. The management board has decided to pay an ordinary dividend (ie a dividend on ordinary shares) which is 50% of profits after tax and preference dividend.

Required

Show the amount in total of dividends and of retained profits, and calculate the dividend per share on ordinary shares.

Solution

	$
Profit after tax	8,400
Preference dividend (7% of $1 × 20,000)	1,400
Earnings (profit after tax and preference dividend)	7,000
Ordinary dividend (50% of earnings)	3,500
Retained earnings (also 50% of earnings)	3,500

The ordinary dividend is 7 cents per share ($3,500 ÷ 50,000 ordinary shares).

The appropriation of profit would be as follows:

	$	$
Profit after tax		8,400
Dividends: preference	1,400	
ordinary	3,500	
		4,900
Retained profit		3,500

As we will see later, appropriations of profit do not appear in the income statement, but are shown as movements on reserves.

2.5 The market value of shares

The par value of shares will be different from their market value, which is the price at which someone is prepared to purchase shares in the company from an existing shareholder. If Mr A owns 1,000 $1 shares in Z Co he may sell them to B for $1.60 each.

This transfer of existing shares does not affect Z Co's own financial position in any way whatsoever, and apart from changing the register of members, Z Co does not have to bother with the sale by Mr A to Mr B at all. There are certainly no accounting entries to be made for the share sale.

Shares in private companies do not change hands very often, hence their market value is often hard to estimate. Companies listed on a stock exchange are quoted, ie it is the market value of the shares which is quoted.

2.6 Loan stock or bonds

Limited liability companies may issue loan stock or bonds. These are long-term liabilities and in some countries they are described as *loan capital* because they are a means of raising finance, in the same way as issuing share capital raises finance. They are different from share capital in the following ways.

(a)   **Shareholders** are **members** of a company, while **providers of loan capital** are **creditors**.

(b)   **Shareholders** receive **dividends** (appropriations of profit) whereas the **holders of loan capital** are entitled to a **fixed rate of interest** (an expense charged against revenue).

(c)   Loan capital holders can take legal action against a company if their interest is not paid when due, whereas **shareholders cannot enforce the payment of dividends**.

(d)   Loan stock is **often secured on company assets**, whereas shares are not.

The holder of loan capital is generally in a less risky position than the shareholder. He has greater security, although his income is fixed and cannot grow, unlike ordinary dividends. As remarked earlier, preference shares are in practice very similar to loan capital, not least because the preference dividend is normally fixed.

Interest is calculated on the par or legal value of loan capital, regardless of its market value. If a company has $700,000 (par value) 12% loan stock in issue, interest of $84,000 will be charged in the income statement per year. Interest is usually paid half-yearly; examination questions often require an accrual to be made for interest due at the year-end.

For example, if a company has $700,000 of 12% loan stock in issue, pays interest on 30 June and 31 December each year, and ends its accounting year on 30 September, there would be an accrual of three months' unpaid interest (3/12 × $84,000) = $21,000 at the end of each accounting year that the loan stock is still in issue.

Question
                                                                                    Share capital

Distinguish between authorised, issued, called-up and paid-up capital.

Answer

Authorised share capital: the maximum amount of share capital that a company is empowered to issue.

Issued share capital: the amount of share capital that has been issued to shareholders.

Called-up share capital: the amount the company has asked shareholders to pay, for the time being, on shares issued to them.

Paid-up share capital: the amounts actually paid by shareholders on shares issued to them.

3 Reserves

FAST FORWARD

Share capital and reserves are 'owned' by the shareholders.
They are known collectively as 'shareholders' equity'.

Shareholders' equity consists of the following.

(a)   The par value of issued capital (minus any amounts not yet called up on issued shares)
(b)   Other equity

The share capital itself might consist of both ordinary shares and preference shares. All reserves, however, are owned by the ordinary shareholders, who own the 'equity' in the company. We looked at share capital in detail above.

'Other equity' consists of four elements.

(a)   Capital paid-up in excess of par value (share premium)
(b)   Revaluation surplus
(c)   Reserves
(d)   Retained earnings

We will look at each in turn.

3.1 The share premium account

In this context, 'premium' means the difference between the issue price of the share and its par value. The account is sometimes called 'capital paid-up in excess of par value'. When a company is first incorporated (set up) the issue price of its shares will probably be the same as their par value and so there would be no share premium. If the company does well, the market value of its shares will increase, but not the par value. The price of any new shares issued will be approximately their market value.

The difference between cash received by the company and the par value of the new shares issued is transferred to the **share premium account**. For example, if X Co issues 1,000 $1 ordinary shares at $2.60 each the book entry will be:

		$	$
DEBIT	Cash	2,600	
CREDIT	Ordinary shares		1,000
	Share premium account		1,600

A share premium account only comes into being when a company issues shares at a price in excess of their par value. The market price of the shares, once they have been issued, has no bearing at all on the company's accounts, and so if their market price goes up or down, the share premium account would remain unaltered.

Key term

> A **share premium account** is an account into which sums received as payment for shares in excess of their nominal value must be placed.

Once established, the share premium account constitutes capital of the company which cannot be paid out in dividends, ie it is a capital reserve. The share premium account will increase in value if and when new shares are issued at a price above their par value. The share premium account can be 'used' – and so decrease in value – only in certain very limited ways, which are largely beyond the scope of your basic financial accounting syllabus. One common use of the share premium account, however, is to 'finance' the issue of bonus shares, which are described later in this chapter. Other uses of this account may depend on national legislation.

Exam focus point

> The share premium account cannot be distributed as dividend under any circumstances.

The reason for creating such non-distributable reserves is to maintain the capital of the company. This capital 'base' provides some security for the company's creditors, bearing in mind that the liability of shareholders is limited in the event that the company cannot repay its debts. It would be most unjust – and illegal – for a company to pay its shareholders a dividend out of its base capital when it is not even able to pay back its debts.

Question

Share issue

AB Co issues 5,000 50c shares for $6,000. What are the entries for share capital and share premium in the statement of financial position?

	Share capital	Share premium
A	$5,000	$1,000
B	$1,000	$5,000
C	$3,500	$3,500
D	$2,500	$3,500

Answer

Did you notice that the shares are 50c each, not $1? The shares were issued for $1.20 each ($6,000/5,000 shares). Of this 50c is share capital and 70c is share premium. Therefore option D is the correct answer.

3.2 Revaluation surplus

We looked at the revaluation of non-current assets in Chapter 9. The result of an upward revaluation is a 'revaluation surplus'. This is **non-distributable** as it represents unrealised profits on the revalued assets. It is another capital reserve. The relevant part of a revaluation surplus can only become realised if the asset in question is sold, thus realising the gain. The revaluation surplus may fall, however, if an asset which had previously been revalued upwards suffered a fall in value in the next revaluation.

3.3 Reserves

In most countries, a distinction must be made between the following.

(a) **Statutory reserves**, which are reserves which a company is required to set up by law, and which are not available for the distribution of dividends.

(b) **Non-statutory reserves**, which are reserves consisting of profits which are distributable as dividends, if the company so wishes.

Statutory reserves are capital reserves (share premium, revaluation) and non-statutory reserves are revenue reserves.

We are concerned here with the latter type, which the company managers may choose to set up. These may have a specific purpose (eg plant and machinery replacement reserve) or not (eg general reserve). The creation of these reserves usually indicates a general intention not to distribute the profits involved at any future date, although legally any such reserves, being non-statutory, remain available for the payment of dividends.

Profits are transferred to these reserves by making an appropriation out of profits, usually profits for the year. Typically, you might come across the following.

	$	$
Profit after taxation		100,000
Appropriations of profit		
Dividend	60,000	
Transfer to general reserve	10,000	
		70,000
Retained earnings for the year		30,000
Retained earnings b/f		250,000
Retained earnings c/f		280,000

3.3.1 Dividends

Key term

> **Dividends** are appropriations of profit after tax.

Shareholders who are also managers of their company will receive a salary as a manager. They are also entitled to a share of the profits made by the company.

Many companies pay dividends in two stages during the course of their accounting year.

(a) In mid year, after the half-year financial results are known, the company might pay an **interim dividend**.

(b) At the end of the year, the company might propose a further **final dividend**.

The total dividend for the year is the sum of the interim and the final dividend. (Not all companies by any means pay an interim dividend. Interim dividends are, however, commonly paid out by larger limited liability companies.)

At the end of an accounting year, a company's managers may have proposed a final dividend payment, but this will not yet have been paid. The final dividend **does not appear in the accounts** but will be disclosed in the notes.

Dividends which have been **paid** are shown in the statement of changes in equity (see Section 3.6). They are not shown in the income statement, although they are deducted from retained earnings in the statement of financial position. **Proposed** dividends are not adjusted for, they are simply disclosed by note.

The terminology of dividend payments can be confusing, since they may be expressed either in the form, as 'x cents per share' or as 'y%. In the latter case, the meaning is always 'y% of the *par value* of the shares in issue'. For example, suppose a company's issued share capital consists of 100,000 50c ordinary shares which were issued at a premium of 10c per share. The company's statement of financial position would include the following.

		$
Ordinary shares:	100,000 50c ordinary shares	50,000
Share premium account	(100,000 × 10c)	10,000

If the managers wish to pay a dividend of $5,000, they may propose either:

(a) a dividend of 5c per share (100,000 × 5c = $5,000); or
(b) a dividend of 10% (10% × $50,000 = $5,000).

Not all profits are distributed as dividends; some will be retained in the business to finance future projects.

Question
Dividend

A company has authorised share capital of 1,000,000 50c ordinary shares and an issued share capital of 800,000 50c ordinary shares. If an ordinary dividend of 5% is declared, what is the amount payable to shareholders?

A $50,000
B $20,000
C $40,000
D $25,000

Answer

B   800,000 × 50c × 5% = $20,000.

3.4 Retained earnings

This is the **most significant reserve** and is variously described as:

(a) Revenue reserve
(b) Retained profits
(c) Accumulated profits
(d) Undistributed profits
(e) Unappropriated profits

These are **profits** earned by the company and not appropriated by dividends, taxation or transfer to another reserve account.

Provided that a company is earning profits, this reserve generally increases from year to year, as most companies do not distribute all their profits as dividends. Dividends can be paid from it: even if a loss is made in one particular year, a dividend can be paid from previous years' retained earnings.

For example, if a company makes a loss of $100,000 in one year, yet has unappropriated profits from previous years totalling $250,000, it can pay a dividend not exceeding $150,000. One reason for retaining some profit each year is to enable the company to pay dividends even when profits are low (or non-existent). Another reason is usually shortage of cash.

Very occasionally, you might come across a debit balance on the retained earnings account. This would indicate that the company has accumulated losses.

3.5 Distinction between reserves and provisions

Key terms

A **reserve** is an appropriation of distributable profits for a specific purpose (eg plant replacement) while a provision is an amount charged against revenue as an expense. A provision relates either to a diminution in the value of an asset or a known liability (eg audit fees), the amount of which cannot be established with any accuracy.

Provisions or allowances (for depreciation etc) are dealt with in company accounts in the same way as in the accounts of other types of business.

3.6 Statement of changes in equity

In the published accounts, a company has to provide a statement of changes in equity which details the movements on its capital and reserves.

Example: Statement of changes in equity

	Share capital	Share premium	Revaluation reserve	Retained earnings	Total
Balance at 1.1.X6	X	X	X	X	X
Changes in accounting policy	-	-	-	(X)	(X)
Restated balance	X	X	X	X	X
Changes in equity for 20X6					
Dividends	-	-	-	(X)	(X)
Total comprehensive income for the year	-	-	X	X	X
Issue of share capital	X	X	-	-	X
Balance at 31.12.X6	X	X	X	X	X

Note that the statement of changes in equity simply takes the equity section of the statement of financial position and shows the movements during the year. The bottom line shows the amounts for the current statement of financial position. Total comprehensive income for the year will be explained in the next chapter. For the moment, treat it as profit for the year.

Dividends paid during the year are not shown on the income statement; they are shown in the statement of changes in equity.

USB, a limited liability company, has the following trial balance at 31 December 20X9.

	Debit $'000	Credit $'000
Cash at bank	100	
Inventory at 1 January 20X9	2,400	
Administrative expenses	2,206	
Distribution costs	650	
Non-current assets at cost:		
Buildings	10,000	
Plant and equipment	1,400	
Motor vehicles	320	
Suspense		1,500
Accumulated depreciation		
Buildings		4,000
Plant and equipment		480
Motor vehicles		120
Retained earnings		560
Trade receivables	876	
Purchases	4,200	
Dividend paid	200	
Sales revenue		11,752
Sales tax payable		1,390
Trade payables		1,050
Share premium		500
$1 ordinary shares		1,000
	22,352	22,352

The following additional information is relevant.

(a) Inventory at 31 December 20X9 was valued at $1,600,000. While doing the inventory count, errors in the previous year's inventory count were discovered. The inventory brought forward at the beginning of the year should have been $2.2m, not $2.4m as above.

(b) No final dividend is being proposed.

(c) 1 million new ordinary shares were issued at $1.50 on 1 December 20X9. The proceeds have been left in a suspense account.

(d) The profit for the period was $3,246,000.

Required

Prepare a statement of changes in equity for the year to 31 December 20X9.

USB
STATEMENT OF CHANGES IN EQUITY FOR THE YEAR ENDED 31 DECEMBER 20X9

	Share capital $'000	Share premium $'000	Retained earnings $'000	Total $'000
Balance at 1 January 20X9	1,000	500	560	2,060
Prior period adjustment*	-	-	(200)	(200)
Restated balance	1,000	500	360	1,860
Profit for the period	-	-	3,246	3,246
Dividends paid	-	-	(200)	(200)
Share issue	1,000	500	-	1,500
	2,000	1,000	3,406	6,406

* See Chapter 16. The previous year's closing inventory was revalued by $200,000. This means that the profits for that period were overstated by $200,000 and this needs to be adjusted.

4 Bonus and rights issues

FAST FORWARD

A company can increase its share capital by means of a **bonus issue** or a **rights issue**.

4.1 Bonus (capitalisation) issues

A company may wish to increase its share capital without needing to raise additional finance by issuing new shares. For example, a profitable company might expand from modest beginnings over a number of years. Its profitability would be reflected in large balances on its reserves, while its original share capital might look like that of a much smaller business.

It is open to such a company to **re-classify some of its reserves as share capital**. This is purely a paper exercise which raises no funds. Any reserve may be re-classified in this way, including a share premium account or other reserve. Such a re-classification increases the capital base of the company and gives creditors greater protection.

4.1.1 Advantages

- Increases capital without diluting current shareholders' holdings
- Capitalises reserves, so they cannot be paid as dividends

4.1.2 Disadvantages

- Does not raise any cash
- Could jeopardise payment of future dividends if profits fall

4.2 Example: Bonus issue

BUBBLES CO
STATEMENT OF FINANCIAL POSITION (EXTRACT)

	$'000	$'000
Shareholders' equity		
Share capital		
$1 ordinary shares (fully paid)		1,000
Reserves		
Share premium	500	
Retained earnings	2,000	
		2,500
		3,500

Bubbles decided to make a '3 for 2' bonus issue (ie 3 new shares for every 2 already held).

The double entry is:		$'000	$'000
DEBIT	Share premium	500	
	Retained earnings	1,000	
CREDIT	Ordinary share capital		1,500

After the issue the statement of financial position is as follows.

	$'000
Share capital: $1 ordinary shares (fully paid)	2,500
Retained earnings	1,000
Shareholders' equity	3,500

1,500,000 new ('bonus') shares are issued to existing shareholders, so that if Mr X previously held 20,000 shares he will now hold 50,000. The total value of his holding should theoretically remain the same however, since the net assets of the company remain unchanged and his share of those net assets remains at 2% (ie 50,000/2,500,000; previously 20,000/1,000,000).

4.3 Rights issues

A **rights issue** (unlike a bonus issue) is **an issue of shares for cash**. The 'rights' are offered to existing shareholders, who can sell them if they wish. This is beneficial for existing shareholders in that the shares are usually issued at a discount to the current market price.

4.3.1 Advantages

- Raises cash for the company
- Keeps reserves available for future dividends

4.3.2 Disadvantages

- Dilutes shareholders' holdings if they do not take up rights issue

4.4 Example: Rights issue

Bubbles Co (above) decides to make a rights issue, shortly after the bonus issue. The terms are '1 for 5 @ $1.20' (ie one new share for every five already held, at a price of $1.20). Assuming that all shareholders take up their rights (which they are not obliged to) the double entry is:

		$'000	$'000
DEBIT	Cash (2,500 ÷ 5 × $1.20)	600	
CREDIT	Ordinary share capital		500
	Share premium		100

Mr X who previously held 50,000 shares will now hold 60,000, and the value of his holding should increase (all other things being equal) because the net assets of the company will increase. The new statement of financial position will show:

	$'000
$1 ordinary shares	3,000
Share premium	100
Retained earnings	1,000
Shareholders' equity	4,100

The increase in funds of $600,000 represents the cash raised from the issue of 500,000 new shares at a price of $1.20 each.

Rights issues are a popular way of raising cash by issuing shares and they are cheap to administer. In addition, shareholders retain control of the business as their holding is not diluted.

Question

Bonus and rights issue

X Co has the following capital structure:

	$
400,000 ordinary shares of 50c	200,000
Share premium account	70,000
Retained earnings	230,000
Shareholders' equity	500,000

Show its capital structure following:

(a)   A '1 for 2' bonus issue
(b)   A rights issue of '1 for 3' at 75c following the bonus issue, assuming all rights taken up

Answer

(a) $

600,000 ordinary shares of 50c	300,000
Retained earnings	200,000
Shareholders equity	500,000

(b) $

800,000 ordinary shares of 50c	400,000
Share premium account	50,000
Retained earnings	200,000
Shareholders equity	650,000

The bonus issue was financed by the whole of the share premium account and $30,000 retained earnings. The share premium account has funds again following the rights issue. Note that the bonus issue leaves shareholders equity unchanged. The rights issue will have brought in cash of $150,000 (200,000 x 75c) and shareholders equity is increased by this amount.

5 Ledger accounts and limited liability companies

Limited companies keep ledger accounts, and the only difference between the ledger accounts of companies and sole traders is the nature of some of the transactions, assets and liabilities for which accounts need to be kept.

For example, there will be an account for each of the following items:

(a)   *Taxation*

    (i)   Tax charged against profits will be accounted for by:

        DEBIT   I/S
        CREDIT   Taxation account

(ii)   The outstanding balance on the taxation account will be a liability in the statement of financial position, until eventually paid, when the accounting entry would be:

DEBIT   Taxation account
CREDIT   Cash

(b)   *Dividends*

A separate account will be kept for the dividends for each different class of shares (eg preference, ordinary).

(i)   Dividends declared out of profits will be disclosed in the notes if they are unpaid at the year end.

(ii)   When dividends are paid, we have:

DEBIT   Dividends paid account
CREDIT   Cash

(c)   *Loan stock*

Loan stock being a long-term liability will be shown as a credit balance in a loan stock account.

Interest payable on such loans is not credited to the loan account, but is credited to a separate payables account for interest until it is eventually paid: ie

DEBIT   Interest account (an expense, chargeable against profits)
CREDIT   Interest payable (a current liability until eventually paid)

(d)   *Share capital and reserves*

There will be a separate account for:

(i)   each different class of share capital (always a credit balance b/f).
(ii)   each different type of reserve (nearly always a credit balance b/f).

Chapter Roundup

- There are some important differences between the accounts of a *limited liability company* and those of sole traders or partnerships.

- In preparing a statement of financial position you must be able to deal with:

    – ordinary and preference share capital
    – reserves
    – loan stock

- Share capital and reserves are 'owned' by the shareholders. They are known collectively as 'shareholders' equity'.

- A company can increase its share capital by means of a bonus issue or a rights issue.

Quick Quiz

1   What is the meaning of limited liability?

   A   Shareholders are responsible for the company's debts.

   B   Shareholders are responsible only for the amount paid on the shares.

2   What is the difference between issued capital and called-up capital?

3   What are the differences between ordinary shares and preferred shares?

4   What are the differences between loan stock and share capital?

5   A company issues 50,000 $1 shares at a price of $1.25 per share. How much should be posted to the share premium account?

   A $50,000

   B $12,500

   C $62,500

   D $60,000

6   Distinguish between a bonus (capitalisation) issue and a rights issue.

7   A company has a balance on share premium account of $50,000 and on retained earnings of $75,000. Issued share capital is 400,000 25c shares. The company decides to make a bonus issue of one for one. What are the closing balances on share premium and retained earnings?

	Share premium	Retained earnings
A	$25,000	Nil
B	$10,000	$15,000
C	Nil	$25,000
D	Nil	$(275,000)

Answers to Quick Quiz

1   B   The maximum amount that a shareholder has to pay is the amount paid on his shares.

2   Issued share capital is the par value of shares issued to shareholders. Called-up share capital is the amount payable to date by the shareholders.

3   Ordinary shares can be paid any or no dividend. The dividend attaching to preferred shares is set from the start.

4   Loan stock are long-term loans, and so loan note holders are long-term payables. Equity shareholders own the company.

5   B. (50,000 × 25c)

6   A bonus issue is financed by capitalising revenue reserves. A rights issue is paid for by the shareholders taking up the shares.

7   C   Capitalisation of 1:1 means a further 400,000 25c share are issued. This represents $100,000. This $100,000 is taken from share premium account first ($50,000) and the balance of $50,000 is taken from retained earnings.

Now try the questions below from the Exam Question Bank

Number	Level	Marks	Time
Q41	Examination	1	1 min
Q42	Examination	2	2 mins
Q43	Examination	2	2 mins
Q44	Examination	2	2 mins

Preparation of
financial statements
for companies

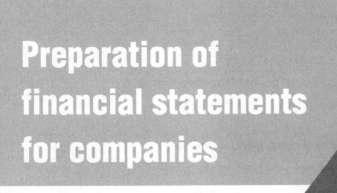

Topic list	Syllabus reference
1 IAS 1: *Presentation of financial statements*	F1(d), F2(a), F2(g)
2 Items in the income statement and statement of comprehensive income	F1(e), F2(a)–(g)
3 Items in the statement of financial position	F1(a), F1(d)
4 The current/non-current distinction	D8(l)
5 Company accounts for internal purposes	F1(d), F2(a), F2(c)
6 IAS 18 *Revenue*	F2(b)
7 Published accounts	F1(d), F2(a), F2(c), F2(d)

Introduction

You now come to the point in your studies for Paper F3 when you can look at the form and content of the financial statements of **limited liability companies**. Your later financial accounting studies will be concerned almost entirely with company accounts so it is vital that you acquire a sound understanding of the basic concepts now.

The financial statements of limited liability companies are usually governed by national legislation and accounting standards. From an international standpoint, however, the **general content** of financial statements is governed by IAS 1 *Presentation of financial statements*. We will look at the standard and explain those items in the financial statements which have not yet appeared in the text.

We will look at another IAS which has a significant impact on the content and form of company accounts, IAS 18 *Revenue.*

All these standards are concerned with financial statements produced for external reporting purposes (ie to external users), but companies also produce financial accounts for internal purposes, and we will look at the different approach in preparing accounts for internal as well as external use.

Study guide

		Intellectual level
D8	**Receivables and payables**	
(l)	Classify items as current or non-current liabilities in the statement of financial position	1
F1	**Statements of financial position**	
(a)	Recognise how the accounting equation and business entity convention underlie the statement of financial position	1
(d)	Prepare extracts of a statement of financial position from given information	1
(e)	Understand why the heading retained earnings appears in a company statement of financial position	1
F2	**Income statements and statements of comprehensive income**	
(a)	Prepare extracts of an income statement and statement of comprehensive income from given information	1
(b)	Understand how accounting concepts apply to revenue and expenses	1
(c)	Calculate revenue, cost of sales, gross profit, profit for the year and total comprehensive income from given information	1
(d)	Disclose items of income and expenditure in the income statement	1
(e)	Record income tax in the income statement of a company including the under and overprovision of tax in the prior year	1
(f)	Understand the interrelationship between the statement of financial position, income statement and statement of comprehensive income	1
(g)	Identify items requiring separate disclosure on the face of the income statement	1

Exam guide

Company financial statements form the foundation for all your future studies. You will be examined on it!

1 IAS 1: Presentation of financial statements

FAST FORWARD

IAS 1 lists the required contents of a company's income statement and statement of financial position sheet. It also give guidance on how items should be presented in the financial statements.

As well as covering accounting policies and other general considerations governing financial statements, IAS 1 *Presentation of financial statements* give substantial guidance on the form and content of published financial statements. The standard looks at the statement of financial position and income statement (the statement of cash flows is covered by IAS 7). First of all, some general points are made about financial statements.

1.1 Profit or loss for the period

The income statement is the most significant indicator of a company's financial performance. So it is important to ensure that it is not misleading.

The income statement will be misleading if costs incurred in the current year are deducted not from the current year profits but from the balance of accumulated profits brought forward. This presents the current year's results more favourably.

IAS 1 stipulates that all items of income and expense recognised in a period shall be included in profit or loss unless a **standard** or an **interpretation** requires otherwise.

Circumstances where items may be excluded from profit or loss for the current year include the correction of errors and the effect of changes in accounting policies. These are covered in IAS 8 (see Chapters 16 and 3 respectively).

1.2 Statement of comprehensive income

The statement of comprehensive income takes the income statement and adjusts it for certain gains and losses. At F3 level, this just means gains on property revaluation. The idea is to present all gains and losses, both those recognised in profit or loss (income statement) as well as those recognised through reserves (other comprehensive income).

IAS 1 allows a company to choose the presentation: one statement (statement of comprehensive income) or two statements (income statement and statement of other comprehensive income). See Section 1.7 for further details.

1.3 How items are disclosed

IAS 1 specifies disclosures of certain items in certain ways.

- Some items must appear on the **face of the statement of financial position or income statement**
- Other items can appear in a **note to the financial statements** instead
- **Recommended formats** are given which entities may or may not follow, depending on their circumstances

Obviously, disclosures specified by **other standards** must also be made, and we will mention the necessary disclosures when we cover each statement in turn. Disclosures in both IAS 1 and other standards must be made either on the face of the statement or in the notes unless otherwise stated, ie disclosures cannot be made in an accompanying commentary or report.

1.4 Identification of financial statements

As a result of the above point, it is most important that entities **distinguish the financial statements** very clearly from any other information published with them. This is because all IFRSs apply *only* to the financial statements (ie the main statements and related notes), so readers of the annual report must be able to differentiate between the parts of the report which are prepared under IFRSs, and other parts which are not.

The entity should **identify each component** of the financial statements very clearly. IAS 1 also requires disclosure of the following information in a prominent position. If necessary it should be repeated wherever it is felt to be of use to the reader in his understanding of the information presented.

- **Name** of the reporting entity (or other means of identification)
- Whether the accounts cover the **single entity** only or a group of entities
- The **reporting date** or the period covered by the financial statements (as appropriate)
- The **reporting currency**
- The **level of precision** used in presenting the figures in the financial statements

Judgement must be used to determine the best method of presenting this information. In particular, the standard suggests that the approach to this will be very different when the financial statements are communicated electronically.

The **level of precision** is important, as presenting figures in thousands or millions of units makes the figures more understandable. The level of precision must be disclosed, however, and it should not obscure necessary details or make the information less relevant.

1.5 Reporting period

It is normal for entities to present financial statements **annually** and IAS 1 states that they should be prepared at least as often as this.

Exam focus point

> IASs do not set out an **obligatory** format for financial statements but it would be best practice to use the **suggested format** of IAS 1.

1.6 Statement of financial position

ABC CO
STATEMENT OF FINANCIAL POSITION AS AT 31 DECEMBER 20X2

	20X2		20X1	
	$'000	$'000	$'000	$'000
Assets				
Non-current assets				
Property, plant and equipment	X		X	
Goodwill	X		X	
Other intangible assets	X		X	
		X		X
Current assets				
Inventories	X		X	
Trade receivables	X		X	
Other current assets	X		X	
Cash and cash equivalents	X		X	
		X		X
Total assets		X		X
Equity and liabilities				
Equity				
Share capital	X		X	
Retained earnings	X		X	
Other components of equity	X		X	
		X		X
Non-current liabilities				
Long-term borrowings	X		X	
Long-term provisions	X		X	
		X		X
Current liabilities				
Trade and other payables	X		X	
Short-term borrowings	X		X	
Current portion of long-term borrowings	X		X	
Current tax payable	X		X	
Short-term provisions	X		X	
		X		X
Total equity and liabilities		X		X

1.7 Statement of comprehensive income

ABC CO
STATEMENT OF COMPREHENSIVE INCOME FOR THE YEAR ENDED 31 DECEMBER 20X2
Illustrating the classification of expenses by function

	20X2 $'000	20X1 $'000
Revenue	X	X
Cost of sales	(X)	(X)
Gross profit	X	X
Other income	X	X
Distribution costs	(X)	(X)
Administrative expenses	(X)	(X)
Other expenses	(X)	(X)
Finance cost	(X)	(X)
Profit before tax	X	X
Income tax expense	(X)	(X)
Profit for the year	X	X
Other comprehensive income:		
Gains on property revaluation	X	X
Total comprehensive income for the year	X	X

Exam focus point

Questions in the exam may refer to an income statement: this means the entries from Revenue to Profit for the year. References to other comprehensive income means the last 3 lines. However a reference to statement of comprehensive income means the whole statement shown above.

1.8 Notes to the financial statements

Exam focus point

These notes are given as illustrations. For your exam, you only need to know five and these are listed in Section 1.9.

(1)   *Accounting policies*

This will generally be the first note to the accounts and is governed by IAS 1 *Presentation of financial statements*. Disclosure of the following policies is likely.

- Depreciation
- Inventories
- Revaluation of long-term assets

(2)   *General statement of financial position disclosures*

- Restrictions on the title to assets
- Security given in respect of liabilities
- Contingent assets and contingent liabilities, quantified if possible
- Amounts committed for future capital expenditure
- Events after the reporting period

(3)   *Property, plant and equipment*

- Land and buildings
- Plant and equipment
- Other categories of assets, suitably identified
- Accumulated depreciation
- Separate disclosure should be made of leaseholds and of assets being acquired on instalment purchase plans.

(4)   *Other non-current assets*

- Include, if applicable, the method and period of depreciation and any unusual write-offs during the period.

- *Long-term investments* stating the market value of listed investments if different from the carrying amount in the financial statements

- *Long-term receivables*

    - Accounts and notes receivable: trade
    - Receivables from directors
    - Other

- Goodwill

- Patents, trademarks, and similar assets

- Development costs capitalised and their movements during the period

(5)   *Investments*

For marketable securities, the market value should be disclosed if different from the carrying amount in the financial statements.

(6)   *Receivables*

- Accounts and notes receivable: trade
- Receivable from directors
- Other receivables and prepaid expenses

(7)   *Cash*

Cash includes cash on hand and in current and other accounts with banks. Cash which is not immediately available for use, for example balances frozen in foreign banks by exchange restrictions, should be disclosed.

(8)   *Shareholders' interests*

The following disclosures should be made separately.

- *Share capital*: disclose the following for each class of share capital.

    - Number of shares issued and partly paid, and issued but not fully paid
    - Par value per share or that the shares have not par value
    - Reconciliation of number of shares outstanding at the beginning and end of the year
    - Rights, preferences, and restrictions with respect to the distribution of dividends and to the repayment of capital
    - Shares in the enterprise held by itself or related companies
    - Shares reserved for future issue under options and sales contracts, including the terms and amounts.
    - Description of the nature and purpose of each reserve
    - Dividends proposed but not formally approved for payment
    - Cumulative preferred dividends not recognised

- Statement of changes in equity

(9)   *Non-current liabilities*

- Exclude the portion repayable within one year.
- Secured loans
- Unsecured loans

A summary of the interest rates, repayment terms, covenants, subordination and conversion features should be shown.

(10)   *Other liabilities and provisions*

The significant items included in other liabilities and in provisions and accruals should be separately disclosed. You are unlikely to meet any items of this nature in your syllabus.

(11)   *Payables*

- Accounts and notes payable: trade
- Payables to directors
- Taxes on income
- Other payables and accrued expenses

1.9 Examinable notes

For the purposes of your syllabus, you need to be able to **produce the following notes** to the accounts.

(a)   Statement of changes in equity (see Chapter 20 of this Study Text)
(b)   Tangible non-current assets (see Chapter 9 of this Study Text)
(c)   Events after the reporting period (Chapter 22)
(d)   Contingent assets and contingent liabilities (Chapter 13)
(e)   Research and development (Chapter 10)

Question	Pro forma

Before we go any further, take a blank sheet of paper and write out the 'pro forma' statement of comprehensive income and statement of financial position shown above. Mark which items are likely to require further disclosure, either by note or on the face of the statements.

FAST FORWARD

You must be able to account for these items when preparing the accounts of limited liability companies.

- Taxation
- Ordinary and preference shares
- Shareholders' equity (share premium, revaluation surplus, reserves and retained earnings)

2 Items in the income statement and statement of comprehensive income

2.1 Revenue

There are important rules on revenue recognition and these are the subject of IAS 18 *Revenue*. We will look at this in detail in Section 6 of this chapter.

2.2 Cost of sales

This represents the summary of the detailed workings we have used in a sole trader's financial statements.

2.3 Expenses

Notice that expenses are gathered under a number of headings. Any detail needed will be given in the notes to the financial statements.

2.3.1 Managers' salaries

The salary of a sole trader or a partner in a partnership is not a charge to the income statement but is an appropriation of profit. The **salary of a manager or member of management board of a limited liability company**, however, is an **expense in the income statement**, even when the manager is a shareholder in the company. Management salaries are included in **administrative expenses.**

2.4 Finance cost

This is interest **payable** during the period. Remember (from the previous chapter) that this may include accruals for interest payable on loan stock.

2.5 Income tax expense

This represents taxation as detailed in 2.6 below. Once again this will include accruals for the tax due on the current year's profits. However, it may also include adjustments for any over or under provision for prior periods (see example 2.6.1 below).

2.6 Taxation

Taxation affects both the statement of financial position and the income statement.

All companies pay some kind of corporate taxation on the profits they earn, which we will call **income tax** (for the sake of simplicity), but which you may find called 'corporation tax'. The rate of income tax will vary from country to country and there may be variations in rate within individual countries for different types or size of company.

Note that because a company has a **separate legal personality, its tax is included in its accounts**. An unincorporated business would not show personal income tax in its accounts, as it would not be a business expense but the personal affair of the proprietors.

(a)   The **charge for income tax on profits for the year** is shown as a **deduction from net profit**.

(b)   In the statements of financial position, **tax payable** to the government is generally shown as a **current liability** as it is usually due within 12 months of the year end.

(c)   For various reasons, the tax on profits in the income statement and the tax payable in the statement of financial position are not normally the same amount.

2.6.1 Example: taxation

A company has a tax liability brought forward of $15,000. The liability is finally agreed at $17,500 and this is paid during the year. The company estimates that the tax liability based on the current year's profits will be $20,000. Prepare the tax liability account for the year.

Solution

TAX LIABILITY ACCOUNT

	$		$
Cash paid	17,500	Balance b/f	15,000
Balance c/f	20,000	Income statement	22,500
	37,500		37,500

Notice that the income statement charge consists of the following:

	$
Under provision for prior year (17,500 – 15,000)	2,500
Provision for current year	20,000
	22,500

Notice also that the balance carried forward consists solely of the provision for the current year.

2.7 Accounting concepts

You will notice from the above that the accounting concepts apply to revenue and expenses. In particular, the matching concept applies and so expect to have to adjust for accruals and prepayments.

2.8 Interrelationship of income statement and statement of financial position

When we were dealing with the financial statements of sole traders, we transferred the net profit to the capital account. In the case of limited liability companies, the net profit is transferred to retained earnings in the statement of changes in equity (SOCIE). The closing balance of the accounts in the SOCIE are then transferred to the statement of financial position.

2.9 Gains on property revaluation

These arise when a property is revalued. The revaluation is recognised in the other comprehensive income part of the statement of comprehensive income.

For example an asset originally cost $5,000 and was revalued to $15,000. The $10,000 goes to revaluation reserve. However, rather than the SOCIE (see Section 5 for a practical example), the $10,000 transfer to the revaluation reserve is recognised in the statement of other comprehensive income.

3 Items in the statement of financial position

3.1 Assets

The assets are exactly the same as those we would expect to find in the accounts of a sole trader. The only difference is that the detail is given in notes and only the totals are shown on the face of the statement of financial position.

3.2 Equity

We looked at share capital and reserves in detail in the previous chapter. Remember that movements must be reported in the SOCIE.

Capital reserves usually have to be set up by law, whereas revenue reserves are appropriations of profit. With a sole trader, profit was added to capital. However, in a limited company, share capital and profit have to be disclosed separately, because profit is distributable as a dividend but share capital cannot be distributed. Therefore any retained profits are kept in the retained earnings reserve.

3.3 Liabilities

Liabilities are split between current and non-current and this is dealt with in detail in the next section.

3.4 Concepts

The statement of financial position makes use of the accounting equation concept that:

Assets = Capital + Liabilities

The statement of financial position is also prepared according to the **business entity** convention (that a business is separate from its owners).

4 The current/non-current distinction

FAST FORWARD

> You should be aware of the issues surrounding the current/non-current distinction as well as the disclosure requirements laid down in IAS 1.

Current assets and current liabilities of various types have been discussed in earlier parts of this Study Text. Users of financial statements need to be able to identify current assets and current liabilities in order to determine the company's financial position. Where current assets are greater than current liabilities, the net excess is often called 'working capital' or 'net current assets'.

4.1 Alternative views of current assets and current liabilities

IAS 1 lays down rules for entities which choose to show the current/non-current distinction. It also states what should happen if they do not do so.

Each entity should decide whether it wishes to present current/non-current assets and current/non-current liabilities as **separate classifications** in the statement of financial position. This decision should be based on the nature of the entity's options. Where an entity does *not* choose to make this classification, it should present assets and liabilities broadly **in order of their liquidity**.

In either case, the entity should disclose any portion of an asset or liability which is expected to be recovered or settled **after more than twelve months**. For example, for an amount receivable which is due in instalments over 18 months, the portion due after more than twelve months must be disclosed.

4.2 Current assets

Key term

> An asset should be classified as a **current asset** when it:
>
> - is expected to be realised in, or is held for sale or consumption in, the entity's normal operating cycle; or
> - is held primarily for the purpose of being traded
> - is expected to be realised within twelve months after the reporting date
> - is cash or a cash equivalent which is not restricted in its use.
>
> All other assets should be classified as non-current assets.   *(IAS 1)*

Non-current includes tangible, intangible operating and financial assets of a long-term nature. Other terms with the same meaning can be used (eg 'fixed', 'long-term').

The term 'operating cycle' is defined by the standard as follows.

Key term

> The **operating cycle** of an entity is the time between the acquisition of assets for processing and their realisation in cash or cash equivalents.   *(IAS 1)*

Current assets therefore include assets (such as inventories and trade receivables) that are sold, or realised as part of the normal operating cycle. **This is the case even where they are not expected to be realised within twelve months**.

4.3 Current liabilities

Key term

> A liability should be classified as a **current liability** when it:
>
> - is expected to be settled in the entity's normal operating cycle; or
> - is due to be settled within twelve months of the reporting date
> - is held primarily for the purpose of being traded.
>
> All other liabilities should be classified as non-current liabilities.   *(IAS 1)*

The categorisation of current liabilities is very similar to that of current assets. Thus, some current liabilities are part of the **working capital** used in the normal operating cycle of the business (ie trade payables and accruals for employee and other operating costs). Such items will be classed as current liabilities **even where they are due to be settled more than twelve months after the reporting date.**

There are also current liabilities which are not settled as part of the normal operating cycle, but which are due to be settled within twelve months of the reporting date. These include bank overdrafts, income taxes, other non-trade payables and the current portion of interest-bearing liabilities. Any interest-bearing liabilities that are used to finance working capital on a long-term basis, and that are not due for settlement within twelve months, should be classed as **non-current liabilities.**

For the differences between liabilities and provisions, see Chapter 13 of this Study Text.

5 Company accounts for internal purposes

The large amount of information in this chapter so far has really been geared towards the financial statements companies produce for external reporting purposes. In particular, the IFRSs discussed here are all concerned with external disclosure. **Companies do produce financial accounts for internal purposes, however.**

It will often be the case that internal use financial accounts look very similar to those produced for external reporting for various reasons.

(a)   The information required by internal users is similar to that required by external users. Any additional information for managers is usually provided by **management accounts**.

(b)   Financial accounts produced for internal purposes can be used for external reporting with very little further adjustment.

It remains true, nevertheless, that **financial accounts for internal use can follow whichever format managers wish**. They may be more detailed in some areas than external financial accounts (perhaps giving breakdown of sales and profits by region or by product), but may also exclude some items, for example the taxation charge and dividend may be missed out of the income statement.

You should always read question requirements carefully to discover whether you are being asked to produce accounts for external or internal purposes. Even when producing the latter, however, it is a good idea to stick to the external statement formats as these show best practice.

Now try this exercise.

Question	Internal accounts

The accountant of Zabit Co has prepared the following trial balance as at 31 December 20X7.

	$'000
50c ordinary shares (fully paid)	350
7% $1 preference shares (fully paid)	100
10% loan stock (secured)	200
Retained earnings 1.1.X7	242
General reserve 1.1.X7	171
Land and buildings 1.1.X7 (cost)	430
Plant and machinery 1.1.X7 (cost)	830
Accumulated depreciation	
Buildings 1.1.X7	20
Plant and machinery 1.1.X7	222
Inventory 1.1.X7	190
Sales	2,695
Purchases	2,152
Preference dividend	7
Ordinary dividend (interim)	8
Loan interest	10

	$'000
Wages and salaries	254
Light and heat	31
Sundry expenses	113
Suspense account	135
Trade accounts receivable	179
Trade accounts payable	195
Cash	126

Notes

(a) Sundry expenses include $9,000 paid in respect of insurance for the year ending 1 September 20X8. Light and heat does not include an invoice of $3,000 for electricity for the three months ending 2 January 20X8, which was paid in February 20X8. Light and heat also includes $20,000 relating to salesmen's commission.

(b) The suspense account is in respect of the following items.

	$'000
Proceeds from the issue of 100,000 ordinary shares	120
Proceeds from the sale of plant	300
	420
Less consideration for the acquisition of Mary & Co	285
	135

(c) The net assets of Mary & Co were purchased on 3 March 20X7. Assets were valued as follows.

	$'000
Investments	231
Inventory	34
	265

All the inventory acquired was sold during 20X7. The investments were still held by Zabit at 31.12.X7.

(d) The property was acquired some years ago. The buildings element of the cost was estimated at $100,000 and the estimated useful life of the assets was fifty years at the time of purchase. As at 31 December 20X7 the property is to be revalued at $800,000.

(e) The plant which was sold had cost $350,000 and had a net book value of $274,000 as on 1.1.X7. $36,000 depreciation is to be charged on plant and machinery for 20X7.

(f) The loan stock has been in issue for some years. The 50c ordinary shares all rank for dividends at the end of the year.

(g) The management wish to provide for:

   (i) loan stock interest due
   (ii) a transfer to general reserve of $16,000
   (iii) audit fees of $4,000

(h) Inventory as at 31 December 20X7 was valued at $220,000 (cost).

(i) Taxation is to be ignored.

Required

Prepare the financial statements of Zabit Co as at 31 December 20X7 including the statement of changes in equity. No other notes are required.

(a) Normal adjustments are needed for accruals and prepayments (insurance, light and heat, loan interest and audit fees). The loan interest accrued is calculated as follows.

	$'000
Charge needed in income statement (10% × $200,000)	20
Amount paid so far, as shown in list of account balances	10
Accrual: presumably six months' interest now payable	10

The accrued expenses shown in the statement of financial position comprise:

	$'000
Loan interest	10
Light and heat	3
Audit fee	4
	17

(b) The misposting of $20,000 to light and heat is also adjusted, by reducing the light and heat expense, but charging $20,000 to salesmen's commission.

(c) Depreciation on the building is calculated as $\dfrac{\$100,000}{50} = \$2,000$.

The NBV of the property is then $430,000 − $20,000 − $2,000 = $408,000 at the end of the year. When the property is revalued a reserve of $800,000 − $408,000 = $392,000 is then created.

(d) The profit on disposal of plant is calculated as proceeds $300,000 (per suspense account) less NBV $274,000, ie $26,000. The cost of the remaining plant is calculated at $830,000 − $350,000 = $480,000. The depreciation allowance at the year end is:

	$'000
Balance 1.1.X7	222
Charge for 20X7	36
Less depreciation on disposals (350 − 274)	(76)
	182

(e) Goodwill arising on the purchase of Mary & Co is:

	$'000
Consideration (per suspense account)	285
Assets at valuation	265
Goodwill	20

This is shown as an asset on the statement of financial position. The investments, being owned by Zabit at the year end, are also shown on the statement of financial position, whereas Mary's inventory, acquired and then sold, is added to the purchases figure for the year.

(f) The other item in the suspense account is dealt with as follows.

	$'000
Proceeds of issue of 100,000 ordinary shares	120
Less nominal value 100,000 × 50c	50
Excess of consideration over par value (= share premium)	70

(g) The transfer to general reserve increases it to $171,000 + $16,000 = $187,000.

We can now prepare the financial statements.

ZABIT CO
STATEMENT OF COMPREHENSIVE INCOME
FOR THE YEAR ENDED 31 DECEMBER 20X7

	$'000	$'000	$'000
Sales			2,695
Less cost of sales			
Opening inventory		190	
Purchases		2,186	
		2,376	
Less closing inventory		220	
			2,156
Gross profit			539
Profit on disposal of plant			26
			565
Expenses			
Wages, salaries and commission		274	
Sundry expenses		107	
Light and heat		14	
Depreciation: buildings		2	
plant		36	
Audit fees		4	
Loan interest		20	
			457
Profit for the year			108
Other comprehensive income:			
Revaluation of non-current assets			392
Total comprehensive income for the year			500

ZABIT CO
STATEMENT OF CHANGES IN EQUITY FOR THE YEAR ENDED 31 DECEMBER 20X7

	Share capital $'000	Share premium $'000	Revaluation surplus $'000	General reserve $'000	Retained earnings $'000	Total $'000
Balance at 1.1.X7	450	-	-	171	242	863
Total comprehensive income for the year	-	-	392	-	108	500
Issue of shares	50	70	-	-	-	120
Dividends paid	-	-	-	-	(15)	(15)
Transfer to general reserve	-	-	-	16	(16)	-
Balance at 1.12.X7	500	70	392	187	329	1,468

ZABIT CO
STATEMENT OF FINANCIAL POSITION AS AT 31 DECEMBER 20X7

	$'000	$'000
ASSETS		
Non-current assets		
Property, plant land and equipment		
Property at valuation		800
Plant: cost	480	
depreciation	182	
		298
Goodwill		20
Investments		231
Current assets		
Inventory	220	
Trade accounts receivable	179	
Prepayments	6	
Cash	126	
		531
Total assets		1,880
EQUITY AND LIABILITIES		
Equity		
50c ordinary shares	400	
7% $1 preference shares	100	
Share premium	70	
Revaluation reserve	392	
General reserve	187	
Retained earnings	319	
		1,468
Non-current liabilities		
10% loan stock (secured)		200
Current liabilities		
Trade accounts receivable	195	
Accrued expenses	17	
		212
Total equity and liabilities		1,880

Tutorial note. A lot of information has been shown on the face of the statement of comprehensive income and statement of financial position. However, for external purposes, most of this would be hidden in the notes.

6 IAS 18 Revenue

IAS 18 *Revenue* is concerned with the recognition of revenues arising from fairly common transactions:

- The sale of goods
- The rendering of services
- The use of others of assets of the entity yielding interest, royalties and dividends.

Generally revenue is recognised when the entity has transferred to the buyer the **significant risks and rewards** of ownership and when the revenue can be **measured reliably**.

6.1 Introduction

Accruals accounting is based on the **matching of costs with the revenue they generate**. It is crucially important under this convention that we establish the point at which revenue is recognised, so that the correct treatment can be applied to the related costs. For example, the costs of producing an item of finished goods should be carried as an asset in the statement of financial position until such time as it is sold; they should then be written off as a charge to the trading account. Which of these two treatments should be applied cannot be decided until it is clear at what moment the sale of the item takes place.

The decision has a **direct impact on profit** since, under the prudence concept, it is unacceptable to recognise the profit on sale until a sale has taken place, in accordance with the criteria of revenue recognition.

Revenue is generally recognised as **earned at the point of sale**, because at that point four criteria will generally have been met.

- The product or service has been **provided to the buyer**.
- The buyer has **recognised his liability** to pay for the goods or services provided. The converse of this is that the seller has recognised that ownership of goods has passed from himself to the buyer.
- The buyer has indicated his **willingness to hand over cash** or other assets in settlement of his liability.
- The **monetary value** of the goods or services has been established.

At earlier points in the business cycle there will not in general be **firm evidence** that the above criteria will be met. Until work on a product is complete, there is a risk that some flaw in the manufacturing process will necessitate its writing off; even when the product is complete there is no guarantee that it will find a buyer.

At later points in the business cycle, for example when cash is received for a credit sale, the recognition of revenue may occur in a period later than that in which the related costs were charged. Revenue recognition then depends on fortuitous circumstances, such as the cash flow of a company's receivables, and can fluctuate misleadingly from one period to another.

However, there are times when revenue is **recognised at other times than at the completion of a sale**. For example, in the recognition of profit on long-term construction contracts. Under IAS 11 *Construction contracts* (not in your syllabus) contract revenue and contract costs are recognised by reference to the stage of completion of the contract activity at the reporting date. You will learn about this later in your studies.

6.2 IAS 18 Revenue

IAS 18 governs the recognition of revenue in specific (common) types of transaction. Generally, recognition occurs when it is probable that **future economic benefits** will flow to the entity and when these benefits can be **measured reliably**.

Income, as defined by the IASC's *Framework* document (see Chapter 3), includes both revenues and gains. Revenue is income arising in the ordinary course of an entity's activities, such as sales, fees, interest, dividends or royalties.

6.3 Scope

IAS 18 covers the revenue from specific types of transaction or events.

- **Sale of goods** (manufactured products and items purchased for resale)
- **Rendering of services**
- Use by others of entity assets yielding **interest, royalties and dividends**

Interest, royalties and dividends are included as income because they arise from the use of an entity assets by other parties.

> **Interest** is the charge for the use of cash or cash equivalents or amounts due to the entity.
>
> **Royalties** are charges for the use of long-term assets of the entity, eg patents, computer software and trademarks.
>
> **Dividends** are distributions of profit to holders of equity investments, in proportion with their holdings, of each relevant class of capital.

The standard specifically **excludes** various types of revenue arising from leases, insurance contracts, changes in value of financial instruments or other current assets, natural increases in agricultural assets and mineral ore extraction.

6.4 Definitions

The following definitions are given in the standard.

> **Revenue** is the gross inflow of economic benefits during the period arising in the course of the ordinary activities of an entity when those inflows result in increases in equity, other than increases relating to contributions from equity participants.
>
> **Fair value** is the amount for which an asset could be exchanged, or a liability settled, between knowledgeable, willing parties in an arm's length transaction. *(IAS 18)*

Revenue **does not include** sales taxes, value added taxes or goods and service taxes which are only collected for third parties, because these do not represent an economic benefit flowing to the entity. The same is true for revenues collected by an agent on behalf of a principal. Revenue for the agent is only the commission received for acting as agent.

6.5 Measurement of revenue

When a transaction takes place, the amount of revenue is usually decided by the **agreement of the buyer and seller**. The revenue is actually measured, however, as the **fair value of the consideration received**, which will take account of any trade discounts and volume rebates.

6.6 Disclosure

The following items should be disclosed.

(a)   The **accounting policies** adopted for the recognition of revenue, including the methods used to determine the stage of completion of transactions involving the rendering of services

(b)   The amount of each **significant category of revenue** recognised during the period including revenue arising from the sources below

      (i)   The sale of goods
      (ii)   The rendering of services
      (iii)   Interest
      (iv)   Royalties
      (v)   Dividends

(c)   The amount of revenue arising from **exchanges of goods or services** included in each significant category of revenue

Any **contingent gains or losses**, such as those relating to warranty costs, claims or penalties should be treated according to IAS 10 *Events after the reporting period* (see Chapter 22).

Given that prudence is the main consideration, discuss under what circumstances, if any, revenue might be recognised at the following stages of a sale.

(a)   Goods are acquired by the business which it confidently expects to resell very quickly.
(b)   A customer places a firm order for goods.
(c)   Goods are delivered to the customer.
(d)   The customer is invoiced for goods.
(e)   The customer pays for the goods.
(f)   The customer's cheque in payment for the goods has been cleared by the bank.

Answer

(a)   A sale must never be recognised before the goods have even been ordered by a customer. There is no certainty about the value of the sale, nor when it will take place, even if it is virtually certain that goods will be sold.

(b)   A sale must never be recognised when the customer places an order. Even though the order will be for a specific quantity of goods at a specific price, it is not yet certain that the sale transaction will go through. The customer may cancel the order, the supplier might be unable to deliver the goods as ordered or it may be decided that the customer is not a good credit risk.

(c)   A sale will be recognised when delivery of the goods is made only when:

(i)   the sale is for cash, and so the cash is received at the same time.
(ii)   the sale is on credit and the customer accepts delivery (eg by signing a delivery note).

(d)   The critical event for a credit sale is usually the despatch of an invoice to the customer. There is then a legally enforceable debt, payable on specified terms, for a completed sale transaction.

(e)   The critical event for a cash sale is when delivery takes place and when cash is received; both take place at the same time.

It would be too cautious or 'prudent' to await cash payment for a credit sale transaction before recognising the sale, unless the customer is a high credit risk and there is a serious doubt about his ability or intention to pay. But in that case, why would the business risk dispatching the goods?

(f)   It would again be over-cautious to wait for clearance of the customer's cheques before recognising sales revenue. Such a precaution would only be justified in cases where there is a very high risk of the bank refusing to honour the cheque.

7 Published accounts

Now work through this example to give you practice in preparing financial statements in accordance with IAS 1. You have already met part of this question in the previous chapter (section 3.6), when you prepared the SOCIE (statement of changes in equity).

Note that very little detail appears in the income statement – all items of income and expenditure are accumulated under the standard headings. Write out the standard proformas and then go through the workings, inserting figures as you go.

USB, a limited liability company, has the following trial balance at 31 December 20X9.

	Debit $'000	Credit $'000
Cash at bank	100	
Inventory at 1 January 20X9	2,400	
Administrative expenses	2,206	
Distribution costs	650	
Non-current assets at cost:		
Buildings	10,000	
Plant and equipment	1,400	
Motor vehicles	320	
Suspense		1,500
Accumulated depreciation		
Buildings		4,000
Plant and equipment		480
Motor vehicles		120
Retained earnings		560
Trade receivables	876	
Purchases	4,200	
Dividend paid	200	
Sales revenue		11,752
Sales tax payable		1,390
Trade payables		1,050
Share premium		500
$1 ordinary shares		1,000
	22,352	22,352

The following additional information is relevant.

(a)   Inventory at 31 December 20X9 was valued at $1,600,000. While doing the inventory count, errors in the previous year's inventory count were discovered. The inventory brought forward at the beginning of the year should have been $2.2m, not $2.4m as above.

(b)   Depreciation is to be provided as follows:

(i)   Buildings at 5% straight line, charged to administrative expenses.
(ii)   Plant and equipment at 20% on the reducing balance basis, charged to cost of sales.
(iii)   Motor vehicles at 25% on the reducing balance basis, charged to distribution costs.

(c)   No final dividend is being proposed.

(d)   A customer has gone bankrupt owing $76,000. This debt is not expected to be recovered and an adjustment should be made. An allowance for receivables of 5% is to be set up.

(e)   1 million new ordinary shares were issued at $1.50 on 1 December 20X9. The proceeds have been left in a suspense account.

Required

Prepare the income statement for the year to 31 December 20X9, a statement of changes in equity and a statement of financial position at that date in accordance with the requirements of International Financial Reporting Standards. Ignore taxation.

USB
INCOME STATEMENT FOR THE YEAR ENDED 31 DECEMBER 20X9

	$'000
Revenue	11,752
Cost of sales (W2)	4,984
Gross profit	6,768
Administrative expenses (W3)	2,822
Distribution costs (650 + 50 (W1))	700
Profit for the year	3,246

USB
STATEMENT OF CHANGES IN EQUITY FOR THE YEAR ENDED 31 DECEMBER 20X9

	Share capital	Share premium	Retained earnings	Total
	$'000	$'000	$'000	$'000
Balance at 1 January 20X9	1,000	500	560	2,060
Prior period adjustment	-	-	(200)	(200)
Restated balance	1,000	500	360	1,860
Total comprehensive income for the year	-	-	3,246	3,246
Dividends paid	-	-	(200)	(200)
Share issue	1,000	500	-	1,500
Balance at 31 December 20X9	2,000	1,000	3,406	6,406

USB
STATEMENT OF FINANCIAL POSITION AS AT 31 DECEMBER 20X9

	$'000	$'000
Non-current assets		
Property, plant and equipment (W5)		6,386
Current assets		
Inventory	1,600	
Trade receivables (876 – 76 – 40)	760	
Cash	100	
		2,460
Total assets		8,846
Equity and liabilities		
Equity		
Share capital		2,000
Share premium		1,000
Retained earnings (W6)		3,406
Current liabilities		
Sales tax payable	1,390	
Trade payables	1,050	
		2,440
Total equity and liabilities		8,846

Workings

1   *Depreciation*

	$'000
Buildings (10,000 × 5%)	500
Plant (1,400 – 480) × 20%	184
Motor vehicles (320 – 120) × 25%	50

2   Cost of sales

	$'000
Opening inventory	2,200
Purchases	4,200
Depreciation (W1)	184
Closing inventory	(1,600)
	4,984

3   Administrative expenses

	$'000
Per T/B	2,206
Depreciation (W1)	500
Irrecoverable debt	76
Receivables allowance ((876 – 76) × 5%)	40
	2,822

4   Property, plant and equipment

	Cost	Acc Dep	Dep chg	NBV
	$'000	$'000	$'000	$'000
Buildings	10,000	4,000	500	5,500
Plant	1,400	480	184	736
Motor vehicles	320	120	50	150
	11,720	4,600	734	6,386

5   Retained earnings

	$'000
B/f per T/B	560
Prior period adjustment (inventory)	(200)
Profit for period	3,246
Dividend paid	(200)
	3,406

One of the competences you require to fulfil performance criteria 10 of the PER is the ability to compile financial statements and accounts in line with appropriate standards and guidelines. You can apply the knowledge you obtain from this section of the text to help demonstrate this competence.

Chapter Roundup

- IAS 1 lists the required contents of a company's income statement and statement of financial position. It also gives guidance on how items should be presented in the financial statements.

- You must be able to account for these items in particular when preparing the accounts of limited liability companies.

    - Taxation
    - Ordinary and preferred shares
    - Shareholders' equity (share premium, revaluation surplus, reserves and retained earnings)

- You should be aware of the issues surrounding the current/non-current distinction as well as the disclosure requirements laid down in IAS 1.

- IAS 18 Revenue is concerned with the recognition of revenues arising from fairly common transactions:

    - The sale of goods
    - The rendering of services
    - The use of others of assets of the entity yielding interest, royalties and dividends.

    Generally revenue is recognised when the entity has transferred to the buyer the significant risks and rewards of ownership and when the revenue can be measured reliably.

Quick Quiz

1   According to IAS 1, entities have to produce their accounts within what period?
    A   Within 6 months of the reporting date
    B   Within 9 months of the reporting date

2   Managers' salaries are appropriations of profit.
    A   True
    B   False

3   Which of the following items are non-current assets?
    (i)   Land
    (ii)   Machinery
    (iii) Bank loan
    (iv)   Inventory
    A   (i) only
    B   (i) and (ii)
    C   (i), (ii) and (iii)
    D   (ii), (iii) and (iv)

4   How is a bank overdraft classified in the statement of financial position?
    A   Non-current asset
    B   Current asset
    C   Current liability
    D   Non-current liability

5   In the published accounts of XYZ Co, the profit for the period is $3,500,000. The balance of retained earnings at the beginning of the year is $500,000. If dividends of $2,500,000 were paid, what is the closing balance of retained earnings?
    A $4,000,000
    B $1,500,000
    C $500,000
    D $1,000,000

Answers to Quick Quiz

1   A

2   B   False. Managers' salaries are an expense charged to the income statement.

3   B   Item (iii) is a liability and item (iv) is a current asset.

4   C   A bank overdraft is strictly payable on demand and so it is a current liability.

5   B

	$'000
Retained earnings	
Opening balance	500
Profit for the period	3,500
	4,000
Dividends paid	(2,500)
Closing balance	1,500

Now try the question below from the Exam Question Bank

Number	Level	Marks	Time
Q45	Examination	2	2 mins

Events after the reporting period

Topic list	Syllabus reference
1 IAS 10 *(Revised) Events after the reporting period*	F3(a)–(c)

Introduction

We will now examine a statement that applies very much to limited liability companies, IAS 10.

You will see in IAS 10 the application of the concept of prudence, which you learnt about in Chapter 3. This IAS is very important for your auditing studies. It is more straightforward in theory than in practice.

Study guide

		Intellectual level
F3	**Events after the reporting period**	
(a)	Define an event after the reporting period in accordance with IFRSs.	1
(b)	Classify events as adjusting or non-adjusting	1
(c)	Distinguish between how adjusting and non-adjusting events are reported in the financial statements.	1

Exam guide

These are extremely important topics that could well be examined.

1 IAS 10 (Revised) Events after the reporting period

FAST FORWARD

Events after the reporting period which provide **additional evidence** of conditions existing at the reporting date, will cause **adjustments** to be made to the assets and liabilities in the financial statements.

The financial statements are significant indicators of a company's success or failure. It is important, therefore, that they include all the information necessary for an understanding of the company's position.

IAS 10 *(Revised) Events after the reporting period* requires the provision of additional information in order to facilitate such an understanding. IAS 10 deals with events **after** the reporting date which may **affect the position at** the reporting date.

1.1 Definitions

The standard gives the following definition.

Key terms

Events after the reporting period are those events, both favourable and unfavourable, that occur between the reporting date and the date on which the financial statements are authorised for issue. Two types of events can be identified:

- those that provide further evidence of conditions that existed at the reporting date; and
- those that are indicative of conditions that arose subsequent to the reporting date.   (IAS 10)

1.2 Events after the reporting period

Between the reporting date and the date the financial statements are authorised (ie for issue outside the organisation), events may occur which show that assets and liabilities at the reporting date should be adjusted, or that disclosure of such events should be given.

1.3 Events requiring adjustment

The standard requires adjustment of assets and liabilities in certain circumstances.

FAST FORWARD

An entity shall adjust the amounts recognised in its financial statements to reflect adjusting events after the reporting period.   (IAS 10)

Where events indicate that the **going concern concept** is no longer appropriate, then the accounts may have to be restated on a break-up basis.

An **example** of additional evidence which becomes available after the reporting date is where a **customer goes bankrupt, thus confirming that the trade account receivable balance at the year end is uncollectable.**

In relation to going concern, the standard states that, where operating results and the financial position have deteriorated after the reporting date, it may be necessary to reconsider whether the going concern assumption is appropriate in the preparation of the financial statements.

1.4 Events not requiring adjustment

Events which do not affect the situation at the reporting date should not be adjusted for, but should be **disclosed** in the financial statements.

The standard then looks at events which do **not** require adjustment.

An entity shall not adjust the amounts recognised in its financial statements to reflect non-adjusting events after the reporting period. (IAS 10)

The **example** given by the standard of such an event is where the **value of an investment falls between the reporting date and the date the financial statements are authorised** for issue. The fall in value represents circumstances during the current period, not conditions existing at the previous reporting date, so it is not appropriate to adjust the value of the investment in the financial statements. Disclosure is an aid to users, however, indicating 'unusual changes' in the state of assets and liabilities after the reporting date.

The rule for **disclosure** of events occurring after the reporting period which relate to conditions that arose after that date, is that disclosure should be made if non-disclosure would hinder the user's ability to made **proper evaluations** and decision based on the financial statements. An example might be the acquisition of another business.

Exam focus point

There was an article on events after the reporting period in *Student Accountant* dated 15 March 2007. We recommend that you read this article.

1.5 Dividends

Dividends proposed or declared (but not paid) are no longer recognised as a liability and do not appear in the accounts.

1.6 Disclosures

The following **disclosure requirements** are given **for events** which occur after the reporting period which do *not* require adjustment. If disclosure of events occurring after the reporting period is required by this standard, the following information should be provided:

(a) The nature of the event
(b) An estimate of the financial effect, or a statement that such an estimate cannot be made

Exam focus point

Expect to be asked whether an item is adjusting or non-adjusting. You may well be asked to adjust for an adjusting item.

Question

State whether the following events occurring after the reporting period require an adjustment to the assets and liabilities of the financial statements.

(a)   Purchase of an investment
(b)   A change in the rate of tax, applicable to the previous year
(c)   An increase in pension benefits
(d)   Losses due to fire
(e)   An irrecoverable debt suddenly being paid
(f)   The receipt of proceeds of sales or other evidence concerning the net realisable value of inventory
(g)   A sudden decline in the value of property held as a long-term asset

Answer

(b), (e) and (f) require adjustment.

Of the other items, (a) would not need to be disclosed at all. Item (c) could need a disclosure if the cost to the company is likely to be material. Item (d) again would be disclosed if material, as would (g) if material.

Assuming that item (d) is material, it would be disclosed by way of the following note to the accounts. (The company year end is 31 December 20X8.)

Events after the reporting period

On 22 January 20X9, there was a fire at the company's warehouse. As a result, inventories costing a total of $250,000 were destroyed. These inventories are included in assets at the reporting date.

Chapter Roundup

- **Events after the reporting period** which provide **additional evidence** of conditions existing at the reporting date, will cause **adjustments** to be made to the assets and liabilities in the financial statements.

- An entity shall adjust the amounts recognised in its financial statements to reflect adjusting events after the reporting period.

  Where events indicate that the **going concern concept** is no longer appropriate, then the accounts may have to be restated on a break-up basis.

- **Events** which **do not affect the situation at the reporting date** should **not be adjusted for**, but should be **disclosed** in the financial statements.

- An entity shall not adjust the amounts recognised in its financial statements to reflect non-adjusting events after the **reporting period**.

1   When does an event after the reporting period require changes to the financial statements?

    A   Never

    B   If it provides further evidence of conditions existing at the reporting date

2   What disclosure is required when it is not possible to estimate the financial effect of an event not requiring adjustment?

    A   No disclosure

    B   A note to the accounts giving what information is available

3   Which of the following items are adjusting events?

    (i)   Inventory found to have deteriorated

    (ii)   Dividends proposed at the year end

    (iii)   A building destroyed by fire after the reporting date

    A   (i) only

    B   (ii) only

    C   (iii) only

    D   None of the above

4   Which of the following items are non-adjusting events?

    (i)   Inventory destroyed by flood two days before the reporting date

    (ii)   A customer goes bankrupt

    (iii)   Fall in value of an investment between the reporting date and the date the financial statements are finalised

    A   (i) only

    B   (ii) only

    C   (iii) only

    D   None of the above

5   A receivable has been written off as irrecoverable. However the customer suddenly pays the written off amount after the reporting date. Is this event

    A   Adjusting

    B   Non-adjusting

Answers to Quick Quiz

1   B   Assets and liabilities should be adjusted for events after the reporting period when these provide additional evidence for estimates existing at the reporting date.

2   B   A statement of the nature of the event and the fact that a financial estimate of the event can not be made.

3   A

4   C

5   A

Now try the questions below from the Exam Question Bank

Number	Level	Marks	Time
Q46	Examination	1	1 min
Q47	Examination	2	2 mins

23

Statements of cash flows

Topic list	Syllabus reference
1 IAS 7 *Statement of cash flows*	F5(a)–(h)
2 Preparing a statement of cash flows	F5(g)

Introduction

In the long run, a profit will result in an increase in the company's cash balance but, as Keynes observed, 'in the long run we are all dead'. In the short run, **the making of a profit will not necessarily result in an increased cash balance.** The observation leads us to two questions. The first relates to the importance of the distinction between cash and profit. The second is concerned with the usefulness of the information provided by the statement of financial position and income statement in the problem of deciding whether the company has, or will be able to generate, sufficient cash to finance its operations.

The importance of the **distinction between cash and profit** and the scant attention paid to this by the income statement has resulted in the development of statements of cash flows.

This chapter adopts a systematic approach to the preparation of statements of cash flows in examinations; you should learn this method and you will then be equipped for any problems in the exam itself.

Study guide

		Intellectual level
F5	**Statements of cash flows (excluding partnerships)**	
(a)	Differentiate between profit and cash flow	1
(b)	Understand the need for management to control cash flow	1
(c)	Recognise the benefits and drawbacks to users of the financial statements of a statement of cash flows	1
(d)	Classify the effect of transactions on cash flows	1
(e)	Calculate the figures needed for the statement of cash flows including: (i) Cash flows from operating activities (ii) Cash flows from investing activities (iii) Cash flows from financing activities	1
(f)	Calculate the cash flow from operating activities using the indirect and direct methods	1
(g)	Prepare extracts from statement of cash flows from given information	1
(h)	Identify the treatment of given transactions in a company's statement of cash flows	1

Exam guide

This topic is very important. You are certain to be examined on it. Exam questions will not ask you to prepare a full statement, but some element of the cash flow will need to be calculated (eg cash flow from financing activities).

1 IAS 7 Statement of cash flows

FAST FORWARD

Statements of cash flows. are a useful addition to the financial statements of a company because accounting profit is not the only indicator of performance. Statements of cash flows concentrate on the sources and uses of cash and are a useful indicator of a company's liquidity and solvency.

It has been argued that 'profit' does not always give a useful or meaningful picture of a company's operations. Readers of a company's financial statements might even be **misled by a reported profit figure**.

(a) Shareholders might believe that if a company makes a profit after tax, of say, $100,000 then this is the amount which it could afford to **pay as a dividend**. Unless the company has **sufficient cash** available to stay in business and also to pay a dividend, the shareholders' expectations would be wrong.

(b) Employees might believe that if a company makes profits, it can afford to **pay higher wages** next year. This opinion may not be correct: the ability to pay wages depends on the **availability of cash**.

(c) Survival of a business entity depends not so much on profits as on its **ability to pay its debts when they fall due**. Such payments might include 'profit and loss' items such as material purchases, wages, interest and taxation etc, but also capital payments for new non-current assets and the repayment of loan capital when this falls due (for example on the redemption of loan stock).

From these examples, it may be apparent that a company's performance and prospects depend not so much on the 'profits' earned in a period, but more realistically on liquidity or **cash flows**.

1.1 Funds flow and cash flow

Some countries, either currently or in the past, have required the disclosure of additional statements based on **funds flow** rather than cash flow. However, the definition of 'funds' can be very vague and such statements often simply require a rearrangement of figures already provided in the statement of financial position and income statement. By contrast, a statement of cash flows is unambiguous and provides information which is additional to that provided in the rest of the accounts. It also lends itself to organisation by activity and not by statement of financial position classification.

Statements of cash flows are frequently given as an **additional statement**, supplementing the statement of financial position, income statement and related notes. The group aspects of statements of cash flows (and certain complex matters) have been excluded as they are beyond the scope of your syllabus.

1.2 Objective of IAS 7

The aim of IAS 7 is to provide information to users of financial statements about an entity's **ability to generate cash and cash equivalents**, as well as indicating the cash needs of the entity. The statement of cash flows provides *historical* information about cash and cash equivalents, classifying cash flows between operating, investing and financing activities.

1.3 Scope

A statement of cash flows should be presented as an **integral part** of an entity's financial statements. All types of entity can provide useful information about cash flows as the need for cash is universal, whatever the nature of their revenue-producing activities. Therefore **all entities are required by the standard to produce a statement of cash flows.**

1.4 Benefits of cash flow information

The use of statements of cash flows is very much **in conjunction** with the rest of the financial statements. Users can gain further appreciation of the change in net assets, of the entity's financial position (liquidity and solvency) and the entity's ability to adapt to changing circumstances by adjusting the amount and timing of cash flows. Statements of cash flows **enhance comparability** as they are not affected by differing accounting policies used for the same type of transactions or events.

Cash flow information of a historical nature can be used as an indicator of the amount, timing and certainty of future cash flows. Past forecast cash flow information can be **checked for accuracy** as actual figures emerge. The relationship between profit and cash flows can be analysed as can changes in prices over time. All this information helps management to control costs by controlling cash flow.

1.5 Definitions

The standard gives the following definitions, the most important of which are **cash** and **cash equivalents**.

Key terms

- **Cash** comprises cash on hand and demand deposits.
- **Cash equivalents** are short-term, highly liquid investments that are readily convertible to known amounts of cash and which are subject to an insignificant risk of changes in value.
- **Cash flows** are inflows and outflows of cash and cash equivalents.
- **Operating activities** are the principal revenue-producing activities of the enterprise and other activities that are not investing or financing activities.
- **Investing activities** are the acquisition and disposal of non-current assets and other investments not included in cash equivalents.
- **Financing activities** are activities that result in changes in the size and composition of the equity capital and borrowings of the entity.

(IAS 7)

1.6 Cash and cash equivalents

The standard expands on the definition of cash equivalents: they are not held for investment or other long-term purposes, but rather to meet short-term cash commitments. To fulfil the above definition, an investment's **maturity date should normally be three months from its acquisition date**. It would usually be the case then that equity investments (ie shares in other companies) are *not* cash equivalents. An exception would be where redeemable preference shares were acquired with a very close redemption date.

Loans and other borrowings from banks are classified as investing activities. In some countries, however, **bank overdrafts** are repayable on demand and are treated as part of an enterprise's total cash management system. In these circumstances an overdrawn balance will be included in cash and cash equivalents. Such banking arrangements are characterised by a balance which fluctuates between overdrawn and credit.

Movements between different types of cash and cash equivalent are not included in cash flows. The investment of surplus cash in cash equivalents is part of cash management, not part of operating, investing or financing activities.

1.7 Presentation of a statement of cash flows

IAS 7 requires statements of cash flows to report cash flows during the period classified by **operating, investing and financing activities.**

The manner of presentation of cash flows from operating, investing and financing activities **depends on the nature of the enterprise**. By classifying cash flows between different activities in this way users can see the impact on cash and cash equivalents of each one, and their relationships with each other. We can look at each in more detail.

1.7.1 Operating activities

This is perhaps the key part of the statement of cash flows because it shows whether, and to what extent, companies can **generate cash from their operations**. It is these operating cash flows which must, in the end pay for all cash outflows relating to other activities, ie paying loan interest, dividends and so on.

Most of the components of cash flows from operating activities will be those items which **determine the net profit or loss of the enterprise**, ie they relate to the main revenue-producing activities of the enterprise. The standard gives the following as examples of cash flows from operating activities.

(a)   Cash receipts from the sale of goods and the rendering of services
(b)   Cash receipts from royalties, fees, commissions and other revenue
(c)   Cash payments to suppliers for goods and services
(d)   Cash payments to and on behalf of employees

Certain items may be included in the net profit or loss for the period which do *not* relate to operational cash flows, for example the profit or loss on the sale of a piece of plant will be included in net profit or loss, but the cash flows will be classed as **financing**.

1.7.2 Investing activities

The cash flows classified under this heading show the extent of new investment in **assets which will generate future profit and cash flows**. The standard gives the following examples of cash flows arising from investing activities.

(a)   Cash payments to acquire property, plant and equipment, intangibles and other non-current assets, including those relating to capitalised development costs and self-constructed property, plant and equipment
(b)   Cash receipts from sales of property, plant and equipment, intangibles and other non-current assets
(c)   Cash payments to acquire shares or debentures of other enterprises
(d)   Cash receipts from sales of shares or debentures of other enterprises
(e)   Cash advances and loans made to other parties
(f)   Cash receipts from the repayment of advances and loans made to other parties

1.7.3 Financing activities

This section of the statement of cash flows shows the share of cash which the enterprise's capital providers have claimed during the period. This is an indicator of **likely future interest and dividend payments**. The standard gives the following examples of cash flows which might arise under these headings.

(a)   Cash proceeds from issuing shares

(b)   Cash payments to owners to acquire or redeem the enterprise's shares

(c)   Cash proceeds from issuing debentures, loans, notes, bonds, mortgages and other short or long-term borrowings

(d)   Cash repayments of amounts borrowed

1.8 Reporting cash flows from operating activities

The standard offers a choice of method for this part of the statement of cash flows.

(a)   **Direct method:** disclose major classes of gross cash receipts and gross cash payments

(b)   **Indirect method:** net profit or loss is adjusted for the effects of transactions of a non-cash nature, any deferrals or accruals of past or future operating cash receipts or payments, and items of income or expense associated with investing or financing cash flows

The **direct method** discloses information, not available elsewhere in the financial statements, which could be of use in estimating future cash flows. However, the **indirect method** is simpler, more widely used and more likely to be examined.

1.8.1 Using the direct method

There are different ways in which the **information about gross cash receipts and payments** can be obtained. The most obvious way is simply to extract the information from the accounting records. The pro-forma is shown below. This may be a laborious task, however, and the indirect method below may be easier.

Formula to learn

	$
Cash receipts from customers	X
Cash paid to suppliers and employees	X
Cash generated from operations	X

1.8.2 Using the indirect method

This method is undoubtedly **easier** from the point of view of the preparer of the statement of cash flows. The net profit or loss for the period is adjusted for the following.

(a)   Changes during the period in inventories, operating receivables and payables

(b)   Non-cash items, eg depreciation, provisions, profits/losses on the sales of assets

(c)   Other items, the cash flows from which should be classified under investing or financing activities.

A **proforma** of such a calculation is as follows and this method may be more common in the exam.

	$
Profit before interest and tax (income statement)*	X
Add depreciation	X
Loss (profit) on sale of non-current assets	X
(Increase)/decrease in inventories	(X)/X
(Increase)/decrease in receivables	(X)/X
Increase/(decrease) in payables	X/(X)
Cash generated from operations	X
Interest (paid)/received	(X)
Income taxes paid	(X)
Net cash flows from operating activities	X

* Take profit before tax and add back any interest expense

It is important to understand why **certain items are added and others subtracted**. Note the following points.

(a)   Depreciation is not a cash expense, but is deducted in arriving at the profit figure in the income statement. It makes sense, therefore, to eliminate it by adding it back.

(b)   By the same logic, a loss on a disposal of a non-current asset (arising through underprovision of depreciation) needs to be added back and a profit deducted.

(c)   An increase in inventories means less cash – you have spent cash on buying inventory.

(d)   An increase in receivables means the company's receivables have not paid as much, and therefore there is less cash.

(e)   If we pay off payables, causing the figure to decrease, again we have less cash.

1.8.3 Indirect versus direct

The direct method is encouraged where the necessary information is not too costly to obtain, but IAS 7 does not demand it. In practice, therefore, the direct method is rarely used. It could be argued that companies ought to monitor their cash flows carefully enough on an ongoing basis to be able to use the direct method at minimal extra cost.

1.9 Interest and dividends

Cash flows from interest and dividends received and paid should each be **disclosed separately**. Each should be classified in a consistent manner from period to period as either operating, investing or financing activities.

Dividends paid by the enterprise can be classified in **one of two ways**.

(a)   As a **financing cash flow**, showing the cost of obtaining financial resources.

(b)   As a component of **cash flows from operating activities** so that users can assess the enterprise's ability to pay dividends out of operating cash flows.

1.10 Taxes on income

Cash flows arising from taxes on income should be **separately disclosed** and should be classified as cash flows from operating activities *unless* they can be specifically identified with financing and investing activities.

Taxation cash flows are often **difficult to match** to the originating underlying transaction, so most of the time all tax cash flows are classified as arising from operating activities.

1.11 Components of cash and cash equivalents

The components of cash and cash equivalents should be disclosed and a **reconciliation** should be presented, showing the amounts in the statement of cash flows reconciled with the equivalent items reported in the statement of financial position.

It is also necessary to disclose the **accounting policy** used in deciding the items included in cash and cash equivalents, in accordance with IAS 1 *Presentation of financial statements*, but also because of the wide range of cash management practices worldwide.

1.12 Other disclosures

All enterprises should disclose, together with a **commentary by management**, any other information likely to be of importance, for example:

(a)   restrictions on the use of or access to any part of cash equivalents;

(b)   the amount of undrawn borrowing facilities which are available; and

(c)   Cash flows which increased operating capacity compared to cash flows which merely maintained operating capacity.

1.13 Example of a statement of cash flows

In the next section we will look at the procedures for preparing a statement of cash flows. First, look at this **example**, adapted from the example given in the standard (which is based on a group and therefore beyond the scope of your syllabus).

1.13.1 Direct method

STATEMENT OF CASH FLOWS (DIRECT METHOD)
YEAR ENDED 20X7

	$m	$m
Cash flows from operating activities		
Cash receipts from customers	30,330	
Cash paid to suppliers and employees	(27,600)	
Cash generated from operations	2,730	
Interest paid	(270)	
Income taxes paid	(900)	
Net cash from operating activities		1,560
Cash flows from investing activities		
Purchase of property, plant and equipment	(900)	
Proceeds from sale of equipment	20	
Interest received	200	
Dividends received	200	
Net cash used in investing activities		(480)
Cash flows from financing activities		
Proceeds from issuance of share capital	250	
Proceeds from long-term borrowings	250	
Dividends paid*	(1,290)	
Net cash used in financing activities		(790)
Net increase in cash and cash equivalents		290
Cash and cash equivalents at beginning of period (Note)		120
Cash and cash equivalents at end of period (Note)		410

* This could also be shown as an operating cash flow

1.13.2 Indirect method

STATEMENT OF CASH FLOWS (INDIRECT METHOD)
YEAR ENDED 20X7

	$m	$m
Cash flows from operating activities		
Net profit before taxation	3,570	
Adjustments for:		
Depreciation	450	
Investment income	(500)	
Interest expense	400	
Operating profit before working capital changes	3,920	
Increase in trade and other receivables	(500)	
Decrease in inventories	1,050	
Decrease in trade payables	(1,740)	
Cash generated from operations	2,730	
Interest paid	(270)	
Income taxes paid	(900)	
Net cash from operating activities		1,560

Cash flows from investing activities		
Purchase of property, plant and equipment	(900)	
Proceeds from sale of equipment	20	
Interest received	200	
Dividends received	200	
Net cash used in investing activities		(480)
Cash flows from financing activities		
Proceeds from issuance of share capital	250	
Proceeds from long-term borrowings	250	
Dividends paid*	(1,290)	
Net cash used in financing activities		(790)
Net increase in cash and cash equivalents		290
Cash and cash equivalents at beginning of period (Note)		120
Cash and cash equivalents at end of period (Note)		410

* This could also be shown as an operating cash flow

The following note is required to both versions of the statement.

Note: Cash and cash equivalents

Cash and cash equivalents consist of cash on hand and balances with banks, and investments in money market instruments. Cash and cash equivalents included in the statement of cash flows comprise the following statement of financial position amounts.

	20X7	20X6
	$m	$m
Cash on hand and balances with banks	40	25
Short-term investments	370	95
Cash and cash equivalents	410	120

The company has undrawn borrowing facilities of $2,000 of which only $700 may be used for future expansion.

2 Preparing a statement of cash flows

You need to be aware of the **format** of the statement as laid out in IAS 7. Setting out the format is the first step. Then follow the **step-by-step preparation procedure**.

Exam focus point

In essence, preparing a statement of cash flows is very straightforward. You should therefore simply learn the format and apply the steps noted in the example below.

Note that the following items are treated in a way that might seem confusing, but the treatment is logical if you **think in terms of cash**.

(a) **Increase in inventory** is treated as **negative** (in brackets). This is because it represents a cash **outflow**; cash is being spent on inventory.

(b) An **increase in receivables** would be treated as **negative** for the same reasons; more receivables means less cash.

(c) By contrast an **increase in payables is positive** because cash is being retained and not used to settle accounts payable. There is therefore more of it.

2.1 Example: Preparation of a statement of cash flows

Colby Co's income statement for the year ended 31 December 20X2 and statements of financial position at 31 December 20X1 and 31 December 20X2 were as follows.

COLBY CO
INCOME STATEMENT FOR THE YEAR ENDED 31 DECEMBER 20X2

	$'000	$'000
Sales		720
Raw materials consumed	70	
Staff costs	94	
Depreciation	118	
Loss on disposal of non-current asset	18	
		(300)
		420
Interest payable		(28)
Profit before tax		392
Taxation		(124)
Profit for the period		268

COLBY CO
STATEMENT OF FINANCIAL POSITION AS AT 31 DECEMBER

	20X2		20X1	
	$'000	$'000	$'000	$'000
Assets				
Property, plant and equipment				
Cost	1,596		1,560	
Depreciation	318		224	
		1,278		1,336
Current assets				
Inventory	24		20	
Trade receivables	76		58	
Bank	48		56	
		148		134
Total assets		1,426		1,470
Equity and liabilities				
Capital and reserves				
Share capital	360		340	
Share premium	36		24	
Retained earnings	716		514	
		1,112		878
Non-current liabilities				
Non-current loans		200		500
Current liabilities				
Trade payables	12		6	
Taxation	102		86	
		114		92
		1,426		1,470

During the year, the company paid $90,000 for a new piece of machinery.

Dividends paid during 20X2 totalled $66,000.

Required

Prepare a statement of cash flows for Colby Co for the year ended 31 December 20X2 in accordance with the requirements of IAS 7, using the indirect method.

Solution

Step 1   **Set out the proforma statement of cash flows** with the headings required by IAS 7. You should leave plenty of space. Ideally, use three or more sheets of paper, one for the main statement, one for the notes and one for your workings. It is obviously essential to know the formats very well.

Step 2   Begin with the **reconciliation of profit before tax to net cash from operating activities** as far as possible. When preparing the statement from statements of financial position, you will usually have to calculate such items as depreciation, loss on sale of non-current assets, profit for the year and tax paid (see Step 4). Note that you may not be given the tax charge in the income statement. You will then have to assume that the tax paid in the year is last year's year-end provision and calculate the charge as the balancing figure.

Step 3   Calculate the cash flow figures for **dividends paid, purchase or sale of non-current assets, issue of shares and repayment of loans** if these are not already given to you (as they may be).

Step 4   If you are not given the profit figure, open up a **working for the trading, income and expense account**. Using the opening and closing balances, the taxation charge and dividends paid and proposed, you will be able to calculate profit for the year as the balancing figure to put in the net profit to net cash flow from operating activities section.

Step 5   You will now be able to **complete the statement** by slotting in the figures given or calculated.

COLBY CO
STATEMENT OF CASH FLOWS FOR THE YEAR ENDED 31 DECEMBER 20X2

	$'000	$'000
Net cash flow from operating activities		
Profit before tax	392	
Depreciation charges	118	
Loss on sale of property, plant and equipment	18	
Interest expense	28	
Increase in inventories	(4)	
Increase in receivables	(18)	
Increase in payables	6	
Cash generated from operations	540	
Interest paid	(28)	
Dividends paid	(66)	
Tax paid (86 + 124 – 102)	(108)	
Net cash flow from operating activities		338
Cash flows from investing activities		
Payments to acquire property, plant and equipment	(90)	
Receipts from sales property, plant and equipment	12	
Net cash outflow from investing activities		(78)
Cash flows from financing activities		
Issues of share capital (360 + 36 – 340 – 24)	32	
Long-term loans repaid (500 – 200)	(300)	
Net cash flows from financing		(268)
Decrease in cash and cash equivalents		(8)
Cash and cash equivalents at 1.1.X2		56
Cash and cash equivalents at 31.12.X2		48

Working: property, plant and equipment

COST

	$'000		$'000
At 1.1.X2	1,560	At 31.12.X2	1,596
Purchases	90	Disposals (balance)	54
	1,650		1,650

ACCUMULATED DEPRECIATION

	$'000		$'000
At 31.1.X2	318	At 1.1.X2	224
Depreciation on disposals		Charge for year	118
(balance)	24		
	342		342

NBV of disposals	30
Net loss reported	(18)
Proceeds of disposals	12

Question	Statement of cash flows

Set out below are the financial statements of Shabnum Co. You are the financial controller, faced with the task of implementing IAS 7 *Statement of cash flows*.

SHABNUM CO
INCOME STATEMENT FOR THE YEAR ENDED 31 DECEMBER 20X2

	$'000
Revenue	2,553
Cost of sales	(1,814)
Gross profit	739
Distribution costs	(125)
Administrative expenses	(264)
	350
Interest received	25
Interest paid	(75)
Profit before taxation	300
Taxation	(140)
Profit for the period	160

SHABNUM CO
STATEMENTS OF FINANCIAL POSITION AS AT 31 DECEMBER

	20X2	20X1
	$'000	$'000
Assets		
Non-current assets		
Property, plant and equipment	380	305
Intangible assets	250	200
Investments	–	25
Current assets		
Inventories	150	102
Receivables	390	315
Short-term investments	50	–
Cash in hand	2	1
Total assets	1,222	948

	20X2	20X1
	$'000	$'000
Equity and liabilities		
Equity		
Share capital ($1 ordinary shares)	200	150
Share premium account	160	150
Revaluation reserve	100	91
Retained earnings	260	180
Non-current liabilities		
Loan	170	50
Current liabilities		
Trade payables	127	119
Bank overdraft	85	98
Taxation	120	110
Total equity and liabilities	1,222	948

The following information is available.

(a) The proceeds of the sale of non-current asset investments amounted to $30,000.

(b) Fixtures and fittings, with an original cost of $85,000 and a net book value of $45,000, were sold for $32,000 during the year.

(c) The following information relates to property, plant and equipment

	31.12.20X2	31.12.20X1
	$'000	$'000
Cost	720	595
Accumulated depreciation	340	290
Net book value	380	305

(d) 50,000 $1 ordinary shares were issued during the year at a premium of 20c per share.

(e) Dividends totalling $80,000 were paid during the year.

Required

Prepare a statement of cash flows for the year to 31 December 20X2 using the format laid out in IAS 7.

Answer

SHABNUM CO
STATEMENT OF CASH FLOWS FOR THE YEAR ENDED 31 DECEMBER 20X2

	$'000	$'000
Net cash flows from operating activities		
Profit before tax	300	
Depreciation charge (W1)	90	
Interest expense	50	
Loss on sale of property, plant and equipment (45 – 32)	13	
Profit on sale of non-current asset investments	(5)	
(Increase)/decrease in inventories	(48)	
(Increase)/decrease in receivables	(75)	
Increase/(decrease) in payables	8	
Cash generated from operating activities	333	
Interest received	25	
Interest paid	(75)	
Dividends paid	(80)	
Tax paid (110 + 140 – 120)	(130)	
Net cash flow from operating activities		73

	$'000	$'000
Cash flows from investing activities		
Payments to acquire property, plant and equipment (W2)	(201)	
Payments to acquire intangible non-current assets	(50)	
Receipts from sales of property, plant and equipment	32	
Receipts from sale of non-current asset investments	30	
Net cash flows from investing activities		(189)
Cash flows from financing activities		
Issue of share capital	60	
Long-term loan	120	
Net cash flows from financing		180
Increase in cash and cash equivalents (Note)		64
Cash and cash equivalents at 1.1 X2 (Note)		(97)
Cash and cash equivalents at 31.12.X2 (Note)		(33)

NOTES TO THE STATEMENT OF CASH FLOWS

Note: Analysis of the balances of cash and cash equivalents as shown in the statement of financial position

	20X2	20X1	Change in year
	$'000	$'000	$'000
Cash in hand	2	1	1
Short term investments	50		50
Bank overdraft	(85)	(98)	13
	(33)	(97)	64

Workings

1 *Depreciation charge*

		$'000	$'000
Depreciation at 31 December 20X2			340
Depreciation 31 December 20X1		290	
Depreciation on assets sold (85 – 45)		40	
			250
Charge for the year			90

2 *Purchase of property, plant and equipment*

PROPERTY, PLANT AND EQUIPMENT

	$'000		$'000
1.1.X2 Balance b/d	595	Disposals	85
Revaluation (100 – 91)	9		
Purchases (bal fig)	201	31.12.X2 Balance c/d	720
	805		805

Exam focus point

In the December 2008 exam, there was a question requiring the calculation of the purchase of property, plant and equipment for the statement of cash flows. Only 38% answered the question correctly. Make sure you use a working to calculate the figure as shown above.

2.2 The advantages of cash flow accounting

The advantages of cash flow accounting are as follows.

(a) Survival in business depends on the **ability to generate** cash. Cash flow accounting directs attention towards this critical issue.

(b)   Cash flow is **more comprehensive** than 'profit' which is dependent on accounting conventions and concepts.

(c)   **Payables** (long and short-term) are more interested in an enterprise's ability to repay them than in its profitability. Whereas 'profits' might indicate that cash is likely to be available, cash flow accounting is more direct with its message.

(d)   Cash flow reporting provides a better means of **comparing the results** of different companies than traditional profit reporting.

(e)   Cash flow reporting **satisfies the needs of all users** better.

    (i)   For **management**, it provides the sort of information on which decisions should be taken: (in management accounting, 'relevant costs' to a decision are future cash flows); traditional profit accounting does not help with decision-making.

    (ii)   For **shareholders and auditors**, cash flow accounting can provide a satisfactory basis for stewardship accounting.

    (iii)   As described previously, the information needs of **creditors and employees** will be better served by cash flow accounting.

(f)   Cash flow forecasts are **easier to prepare**, as well as more useful, than profit forecasts.

(g)   They can in some respects be **audited more easily** than accounts based on the accruals concept.

(h)   The accruals concept is confusing, and cash flows are **more easily understood**.

(i)   Cash flow accounting should be both retrospective, and also include a forecast for the future. This is of **great information value** to all users of accounting information.

(j)   **Forecasts** can subsequently be **monitored** by the publication of variance statements which compare actual cash flows against the forecast.

Question

Can you think of some possible disadvantages of cash flow accounting?

Answer

The main disadvantages of cash accounting are essentially the advantages of accruals accounting (proper matching of related items). There is also the practical problem that few businesses keep historical cash flow information in the form needed to prepare a historical statement of cash flows and so extra record keeping is likely to be necessary.

2.3 Criticisms of IAS 7

The inclusion of **cash equivalents** has been criticised because it does not reflect the way in which businesses are managed: in particular, the requirement that to be a cash equivalent an investment has to be within three months of maturity is considered **unrealistic**.

The management of assets similar to cash (ie 'cash equivalents') is not distinguished from other investment decisions.

Exam focus point

You could be asked to consider the usefulness of a statement of cash flows as well as having to prepare one.

One of the competences you require to fulfil performance objective 11 of the PER is the ability to analyse and interpret financial data. You can apply the knowledge you obtain from this chapter to help to demonstrate this competence.

Chapter Roundup

- **Statements of cash flows** are a useful addition to the financial statements of companies because it is recognised that accounting profit is not the only indicator of a company's performance.

- Statements of cash flows concentrate on the sources and uses of cash and are a useful indicator of a company's **liquidity and solvency**.

- You need to be aware of the **format** of the statement as laid out in **IAS 7**. Setting out the format is the first step. Then follow the **step-by-step preparation procedure**.

Quick Quiz

1   What is the objective of IAS 7?
    A   To provide additional information about profit and losses
    B   To provide additional information about generation of cash
2   What are the benefits of cash flow information according to IAS 7?
3   Define cash and cash equivalents according to IAS 7.
4   Which of the following headings is not a classification of cash flows in IAS 7?
    A   Operating
    B   Investing
    C   Administration
    D   Financing
5   A company has the following information about property, plant and equipment.

	20X7	20X6
	$'000	$'000
Cost	750	600
Accumulated depreciation	250	150
Net book value	500	450

Plant with a net book value of $75,000 (original cost $90,000) was sold for $30,000 during the year.
What is the cash flow from investing activities for the year?
    A $95,000 inflow
    B $210,000 inflow
    C $210,000 outflow
    D $95,000 outflow
6   A company has the following extract from a statement of financial position.

	20X7	20X6
	$'000	$'000
Share capital	2,000	1,000
Share premium	500	–
Loan stock	750	1,000

What is the cash flow from financing activities for the year?
    A $1,250 inflow
    B $1,750 inflow
    C $1,750 outflow
    D $1,250 outflow

7   When adjusting profit before tax to arrive at cash generated from operations, a decrease in receivables is added to profit before tax. Is this statement

  A   True
  B   False

Answers to Quick Quiz

1   B   To provide information to users about the company's ability to generate cash and cash equivalents.

2   Further information is available about liquidation and solvency, of the change in net assets, the ability to adapt to changing circumstances and comparability between entities.

3   See Para 1.5, Key Terms.

4   C   Administration costs are a classification in the income statement, not the statement of cash flows.

5   C   PROPERTY, PLANT AND EQUIPMENT

	$'000		$'000
Opening balance	600	Disposals	90
Purchases (balancing figure)	240	Closing balance	750
	840		840

	$'000
Purchase of property, plant and equipment	240,000
Proceeds of sale of property, plant and equipment	(30,000)
Net cash outflow	210,000

6   A

	$'000
Issue of share capital (2,000 + 500 – 1,000)	1,500
Repayment of loan stock (1,000 – 750)	(250)
Net cash inflow	1,250

7   A   True

Now try the questions below from the Exam Question Bank

Number	Level	Marks	Time
Q48	Examination	2	2 mins
Q49	Examination.	2	2 mins
Q50	Examination	2	2 mins

Miscellaneous topics

Information technology

Topic list	Syllabus reference
1 Accounting packages	C3(d)–(e)
2 Accounting modules	C3(b)–(e)
3 Databases	C3(b)
4 Practical experience	C3(b)

Introduction

We have referred briefly to computerised accounting systems earlier in the text. These days, most accounting systems are computerised and anyone training to be an accountant should be able to work with them.

The most important point to remember is that the principles of computerised accounting are the same as those of manual accounting. You should by now have a good grasp of these principles.

The first section of this chapter talks about accounting **packages**. This is a rather general term, but most of us can probably name the accounting package that we use at work.

An accounting package consists of several accounting **modules**, eg receivables ledger, cash book. An exam question may take one of these modules and ask you to describe inputs, processing and outputs. Alternatively, you may be asked to outline the advantages of computer processing over manual processing, for example, for receivables or payroll.

Questions may ask you to discuss the advantages and disadvantages of **databases**. These are discussed in Section 3.

Study guide

		Intellectual level
C3	**Accounting systems and the impact of information technology on financial reporting**	
(b)	Understand the basic function and form of accounting records in a typical computerised system	1
(c)	Compare manual and computerised accounts systems	1
(d)	Identify advantages and disadvantages of computerised accounts systems	1
(e)	Understand the uses of integrated accounting system packages	1

Exam guide

You should be prepared for questions comparing computer systems with manual systems. Do not neglect this chapter. You need to study the **full range** of the syllabus.

1 Accounting packages

FAST FORWARD

Computer software used in accounting may be divided into two types.

- Dedicated accounting packages.
- General software, such as spreadsheets, which can be used for accounting.

The syllabus for this paper requires you to know about the use of computers in financial accounting practice.

Exam focus point

Questions will *not* be set on the technical aspects of how computers work. A typical question might be to give advantages and disadvantages of computerised accounting systems over manual systems.

We shall assume, therefore, that you know that a modern computer generally consists of a keyboard, a television-like screen, a box-like disk drive which contains all the necessary electronic components for data processing, and a printer. This is the computer hardware.

The computer hardware described above is also known as a personal computer (PC), but the technical name is a **micro-computer.**

Key term

Computer programs are the instructions that tell the electronics how to process data. The general term used for these is software.

Software is what we are concerned with in this text, and in particular 'applications software', that is packages of computer programs that carry out specific tasks.

(a) Some applications are devoted specifically to an accounting task, for example a payroll package, a non-current asset register or an inventory control package.

(b) Other applications have many uses in business, including their use for accounting purposes. Packages of this sort that we shall describe are databases.

1.1 Accounting packages

FAST FORWARD

One of the most important facts to remember about computerised accounting is that **in principle, it is exactly the same as manual accounting.** However, it has certain advantages.

Accounting functions retain the same names in computerised systems as in more traditional written records. Computerised accounting still uses the familiar ideas of day books, ledger accounts, double entry, trial balance and financial statements. The principles of working with computerised sales, purchase and nominal ledgers are exactly what would be expected in the manual methods they replace.

The only difference is that these various books of account have become invisible. Ledgers are now computer files which are held in a computer-sensible form, ready to be called upon.

1.1.1 Advantages

However, the advantages of accounting packages compared with a manual system are as follows.

(a)   The packages can be used by **non-specialists**.

(b)   A large amount of **data can be processed very quickly**.

(c)   Computerised systems are **more accurate** than manual systems.

(d)   A computer is capable of handling and processing **large volumes** of data.

(e)   Once the data has been input, computerised systems can **analyse data** rapidly to present useful control information for managers such as a trial balance or a trade accounts receivable schedule.

1.1.2 Disadvantages

The advantages of computerised accounting system far outweigh the disadvantages, particularly for large businesses. However, the following may be identified as possible disadvantages.

(a)   The initial **time and costs** involved in installing the system, training personnel and so on.

(b)   The need for **security checks** to make sure that unauthorised personnel do not gain access to data files.

(c)   The necessity to develop a **system of coding** (see below) and checking.

(d)   **Lack of 'audit trail'**. It is not always easy to see where a mistake has been made.

(e)   Possible **resistance** on the part of staff to the introduction of the system.

1.2 Coding

Computers are used more efficiently if vital information is expressed in the form of codes. For example, nominal ledger accounts will be coded individually, perhaps by means of a two-digit code: eg

00	Ordinary share capital
01	Share premium
05	Income and expenses account
15	Purchases
22	Receivables ledger control account
41	Payables ledger control account
42	Interest
43	Dividends etc

In the same way, individual accounts must be given a unique code number in the receivables ledger and payables ledger.

1.3 Example: Coding

When an invoice is received from a supplier (code 1234) for $3,000 for the purchase of raw materials, the transaction might be coded for input to the computer as:

| | Nominal ledger | | | Inventory | |
Supplier Code	Debit	Credit	Value	Code	Quantity
1234	15	41	$3,000	56742	150

Code 15 might represent purchases and code 41 the payables control account. This single input could be used to update the purchase ledger, the nominal ledger, and the inventory ledger. The inventory code may enable further analysis to be carried out, perhaps allocating the cost to a particular department or product. Thus the needs of both financial accounting and cost accounting can be fulfilled at once.

> If you are not already using one, get some experience between now and the exam, of using an accounting package.

One of the competences you require to fulfil performance objective 6 of the PER is the ability to use standard software packages including work processing and spreadsheet applications. You can apply the knowledge you obtain from this section of the text to help to demonstrate this competence.

1.4 Modules

Key term

> A **module** is a program which deals with one particular part of a business accounting system.

An accounting package will consist of several modules. A simple accounting package might consist of only one module (in which case it is called a stand-alone module), but more often it will consist of several modules. The name given to a set of several modules is a **suite**. An accounting package, therefore, might have separate modules for some or all of the following.

(a) Invoicing
(b) Inventory
(c) Receivables ledger
(d) Payables ledger
(e) Nominal ledger
(f) Payroll
(g) Cash book
(h) Job costing
(i) Non-current asset register
(j) Report generator

1.5 Integrated software

Each module may be integrated with the others, so that data entered in one module will be passed automatically or by simple operator request through into any other module where the data is of some relevance. For example, if there is an input into the invoicing module authorising the despatch of an invoice to a customer, there might be **automatic links**:

(a) To the sales ledger, to update the file by posting the invoice to the customer's account.

(b) To the inventory module, to update the inventory file by:

   (i) reducing the quantity and value of inventory in hand
   (ii) recording the inventory movement

(c) To the nominal ledger, to update the file by posting the sale to the sales account.

(d) To the job costing module, to record the sales value of the job on the job cost file.

(e) To the report generator, to update the sales analysis and sales totals which are on file and awaiting inclusion in management reports.

A diagram of an **integrated accounting system** is given below.

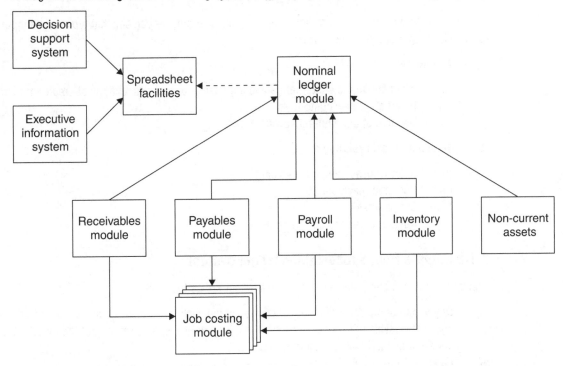

1.5.1 Advantages

(a)   It becomes possible to make just one entry in one of the ledgers which automatically updates the others.

(b)   Users can specify reports, and the software will automatically extract the required data from *all* the relevant files.

(c)   Both of the above simplify the workload of the user, and the irritating need to constantly load and unload disks is eliminated.

1.5.2 Disadvantages

(a)   Usually, it requires more computer memory than separate (stand-alone) systems – which means there is less space in which to store actual data.

(b)   Because one program is expected to do everything, the user may find that an integrated package has fewer facilities than a set of specialised modules. In effect, an integrated package could be 'Jack of all trades but master of none'.

2 Accounting modules

FAST FORWARD

An accountancy package consists of a number of **modules** which perform all the tasks needed to maintain a normal accounting function like payables ledger or payroll. In modern systems the modules are usually integrated with each other.

In this section we shall look at some of the accounting modules in more detail, starting with the receivables ledger.

2.1 Accounting for trade accounts receivable

A computerised receivables ledger will be expected to keep the receivables ledger up-to-date, and also it should be able to produce certain output (eg statements, sales analysis reports, responses to file interrogations etc). The output might be produced daily (eg day book listings), monthly (eg statements), quarterly (eg sales analysis reports) or periodically (eg responses to file interrogations, or customer name and address lists printed on adhesive labels for despatching circulars or price lists).

2.1.1 Inputs to a receivables ledger system

Bearing in mind what we expect to find in a receivables ledger, we can say that typical data input into receivables ledger system is as follows.

(a) **Amendments**

    (i)   Amendments to customer details, eg change of address, change of credit limit

    (ii)   Insertion of new customers

    (iii)   Deletion of old 'non-active' customers

(b) **Transaction data relating to:**

    (i)   Sales transactions, for invoicing

    (ii)   Customer payments

    (iii)   Credit notes

    (iv)   Adjustments (debit or credit items)

2.1.2 Outputs from a receivables ledger system

Typical outputs in a computerised receivables ledger are as follows.

(a) **Day book listing**. A list of all transactions posted each day. This provides an audit trail – ie it is information which the auditors of the business can use when carrying out their work. Batch and control totals will be included in the listing.

(b) **Invoices** (if the package is one which is expected to produce invoices.)

(c) **Statements**. End of month statements for customers.

(d) **Aged accounts receivable list**. Probably produced monthly.

(e) **Sales analysis reports**. These will analyse sales according to the sales analysis codes on the receivables ledger file.

(f) **Reminder letters**. Letters can be produced automatically to chase late payers when the due date for payment goes by without payment having been received.

(g) **Customer lists** (or perhaps a selective list). The list might be printed on to adhesive labels, for sending out customer letters or marketing material.

(h) **Responses to enquiries**, perhaps output on to a VDU screen rather than as printed copy, for fast response to customer enquiries.

(i) **Output onto disk file for other modules** – eg to the inventory control module and the nominal ledger module, if these are also used by the organisation, and the package is not an integrated one.

2.1.3 The advantages of a computerised trade accounts receivable system

The advantages of such a system, in addition to the advantages of computerised accounting generally, are its ability to assist in sales administration and marketing by means of outputs such as those listed above.

2.2 Payables ledger

A computerised payables ledger will certainly be expected to keep the payables ledger up-to-date, and also it should be able to output various reports requested by the user. In fact, a computerised payables ledger is much the same as a computerised receivables ledger, except that it is a sort of mirror image as it deals with purchases rather than sales.

Question	Payables ledger

What sort of data would you expect to be held on a payables ledger file?

The payables ledger will consist of individual records for each supplier account. Just as for customer accounts, some of the data held on record will be *standing* data, and some will be *variable* data.

Standing data will include:		Variable data will include:	
(a)	Account number	(a)	Transaction date
(b)	Name	(b)	Transaction description
(c)	Address	(c)	Transaction code
(d)	Credit details	(d)	Debits
(e)	Bank details (eg method of payment)	(e)	Credits
(f)	Cash discount details, if appropriate	(f)	Balance

2.2.1 Inputs to a payables ledger system

Bearing in mind what we expect to see held on a payables ledger, typical data input into a payables ledger system is:

(a)   Details of purchases recorded on invoices
(b)   Details of returns to suppliers for which credit notes are received
(c)   Details of payments to suppliers
(d)   Adjustments

2.2.2 Processing in a payables ledger system

The primary action involved in updating the payables ledger is adjusting the amounts outstanding on the supplier accounts. These amounts will represent money owed to the suppliers. This processing is identical to updating the accounts in the receivables ledger, except that the receivables ledger balances are debits (receivables) and the payables ledger balances are credits (payables). Again, the open item approach is the best.

2.2.3 Outputs from a payables ledger system

Typical outputs in a computerised payables ledger are as follows.

(a)   **Lists of transactions posted** – produced every time the system is run.

(b)   An **analysis of expenditure** for nominal ledger purposes. This may be produced every time the system is run or at the end of each month.

(c)   **List of payable balances** together with a reconciliation between the total balance brought forward, the transactions for the month and the total balance carried forward.

(d)   **Copies of suppliers' accounts**. This may show merely the balance b/f, current transactions and the balance c/f. If complete details of all unsettled items are given, the ledger is known as an **open-ended ledger**. (This is similar to the open item or balance forward methods with a receivables ledger system.)

(e)   Any payables ledger system can be used to produce details of payments to be made.

   (i)   Remittance advices (usually a copy of the ledger account)
   (ii)   Cheques
   (iii)   Credit transfer listings

(f)   Other special reports may be produced for:

   (i)   Costing purposes
   (ii)   Updating records about non-current assets
   (iii)   Comparisons with budget
   (iv)   Aged accounts payable list

2.3 Nominal ledger

The nominal ledger (or general ledger) is an accounting record which summarises the financial affairs of a business. It is the nucleus of an accounting system. It contains details of assets, liabilities and capital, income and expenditure and so profit or loss. It consists of a large number of different accounts, each account having its own purpose or 'name' and an identity or code.

A nominal ledger will consist of a large number of coded accounts. For example, part of a nominal ledger might be as follows.

Account code	Account name
100200	Plant and machinery (cost)
100300	Motor vehicles (cost)
100201	Plant and machinery depreciation
100301	Vehicles depreciation
300000	Total receivables
400000	Total payables
500130	Wages and salaries
500140	Rent and local taxes
500150	Advertising expenses
500160	Bank charges
500170	Motor expenses
500180	Telephone expenses
600000	Sales
700000	Cash

A business will, of course, choose its own codes for its nominal ledger accounts. The codes given in this table are just for illustration.

It is important to remember that a **computerised nominal ledger works in exactly the same way as a manual nominal ledger**, although there are some differences in terminology. For instance, in a manual system, the sales and receivables accounts were posted from the sales day book (not the sales ledger). But in a computerised system, the sales day book is automatically produced as part of the 'receivables ledger module'. So it may **sound** as if you are posting directly from the receivables ledger, but in fact the day book is part of a computerised receivables ledger.

2.3.1 Inputs to the nominal ledger

Inputs depend on whether the accounting system is integrated or not.

(a)   If the system is integrated, then as soon as data is put into the sales ledger module (or anywhere else for that matter), the relevant nominal ledger accounts are updated. There is nothing more for the system user to do.

(b)   If the system is not integrated then the output from the sales ledger module (and anywhere else) has to be input into the nominal ledger. This is done by using journal entries. For instance.

DEBIT	A/c 300000	$3,000	
CREDIT	A/c 600000		$3,000

Where 600000 is the nominal ledger code for sales, and 300000 is the code for receivables.

Regardless of whether the system is integrated or not, the actual data needed by the nominal ledger package to be able to update the ledger accounts includes:

(a) Date
(b) Description
(c) Amount
(d) Account codes (sometimes called distinction codes)

2.3.2 Outputs from the nominal ledger

The main outputs apart from listings of individual nominal ledger accounts are:

(a) trial balance;
(b) financial statements.

3 Databases

FAST FORWARD

A database is a file of data structured in such a way that it can serve a number of applications without its structure being dictated by any particular function.

A database may be described as a 'pool' of data, which can be used by any number of applications. Its use is not restricted to the accounts department. A stricter definition is provided in the *Computing Terminology* of the Chartered Institute of Management Accountants (CIMA).

Key term

'Frequently a much abused term. In its strict sense a **database** is a file of data structured in such a way that it may serve a number of applications without its structure being dictated by any one of those applications, the concept being that programs are written around the database rather than files being structured to meet the needs of specific programs. The term is also rather loosely applied to simple file management software.'

3.1 Objectives of a database

The main virtues of a database are as follow.

(a) There is **common data** for all users to share.
(b) The extra effort of keeping **duplicate files** in different departments is avoided.
(c) Conflicts between departments who use **inconsistent data are avoided**.

A database should have four major objectives.

(a) It should be **shared**. Different users should be able to access the *same data* in the database for their own processing applications (and at the *same time* in some systems) thus removing the need for duplicating data on different files.
(b) The **integrity** of the database must be preserved. This means that one user should not be allowed to alter the data on file so as to spoil the database records for other users. However, users must be able to update the data on file, and so make valid alterations to the data.
(c) The database system should provide for the needs of different users, who each have their own processing requirements and data access methods. In other words, the database should provide for the **operational requirements of all its users**.
(d) The database should be capable of **evolving**, both in the short term (it must be kept updated) and in the longer term (it must be able to meet the future data processing needs of users, not just their current needs).

3.2 Example: Non-current assets and databases

An organisation, especially a large one, may possess a large quantity of non-current assets. Before computerisation these would have been kept in a manual non-current asset register. A database enables this non-current asset register to be stored in an electronic form. A database file for non-current assets might contain most or all of the following categories of information.

(a)   Code number to give the asset a unique identification in the database
(b)   Type of asset (motor car, leasehold premises), for published accounts purposes
(c)   More detailed description of the asset (serial number, car registration number, make)
(d)   Physical location of the asset (address)
(e)   Organisational location of the asset (accounts department)
(f)   Person responsible for the asset (in the case of a company-owned car, the person who uses it)
(g)   Original cost of the asset
(h)   Date of purchase
(i)   Depreciation rate and method applied to the asset
(j)   Accumulated depreciation to date
(k)   Net book value of the asset
(l)   Estimated residual value
(m)   Date when the physical existence of the asset was last verified
(n)   Supplier

Obviously, the details kept about the asset would depend on the type of asset it is.

Any kind of computerised non-current asset record will improve efficiency in accounting for non-current assets because of the ease and speed with which any necessary calculations can be made. Most obvious is the calculation of the depreciation provision which can be an extremely onerous task if it is done monthly and there are frequent acquisitions and disposals and many different depreciation rates in use.

The particular advantage of using a database for the non-current asset function is its flexibility in generating reports for different purposes. Aside from basic cost and net book value information, a database with fields such as those listed above in the record of each asset could compile reports analysing assets according to location, or by manufacturer. This information could be used to help compare the performance of different divisions, perhaps, or to assess the useful life of assets supplied by different manufacturers. There may be as many more possibilities as there are permutations of the individual pieces of data.

4 Practical experience

Reading about computer systems and packages is no substitute for using them, and you should make every effort to gain experience in using an accounting package.

Chapter Roundup

- Computer software used in accounting may be divided into two types.

    - Dedicated accounting packages.
    - General software, such as spreadsheets, which can be used for accounting.

- One of the most important facts to remember about computerised accounting is that **in principle, it is exactly the same as manual accounting.** However, it has certain advantages.

- An accountancy package consists of a number of **modules** which perform all the tasks needed to maintain a normal accounting function like payables ledger or payroll. In modern systems the modules are usually integrated with each other.

- A database is a file of data structured in such a way that it can serve a number of applications without its structure being dictated by any particular function.

Quick Quiz

1   What is one of the advantages of computerised accounting?

    A   Use by non-specialists

    B   Need for security checks

2   What are the disadvantages?

3   What is an accounting suite?

    A   Where accounting information is produced

    B   A set of several different modules

4   What sort of data is input into a receivables ledger system?

    A   Amendments

    B   Transaction data

    C   Adjustments to terms

    D   All of the above

5   What is the open item method of processing?

6   What should be the four major objectives of a database?

7   What are the advantages of using a database to maintain non-current asset records?

    A   Amount of detail

    B   Ease of calculation

    C   Both of the above

Answers to Quick Quiz

1   A

2   See Paragraph 1.1.2.

3   B   A set of several different modules.

4   D

5   Payments are credited to specific invoices, so that late payment of invoices can be identified.

6   See Paragraph 3.1.

7   C   The amount of detail that can be kept about each individual asset and the ease in analysing this information into different reports and calculations (eg depreciation, profit on sale).

Now try the question below from the Exam Question Bank

Number	Level	Marks	Time
Q51	Examination	1	1 min

Exam question and answer bank

1   Which of the following are differences between sole traders and limited liability companies?

(1)   A sole traders' financial statements are private; a company's financial statements are sent to shareholders and may be publicly filed

(2)   Only companies have capital invested into the business

(3)   A sole trader is fully and personally liable for any losses that the business might make; a company's shareholders are not personally liable for any losses that the company might make.

A   1 and 2 only
B   2 and 3 only
C   1 and 3 only
D   1, 2 and 3

(2 marks)

2   What is the role of the International Financial Reporting Interpretations Committee?

A   To create a set of global accounting standards
B   To issue guidance on the application of International Financial Reporting Standards

(1 mark)

3   In times of rising prices, what effect does the use of the historical cost concept have on a company's asset values and profit?

A   Asset values and profit both understated
B   Asset values and profit both overstated
C   Asset values understated and profit overstated
D   Asset values overstated and profit understated.

(2 marks)

4   The IASB's *Framework for the preparation and presentation of financial statements* gives qualitative characteristics that make financial information reliable.

Which of the following are examples of those qualitative characteristics?

A   Faithful Representation, neutrality and prudence
B   Neutrality, comparability and true and fair view
C   Prudence, comparability and accruals
D   Neutrality, accruals and going concern

(2 marks)

5   A company has made a material change to an accounting policy in preparing its current financial statements.

Which of the following disclosures are required by IAS 8 *Accounting policies, changes in accounting estimates and errors* in the financial statements?

1   The reasons for the change.
2   The amount of the adjustment in the current period and in comparative information for prior periods.
3   An estimate of the effect of the change on the next five accounting periods.

A   1 and 2 only
B   1 and 3 only
C   2 and 3 only
D   1, 2 and 3

(2 marks)

6   Which of the following statements are correct?

        (1)   Materiality means that only items having a physical existence may be recognised as assets.
        (2)   The substance over form convention means that the legal form of a transaction must always
                be shown in financial statements even if this differs from the commercial effect.
        (3)   The money measurement concept is that only items capable of being measured in monetary
                terms can be recognised in financial statements.

        A   2 only
        B   1, 2 and 3
        C   1 only
        D   3 only

                                                                                                (2 marks)

7   Which of the following explains the imprest system of operating petty cash?

        A   Weekly expenditure cannot exceed a set amount.
        B   The exact amount of expenditure is reimbursed at intervals to maintain a fixed float.
        C   All expenditure out of the petty cash must be properly authorised.
        D   Regular equal amounts of cash are transferred into petty cash at intervals.

                                                                                                (2 marks)

8   Which of the following documents should accompany a payment made to a supplier?

        A   Supplier statement
        B   Remittance advice
        C   Purchase invoice

                                                                                                 (1 mark)

9   The business entity concept requires that a business is treated as being separate from its owners

        Is this statement true or false?

        A   True
        B   False

                                                                                                 (1 mark)

10   A company's motor vehicles at cost account at 30 June 20X6 is as follows:

                                        MOTOR VEHICLES – COST

                                        $ $
        Balance b/f   35,800   Disposal   12,000
        Additions   12,950   Balance c/f   36,750
                                        48,750   48,750

        What opening balance should be included in the following period's trial balance for motor vehicles
        – cost at 1 July 20X6?

        A $36,750 DR
        B $48,750 DR
        C $36,750 CR
        D $48,750 CR

                                                                                                (2 marks)

11   Sales tax should be included in the income statement of a registered trader.

        Is this statement true or false?

        A   True
        B   False

                                                                                                 (1 mark)

12   According to IAS 2 *Inventories*, which of the following costs should be included in valuing the
      inventories of a manufacturing company?

      (1)   Carriage inwards
      (2)   Carriage outwards
      (3)   Depreciation of factory plant
      (4)   General administrative overheads

      A   All four items
      B   1, 2 and 4 only
      C   2 and 3 only
      D   1 and 3 only

                                                                                            (2 marks)

13   A company values its inventory using the first in, first out (FIFO) method. At 1 May 20X5 the
      company had 700 engines in inventory, valued at $190 each.

      During the year ended 30 April 20X6 the following transactions took place:

      20X5
      1 July   Purchased   500 engines   At $220 each
      1 November   Sold   400 engines   For $160,000

      20X6
      1 February   Purchased   300 engines   At $230 each
      15 April   Sold   250 engines   For $125,000

      What is the value of the company's closing inventory of engines at 30 April 20X6?

      A $188,500
      B $195,500
      C $166,000
      D $106,000

                                                                                            (2 marks)

14   At 31 December 20X4 Q, a limited liability company, owned a building that cost $800,000 on 1
      January 20W5. It was being depreciated at two per cent per year.

      On 1 January 20X5 a revaluation to $1,000,000 was recognised. At this date the building had a
      remaining useful life of 40 years.

      What is the depreciation charge for the year ended 31 December 20X5 and the revaluation reserve
      balance as at 1 January 20X5?

	Depreciation charge for year ended 31 December 20X5	Revaluation reserve as at 1 January 20X5
	$	$
A	25,000	200,000
B	25,000	360,000
C	20,000	200,000
D	20,000	360,000

                                                                                            (2 marks)

15   The plant and machinery account (at cost) of a business for the year ended 31 December 20X5 was
      as follows:

PLANT AND MACHINERY – COST

20X5	$	20X5	$
1 Jan Balance	240,000	31 March Transfer disposal account	60,000
30 June cash – purchase of plant	160,000	31 Dec Balance	340,000
	400,000		400,000

The company's policy is to charge depreciation at 20% per year on the straight line basis, with proportionate depreciation in the years of purchase and disposal.

What should be the depreciation charge for the year ended 31 December 20X5?

A $68,000
B $64,000
C $61,000
D $55,000

(2 marks)

16   Gareth, a sales tax registered trader purchased a computer for use in his business. The invoice for the computer showed the following costs related to the purchase:

	$
Computer	890
Additional memory	95
Delivery	10
Installation	20
Maintenance (1 year)	25
	1,040
Sales tax (17.5%)	182
	1,222

How much should Gareth capitalise as a non-current asset in relation to the purchase?

A $1,222
B $1,040
C $890
D $1,015

(2 marks)

17   What is the correct double entry to record the depreciation charge for a period?

A   DR   Depreciation expense
         CR   Accumulated depreciation

B   DR   Accumulated depreciation
         CR   Depreciation expense

(1 mark)

18   Which of the following statements are correct?

(1)   Capitalised development expenditure must be amortised over a period not exceeding five years.

(2)   Capitalised development costs are shown in the statement of financial position under the heading of Non-current Assets

(3)   If certain criteria are met, research expenditure must be recognised as an intangible asset.

A   2 only
B   2 and 3
C   1 only
D   1 and 3

(2 marks)

19 Theta prepares its financial statements for the year to 30 April each year. The company pays rent for its premises quarterly in advance on 1 January, 1 April, 1 July and 1 October each year. The annual rent was $84,000 per year until 30 June 20X5. It was increased from that date to $96,000 per year.

What rent expense and end of year prepayment should be included in the financial statements for the year ended 30 April 20X6?

	Expense	Prepayment
A	$93,000	$8,000
B	$93,000	$16,000
C	$94,000	$8,000
D	$94,000	$16,000

(2 marks)

20 A company receives rent from a large number of properties. The total received in the year ended 30 April 20X6 was $481,200.

The following were the amounts of rent in advance and in arrears at 30 April 20X5 and 20X6:

	30 April 20X5	30 April 20X6
	$	$
Rent received in advance	28,700	31,200
Rent in arrears (all subsequently received)	21,200	18,400

What amount of rental income should appear in the company's income statement for the year ended 30 April 20X6?

A $486,500
B $460,900
C $501,500
D $475,900

(2 marks)

21 At 30 June 20X5 a company's allowance for receivables was $39,000. At 30 June 20X6 trade receivables totalled $517,000. It was decided to write off debts totalling $37,000 and to adjust the allowance for receivables to the equivalent of 5 per cent of the trade receivables based on past events.

What figure should appear in the income statement for the year ended 30 June 20X6 for these items?

A $61,000
B $22,000
C $24,000
D $23,850

(2 marks)

22 How should a contingent liability be included in a company's financial statements if the likelihood of a transfer of economic benefits to settle it is remote?

A Disclosed by note with no provision being made
B No disclosure or provision is required

(1 mark)

23   The following control account has been prepared by a trainee accountant:

RECEIVABLES LEDGER CONTROL ACCOUNT

	$		$
Opening balance	308,600	Cash received from credit customers	147,200
Credit sales	154,200	Discount allowed to credit customers	1,400
Cash sales	88,100	Interest charged on overdue accounts	2,400
Contras against credit balance in payable ledger	4,600	Irrecoverable debts written off	4,900
		Allowance for receivable	2,800
		Closing balance	396,800
	555,500		555,500

What should the closing balance be when all the errors made in preparing the receivables ledger control account have been corrected?

A $395,200
B $304,300
C $309,500
D $307,100

(2 marks)

24   Alpha received a statement of account from a supplier Beta, showing a balance to be paid of $8,950. Alpha's payables ledger account for Beta shows a balance due to Beta of $4,140.

Investigation reveals the following:

(1)   Cash paid to Beta $4,080 has not been allowed for by Beta
(2)   Alpha's ledger account has not been adjusted for $40 of cash discount disallowed by Beta.

What discrepancy remains between Alpha's and Beta's records after allowing for these items?

A $690
B $770
C $9,850
D $9,930

(2 marks)

25   Mountain sells goods on credit to Hill. Hill receives a 10% trade discount from Mountain and a further 5% settlement discount if goods are paid for within 14 days. Hill bought goods with a list price of $200,000 from Mountain. Sales tax is at 17.5%.

What amount should be included in Mountain's receivables ledger for this transaction?

A $235,000
B $211,500
C $200,925
D $209,925

(2 marks)

26   The total of the list of balances in Valley's payables ledger was $438,900 at 30 June 20X6. This balance did not agree with Valley's payables ledger control account balance. The following errors were discovered:

(1)   A contra entry of $980 was recorded in the payables ledger control account, but not in the payables ledger.
(2)   The total of the purchase returns daybook was undercast by $1,000.
(3)   An invoice for $4,344 was posted to the supplier's account as $4,434.

What amount should Valley report in its statement of financial position as accounts payable at 30 June 20X6?

A $436,830
B $438,010
C $439,790
D $437,830

(2 marks)

27   The following bank reconciliation statement has been prepared by a trainee accountant:

	$
Overdraft per bank statement	3,860
less: Outstanding cheques	9,160
	5,300
add: Deposits credited after date	16,690
Cash at bank as calculated above	21,990

What should be the correct balance per the cash book?

A $21,990 balance at bank as stated
B $3,670 balance at bank
C $11,390 balance at bank
D $3,670 overdrawn.

(2 marks)

28   In preparing a company's bank reconciliation statement at March 20X6, the following items are causing the difference between the cash book balance and the bank statement balance:

(1)   Bank charges $380
(2)   Error by bank $1,000 (cheque incorrectly debited to the account)
(3)   Lodgements not credited $4,580
(4)   Outstanding cheques $1,475
(5)   Direct debit $350
(6)   Cheque paid in by the company and dishonoured $400.

Which of these items will require an entry in the cash book?

A   2, 4 and 6
B   1, 5 and 6
C   3, 4 and 5
D   1, 2 and 3

(2 marks)

29   The debit side of a company's trial balance totals $800 more than the credit side.

Which one of the following errors would fully account for the difference?

A $400 paid for plant maintenance has been correctly entered in the cash book and credited to the plant asset account.
B   Discount received $400 has been debited to discount allowed account
C   A receipt of $800 for commission receivable has been omitted from the records
D   The petty cash balance of $800 has been omitted from the trial balance.

(2 marks)

30   A company's income statement for the year ended 31 December 20X5 showed a net profit of $83,600. It was later found that $18,000 paid for the purchase of a motor van had been debited to the motor expenses account. It is the company's policy to depreciate motor vans at 25 per cent per year on the straight line basis, with a full year's charge in the year of acquisition.

What would the net profit be after adjusting for this error?

A $106,100
B $70,100
C $97,100
D $101,600

(2 marks)

31   Q's trial balance failed to agree and a suspense account was opened for the difference. Q does not keep receivables and payables control accounts. The following errors were found in Q's accounting records:

(1)   In recording an issue of shares at par, cash received of $333,000 was credited to the ordinary share capital account as $330,000

(2)   Cash $2,800 paid for plant repairs was correctly accounted for in the cash book but was credited to the plant asset register

(3)   The petty cash book balance $500 had been omitted from the trial balance

(4)   A cheque for $78,400 paid for the purchase of a motor car was debited to the motor vehicles account as $87,400.

Which of the errors will require an entry to the suspense account to correct them?

A   1, 2 and 4 only
B   1, 2, 3 and 4
C   1 and 4 only
D   2 and 3 only

(2 marks)

32   The bookkeeper of Field made the following mistakes: Discounts allowed $3,840 was credited to the discounts received account Discounts received $2,960 was debited to the discounts allowed account

Which journal entry will correct the errors?

		DR	CR
A	Discounts allowed	$7,680	
	Discounts received		$5,920
	Suspense account		$1,760
B	Discounts allowed	$880	
	Discounts received	$880	
	Suspense account		$1,760
C	Discounts allowed	$6,800	
	Discounts received		$6,800
D	Discounts allowed	$3,840	
	Discounts received		$2,960
	Suspense account		$880

(2 marks)

33   A sole trader took some goods costing $800 from inventory for his own use. The normal selling price of the goods is $1,600.

Which of the following journal entries would correctly record this?

		Dr $	Cr $
A	Drawings account	800	
	Inventory account		800
B	Drawings account	800	
	Purchases account		800
C	Sales account	1,600	
	Drawings account		1,600

(1 mark)

34   Which of the following calculates a trader's net profit for a period?

A   Closing net assets + drawings – capital introduced – opening net assets
B   Closing net assets – drawings + capital introduced – opening net assets
C   Closing net assets – drawings – capital introduced – opening net assets
D   Closing net assets + drawings + capital introduced – opening net assets.

(2 marks)

35   A fire on 30 September destroyed some of a company's inventory and its inventory records. The following information is available:

	$
Inventory 1 September	318,000
Sales for September	612,000
Purchases for September	412,000
Inventory in good condition at 30 September	214,000

Standard gross profit percentage on sales is 25%

Based on this information, what is the value of the inventory lost?

A $96,000
B $271,000
C $26,400
D $57,000

(2 marks)

36   The inventory value for the financial statements of Q for the year ended 31 May 20X6 was based on an inventory count on 4 June 20X6, which gave a total inventory value of $836,200.

Between 31 May and 4 June 20X6, the following transactions took place:

	$
Purchases of goods	8,600
Sales of goods (profit margin 30% on sales)	14,000
Goods returned by Q to supplier	700

What adjusted figure should be included in the financial statements for inventories at 31 May 20X6?

A $838,100
B $853,900
C $818,500
D $834,300

(2 marks)

37 Annie is a sole trader who does not keep full accounting records. The following details relate to her transactions with credit customers and suppliers for the year ended 30 June 20X6:

	$
Trade receivables, 1 July 20X5	130,000
Trade payables, 1 July 20X5	60,000
Cash received from customers	686,400
Cash paid to suppliers	302,800
Discounts allowed	1,400
Discounts received	2,960
Contra between payables and receivables ledgers	2,000
Trade receivables, 30 June 20X6	181,000
Trade payables, 30 June 20X6	84,000

What figure should appear in Annie's income statement for the year ended 30 June 20X6 for purchases?

A $331,760
B $740,800
C $283,760
D $330,200

(2 marks)

38 P and Q are in partnership, sharing profits equally.

On 30 June 20X5, R joined the partnership and it was agreed that from that date all three partners should share equally in the profit.

In the year ended 31 December 20X5 the profit amounted to $300,000, accruing evenly over the year, after charging a bad debt of $30,000 which it was agreed should be borne equally by P and Q only.

What should P's total profit share be for the year ended 31 December 20X5?

A $ 95,000
B $122,500
C $125,000
D $110,000

(2 marks)

39 Goodwill should never be shown on the statement of financial position of a partnership.

Is this statement true or false?

A   True
B   False

(1 mark)

40 A and B are in partnership sharing profits and losses in the ratio 3:2 respectively. Profit for the year was $86,500. The partners' capital and current account balances at the beginning of the year were as follows:

	A	B
	$	$
Current accounts	5,750CR	1,200CR
Capital accounts	10,000CR	8,000CR

A's drawings during the year were $4,300, and B's were $2,430.

What should A's current account balance be at the end of the year?

A   57,650
B   51,900
C   61,950
D   53,350

(2 marks)

41 Should dividends paid appear on the face of a company's income statement?

A Yes
B No

(1 mark)

42 Which of the following journal entries are correct, according to their narratives?

	Dr $	Cr $
1 Suspense account	18,000	
Rent received account		18,000

Correction of error in posting $24,000 cash received for rent to the rent received amount as $42,000

2 Share premium account	400,000	
Share capital account		400,000

1 for 3 bonus issue on share capital of 1,200,000 50c shares

3 Trade investment in X	750,000	
Share capital account		250,000
Share premium account		500,000

500,000 50c shares issued at $1.50 per share in exchange for shares in X

A 1 and 2
B 2 and 3
C 1 only
D 3 only

(2 marks)

43 Which of the following should appear in a company's statement of changes in equity?

1 Profit for the financial year
2 Amortisation of capitalised development costs
3 Surplus on revaluation of non-current assets

A All three items
B 2 and 3 only
C 1 only
D 1 and 2 only

(2 marks)

44 At 31 December 20X4 a company's capital structure was as follows:

	$
Ordinary share capital(500,000 shares of 25c each)	125,000
Share premium account	100,000

In the year ended 31 December 20X5 the company made a rights issue of 1 share for every 2 held at $1 per share and this was taken up in full. Later in the year the company made a bonus issue of 1 share for every 5 held, using the share premium account for the purpose.

What was the company's capital structure at 31 December 20X5?

	Ordinary share capital $	Share premium account $
A	450,000	25,000
B	225,000	250,000
C	225,000	325,000
D	212,500	262,500

(2 marks)

45   At 31 December 20X5 the following require inclusion in a company's financial statements:

(1)   On 1 January 20X5 the company made a loan of $12,000 to an employee, repayable on 1 January 20X6, charging interest at 2 per cent per year. On the due date she repaid the loan and paid the whole of the interest due on the loan to that date.

(2)   The company has paid insurance $9,000 in 20X5, covering the year ending 31 August 20X6.

(3)   In January 20X6 the company received rent from a tenant $4,000 covering the six months to 31 December 20X5.

For these items, what total figures should be included in the company's statement of financial position at 31 December 20X5?

	Current assets	Current liabilities
	$	$
A	10,000	12,240
B	22,240	Nil
C	10,240	Nil
D	16,240	6,000

(2 marks)

46   Should details of material adjusting or material non-adjusting events after the reporting period be disclosed in the notes to financial statements according to IAS 10 *Events After the Reporting Period*?

A   Adjusting events
B   Non-Adjusting events

(1 mark)

47   Which of the following material events after the reporting period and before the financial statements are approved are adjusting events?

(1)   A valuation of property providing evidence of impairment in value at the reporting date.
(2)   Sale of inventory held at the reporting date for less than cost.
(3)   Discovery of fraud or error affecting the financial statements.
(4)   The insolvency of a customer with a debt owing at the reporting date which is still outstanding.

A   1, 2, 3 and 4
B   1, 2 and 4 only
C   3 and 4 only
D   1, 2 and 3 only.

(2 marks)

48   Part of a company's statement of cash flows is shown below:

	$'000
Operating profit	8,640
Depreciation charges	(2,160)
Increase in inventory	(330)
Increase in accounts payable	440

The following criticisms of the extract have been made:

(1)   Depreciation charges should have been added, not deducted.
(2)   Increase in inventory should have been added, not deducted.
(3)   Increase in accounts payable should have been deducted, not added.

Which of the criticisms are valid?

A   2 and 3 only
B   1 only
C   1 and 3 only
D   2 only

(2 marks)

49   Which of the following items could appear in a company's statement of cash flows?

(1)   Surplus on revaluation of non-current assets
(2)   Proceeds of issue of shares
(3)   Proposed dividend
(4)   Dividends received

A   1 and 2
B   3 and 4
C   1 and 3
D   2 and 4

(2 marks)

50   Which of the following statements are correct?

(1)   A statement of cash flows prepared using the direct method produces a different figure for operating cash flow from that produced if the indirect method is used.
(2)   Rights issues of shares do not feature in statements of cash flows.
(3)   A surplus on revaluation of a non-current asset will not appear as an item in a statement of cash flows.
(4)   A profit on the sale of a non-current asset will appear as an item under Cash Flows from Investing Activities in a statement of cash flows.

A   1 and 4
B   2 and 3
C   3 only
D   2 and 4

(2 marks)

51   A computerised accounting system operates using the principle of double entry accounting.

Is this statement true or false?

A   True
B   False

(1 mark)

1	C	A sole trader also invests capital in his or her business.
2	B	
3	C	
4	A	
5	A	IAS 8 does not require prospective future information, so 3 is never correct.
6	D	
7	B	
8	B	A remittance advice gives details of the invoices covered by the payment.
9	A	
10	A	Balance carried forward from previous period shows debits exceed credits and so it is a debit balance brought forward for the new period.
11	B	False. Sales tax for a registered trader is removed from income and expenses.
12	D	Carriage outwards is a selling expense.
13	A	(300@230) + (500@220) + (50@190) = 188,500
14	B	1,000,000/40years = 25,000; 1,000,000 − (800,000 − (800,000 × 2%*10years)) = 360,000
15	D	(240,000*20%) + (6/12*160,000*20%) − (9/12*60,000*20%) = 55,000
16	D	890 + 95 + 10 + 20 = 1,015 Maintenance is revenue expenditure and the sales tax is reclaimed.
17	A	
18	A	Research expenditure must be charged to the income statement.
19	D	(84,000 × 2/12) + (96,000 × 10/12) = 94,000; 96,000 × 2/12 = 16,000

20   D

RENT RECEIVABLE

	$		$
O/Balance	21,200	O/Balance	28,700
Income statement	475,900	Cash received	481,200
C/Balance	31,200	C/Balance	18,400
	528,300		528,300

21	B	37,000 + ((517,000 − 37,000) × 5%) − 39,000) = 22,000. New allowance required is $24,000, so the allowance is reduced by $15,000.
22	B	

23   D

RECEIVABLES LEDGER CONTROL ACCOUNT

	$		$
Opening balance	308,600	Contras	4,600
Credit sales	154,200	Cash received	147,200
Interest charged	2,400	Discounts allowed	1,400
		Irrecoverable debts	4,900
		Closing balance	307,100
	465,200		465,200

24	A	(8,950 − 4,080) − (4,140 + 40) = 690

25   D

	$
List Price	200,000
Trade discount	(20,000)
	180,000
Sales tax (17.5% × 95% × 180,000)	29,925
	209,925

26	D	438,900 – 980 – 90 = 437,830 The figure of $90 is $4,434 – $4,344.
27	B	– 3,860 – 9,160 + 16,690 = 3,670. Remember that the opening bank balance is overdrawn.
28	B	Items 2 to 4 are adjustments to the bank balance per the statement.
29	B	
30	C	83,600 + 18,000 – (18,000*25%) = 97,100 Add back the capital expenditure, but charge depreciation for the year.
31	B	
32	B	
33	B	The inventory account is only changed at the end of the accounting period.
34	A	Remember the business equation: $P = I + D – C_i$
35	D	(318,000 + 412,000 – 214,000) – (612,000 × 75%) = 57,000
36	A	836,200 – 8,600 + (14,000 × 70%) + 700 = 838,100
37	A	

37   A

PAYABLES LEDGER

	$		$
Cash paid	302,800	O/Balance	60,000
Discounts received	2,960	Purchases (bal.. fig.)	331,760
Contra	2,000		
C/Balance	84,000		
	391,760		391,760

38	B	((300,000 + 30,000) / 2 × ½) + (300,000 + 30,000) / 2 × 1/3) – (30,000 × ½)) = 122,500
39	A	Goodwill is usually brought in under the old PSR and written off in the new PSR.
40	D	5,750 + (86,500 × 3/5) – 4,300 = 53,350
41	B	Dividends appear in the SOCIE.
42	D	
43	C	Item 2 is charged to the income statement, and item 3 to 'other comprehensive income'.
44	B	125,000 + (500,000 × 1/2 × 25c) + (750,000 × 1/5 × 25c) = 225,000; 100,000 + (500,000 × 1/2 × 75c) – (750,000 × 1/5 × 25c) = 250,000
45	B	12,000 + (12,000 × 2%) + (9,000 × 8/12) + 4,000 = 22,240
46	B	
47	A	All these items provide additional information about conditions at the reporting date.
48	B	
49	D	Items (1) and (3) do not involve movements of cash.
50	C	
51	A	

Index

Note: **Key terms** and their page references are given in **bold**.

Review Form & Free Prize Draw – Paper F3 Financial Accounting (International) (6/09)

All original review forms from the entire BPP range, completed with genuine comments, will be entered into one of two draws on 31 January 2010 and 31 July 2010. The names on the first four forms picked out on each occasion will be sent a cheque for £50.

Name: _____   **Address:** _____

_____

_____

How have you used this Text?
(Tick one box only)

☐ Home study (book only)

☐ On a course: college _____

☐ With 'correspondence' package

☐ Other _____

Why did you decide to purchase this Text? *(Tick one box only)*

☐ Have used BPP Texts in the past

☐ Recommendation by friend/colleague

☐ Recommendation by a lecturer at college

☐ Saw advertising

☐ Saw information on BPP website

☐ Other _____

During the past six months do you recall seeing/receiving any of the following?
(Tick as many boxes as are relevant)

☐ Our advertisement in *ACCA Student Accountant*

☐ Our advertisement in *Pass*

☐ Our advertisement in *PQ*

☐ Our brochure with a letter through the post

☐ Our website www.bpp.com

Which (if any) aspects of our advertising do you find useful?
(Tick as many boxes as are relevant)

☐ Prices and publication dates of new editions

☐ Information on Text content

☐ Facility to order books off-the-page

☐ None of the above

Which BPP products have you used?

Text	☑	Success CD	☐	Learn Online	☐
Kit	☐	i-Learn	☐	Home Study Package	☐
Passcard	☐	i-Pass	☐	Home Study PLUS	☐

Your ratings, comments and suggestions would be appreciated on the following areas.

	Very useful	Useful	Not useful
Introductory section (Key study steps, personal study)	☐	☐	☐
Chapter introductions	☐	☐	☐
Key terms	☐	☐	☐
Quality of explanations	☐	☐	☐
Case studies and other examples	☐	☐	☐
Exam focus points	☐	☐	☐
Questions and answers in each chapter	☐	☐	☐
Fast forwards and chapter roundups	☐	☐	☐
Quick quizzes	☐	☐	☐
Question Bank	☐	☐	☐
Answer Bank	☐	☐	☐
Index	☐	☐	☐

Overall opinion of this Study Text: Excellent ☐ Good ☐ Adequate ☐ Poor ☐

Do you intend to continue using BPP products? Yes ☐ No ☐

On the reverse of this page are noted particular areas of the text about which we would welcome your feedback.
The BPP author of this edition can be e-mailed at: janiceross@bpp.com

Please return this form to: Nick Weller, ACCA Publishing Manager, BPP Learning Media Ltd, FREEPOST, London, W12 8BR

Review Form & Free Prize Draw (continued)

TELL US WHAT YOU THINK

Please note any further comments and suggestions/errors below

Free Prize Draw Rules

1 Closing date for 31 January 2010 draw is 31 December 2009. Closing date for 31 July 2010 draw is 30 June 2010.

2 Restricted to entries with UK and Eire addresses only. BPP employees, their families and business associates are excluded.

3 No purchase necessary. Entry forms are available upon request from BPP Learning Media Ltd. No more than one entry per title, per person. Draw restricted to persons aged 16 and over.

4 Winners will be notified by post and receive their cheques not later than 6 weeks after the relevant draw date.

5 The decision of the promoter in all matters is final and binding. No correspondence will be entered into.